THE 'BABY DOLL' SERIAL KILLER

THE JOHN ERIC ARMSTRONG HOMICIDES

MURDERS IN THE MOTOR CITY, BOOK ONE

B.R. BATES

WITH GERALD CLIFF, PHD.

WILDBLUE
PRESS

WildBluePress.com

THE 'BABY DOLL' SERIAL KILLER published by:
WILDBLUE PRESS
P.O. Box 102440
Denver, Colorado 80250

WILDBLUE PRESS is registered at the U.S. Patent and Trademark Offices.

ISBN 978-1-960332-98-1 Trade Paperback
ISBN 978-1-960332-96-7 eBook
ISBN 978-1-960332-97-4 Hardback

THE
'BABY DOLL'
SERIAL KILLER

As the research for this book was winding down, former Detroit Police Chief Benny Napoleon, who was instrumental in the formation of the task force, as well as in the procedure of this case, lost his battle with COVID-19. Napoleon had graciously done an interview for this book only a few months earlier, and for that we are very grateful, and we express our condolences to his family. We dedicate this book to his memory, as well as to the memory of all the women who lost their lives in this story.

A portion of the profits from sales of this book support Covenant House Michigan, an organization providing homeless, runaway and at-risk youth, as well as youth who have aged out of foster care, with shelter, educational and vocational programs and seeks to remove and overcome barriers such as homelessness, unemployment, inadequate education, violence, drugs, human trafficking and gang activity that prevent young people from successfully transitioning into adulthood. Visit CovenantHouseMI.org to learn more about this organization.

CONTENTS

FOREWORD

By Gerald Cliff, Ph.D

Just a few short words about how this book came to be, from my own perspective as part of the Detroit side of this case involving multiple jurisdictions. In late 1999, I had the honor of being promoted into the executive ranks of the Detroit Police Department and appointed commanding officer of the Violent Crimes Section. Little did I know at the time, the incredible nature of the professional investigators from multiple law enforcement agencies (local, state, and federal) I was about to have the privilege to work with.

The Violent Crimes Section is one of those exceptional groups of extremely talented people, hand selected for their demonstrated expertise, working almost seamlessly together as one well-honed investigative tool in one of the most violent cities in the United States. What was accomplished in this investigation is not the work of one or two superstar detectives; it was the result of an extremely talented, well-led, well-organized investigative team run by the Detroit Police Department, consisting of county sheriff deputies, state troopers, and federal agents from multiple agencies, working this case like no other unit could have. It was talent, leadership, and administrative support from top to bottom of all the combined agencies that made the existence of such a team possible.

The success of the Violent Crimes Section was due to multiple factors coming together in the best possible blend—talented detectives, good supervision, inspirational leadership—but none of it would have worked if we hadn't had a truly great chief of police whose unwavering support for our work made it all possible.

The unit was that "big gun" the chief pulled out whenever something high profile hit the city. If an investigation was too big for Detroit Homicide, the Armed Robbery Section, or the Sex Crimes Unit, it went to the Violent Crimes Section. If the crime became a serial, or exceeded the city border, state lines, or, as in this case, even national boundaries, the chief pulled the trigger on his "big gun," and usually, the bad guys were in custody in very short order. So if a high-profile case was considered unsolvable, it came to the Violent Crimes Section and usually, someone went to prison.

Working as the Detroit C.O. of this incredible group, I had the privilege of working with them to investigate and solve countless cases of such significance that nothing on TV came close to the work that was being done. With the nature of the investigations, I wanted to somehow see that credit for the incredible work and these talented people came to light.

Twenty years and two careers later, I found myself retired, and decided it was time think about committing this all to print. It was at that time that I was introduced to B.R. Bates. An accomplished author and incredible researcher in her own right, she was interested in taking on this project. We discussed the case, she read the files, and it seemed she was "bitten by the bug," one might say, to dig deeper and draw out the details of this truly incredible story.

After three years of intense background research, tracking down witnesses, victims' relatives, the killer's relatives, talking with the killer himself, and skillfully blending it all into this impeccably researched and detailed story which you are about to read.

I wish we could do justice to the work of every individual member of the Violent Crimes Section and to the Headquarters Surveillance unit of the Detroit Police Department that made it possible to remove what was described at the time as a veritable "killing machine" from the streets of Detroit. Unfortunately, that would be logistically impossible. It is my hope that the reader will keep in mind the incredible degree of talent, organization, leadership, and motivation it takes to make a unit like this function.

It is my sincerest hope that those members of the group whose individual contribution to the investigation may not specifically be spotlighted here are at least aware that we tried to give credit where credit is due and that is to the unit as a whole because without any one part, the entire thing would not have worked.

For me, having the honor to have led this group even for a short time was one of the high points in a forty-year career in law enforcement.

Gerry

PROLOGUE

January 2, 2000, evening

Dearborn Heights Police Department

Dearborn Heights, Michigan

"What do you think should happen to the person that did something like this?"

"I don't know. I've never had to experience it. I don't really know what ... what the person should get. I don't know."

"You don't know?"

"I don't know. Umm ..."

"If you were going to—I mean, we have to go find out who she is, obviously. We have to find her mother, father, relatives, next of kin. You know, it's going to be something where she's somebody's daughter somewhere. I don't know what type of person she is. I don't know exactly what kind of life she led. What led up to what happened to her, or what have you. What kind of impression did you get when you looked down at her? What kind of a person did you think she was?" Pause. "Did you remember what she was wearing or anything?"

"I don't know ... I can't judge. I can't judge people."

"Not asking you to judge, just asking to give me your first impression, you know, when you looked down and you saw that. What did you think?"

"Maybe she had a life. I don't know. Maybe she had a good job."

"She looked like that type of person, a working person, a person that lived her life every day trying to, you know, carry on? Be a good person?"

"Probably. I don't know."

"So you don't think that whoever did this to her should go to jail for the rest of their life or anything?"

"Oh, yeah, they should have to, they should."

"You think of any circumstances where if somebody did something like this, why they shouldn't go to jail?"

"Why they shouldn't?"

"Right. Any circumstances, do you think?"

"Couldn't tell you."

"Okay. What are you sighing for?"

"Not knowing anything, I guess."

"Not knowing anything, or is there maybe some things that you want to tell us that you're afraid somebody else might find out? About a way of life? A lifestyle? Something that could be weighing heavily on your mind? Something that you don't want your family to find out? Something that can be explained? Something that people can look at and say I understand why certain things happened? Certain things happen for certain reasons. Sometimes we don't plan them; they happen that way. Sometimes—for all we know, this girl could have fell off the bridge. You know, she could have made a mistake herself. She could have been fighting with somebody, gotten into an argument with somebody, and been trying to do it herself. As you know, people try to commit suicide. You know, you have got firsthand knowledge. People's lives get so messed up sometimes that they don't see a way out. They don't see the light at the end of the tunnel. You know what I'm saying? And sometimes holding all that in is just going to make it a lot worse. You know what I'm saying?"

"Yeah."

"You know if there was a situation where we were to find out that she was with you, that's going to make a whole different story. But if you're going to tell us that she was with you, maybe there's an explanation for what happened on that bridge. Maybe there's an explanation of why certain things that we're going to find out later, witnesses that say that she was in the Jeep with you, or you were talking to her on the bridge. Don't try to cover up now for something that might not be nothing. You know what I mean? You know, if there was an accident that happened, if you were talking to her, and she fell off the bridge, or jumped off the bridge, that's a viable explanation. But if we find out something later on that is questionable—don't try to hide nothing from us. You know what I'm saying? You know what I mean? If this was somebody you knew from work, or we're going to somehow find out that you guys knew each other, and now she's in there, that's going to be a different story, right? You know what I mean?"

"Yeah, but I didn't know her. She wasn't in the Jeep with me."

"She wasn't in the Jeep with you at all?"

"No, sir."

"And she wasn't on the bridge with you at all?"

"No, sir."

"And you just pulled up, and you were going to throw up, and she was laying down there?"

"Yeah, I had to vomit."

"Yeah."

Pause. "Yes, I had to vomit. No, I did not know her. And no, she wasn't in the Jeep with me."

"Not at any point during the day?"

"No. Because she wasn't."

"You didn't meet her after work?"

More insistent: "No, I didn't. This is the same thing that happened in Novi."

MONICA JOHNSON

Thursday, December 2, 1999
It's not the date when this case in Detroit actually begins,
but it's where we'll begin our tale of five women.
The five who lost their lives.

Her boyfriend Cliff went with her that night.

It was pretty temperate, for a Michigan December. Around fifty degrees. No precipitation. The dark of winter was coming earlier and earlier this time of year. Soon it would be the holidays and all that entails, then it would be January's harsher temps and the real dead of winter. For right now, though, Monica Teresa Johnson was out on the street, trying to get some cash. She was thirty-one years old, born in June 1968. She was a female of color, with black hair having red highlights, and salon nails painted red. Even her toenails were painted red that night, the medical examiner would later note.

December 2. Monica and Cliff pulled up to Michigan Avenue and Sharon Street, deep into the 'hood, right where business was booming. She got out of the car and walked off. Off to do her thing. He waited in the car. He fell asleep. When he woke up, she had not returned and had not even called, it was four a.m.; he just went home. And he did not see her again.

Monica Johnson had four kids. They were all pretty young at this point in 1999—babies, really. One was eight, one was ten, one was seven, and one was three.

Monica had a mom who worried about her and other family members who might have wondered how she was doing that night in 1999. Monica's parents raised her and her siblings in the city of Detroit, mostly east side. Park Grove near Linnhurst at one point. St. Clair and Shoemaker. Sanford off of Gunston, over by the Ninth Precinct and not far from the suburbs of Harper Woods and Hamtramck. The kids went to Kettering High School, up by Interstate 94. The siblings still live around the metro area.

A couple of those siblings were reached via phone for this book. One politely declined to speak. The other spoke willingly, freely, with very evident, very deep pain and trauma, but then couldn't be reached later for follow-up and so respectfully will not be quoted here. This sister held a special place in their hearts, it was evident. Too special to even think about at times. And there are other sorts of things that factor in in a situation like this.

Monica was a dedicated worker who held down a variety of jobs over the years, working at banks, burger joints, a watch company. Who knows what put her out there on that night, doing this lifestyle like so many other women, particularly in a place like Detroit. Often it's drug addiction, sometimes it's just a need for money—in the easiest way you can get it. At least some women would call it easy. Some wouldn't.

Monica had no idea that late on the night of December 2 and early morning of December 3, she would become the first fatal strike (the first one in Detroit at least) of a killer who had relocated here with his family just months earlier.

***

US 12 is a major artery cutting across the lower part of Michigan, stretching from downtown Detroit on the east edge of the state all the way west to the Indiana border, touching the southwestern-most tip of the state's mitten shape. From there it crosses the state line and continues toward Chicago. It's a historic highway, an evolution of old Native American trails once twisting and winding in various directions in and out of the state. For the city of Detroit and its western suburbs, US 12 is known as the sprawling, westward boulevard Michigan Avenue.

Sprouting at the nation's first concrete-paved road, Woodward Avenue, the stalwart Michigan Ave cuts across Interstates 94, 75, and 275 in its determined path west, also crossing other major arteries like the Southfield Freeway and Telegraph Road. It is the street of long-loved and/or long-past sites like the old Tiger Stadium, and the once-grand Michigan Central Train Depot (commonly called "the train station"). It's home to the two famous competing Coney Island restaurants, and the yummy and historic sandwich shop Hygrade Deli, open only through breakfast and lunch and closed on Sundays, where scenes have been shot for several movies including *Batman v Superman: Dawn of Justice*. And beyond those well-regarded locales on Michigan Avenue are scattered myriad gas stations, liquor stores, fast-food joints, used car lots, the occasional old bank building or ornate old church building with a congregation that's determined not to move, and other assorted businesses brave enough to stay there. The street is bustling, for sure, and there's commerce to be had. But you see, Michigan Ave can get pretty rough. Its stretch through suburbs like Dearborn is calmer and more akin to civilized strip malls, car washes, hair salons, doctor's and dentist's offices, coffee shops, large retailers like Kroger, and even two suburban police stations that investigated this case (Dearborn and Dearborn Heights). But within the big city's borders, it's a different world. Here, Michigan Ave is also home to the industry of strip clubs and prostitution. It was true back when our story takes place and it remains true today. Detroit has always had its other pockets of prostitution, like certain parts of the aforementioned Woodward, or the notorious Cass Corridor, which you'd think would be far more innocent right there in the midst of the Wayne State University campus. Apart from those other places, though, this stretch of Michigan Ave running through the west side of town has its own unique flavor.

And as with most of those involved in our story, Michigan Ave was where Monica Johnson's killer first spotted her.

It was near the two used car lots on Michigan that night, he would tell police months later. That's how he put it in his statement: "near the two used car lots." This was where Lawndale crossed Michigan, not far from Lonyo.

He described Monica as a Black female with a medium complexion and black hair, five-foot-eight, around one hundred and twenty pounds. She wore orange pants and a black vinyl jacket, and had black hair, he said, maybe with a partial wig.

To her, he no doubt looked like a typical john. Maybe a tad more innocent-seeming. White boy. Probably from the suburbs. A lot of them were. Pretty big guy too. Wireframe glasses. Reddish hair. Many folks who knew him said he looked like the boy next door.

"I pulled over to her and she jumped into my Jeep," the killer later told police. It was a 1998 Jeep Wrangler, dark-bluish-gray, black soft top, two-door. Gray interior with a muted multicolor pattern on the soft upholstery. Purchased recently.

He estimated the time to be around eleven p.m. "She directed me to drive to Springwells and the I-94 service drive." This was just a few blocks away, on the other side of the freeway. Fairly quiet that time of night, a little away from Michigan Ave and off the beaten path. "I parked and she told me that she charged fifty dollars for straight sex. I paid her the money."

For their encounter, Monica Johnson suggested to her last john this stretch of the I-94 service drive, between Springwells and Lumley, on the north side of the freeway. The west-bound street is short and contains a secluded alley. For more photos from the case, see the gallery on the WildBlue Press website.

Their transaction for this traditional sex act then proceeded, but things went wrong.

"After we had sex," he said, "for some reason I started strangling her. I don't know why."

And Monica was no match for this man's six-foot-two, two-hundred-and-thirty-pound frame.

"At some point while I was strangling her," he continued, "she stopped breathing, so I placed her on the sidewalk. I then left and went home and took a shower."

He remembered leaving her face down on the sidewalk. It was twelve-thirty or twelve-forty-five a.m. as he made his way home, and he threw the condom he had used with her into a garbage can a couple miles from the scene.

"Did you intend to kill her after sex?" police asked him these several months later.

"No." And Monica had done nothing to provoke the attack, he said.

"How did you feel after killing her?"

"I felt awful, very hurt and very sorry."

***

Monica was not dead at the point that John Eric Armstrong left her on the sidewalk, however. She was still breathing. A thirty-something man named Allen was driving home from work, just hitting the I-94 service drive right there, and he saw what looked like a person lying along the side of the street. He backed the car up and confirmed it; this was a woman. Was she still alive? What had happened? He called 911 and waited for police and EMS to arrive. Nobody else was around in these early-morning hours. Had she been left there by someone? Did she just have some kind of attack and pass out?

Police from the Fourth Precinct arrived at about four a.m., ironically the same time her boyfriend was heading home blocks away. Police found her lying prone at the curb in the alley between Springwells and Lumley, they would later report. An ambulance arrived. They tried to resuscitate her. She died at about five a.m., just arriving at the hospital, never able to tell authorities about her killer.

Just a few hours later, at 10:33 on Friday, December 3, she was with the Office of the Wayne County Medical Examiner, having at first been Unknown Female No. 72, E.R. Female No. 39502916, and M.E. Case No. 99-11157, then becoming Monica T. Johnson.

"It is my opinion that death was caused by strangulation," Carl J. Schmidt, MD, deputy chief medical examiner, wrote in the report. "Petechiae, or tiny hemorrhages, were present around the eyes and in the tissue surrounding the eyes. There was extensive hemorrhage in the muscles of the left side of the neck, and the hyoid bone was fractures *[sic]*. This indicates great force was applied to the neck." Indeed, when the hyoid bone, a horseshoe-shaped bone in the neck that aids in tongue movement and swallowing, is broken or dislodged, it's an indication of manual strangulation.

"The tears in the perineum are consistent with sexual abuse." The report also noted rectal tears.

"The manner of death is homicide."

The toxicology lab report was negative for all four substances tested: alcohol, benzodiazepines, cocaine, and opiates.

She had been put into a hospital gown en route, and her death was noted as occurring in the ambulance at two minutes after five a.m. The scene at the I-94 service drive was photographed by evidence techs, her clothing bagged as evidence.

Monica was logged as another Detroit homicide, one of more than four hundred in the city in 1999, and life went on.

The impact on the Johnson family, however, was much more deeply felt.

Monica's heartbroken mother had the chore of identifying her daughter at the morgue. Her siblings were left in shock as to how she could have died so young and in such a tortuous way. Monica used to watch the kids of one of her siblings and he would watch her kids when needed. They were six years apart in age but very close. Now she was gone.

After her death, Monica's two sons and two daughters were raised in their grandparents' household. Then Monica's mom died in 2005; her dad not long after.

In the two decades since Monica's murder, her kids have gone separate ways. Two have lived in Ohio in recent years. The older son is doing well, it's been said. He's handsome, has a good head on his shoulders. A college grad. For the younger son, though, who was eight when Monica was killed, it's a different story. He got in trouble with the law. He's been incarcerated in Michigan and has been repeatedly "flopped"—denied—when coming up for parole. This younger son of Monica also lost his father along the way.

Then there's the youngest of the four kids, a little girl of three years old, who had no idea at the time what happened to her mother. A girl who grew up without a mom.

And though the painful mark that Monica's death left on her family members still drums loudly decades later, back then in 1999, in the big city of Detroit, this killer was just getting started.

WENDY JORDAN

In our tale of five women in Detroit, none had more public support from family members after death, more fervent, tearful, stalwart, *very* public support than Wendy Jordan.

Her sisters Bonnie and Judy were there every day of the trial, watching tearfully, making sure their sister's death was brought to an appropriate closure, speaking at the sentencing hearing, speaking to the news reporters at the time, speaking even to Nancy Grace, speaking up during later television specials that would be done on the case. Speaking up now, for this book.

Speaking up for Wendy.

In the photos of the trial that popped up in newspaper stories and TV reports, Bonnie and Judy Jordan gave a face to the horrors of the case. Whereas the family members of at least one of the other four women—maybe two of them—disowned and disavowed them, Wendy was well-represented. It was clear she was loved, no matter the circumstances.

Wendy Jordan was a little older than the other four women we're discussing, about to turn forty in the year 2000, a little past the age you might picture someone working the streets. But Wendy didn't really belong on the streets, and her sisters made that clear in any interview they did. Her life was about a lot of other things, and she was always pulled in more positive directions.

Wendy, right, and her sister Bonnie in happier times. Image courtesy of Bonnie Jordan.

Born in April 1960, Wendy Zelane Jordan was the oldest of five sisters growing up, along with an older brother, on Helen Street on the east side of Detroit. Bonnie was closest to Wendy back then, being only a year younger. In 1970, when Wendy was ten and Bonnie nine, their mom died, and their dad raised all of the kids with the help of his sister, their Aunt Clyde (Bonnie finding it so amusing even years later to have a Bonnie and a Clyde in the same household). The kids attended East Catholic High School for a while, then switched schools.

When asked how she might describe Wendy back then, when they were kids, to someone who had never met her, Bonnie said, "Very, very friendly. When I say she would give you the shirt off her back, it was true. It was true. She was just a sweetie. It was five girls and all of us are still alive. Not one of those other sisters could replace her."

Bonnie could see a change happening in her sister when they were in high school. Around age seventeen or eighteen, Wendy started gravitating toward what Bonnie called "street life"—smoking marijuana, wanting to go to the cabaret, as she put it.

"Me and Wendy were the closest, but when I started realizing that she was liking street life, I just, I couldn't do it. I didn't want to do street life. But up until that point, I was so close to her."

Wendy graduated in 1978 from John Pershing High School, then went on to an executive secretary's school in New York City. From Bonnie's perspective, it was that trip to New York that was a turning point in Wendy's life. Wendy was staying with the girls' maternal aunt, their mom's only sister, Aunt Carol, while attending the school there. In the midst of the big-city allure, she was exposed to a variety of things and found herself at one point on the top of a tall apartment building, doing drugs with a guy who ended up jumping off the building right before her eyes.

"Wendy saw that. She witnessed it. I'm thinking she was around, maybe twenty-one, twenty-two. By the time she was twenty-four, she was back living here. She was done with New York, didn't go back to New York, at age twenty-four. And she was just different. That changed her. She was different. She still was sweet, but she wasn't focused."

Bonnie didn't know the details, but she knew it was a drug situation.

"She was doing—I don't know what her drug of choice was, to be honest. Even up until her death, I still don't know what was her drug of choice." Bonnie thought it might be crack, but she couldn't be sure because she never actually saw Wendy doing whatever it was. "She kept herself away from us when she was doing that stuff. And you know, I just didn't want to know. I never asked her. I just really don't know, really, what her drug of choice was. Which is so weird to me. And I wouldn't have asked her."

Wendy had good jobs over the years, like working as a secretary for the former NBD (National Bank of Detroit, now Chase Bank) in downtown Detroit. But the street kept calling her, despite her best efforts. She fought the addiction through the '80s and '90s. There were even some run-ins with the law: a prostitution arrest in Ferndale in 1984, larceny charges in Harper Woods in 1988 and Detroit in 1995, the latter of which got Wendy two years of probation and a drug program. Sister Judy was raising Wendy's kids. There was one time, Bonnie said, when the family didn't see Wendy for about three years.

"I was at my father's house and the phone rang. I just happened to go over there, so the phone rang, I answered the phone. And it was a guy. I don't know his name or anything. And he said, 'Do you have a sister named Wendy?' I said, yeah. I said, omigod. And he said, 'I know where she is.' I said, 'Where is she at? We've been looking for her for a couple years!' And he said, 'She's over at my house.' I said, 'Where's your house at?' And he said it was on Seminole and Forest. He gave me the address, and I went over there and got her. Omigosh, she looked horrible. She was skin and bones."

Bonnie continued, "We had gone to East Catholic High School, so I put her in the Catholic church that we used to go to when we were kids because they had a rehab program. So she was there for like sixty days. She was doing so good. I forget the name of it, but I know exactly where it's at— it's on Maxwell and Sylvester. And so she was doing really well there. I was visiting her every day and we were talking. So when she came home from there, she came to my bed, talking, and we just knew."

The family could feel Wendy's fighting spirit, no matter what she was into, no matter the life she was living. As with the other women in our story, there were always times spent in a better life. Always the *desire* for a better life.

"You know, we had let her babysit our kids (we had little kids at the time)," Bonnie went on. "And we just knew she was tired of that, being out there. She was living in houses that were vacant. You know, she was a real pretty girl, so people were jealous of her; somebody had busted her upside her head. Right behind her ear, she had to get all these stitches."

Wendy's family was happy she was home again, but bewildered at the lifestyle they knew she was engaging in. "I asked her—I said, 'As sheltered as we were'—and we didn't want for nothing; my father had a good living, my father was a brickmaker—I said, 'How could you ever be out there like that? Living in vacant houses?' You know, we had canopy beds. I said, 'How could you ever live like that?' I could not—for the life of me, I couldn't figure it out, how she could do it. I just couldn't."

It was not the life they had growing up.

"I mean, we just had the best. We went shopping every week. Every Saturday, we went shopping downtown, Hudson's and Crowley's. You know? And I was just like, how could you just be sleeping anywhere, you know? Not being in a nice house, all nice furniture, you know? Omigosh. That was just really something for me."

But that is the nature of addiction, so central to the story of our five women. So many times the reason they're out there on the street.

"Yep, it was the addiction," Bonnie said. "And that's why in my own mind, I said, there's one drug that makes you turn your back on your kids. She had a set of twins, and she had her oldest son; she really was a good mother to him. Because she had him before any of this addiction crap. She had him when we were in high school. She was in the twelfth grade. That's when she had him. So it's like, the only thing I know to make a mother turn her back on her kids is crack. So I know she had to be doing crack at some point."

Back then, in the '90s, crack was the drug of choice for girls on the street, but heroin was in the mix too, and is becoming much more pervasive these days. But whatever the drug, sometimes when you've got a family member deep in that life, you don't really want them around, even though you're worrying about them. Besides the general disappointment of where they're at, and the pain of having to watch it, maybe even your own regrets over what you think you could have done differently for them, you've also been burned in other ways. They have stolen from you, for instance. They have lied to you, then skipped out. But it was a little different for Wendy's family. Somehow Wendy managed a separation of her various lives, a separation between what she was doing and the people she did not want it to affect.

"I think some of these girls, though, I mean, they made their choices, but some of them you've got to respect," Bonnie said. "They took it away from the families. They had children; they left their children with the fathers. You know what I mean? I can speak for Wendy anyway. Her drug life, all that, her street life, all that, we didn't know where she was at for three years at one point. So, I didn't like that, but I respected it because a lot of times they do so much to the family, stealing and all of that, you don't even want to see them coming. See, we always wanted to see her coming because she didn't do that to us."

Years after this case was resolved, in 2012, Investigation Discovery's *Very Bad Men* series would do an episode on John Eric Armstrong. There were Bonnie and Judy front and center, the only victim family members interviewed.

"Wendy was the kind of sister who would give you her shirt off her back," Bonnie said, just as she told me a few years later.

Judy echoed, "I thought Wendy was so pretty. I always thought, when I grow up, I'm going to be like Wendy. I'm going to wear my hair like Wendy, and I'm going to act like Wendy."

Back then, the Jordan siblings had gotten together for a couple hours on New Year's Eve 1999, the TV episode explained. The last time they saw Wendy alive, she was leaving their dad's house and the next day, New Year's Day, Bonnie didn't hear from Wendy for their regular phone call.

"I felt something … I don't want to say was wrong," Bonnie told the viewing audience. "But I felt something. I felt something."

***

New Year's Day 2000

The world didn't explode after all. Y2K fears were put to rest. Life proceeded as normal. And for Wendy Jordan, that "normal" translated into the streets that welcomed her back, that familiar, sometimes-normal she had tried so hard to stay out of for so many years. Her oldest son was attending Michigan State University at the time and she had been seeing all of her kids regularly. She was staying with her father and working at a gas station. The family thought she was clean again.

She wore black leather that night—miniskirt, jacket. Black hosiery. Gold-colored high-heeled pumps. (Sadly, it would be portrayed rather accurately years later by the actress in the *Very Bad Men* episode.)

It was forty-five degrees at eleven p.m., no precipitation, low winds. Not quite as cold as it should be for the Michigan winter that had rolled onward since the day Monica Johnson was killed the previous month. It stayed in the mid-forties all night on New Year's.

Wendy's killer had just left work, he would tell police months later, second shift hours, maybe ten-thirtyish or eleven. He was driving down Warren Avenue in Detroit going toward the western suburb of Dearborn Heights where he lived, west from the city. It seems counterintuitive, looking at it years later, because he both worked and lived west of Detroit. Something had taken him east, into the city, then back toward home. He could have been cruising for hours. He could have gone home and back out again a couple hours later. Armstrong's next-door neighbor would later tell police she heard a car start in his driveway and take off in the early-morning hours. And an employee at the Sunoco at Warren and Evergreen told police he saw Wendy in the gas station at four-thirty that morning. A police sergeant working the midnight shift observed Wendy in the area of Warren and Heyden around three a.m. But whatever the time, Armstrong told police he saw Wendy Jordan and picked her up. She quoted him sixty dollars for oral sex and what he again referred to as "straight sex."

"We pulled down one of the side streets off of Warren by a funeral home that starts with a *Z*," he said. "We parked. I gave her the money."

He remembered her wearing the black leather jacket and skirt.

"I asked if she had a rubber. She said no and that she was clean."

Business proceeded in the passenger seat of John Eric Armstrong's Jeep.

"After sex," he continued in his statement, "I put my hands around her neck and I strangled her. Then I drove down to near where I live at in Dearborn Heights and I dumped her in the Rouge River from the bridge on Ann Arbor Trail near Parkland Park."

The fact that he drove a couple miles with Wendy in his car would turn out to be unusual for him, and that choice to dump her just about in his own backyard—he lived literally around the corner—would prove to be a very interesting one, from a psychological perspective, along with the events that followed the next day. More on that in a later chapter.

"Then I went home, took a shower, and went to bed."

Armstrong remembered Wendy as a Black female about age forty, five-foot-eight or nine, one hundred and forty or so pounds, "with fake hair." He estimated it was about one a.m. on January 2 that he left her at the river.

"Did you know you killed her?" police would later question.

"Yes, because her chest wasn't moving up and down."

"How did you feel when you threw her over the bridge?"

"Guilty, sorry, angry."

***

Ironically, Wendy's killer would be the one who would report sighting her body there, encased in icy water, face-up, in the Rouge River in Dearborn Heights. It was another strange detail for this case, one that remains quite strange to this day.

The 911 call came in on the afternoon on January 2, and Dearborn Heights police investigated at the bridge scene on Ann Arbor Trail.

Bonnie Jordan, meanwhile, was feeling a very strange feeling, since she normally would have talked to her older sister Wendy by now. But she wasn't assuming anything bad had happened. Things had seemed to turn around for Wendy recently. So there couldn't be anything wrong. Right?

"We thought she was done. She said she was, and we hoped it. I'm not going to say we thought it. We just hoped it. And we didn't have enough time to say she wasn't. And then she was dead. We didn't have enough time. Because everything was just boom-boom-boom."

Bonnie received a phone call at seven p.m., she would later testify in court, probably on January 3 but it's possible it was on January 2. The details were understandably hard to grasp amid the trauma that resulted. Police had determined who Wendy was through fingerprints. Now it was time for the next step.

Bonnie said then she and all of her sisters went to the Dearborn Heights Police Department to identify a photo of Wendy. The next day she went to the morgue to make another identification. The Jordan girls drove there "thinking positive" that the body found wasn't Wendy. They ID'd their sister on a view screen, but Bonnie insisted on seeing the scar on Wendy's leg to know for sure it was her.

In the *Very Bad Men* episode, Judy described the ride home from the morgue: "We are in the truck. Nobody had really cried yet. And everybody in the car fell apart. That's when the reality set in."

As with Monica Johnson, Dr. Carl Schmidt performed the autopsy at the Office of the Wayne County Medical Examiner. "It is my opinion that death was caused by manual strangulation," he wrote in the report. "There were scratch marks on the neck and multiple conjunctival and periorbital petechiae (capillary hemorrhage). The orbits were unroofed, and more periorbital petechiae were seen. The manner of death is homicide."

The tox screen was negative for alcohol, benzodiazepines, and cocaine; positive for opiates and morphine in her blood, determined to be from heroin.

For a moment she had the unwanted privilege of being Unknown Female No. 1 for Wayne County in this brand-new millennium.

Then, not too long after her family claimed her, they faced another unseen horror. To this day, they don't know where her remains are. Or were. There was a mix up at the funeral home, perhaps a misunderstanding. The family had purchased a plot for her at a local cemetery. The funeral director had Wendy's body embalmed at one location on Detroit's east side, then moved her to a newer building in town for the funeral service. But the family does not know exactly what happened after that, only that she was evidently cremated. And no one from the family ever received her remains. The funeral director had no answer, just that the remains were lost. Understandably, Bonnie is livid to this day.

"I think he just did what he wanted to do. I think he just took the money, and had some gravediggers, dirty. And stuck her wherever."

It seems ludicrous, but in a city where in more recent years two funeral homes were in the news after bodies of children were found hidden in the walls and ceilings, maybe not.

"I'm going to tell you what happened," Bonnie said of her conversations between the cemetery office and the funeral home. "I went, because we were going to do a plot. I mean, you know, the thing, the statue, we were going to do that. And so I'm in the office, and I'm talking to the lady, and I'm giving her what she gave me. And she looked that stuff up; she said, that's not your sister. That's a different Wendy Jordan there. And that's when I knew he had done something. And I said, oh my God. Yeah. And I called him. I went to him. I said, 'Where is my sister?' I even had reached out to an attorney because I thought that was just horrible that he would act like he buried her in this plot and she is not there. So where are her remains? And maybe they are there, not legally. And none of that was necessary because like I said, we had money."

Bonnie has to wonder if perhaps her sister actually is in the plot they purchased, but with someone else the funeral director had placed there to save costs or whatever. "Because he did it dirty." She said, "It was just so overwhelming, I don't even know what happened after that."

It's all a little hard to understand. But sometimes it's a matter of the wrong assumptions being made. A murder happens. It becomes known under what circumstances the victim was murdered. The killer is not known yet, so this seems like just another Detroit casualty. Just more of what happens here.

"I told him," Bonnie said of the funeral director, "I said, I didn't need anything from you. You didn't do me no favors. We weren't begging. My father had money. We were not begging. My nephew had a life insurance policy. We were not begging anybody. We were grateful for the things that people, you know, donations and stuff like that. But begging, never! I said, somebody donated a plot to me; I turned it down because I figured, why do I need two? Give it to somebody else that's going to come up and need it. You know, I wasn't being ungrateful; I did not need it."

She continued, "I heard that the same person did that to several people. And he's thinking he's doing you a favor, burying them for cheap, or putting it in that way. That might have been their story; that wasn't ours. Now that's worse than—that's worse than the murder, to me."

Bonnie has endured even more than that, though. Years after Wendy's murder, at her job for a medical lab in the suburbs, she encountered, by chance, working for the same lab as a courier, the wife of her sister's killer.

"When we ran into each other, we didn't say anything to each other. We were both so shocked."

When this author first called Bonnie for this interview and I explained what I was doing, the first words she said at the mention of the name of her sister's killer were "Oh my God." And as we talked, she said she might write to him in prison. She wonders what he thinks about it all, these days. If he feels any remorse.

"He should die in there, right?" she asked me. "He won't ever get out, right?"

And … another twisted detail: as we talked in fall 2019, Bonnie told me how her best friend Angela's aunt was murdered by a serial killer too, a man who had been arrested in Detroit just weeks earlier. He was being dubbed the East Side Killer in the media and he was suspected of killing prostitutes in their fifties, leaving them in abandoned houses in the city.

"What are the chances of two best friends having their family members killed by freakin' serial killers?" she said incredulously. "I said, what kind of hell life is we having here? I still cannot believe it."

Wendy's father, now deceased, never recuperated from his daughter's murder. He couldn't bring himself to attend the trial of her killer, he was so heartbroken. Couldn't even watch it on the news. Not all of the siblings really want to talk about it these days, Bonnie said. The youngest sister is special-needs, and she has always had difficulty with it because she really looked up to Wendy. All of Wendy's sisters, however, remain her loving supporters to this day.

"She's all over my walls, in my house, pictures of her," Bonnie said in the ID episode. "Us sisters, we talk about her. We tell her granddaughter about her. She is never forgotten. Wendy is never forgotten."

ROSE MARIE FELT

Her story might seem typical. Predictable. Kinda like a stereotype.

Growing up in a tough inner city. Having a difficult home life, then leaving home altogether. Dropping out of high school. Getting pregnant at fifteen. Falling into drugs.

All the key ingredients that could possibly lead a girl to the streets, it would seem.

But as with the other women in our story, included in the life of Rose Marie Felt are glimpses at a regular, stable life.

Rose was born in October 1967; her father was in the military at the time, her parents staying at a base in Hawaii. There's even a story in the family about Elvis Presley performing for the soldiers at the base and during the performance, asking to hold the precious young Rose this young couple was cradling in the audience. Rose's parents are now deceased, but she had siblings, such as a brother named Scott, two years younger, whom she was very close to. And yes, he confirms the Elvis story—the famous singer kissed his sister on the cheek. "That is the truth," he said, laughing, when reached via phone for this book in 2021, "because my mother told me millions of times."

Rose's parents divorced when she was about two years old, and she, baby Scott, and their two sisters then settled with their mom and stepdad in Tennessee. But things were sometimes difficult. Scott told the story of one particular time his mom and stepdad got into an argument and the four kids packed up all their things and ran away. "We were done," he said. "I mean, there was a lot of drama." The family was touched by alcohol as well as drugs.

When Scott was about five and Rose was seven, the family settled on Military Street in Southwest Detroit, around the area known as Mexicantown. A few years later, they lived at Vinewood and Toledo Streets, not far away. Rose attended Earhart Elementary-Middle School, named after Amelia Earhart. She would have attended Western International High School where her brother attended for a time, right there in that same area on Scotten Street near Vernor Highway, but she didn't make it that far.

As a teen, Rose met a guy named Alex, who grew up around that same area. Rose was actually closer to the age of Alex's little brother, Danny. She and Alex became involved. He was the older to her younger; he was Hispanic to her white. They were different yet bound together by the area they grew up in. They started living together. They had a baby daughter, Jeniffer. That was 1983 and Rose was turning sixteen that year.

"I met Rose when she was fourteen," Alex said via phone in 2019 from across the country, at this point settled in the Pacific Northwest for quite a few years. "Rose was fourteen. I was eighteen. We never went to high school together. I was like five years older than her. Actually, she never went to school. Rose never went to school. Her parents were very poor people in the southwest side of Detroit, where I was living at the time. And I met her there through a mutual friend, who introduced me to her. And at the time, Rose was a young beautiful woman. And of course, I was like, you know, a handsome guy, I guess. You could say. We kinda hit it off. And we started talking. One thing led to another."

Alex asked Rose's mom back then for permission to date her daughter. "When I met her and I found out how old she was, I went to talk to her mother. And told her mom,

'Listen, I want to date your daughter, but she's only fourteen years old. You know, I'm eighteen, and this is going to be a problem here.' And she said, 'Oh no, no, no, there won't be no problems. It's okay.' 'It's okay?' She said, 'Yeah, it's okay, it's okay. She can stay with you if you want, start a life with her,' this and that. And I was working, doing HVAC—heating and air conditioning. Work was picking up on the southwest side in Detroit. And I was there in that line of work, so me and Rose started hanging out and stuff. Then I got her pregnant."

A couple snapshots of Rose texted by her brother, Scott, for this book. Image courtesy of Scott Felt.

Alex spoke very honestly—directly— in laying out the details of two lives marked by various difficulties over the years. "We stayed together for a number of years. A number of years. Well, then I went to prison. I went to prison back in 1989, in the Eastern District of Michigan, federal prison. I went to prison for ten years. And, well, I didn't see her those years that I was gone."

Court records show that Rose filed a complaint against Alex for support for their daughter in 1989. And to make ends meet, Rose tried jobs around town, like waiting tables at a bar on Michigan Avenue while renting the apartment upstairs. A family member of Alex's who knew Rose back then, Loretta, remembered that. Loretta recalled that Rose had a pretty rough upbringing, and it wasn't just about being raised in a city like Detroit in an era just after the famous riots. Rose didn't get along with her mother and left the house as she dropped out of school.

"She left home very young," Loretta said. "Very, very young age. And she was pretty much on her own."

And of course, it's hard to get a decent job without an education—even a high school diploma—and even harder to support a young daughter of your own.

"I was talking to my daughter," Alex said of those years he was incarcerated, "and my daughter was always in communications with Rose. And it was just, you know, what is she doing? And she told me, Mom's doing bad and she's doing this, she's doing that, she's in the streets. She was smoking crack, and she was in a lot of shit. And it was like, wow, it's crazy. I was down in Texas at the time. The federal government sent me down there to USP Beaumont. I was down there in Beaumont, Texas. And then she, ah … she actually gave my daughter up to my mother. She signed papers legally and gave my mother legal consent for my daughter. Because she was, Rose was a young woman that had a child at a young age. She never really lived. And I don't blame her for what she did, you know, because I mean, she just couldn't handle it. She couldn't handle the responsibility of raising a child. She was a child herself. So my mother took that responsibility on her. She raised my daughter. She was a blessing, because she came out good."

Loretta recalled, "Alex's mother raised Jeniffer for a good portion of her life. Because Alex was in and out of custody, and Rose, you know, she was just barely a kid." Still, Loretta remembered her with fondness. "I liked Rose. She was a sweet person."

So how old was Rose when she started using? I had to wonder.

"Oh, hell, I can tell you exactly how old she was," Alex replied matter-of-factly, "because I was the one who introduced her."

He went on: "Yes. Yes, I can tell you exactly how old she was. She was seventeen. She was seventeen years old. Jeniffer was a little over a year old. And she was living over on Military Street in Southwest Detroit. She had an apartment over there. I used to pay for the apartment. I was selling cocaine. I was selling a lot of cocaine in those days, making a lot of money. That's why I went to federal prison. And I mean, it was part of our life. It was both of us, not just her. I was doing it too. We were both doing coke. We were getting high. But we never smoked it. I never smoked cocaine or smoked crack. And you know, we would just sniff it."

Amid all that, there were still those glimmers of hope, times when Rose tried to break free and make a better life. "I remember we went to Disney World one year," Alex said. "I took them to Disney World. We went down there, me, Jeniffer, and her. Because she had OD'd on coke. I took her to the hospital. It scared me. I thought she was going to die, but she didn't. And she got out of the hospital, and I said, listen, let's take a vacation. So I took them to Disney World. We went down to Disney World for a week or ten days. I forget when it was I took them down there. It was '87? '87, yeah. We went down there and had a good time. And I didn't let her take no drugs. We went down there and we stayed for two weeks. She got clean. She was feeling happy again. She was looking more beautiful than ever. I was just real content with her, because I loved her a lot. She was a good person. And then we got back home, chasing the bug again. 'Let me have some coke, Daddy, let me have some coke.' I'm like, you have to stop, you have to stop. This is killing you, man. It's making you crazy."

And things just happened. Life happened, for both of them.

"Well, I ended up going to prison in the state over there," he said. "In 1988, I went to the state prison, for, I don't know what the time was, I think I got one to five on a pistol case. And I went to prison. And she never wrote me." He sorta chuckled. "She never wrote me the whole time I was there. So when I got out, I didn't look for her—you know what I mean? I kinda did, but I didn't. That's when I met another woman. You know, our lives were like that. She was like, 'I'll still love you, I love you.' 'I know; I love you too. But we're never going to be together again.' I found the person I love, who loved me. I was young. We were two people. She went on with her life and her life took her to the streets. She started prostituting and things like that. I guess that was what she was doing. I don't know, I really don't know."

Alex's new girlfriend formed her own relationship with Jeniffer. He sent his daughter to Catholic school in Detroit but always made sure Rose could see her when she wanted to. "You know, I never, ever spoke bad to Jeniffer about her mother. Because that's her mother, you know? She loves her. I didn't want her to ever think anything bad of her. I mean, she was a good person. She had a problem. Addiction led her."

It's hard to pinpoint exactly when Rose was drawn to the streets to try to make money, but estimates were it was a good ten years before she was killed. On and off. Jeniffer would sometimes go stay with Rose for overnighters through the years, from where she lived with Alex's mom, but for the most part Rose lived away from her daughter. And the drugs? Loretta wasn't quite sure what it was Rose was using at the time, but she knew it was something.

"I lost contact with her after her and Alex broke up," Loretta said, "and would see her for a few minutes at a time when I'd drop Jeniffer off to visit her on occasion."

But what friends and acquaintances could only guess at, only see hints of, would be revealed, unfortunately, by the coroner. And confirmed by the man who loved her. "It was the dope that led her life. That's what took her to hell."

As we spoke, Alex was rather intent on setting the record straight on Rose Marie Felt. He was very interested in showing another, better side of what would seem, on paper, a life so unfortunate. Predictable. A life that, as we said at the outset, would seem just another inner-city statistic.

"I hope you don't write anything bad about her," he said somberly near the end of our call. "The addiction led her. But in her heart, she was great."

It's the truth I'm after, I assured him.

"I don't want anybody writing anything bad about Rose," he reiterated. "There's nothing to say bad about her. She had a problem with drugs, and she met an evil person who killed her. And that's what happened."

***

Rose Marie Felt was thirty-two years old and working the area of Michigan Avenue and Livernois when she was picked up by her final john. Her killer would later describe her for police—his first confession after being arrested—as tall, between five-foot-nine or eleven, white, with a medium build, maybe a little thick, and dirty blond hair. She had a deep voice, he remembered. She was wearing "black stretch pants" and a black jacket.

It was mid-March 2000. The time was around midnight.

"I picked her up at the Comerica Bank on Michigan," he told police, "then she took me up there near the railroad tracks. She offered me sex for fifty dollars. I gave it to her, then we started having sex. I took my clothes off. She had a rip in the crotch area of her black stretch pants, and she got on top inside of my Jeep. Next thing I knew, she was sitting on the passenger seat and she wasn't breathing. So I got out of the Jeep and I tossed her out the Jeep to the side of the hill, then I left."

He said he didn't remember strangling her. Police asked what happened to her shoes, and he said he thought he tossed them outside the Jeep as well.

He did not return to the body later, he said, and he had never picked this girl up before.

"I don't know why I did it," he said. "I'm sorry."

He had used a condom with her and he threw it out the window on the drive home, he said. He went home and got in the shower "because I felt dirty."

When asked by police why Rose was found with her legs spread open, he seemed to contradict his statement of a moment ago, "Because I did it to her again after she was dead." The assumption, however, is that he had sex with her again, as she lay there dead, before driving home.

Why? "I don't know."

Did you use a condom the second time you had sex with her, after she was dead? police asked.

"I used the same one," he replied.

He had no weapons in the Jeep the night of Rose's murder, he told police, and that day before it happened, he had gone to school like usual then to his job at the time, at a Target store. He had just gotten off work when he picked up Rose; he was still clad in his khaki work pants and red Target team shirt. (Whether or not Armstrong still had his job at Target at this point in mid-March is iffy.)

"What was your reason for picking her up?" police pressed on.

"Because my wife doesn't have sex with me at home."

***

Rose Felt would be the second of three women found on the same day at the railroad tracks at Military and John

Kronk Streets in Detroit the following month. You'll meet the others next. Police were able to surmise right away, due to her more advanced decomposition, that Rose was the first one left there. She had been the one to show her killer this secluded spot, having known the area, having grown up not too far away, and he followed suit with his next two victims, dumping them there as well.

Rose's autopsy was performed by Yung Chung, MD, assistant medical examiner, on April 11. She died of manual strangulation. The autopsy showed multiple irregular abrasions and scratches in the lateral neck, consistent with pressure marks on the neck. Internal exam of the neck showed fracture of the hyoid bone and soft tissue hemorrhages in the front of the upper neck. No other injuries or evidence of natural disease were present.

She was logged at first as Unknown Female No. 20, Case No. 00-3590, then ID'd by her fingerprints from prior arrest records.

She was wearing two rings: the ring on her left thumb was described as "yellowtone"; the one on her right middle finger was silver-tone with a clear stone and a heart design (though that second ring was noted by the medical examiner as being on her left middle finger). She wore a silver-tone ankle bracelet on her left ankle. Her toenails were painted. Dr. Chung measured her body at five-foot-seven, shorter than her killer's estimate, and one hundred and fifty pounds. She was indeed blond.

Her stomach was empty, and she tested positive for alcohol and cocaine, negative for opiates and benzodiazepines.

A fellow prostitute named Debra would later tell just a little bit more about Rose when interviewed by police. Just a little. Rose had been noted as missing on the street by the girls. Debra described Rose as homeless, doing her "stuff" in the hotels on Michigan. She had been around that area two or three years. She would sometimes wear a large, dark-brown men's coat. She had no tattoos. No boyfriend. Didn't dance like some of the other girls. (Rose's brother Scott said he did learn after her death that she actually was dancing in a club to get by.)

Rose's daughter Jeniffer lost her paternal grandmother later that same year, in July 2000. So then the girl, just about the age her mom was when she had her, went to live with others in the family. She lived with Loretta for a while and was good friends with Loretta's daughter, her cousin. She sometimes lived with Alex and the girlfriend he had become involved with after Rose. Over the years, Alex moved out west.

"After her grandmother passed away," Loretta said of Jeniffer, "she stayed here until she eventually moved out to Seattle, Washington, where her father was. Jeniffer was in her twenties when she left Michigan. Her early twenties."

And now, years later, Jeniffer carries with her a particular memory of her mother that is haunting, yet not uncommon for the family members of these five women. In fact, you'll read something similar in the chapter that follows.

"She just started prostituting; within the first two weeks of her doing so she was killed," Jeniffer said via text in 2021, remembering her mom as not out there on the streets very long at all. "I knew something was wrong with her 'cuz no matter what, every holiday and birthday she always called me, wished me a happy birthday or Merry Christmas or whatever. It was even if she was drunk and it was three a.m. she always still called. But that birthday that year, no call." It was March 2000.

"I knew something wasn't right. Even my grandma said, 'Mija, your mom didn't call on your birthday; I hope she's OK.' And see, I was waiting for her to call because I spoke to her a week before and she was crying and saying she had nowhere to live and told me that she started prostituting, and she asked me can I come stay with u so I can get clean and not do this anymore. I said, 'I don't know, Mom. I'll have to talk to my grandma.' And she said OK and asked me to go visit her, but being the stupid person I was, told her no, I had plans with my friends for my birthday. I regret that so much. I wish I would have gone and visited her 'cuz I never seen or heard from her again. And I was waiting for her to call me 'cuz I spoke to my grandma and asked if my mom could come stay with us and she said, 'Of course she can; your mom is always welcome here.' I was so happy, and she never called so I could tell her. I blamed myself for a very long time that if I hadn't been a selfish little brat and went to go visit her instead of going to hang out with my friends that she would probably still be alive today."

Scott has his own story of regret; he couldn't hold his tears as he shared it with this author. "My sister Rose, she called me about two or three months before she was murdered. She was struggling with her problems, and at the time I lived in Pennsylvania. And I was married and I had a daughter; she was like seven, eight months old. And Rose called me and said she needed help. She had no place to go. And she asked me if she could move to my house and I could help her get on her feet. Do the right thing. That's what she wanted to do. And I was like, 'Yes! Most definitely!' But my ex-wife, at the time she didn't approve of it. And I looked at her side and my side, and I had to tell Rose no. And then a couple months later, she was murdered. And I felt so bad, like I could have maybe made a difference. She would still be alive. I don't know. But it hurt. It still hurts."

But in the difficult slippery slope of could-have, would-have, should-have, there can be no guilt or condemnation. Just moving forward. Focusing on the positive, like the fact that if Rose were alive today, she would be a grandmother. And that could only be a good thing.

Rose's brother is someone who is determined to stay positive and keep moving forward. He is a survivor, even though his father died not long after his sister, then one of his other sisters died of cancer, then his mother died of cancer—a mom he moved back to Michigan to take care of. He's had his own troubles. He knows what the streets are like. Knows what Detroit was like when he and Rose were teens. He remembers being propositioned by a prostitute when he was thirteen or fourteen. He's been shot twice. He's hung out with the wrong people.

"Detroit has been through so much," Scott said. "There's good people in Detroit and there's bad people in Detroit."

Much like Rose, he encountered stuff he wouldn't wish on anybody. "Me and my sister Rose were very close. I struggled as a teenager. I went through trouble myself. Not saying that nobody's perfect. I wasn't perfect. I lived with my mother and three sisters, and my father wasn't there, so I didn't have a father figure or the discipline. And once I got that certain age, my mother couldn't control me. She had health issues as well. So I got involved in things I shouldn't have, which I regret then, but I don't now because I made a difference in my life … It's been rough for me too, but I stay strong. I have to."

And no matter which direction Rose's life took, she will always be his sister. The lovely, lively girl whose favorite color was purple. "She was a good person when she was sober. Once she got into the drugs …" His voice trails. "My nickname for my sister was 'Wild Thing.' She was wild. I mean, she was a tomboy. She would fight a man. And of course, Armstrong was a big guy, so he overpowered her, for sure. And I know my sister would fight. She's a fighter. Always has been."

Scott added, with quite a degree of resolution, "There a reason for everything in life. I do believe that."

So fervently devoted to his sister was he that his family members had to step in at the time of Armstrong's trial to prevent another tragedy from happening.

"I was hogtied by my uncle, brother-in-law, and a couple of my cousins," he said. "I was going to go downtown, and I was going to shoot this man. I was going to get on top of a rooftop, because I've hunted throughout my life. I was going to do that, and they hogtied me. They tied me up. ... At the time I had so much anger. Honest to God, it's the truth. I was going to kill this man. But my family tied me up. And they saved my life because it would have been a mistake. Now that I think about it now. All the anger, the hatred I had toward this person. It's ... omigoodness. I'm glad they tied me up."

Maybe Rose would be surprised, or just happy, to hear how her family members speak of her. How they understand that a person's life is not equal to his or her bad decisions, or bad circumstances. Maybe she would be surprised to hear what her one-time love said about her, how he spoke up for her here.

"She was an awesome person," Alex said. "She's a beautiful person. I miss her every day."

KELLY JEAN HOOD

She was a girl who loved animals of all kinds.

"We had thirty, forty stray dogs and cats in our yard every day," recalled the oldest of Kelly Jean Hood's three children, Kyle. "You know, growing up, I had ducks, chickens, lizards, rats, mice. Almost any kind of animal you could picture as a pet, we had it."

And that was in the inner city of Detroit, believe it or not. It was a sentiment echoed by Kelly's sister, Shannon Wilson. "Oh yeah, if there was a stray, he would end up coming home with Kelly," Shannon said with a laugh. "Yeah. Oh yeah."

Born in February 1966 in Bay City and raised in Muskegon, a smallish town near Lake Michigan on Michigan's western edge, Kelly Jean Hood was the second oldest of four kids in the family—two boys and two girls. She attended Muskegon High School but dropped out by her junior year.

"Honestly, she was a free spirit," Shannon said. "Kelly hated school. She really did. She worked. She was a hard worker. I remember her starting to babysit when she was twelve years old."

Later, she began bartending and waitressing in Muskegon. But that free spirit would pull her away from the more peaceful surrounds of Muskegon to the opposite side of the state. "Kelly just loved the big city life. She loved 'busy-busy.' And Muskegon, Michigan, is not a busy-busy town. And she always liked the bar scene. She loved bartending. She loved people. She loved to socialize."

Detroit had some big things in store for this lovely young blond girl. And a lot of it was good.

"She met her husband in Detroit," Shannon said. "Her best friend that she grew up with, like all through school, had moved to Detroit when she met her own husband. And that's how Kell met her husband, was through her best friend."

Kelly Jean Hood with her two boys, before the birth of her daughter and a few years before her death. Image courtesy of the family.

With her future husband Tony, Kelly began to have kids, through her twenties. First a boy, then another boy, then a girl. They got married in 1997. Kelly worked jobs such as cleaning hotel rooms. It was a pretty normal life. The family lived for a while in a house on Pittsburg Street in Detroit in the earlier 1990s, then in a house down the street from the home of Tony's mom Rosa in Detroit, on Casper not far off Michigan Ave.

But, as with Armstrong's other victims in Detroit, something went wrong. There was something that put Kelly, like so many others, on the street, living a life very much at risk.

"I'm not going to lie," Shannon said. "Kelly got hooked on crack cocaine. Kelly was always a partier, drinking or smoking the weed. But I want to say ... probably in the last year that she was alive, is when she got hooked on it."

Kyle remembered his mom starting to do crack after his sister was born, probably around 1994, then moving on to other substances, such as heroin and pills, and that things intensified in the year before her death.

It all put a strain on her marriage, Shannon said. "Tony was trying everything he could to learn to deal with it, to help her. But when they don't want the help, what do you do?"

It's unclear just how long Kelly was working the streets. Fellow prostitute Debra, interviewed by police about Rose and Kelly, said she had seen Kelly around for two or three years, that she was homeless like Rose and worked out of the hotels on Michigan Avenue, and that she was a dancer in the nearby clubs. Debra also remembered Kelly as twenty-four, much younger than she was at the time.

Kyle remembered his mom starting to prostitute around 1997 or 1998.

Kelly's sister attested that her time in prostitution was rather short-lived. "She had never done that kind of stuff until she got hooked on the crack." She added, "Otherwise, she was all about her kids. And being a family and being with Tony, until she met that drug."

It was a transition very sad for a younger sister to watch. One can't imagine how difficult it is to see a loved one make these choices and feel helpless to change anything about it, right?

"Right. Right," Shannon said. "And that's what I mean—you go from the loving, caring mom that you are, do everything and anything with your kids, and they're with you 24/7. And now, all of a sudden, you know, I don't care. I don't care who I'm with, you know, not spending time with the kids, anything like that."

Tony filed for divorce from Kelly in June 1999, less than a year before she would be killed. Custody of the kids was determined in October.

Kyle also remembers vividly the grip that the drugs had on his mom. He has also chosen to remember who she was beyond the drugs. "She was a very generous mind," he said. "Even though she was on drugs very heavy, she had a great heart. She helped anybody in need, fed anybody."

Kelly's mother-in-law Rosa gave a statement to police on April 11, 2000, that the last time she saw Kelly was two weeks earlier. Kelly was on the street at Michigan and Cecil—and she had a black eye on her left side. Rosa said Kelly had been staying with an older prostitute friend named Cheryl, who would hang out at Michigan and Central, "near the bank," and whom Rosa just saw the day before she talked to police. Police went to Michigan and Central that same day and spoke with a couple other prostitutes: a different prostitute named Deborah had not seen her for a week to ten days, and Angela said Kelly usually worked Michigan between Addison and Livernois.

Kelly's three children last saw their mom on March 26. By that point, though Tony had custody of the kids, Kelly still came around "once in a while" to see them, Rosa told police.

"He left her because of her drugs and working the street," Rosa's statement said.

In the week before Kelly disappeared, she was hospitalized. It was a critical juncture; it was a point in Kelly's life where her sister and her family offered a lifeline, a way to get help, though it had happened many times before, Shannon said, with Kelly's sisters-in-law fighting to get her into rehab, to no avail. This time, though, in this week in early April 2000, if Kelly would have accepted that lifeline offered to her over the phone, it would have saved her life in more ways than one.

"I had talked to her earlier that week," Shannon explained. "She had been in the hospital. She'd been really sick with pneumonia. And she called me, I want to say it was like Monday or Tuesday. She knew she was going to be getting released from the hospital from being so sick. And I told her then, 'Let me come up and get you and bring you home so we get you in rehab. I'll call off from work; I'll come and get you. You know, you're driving Mom absolutely crazy.' And she's like, 'I will, but, you know, I'm not going to come unless I bring Tiffany,' and then, sister-sibling fight, because I refused to just bring—I wasn't going to split her kids up. Because she wanted me to bring Tiffany with me and have me take care of Tiffany while she went to rehab. Like, your boys will be just distraught. You know? And Tony's always been a great dad to his kids. I wasn't going to do that. That was Kelly's way of, 'Well, I'm not going to come and do rehab unless you do this.'"

It was that Friday, April 7, that her sister remembered Kelly as disappearing. Kelly was thirty-four years old.

***

So around that time in the first week of April 2000, the exact date still unconfirmed, John Eric Armstrong said he picked up Kelly Jean Hood behind a gas station at Michigan and Livernois between midnight and twelve-thirty, after he got off work at around eleven or eleven-thirty p.m. He estimated he encountered Kelly a week or two after he killed Rose Felt. He remembered Kelly as "white, short, about one hundred and twenty, one hundred and thirty pounds, with short hair with curls. I believe it was brunette." He thought she was wearing jeans, then corrected that to a black warmup suit with a white zip-up shirt underneath. As with his other confessions, Armstrong seemed to be able to recall quite a few details, though not always super accurately.

Kelly directed him to "that hill by the railroad tracks" where he had left his previous victim, Armstrong told police. It seemed to be a well-known spot for this sort of business. Armstrong said they parked about twenty or thirty feet away from Rose's body.

He paid Kelly forty dollars for "straight sex." She was on her back in the passenger seat, he said. "The next thing I remember is me on top of her trying to strangle her," Armstrong told police. "I let go when I realized what I was doing."

Kelly was still alive at this point, Armstrong said, but he couldn't remember what came next. But when pressed further in this interrogation by the officers: "After I stopped strangling her, I placed her right where the woods start next to the tracks. She was still alive when I placed her there."

Armstrong then left, not knowing if Kelly would attempt to get up or if she would survive. "I went home and got into the shower. I felt real dirty," he told police.

"Did she scream or plead for her life?" officers asked.

"Not that I know of."

The officers said Kelly's body was found at the bottom of the hill, there by the railroad tracks, and they asked if Armstrong put her there. No, he said.

"Why did you kill her?" they pressed.

"I didn't. She was still alive."

Amid several other questions, officers asked if Kelly was bleeding when he left her there.

"I think she had a split lip."

Kelly lay there an undetermined number of days—probably not many—before being found with the other two women at the railroad tracks at Military and John Kronk. The autopsy for Kelly, logged first as Unknown Female No. 21, before fingerprints paired her to earlier records, as with Rose, showed signs of manual strangulation, along with "bruises superimposed on postmortem injuries and dryness" on her legs, and abrasions and linear scratches on the face and wrists. The tox screen covered a variety of substances, even the phencyclidine/PCP/angel dust more widely seen in the '70s. Kelly was positive for cocaine and opiates; negative for alcohol, benzodiazepines, barbiturates, PCP. Noted were Kelly's tattoos, a rose on the left side of her chest, a heart on her right shoulder blade.

Back at his grandma's home a few blocks off Michigan Ave, Kyle received the news of his mom's death.

"They contacted my grandmother, Rosa. After they contacted her, me, my brother and my sister and my father were living with my grandmother at the time. She owned a duplex, a flat, a whole house. So we were living in the upstairs flat at the time. We were just having dinner. And then my grandmother comes walking up the stairs and the first thing out of her mouth is, 'They found your mother.' So after they said that, I kind of was like, 'What?' And then she's like, 'Your mother's gone,' this and that. Just went on to say it that way. At the time I knew what death was. I was nine. I had gone through a lot of stuff already at that time. I had to grow up fast. So I knew what was going on. But I didn't process it right away. I didn't show any real emotion when I was told. But yeah, that's how we found out with the police."

He learned another detail so disturbing. "I heard my other grandmother, her mother, my mother's mother, and my aunt all heard that she was in the hospital before she passed. And she got in contact with them. She got in contact with my grandmother, my great aunt, and my aunt, her sister, told them what was going on. They begged her to come back to Muskegon, Michigan. 'We'll help you; come stay with us.' But she didn't want to."

***

A couple decades after his mom's death, Kyle sometimes uses her maiden name before his own last name on Facebook, where he has also posted photos of the two of them. Not all of his Facebook friends know the story of his mom and he's not eager to share it. He's the oldest of her three children, remembering her well and having had a glimpse into her life that perhaps his two siblings did not.

"I went everywhere with her," he said. "I've seen everything. I've got all this shit in my head I've been trying to block out. ... But again, my mother got into a certain lifestyle because it had such a hold on her. She didn't want to give up the drugs. And she was offered help a couple times from her side of the family in Muskegon, but she loved her drugs too much."

It's a sentiment reinforced by his uncle in an online comment to a blog post about the case: "She left behind three kids; till [sic] this day they miss their mother. She had a drug addiction, and she knew what she was doing was wrong; she was trying to get help. Armstrong took all that away from her and he took her away from her kids."

Kelly's sister-in-law Alma offered a similar statement at Armstrong's sentencing in June 2001: "She was labeled as a prostitute, but to us she was a person with a drug problem who had to find her way to make money to support her problem. You had no right to take her life away."

Still, time has been doing its own job of healing. "I've just recently come to terms with my mother being gone," her son said. "Just started to really open up the past five years. When she first passed, I didn't even visit her gravesite after her funeral and her burial. I didn't even visit her for like almost ten years."

NICOLE YOUNG (AKA ROBIN BROWN)

She was working the Detroit streets for only a short time before she disappeared. That's how she was remembered, as a recent face in town, come over from Chicago. She had been spotted at the all-night burger joint on Michigan Ave. "That little Black girl, she wasn't out there long," said Sheryl Yike, who worked the counter there. "She wasn't. She was gone. I mean, it seemed to be like a week or two."

And this new girl was young, the youngest one of the five women in our story, having just turned twenty in January. Or so it seemed.

Robin Brown, spelled sometimes as Robbin, but real name evidently Nicole Young. Or was it the other way around? Which was the street name? It's hard to say, based on news reports and whatever other information can be scraped together. Also, was she really born in January 1980? Or was she even younger than she told police? She didn't show them any sort of driver's license. Nevertheless, she was a Black female of medium complexion, brown eyes, black hair, with a tattoo of "Jason" on her left leg, according to her arrest records. Five-foot-three on one police report, five-foot-two on another, and one hundred and fifteen or one hundred and twenty pounds. The address she gave police was to a condo on West Gunnison in Chicago, near the Chicago River North Branch.

Mug Photo#:127896
AIJ #:
Last: BROWN
First: ROBBIN
Arr Date: 07 /29 / 1999
DOB:
Sex: F FEMA
Race\Nat\BLACK
Height: 502
Weight: 120
Hair: BRO
Eyes: BRO
Glasses: N

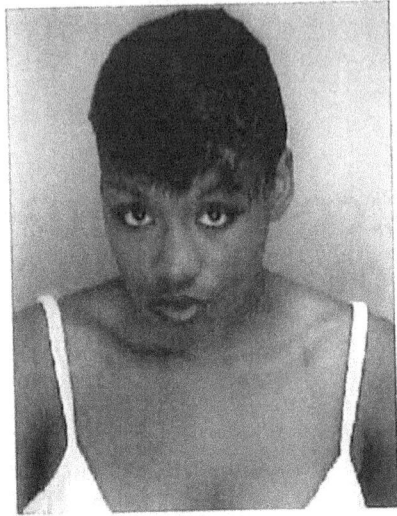

One of Robin's arrest records. Image: Detroit police files.

The story goes that Robin came to Detroit with her boyfriend and started working the streets there. One news story of the time, by Mark Gribben, said she was brought to Detroit by her boyfriend, forced into prostitution and abandoned. A *Detroit Free Press* story said the two split up and the boyfriend returned to Chicago, leaving her stranded here. The girl's mother lived in a Chicago halfway home, the story said. A YouTube commenter named Judy clarified that Robin's boyfriend was a drug dealer, not a prostitute, and that Robin had been raped by a caregiver's boyfriend at age thirteen. She became a ward of the state. A state that abandoned her, Judy said, not even prosecuting her rapist.

Chicago arrest records show police picked her up on June 25 and July 7, 1999, for prostitution or soliciting a ride on a roadway. Then, coming to Michigan, she was arrested by Dearborn police on July 29 for sex offenses. Detroit police picked her up for disorderly conduct and what they call "flagging" (soliciting for an act of prostitution) on

August 7, 1999. She had given her birthplace as Waukegan, Illinois.

Maybe she was envisioning Detroit as a fresh start. We don't know, because family members reportedly wouldn't even claim her body when contacted, and no family members or friends could be reached for this book. The name of her boyfriend surfaced, through some digging, but he wouldn't answer the messages sent.

So unfortunately, we have no one to directly speak for Robin. (Which perhaps is the subject of a whole other book, though we'll get into it a bit.)

We'll just leave it with what Judy said on YouTube: "She had a hard life. She loved to dance and always had a smile on her dimple face in good times. May she rest in peace."

***

The man who confessed to Robin's murder remembered her as five-foot-six, one hundred to one hundred ten pounds, dark complexion with short hair. She was wearing two jackets. The jacket on the outside was black, the one on the inside was red. She had on a skin-tight shirt. "I don't remember the color," he told police. "I believe she had on black pants and tight stockings underneath it. She had on boots."

Again, lots of details. Not always super accurate. But lots of recall.

As with Monica Johnson, Armstrong said he picked up Robin near the two used car lots on Michigan Avenue. He approached her, he said, and she said nothing, just got into his Jeep. She then offered him sex for sixty dollars.

"How did she get to the railroad tracks?" police asked him.

"I took her up there. She asked me if I knew a spot. I told her yes. She said okay and I took her there." Rose Felt's suggestion would serve him a third time, unfortunately.

"Why did you take her to the spot where the other two bodies were?" police asked him.

"That's the only place I knew."

By this point, Armstrong was already a little agitated with Robin, however.

"How did this make you feel that she was offering sex to you for money?" police said.

"Very upset, very angry."

"What did you want to do to her when she offered you sex for money?" the officers prodded.

"I wanted to hit her."

He did not hit her, however, and the two proceeded with their business. But things were a little different with Robin. "She started making fun of me," he said. "She said that I had a small penis and didn't know how to use it."

He then strangled her, he said. "The next thing I knew, I was driving off."

"You killed her because she made fun of your penis?" police pressed.

"Yes. She said I didn't know how to use it; I was a stupid white boy."

This time, Armstrong used a ligature to strangle his victim: the stockings she wore. "She was trying to fight me at first. That's all I remember."

Armstrong did not recall how Robin got out of the Jeep and onto the ground near the railroad tracks that night. He only remembered driving away and seeing her body lying there through his rearview mirror.

He threw the condom he had worn out on Ford Road near Wyoming, near the drive-in movie theater, he said. That was in Dearborn. He threw her shoes down a side street in Detroit. He then went home and took a shower for about thirty to forty minutes.

Armstrong said this all took place on "Monday night," but he misspoke as he was trying to remember. We know it would have been the night of Sunday, April 9, 2000, and the morning of Monday, April 10. It was about one or two a.m., he estimated.

Robin, the last of the three women placed there at the site, would be found first, lying near the tracks with her own stocking around her neck. It would be only a few hours after he left her on this Monday morning.

And the following day, on April 11, Dr. Yung Chung would determine that she died of ligature strangulation, a deep skin groove encircling her neck but no soft tissue hemorrhages in the neck. The white elastic hosiery, as Chung described in the report, was wound around her neck twice and secured in front by a half square knot.

Robin's autopsy pegged her as one hundred and thirty-four pounds but five-foot-six rather than the shorter height of her arrest records. She appeared "about the recorded age of twenty years." Several of her pearl-colored fake fingernails were missing: fifth finger of left hand, and index, middle, and fifth finger from right hand. And there was the tattoo on her leg of "Jason," its *A* turned upside-down as a *V*. Her tox screens came up negative for everything, alcohol and whatever kind of drugs, though undetermined for phenobarbital.

An addendum dated April 27 answered two of our questions: Her real name was indeed Nicole Marie Young, and she was only seventeen, born in January 1983. She had managed to fool the police on those details.

She fooled the police on her address too. The landlady at the address she gave police on West Gunnison in Chicago said, when contacted for this book, that the FBI came knocking at her door there that year. They ended up interviewing her son's friend Ronnie, who knew Nicole. "She never lived here," the landlady said. "And my son said at that time she didn't have a house. She used their address because my son was staying here at the time, so that she could receive whatever help that she was getting. It was going to their address. Because I know she never lived here. I never knew that either, until he told me."

In 2021, this comment about Nicole turned up on a YouTube video about the case: "Nicole Young aka Robin Brown was not 18 years old. She was only a 17 years old beautiful girl who was a ward of the state. She was rape *[sic]* as a 13 child by a boyfriend of a caregiver and the state attorney thought she was not important enough to prosecute the abuser. She did have issues and thought she was useless when they didn't come to her defense. DCFS didn't even attend the meeting with police and attorney or get her the needed help after the ordeal. Not only did John Armstrong killed her the state deserted her. I blame them both. Oh yeah her boyfriend was a drug dealer not a pimp (which is not much better but I want the truth about her to be told). She had a hard life. She loved to dance and always had a smile on her dimple face in good times. May she rest in peace."

At any rate, the girl we'll now refer to as Nicole would be the last person John Eric Armstrong would ever kill. Maybe not the last person he would attack, though. We can't be sure about that. A lot can happen in a day or two.

LIVED TO TELL: NATASHA OLEJNICZAK

Now we need to step back from our tale of five women in Detroit. Backward, actually, several months. Because these five women were not the only ones to encounter John Eric Armstrong on the streets in the Motor City—not by any means, and we'll talk more on that later. But months before the first of our five ever met Armstrong, another woman working the streets of Detroit did. And she lived to tell a story that wouldn't be known publicly until after Armstrong's arrest.

***

Natasha Olejniczak was different from a lot of the prostitutes in town because drugs were not part of the picture for her. She was not out there feeding a habit. She was clean. She was out there simply to get some money, as she openly admits to this day. She lived in Grand Rapids, actually, in the western part of the state, and she would drive the couple hours to Detroit for a stretch of days, working out of a hotel on Michigan Avenue near the border of Detroit and Dearborn. She would stay for a while and when she felt she had made enough money, she would go back home to the other side of the state. She had a boyfriend she would come back to in Grand Rapids, a pimp who worked with girls over in that area.

Maybe it was the hotel room that made her would-be killer a bit nervous. When you read the later chapter "The

Unknown and the Unconfirmed," however, you wouldn't think so. He had evidently met with other women at hotels and motels. Maybe it was just that he was new in Detroit and still finding his way around, still getting his "sea legs," to use a term a former Navy man like him would appreciate. For whatever reason, he was nervous the night he met Natasha Olejniczak. And who knows—it may have helped save her life.

It was August 15, 1999. Around midnight, probably. John Eric Armstrong had moved to metro Detroit with his wife Katie and baby son only weeks before, a few months after he and Katie were discharged from the Navy. Natasha could have been his first prostitute encounter in Detroit and she is likely his first assault in Detroit. She is the first one we know of anyway.

Natasha was about to turn twenty-six that year, born ironically the same year as Armstrong, within a couple weeks, actually. She was described as a leggy blond in one media story of the time. When this author read that description to her over the phone a couple of decades later, she sorta laughed. Yeah, she was a blond at the time. Not very tall, though, maybe five-foot-four. I read the same writer's description of her as wearing a short skirt and a shirt tied up under her breasts. That sounded right, she said. She looked pretty "money" at the time. Fur coats, fur-trimmed heels. Maybe that's part of what made her stand out to Armstrong as she was walking along Michigan Avenue that night.

"He drove around. There was a lot of us out there. And maybe I was just the one, you know?"

She explained, "I was just trying to get money and everything. And you know. It was ... I don't know, I was young and stuff. I was twenty-six years old. And I had two kids, but they were in Grand Rapids with my mother and them. Me and my girlfriend and all of us, we used to just go back and forth to Detroit and get money, and come back to

Grand Rapids. Then we went to New York. Then we went to Vegas. We traveled."

So that night in August, Armstrong spotted Natasha walking just down the street from her hotel, a Days Inn that once sat on Michigan between Oakman and Miller in Dearborn, very close to the city border. The site is now an empty lot.

"There was a lot of prostitution going on," Natasha remembered of the locale in 1999. "That place was full of prostitutes there. That strip was."

They met that night at about Michigan and Lonyo, Natasha would later tell the police. This was about a mile east of her hotel. She got into Armstrong's Jeep and directed him back toward the hotel. Room 121, it would be. There was something about this john that was different, however.

"I just had a feeling about him when I first met him, that feeling like, '*ahhh* ...' You know, he wasn't feeling comfortable."

What might have made him seem that way?

"I don't know; maybe I made him feel nervous or something. He made me feel real nervous too. I don't know. It was odd, too odd for me."

When the two reached her hotel room, she would later testify at Armstrong's trial, he used the bathroom for a few minutes. Then he came out of the bathroom and told her he didn't feel right there. He said he had to leave.

"We were talking and everything," she recalled to me. "He made a deal with the money situation, and I said, okay, fine. He said, 'I forgot something in my car.' And I said okay." But it was all pretty strange. Was this john going to drive away? Or was he really just running out to his car for something? She was unsure, by the way he was acting.

"I can't do this; I don't trust this," she remembered Armstrong saying when she spoke to police that night.

As Armstrong was leaving the room, Natasha told him not to forget his hat, which he had set on the bed. She also remembered that he had on his uniform from the security job he was working at the time.

"He said, 'Did you want a ride?'" she said. "''Do you want a ride back?' And I said no, because I don't need no ride back. So he left out of the room."

She turned to use the phone, but then heard a knock on the door. She went to the window and peered out through the drapes, seeing it was this strange john again. Why was he back at the door? Maybe he really did just need something from his car, or maybe he changed his mind his mind about leaving.

"I opened it," she said, "and that's when all the action happened."

Opening the door is a regret she has felt deeply over the years, especially given the fact that she had been thinking about returning to Grand Rapids earlier in the day. But it was the money that had motivated her to open that door back up and perhaps other stuff was on her mind.

"I had got into an argument that day with my boyfriend. And I got out there on the street. That day was just a bad day. I should have never let him come back in. ... I should have never opened my door back open, but ... I looked out my window, and he's like, 'Open it up, it's me, John,' you know. Yup. And that's when everything went ... He must have went back to his truck, because I was getting ready to call a cab. And then there was a knock at the door. Yup. I remember it. Because he left and he came back; that's when he had that knife. He must have went and got it out of his truck. He was in a Jeep."

(For both her testimony in court in 2001 and her recount of the incident for this book, Natasha remembered Armstrong giving his name as John that night, which is interesting from a psychological standpoint, as you'll see.)

Once back inside the room, Armstrong showed Natasha that he had a knife. "Don't scream," he warned.

"What's the problem?" she asked. "I didn't do anything to you."

"Shut up," he replied.

"Please don't kill me; I've got kids."

He came at her. She backed up toward the bathroom. She was tripping out; he was a lot bigger than her one-hundred-and-twenty-pound frame. He grabbed her by the neck and began to choke her.

"So we were just tousling and everything," she said, "and I slipped with my boots on. I got on the floor and the knife fell out of his hand."

As they were struggling, Natasha received knife cuts on her hand and on her face, and all around her head. She got rug burns on her back. Armstrong picked her up and slammed her on her back on the bed, she remembered.

"I was like, oh, I'm hit, I'm going to die."

Armstrong forced his knees on her chest and was trying choke her with his bare hands, she said. "I hate hookers," she recalled him saying. "I hate hookers."

Then, "after I heard 'hooker,' I passed out," she said in court.

But Natasha remembered another small detail so many years later, when first recalling the incident for this book. Something that didn't come up in court. She remembered, amid her struggling to keep conscious as Armstrong was choking her, that she had also made the decision to play dead.

"We were—me and him—I was fighting with the man! Hanging with him, and the next moment I knew, he got me on the bed. And he grabbed for the knife, so I kicked it then. And that's when, like, the telephone cord, that's when he wrapped that around my neck. And then, I played like I was dead. He didn't even—he didn't touch me to see if I was alive or anything. I did like an act on it, basically."

That one choice on her part might have saved her life, causing her would-be killer to stop just as she was passing out.

"And when I woke up, I was on my stomach with a telephone cord wrapped around my neck so tight I was biting my tongue, saying my kids' names."

Her attacker was gone. Natasha managed to get up and run out of the room. She told the other street girls she knew about the encounter.

The person at the front desk of the hotel called the police. The Dearborn Police Department report gives it as one a.m. on August 15. Officers Kanitra, MacDonell, and Nicklowitz of Dearborn PD responded. They spoke with the hotel manager, who said he had been told there was a woman wandering the parking lot, bleeding and disoriented. They interviewed witnesses there, including the front desk clerk and a friend of Natasha who was sharing the room with her. They noted the red marks around Natasha's neck, the bruising on the back of her neck, the lacerations on her right ring finger and middle finger. She was transported to Oakwood Hospital.

Officer Anthony Domek processed the hotel room for evidence, and he did collect one very interesting item: a silver-tone belt buckle with the word INITIAL on it in black lettering. It was lying on the floor of the room. He bagged it and had it placed in an evidence locker. Natasha recalled, years later, that Armstrong had left a belt buckle behind in her room, and the detail would be picked up in later news reports about the case.

The description of the perp she gave police: white male, age twenty-five to twenty-six, tall, two hundred and twenty pounds, muscular or fit build, light complexion, eyeglasses, short brown hair, brown mustache, no accent. He told her he was from Oklahoma, she said, which struck her as a fabrication because he seemed to know the area pretty well. He wore a Nike hat, a black and green checkered shirt, and black boots. She remembered the knife having a blade that was three-and-a-half-inches long. In the days that followed, as she spoke further with police, particularly Allan Ruprecht and William Sullivan, who had been assigned to the case, she was pretty sure this guy had driven a Jeep Wrangler. Blue in color.

But Natasha also recalled the feeling that though they investigated the scene and photographed her injuries, police were suspicious of her that night, given her line of work.

"The police were like, are you on drugs? Because, you know, they checked the room. They thought they were going to find, like, crack pipes. There was not a drug in there. Not a pipe or nothing."

Dearborn PD's report says Domek "processed the scene" but doesn't go into detail as to what that included. There are only notes that he shot a roll of 35mm film and picked up the belt buckle.

Natasha realized that night her attacker had stolen the money she had accumulated that she was about to take back home. "I had it in my sock," she recalled. "Something was going on with me that day. I'm like, shit, I'm going to get up out of here, go back to Grand Rapids. I said, no, I'm going to turn one more day, then I'm going to leave. So he did get my money, five hundred dollars."

But perhaps the lost money was the least of the effects of that night.

"My girlfriends came over and they were like, oh! Because my eyes were bloodshot. Red. Because you know, from the strangling ... I thought, dang, this is really crazy. This is crazy. I was out of it for a couple days until I really got back, you know, focus. Because I couldn't really talk good, because he strangled me ... My vocal cords were really swollen and I just couldn't say much, you know?"

On August 19, Detective Sullivan contacted the Sex Crimes Unit at the Detroit Police due to the fact that Natasha had first encountered this john in the city limits. A copy of Dearborn's case report was faxed to Detroit.

Several months after the assault, going on a year, actually, Natasha saw Armstrong's photo in the *Grand Rapids Press* after his arrest made national news. Certainly, she freaked out. She contacted police. This is the guy, she told them. The guy that tried to kill me. Sullivan had seen the report himself a day or two after the arrest. He made the connection between his case and the description of Armstrong and the crimes in the media, but he was giving it a few days to see if Natasha would call him first. Indeed, she did.

Nowadays, Natasha thinks about that decision to play dead with her would-be killer. It surprises her, that in such a shocking and traumatic moment, she could have the wherewithal. But it came from a place deep inside her that she barely remembered.

"Yeah, I don't know what made me do that. I don't know. Because when I used to be little and stuff, I used to play, I said, I'm going to be like, if somebody ever does something to me, I would always say, I'm going to play like I was dead. You know, if someone tries to do something wrong or anything? And I was always saying stuff like that to myself, to nobody else. I always said if something bad happens to me, and I had to come into a situation, I was always going to play like I was dead."

As with Monica Johnson a few months later, and Kelly Jean Hood after that, and possibly others before all this, as we would later learn, Armstrong left Natasha without knowing whether or not she was actually dead. Left because he assumed death, or the kind of near death a person can't come back from? Left because he feared he would get caught? Hurried out because he couldn't stand the sight of it all anymore? Because he was feeling remorse? Who knows. Whatever the reason, this time the victim survived.

The presence of the knife might seem unusual in this case, but you will see later that knives were found in his Jeep by police at different times and were mentioned by a couple other survivors. In Natasha's case, was the weapon meant merely to subdue her but not to kill her? A later survivor account will back up that idea.

Had he intended to strangle her all along and just used the knife as a threat? Why? And why did he even go back to the hotel room in the first place when he just could have left, without any suspicion, no harm no foul, if he was feeling so uncomfortable?

***

After the assault, Natasha had to have two fingertips sewn back on. She had stitches around her face and skull. But her scars went much deeper than that. Though she turned away from the streets, left Detroit and never came back, out of the biz and back home to Grand Rapids for good, she has had to rely on medication over the years to help calm her. She has suffered from post-traumatic stress disorder. She has worked regular jobs, tried to lead a regular life with her kids and family. As her kids got older, she told them more of what happened to her. Her kids are now grown and she has five grandkids. She was working as a homecare aide when first interviewed for this book, then got a different job in a factory. But she has found it hard to get by. She forgets a lot of things, she told me. The memories of those days in Detroit, however, are never far away.

She remembers showing up in court, testifying against Armstrong along with a few other assault survivors. What was his demeanor when she saw him in court?

"Just evil. He had that look, like 'yeah.' He couldn't look at me. He turned his head and looked the other way."

How did that feel?

"Like, I was, you know, just sweating and nervous. There was a lot going through my head. And I was like, 'just relax, it'll be all right.' I'm like … Because I'm suffering through a lot of things right now."

You mean in the courtroom, or right now?

"Just from what he did to me. Because I'm not the same person like I used to be."

She elaborated: "I don't like to be around a lot of people no more. I'm not that people person. I'm all medicated up from the incident. Like, I don't trust anybody. I live by myself. You know, my kids, that's all I trust. I used to have friends come around and spend the night; I won't let nobody stay with me. I've been knowing them for years; I don't trust nobody. So a lot of no-trusting. And like if I see a big tall white guy with glasses, you know … it backflashes. Yeah, you know, he took me apart from a lot of things. I don't even like to leave my drinks around nobody, like my cups or anything."

She fears tampering; she fears an attempt on her life in even that sort of premeditated, nonviolent way.

And at the time of Armstrong's trials, Natasha said she was given promises that weren't kept.

"And then, you know, I was in a bind where like, you know, I think, if I'm a survivor, I think you guys should take care of me off of this. I'm coming to testify. I had no income coming in. They promised me they were going to pay me, and they never paid me."

She went on, "Then I filed for my disability. That's how I got on disability, because of PTSD. Because I've always had—before I went in the streets, I was a machine operator, I always had good jobs. But I just wanted to try the streets. No guy led me into anything. I did this on my own."

In Natasha's day-to-day struggles, when I initially spoke with her via phone, she was having a conflict with a neighbor at her apartment complex, a woman who had been in and out of jail and was verbally harassing her. It wasn't helping Natasha's general state of worry.

"So just imagine, like, when I hear loud noises and things and reactions, I get fidgety and worry; like, what's going to happen next? You know? So whatever happens, I feel like—I feel something ain't right. Because I'm always looking over my shoulder. I never used to do that. Never."

And it has, of course, affected her family.

"My youngest boy, he said if he could meet the man, you know, he would hurt him. Because he has a little temper."

Wanting so much to protect Mom.

"Yeah, but I tell my kids, I'm all right, I'll be all right. You just can't keep … I've got to keep moving on. You know, it's just like I said, life is not like it used to be. I mean, sometimes I get into a mood where I wish this would have never happened."

Her oldest son Kenny talked openly about what his mom's assault has meant to him as we all met up in Grand Rapids. He remembered it pretty well. He saw her right after it happened.

"I remember—my mom has naturally blond hair," he said as we all talked over lunch in summer 2019. "But she always had this color, maybe like more bleachy-blond. She had come home; her whole head was red as blood."

He continued, "And I remember that day. I was seven years old. We had a whole house, where we were at. My aunt, her sister, brought me upstairs. I went to see my mom, me and my little brother Ronnie. … He was just a baby, three years old. He doesn't remember much. When I went upstairs, went into her room, she hugged me, and then I remember grabbing her face. I said, 'What happened to your face, Mama?' He was cutting her face with a knife. At least over a hundred stitches. Her whole face was stitched up."

After that, Kenny said, things were different for his mom. "I feel like after Eric Armstrong, our whole lives collapsed. … I feel like he destroyed something with her. I feel like he took a lot from us. My mom hasn't slept in her own room. She's just now starting to. For twenty years, she slept on the couch."

Why did you feel safer on the couch? I asked Natasha.

"I don't know."

As the assault changed the way his mom lived, it changed the direction of Kenny's life too. A solidly built man of twenty-seven as we spoke, you could tell he once played football. He was a Division-1 athlete at one time, but because things had changed so much for the family and they were living differently, struggling for money, college was not an option for him.

"It was either go to school or survive," he said. He turned to the easiest way he could figure to support himself—selling drugs. He talked about watching one particular gang in Grand Rapids come and take over his neighborhood with the drug trade.

"I hated drug dealers," he said. "My dad was a drug dealer. I hated drug dealers. They say sometimes you become what you hate." Ironically, "my little brother had wanted to be a cop. Seriously. I had wanted to be a firefighter."

Kenny started out dealing with weed, then crack cocaine, heroin.

"I hated that. I just wanted to overcome all that. And then reality sunk in. The recession hit. I had to do something. I moved out from my mom's house at seventeen. I had my own apartment. Just from dealing drugs. By the time I was seventeen, I was in my own place. I grew up fast."

Later, in his twenties, the drug trade led him to jail time in Kent County. It could have been worse but for the compassion of a judge. Kenny had completed a drug sentence when he was younger, then on the later charge he encountered the same judge, who gave him a choice of boot camp or a work release program. He chose the latter, which allowed him to still be a provider to his son. Kenny had become a father when he was still a teen.

"I was working for fourteen dollars an hour, fifty-plus hours a week. And I'd be out of jail every day, but it was hard work." And when he was released, which was only a couple months before our interview, he got a fresh perspective. He went into legit work, partnering with a car dealership and doing detailing.

"I respect the working man. I really do. Nobody knows the stress a man goes through trying to be a provider."

As he told of the turns his young life has taken, his demeanor was positive. Determined. He has felt a lot of anger toward Armstrong but has worked through it. He said he hoped Armstrong could read this, could know the effects his actions had not just that night in 1999 but for years afterward. He will, I assured Kenny. He'll know it. Or he already does, without having to read anything at all. And this young man, just past the age his mom was when she was attacked, still continued to share a positive perspective, one helped along by a faith in God, whom he had recently asked, simply, to just show him a better way.

"I sat down this time and started reevaluating my own life," he said. "I spent twenty months in jail in the last four years. No more. I made a promise to God this time. I told God, show me a different way. I don't ask Him for much. I asked Him to keep me out of prison; He did."

He said both his mother and his father were recently baptized. "It took my mother and father until they were in their forties to change, so I knew it wasn't too late for me."

And his own family? "I love my son. He's going on twelve now. He's just the greatest kid. He's enjoying life. I tell him not to grow up too fast. I didn't get to enjoy my childhood, so I'm enjoying watching him. I had to watch over my little brother a lot."

Kenny said he's at peace now, not looking over his shoulder anymore. He thinks a lot about what the situation could be, for him, if he still chose the *other* way.

"Thank God I'm not into drugs or anything now. A lot of my friends right now are overdosing, dying. I just had a buddy that died two weeks ago. Overdosed. Last year I had a buddy overdose. One of my friends got killed right here at this gas station last Saturday." He pointed across the street.

He has a dream to start a youth football program for kids, kids who might go in the wrong direction like him.

And even though Kenny's mom was clean back in those days in Detroit, illegal drugs have since become a part of the story for her, a time or two. But, said Kenny, ever protective at her side as we talked, honest and matter of fact, she is not into that anymore. She was dealing with an alcohol problem at times. But "my mom is a very strong woman."

As Kenny said all this, Natasha nodded. Quietly confirmed it, didn't really add to it. She was nervous about this meeting, she told me later, very nervous, even though she had already talked with me about the assault a few times over the phone in the year leading up to our lunch. It's something that probably can't easily be explained, surviving an attempted murder, and even though you're twenty years beyond it, you've still been sleeping on the couch, you're still wondering how people might perceive you. If they would judge you. You're just scared.

Over the years, the doctors have pushed the medication for her. But like in those days in Detroit, Natasha deep down really doesn't want to be on any substances.

"I don't want to be all medicated up. I can't. I don't want to walk around here and be looking like no zombie." The prescribed drugs that she has taken have given her side effects that made her uneasy anyway.

"A lot of those girls were on drugs bad," she recalled of those days on the street. "I can't believe how many of them girls I used to see out there. They would go and stand in the corner hitting the pipe. I wasn't thinking about no drugs; I was thinking about money."

Natasha has seen Armstrong's most recent online prison picture.

"I think he still looks the same; he's just got the bald head. I really do. And he's still a hefty big guy. I think he's not as big as when he was out. But he's probably like, I don't know … I don't know what goes through his head."

She has seen some information about her attacker online. Though she doesn't use the Internet much, a friend played for her a podcast or two about the case, and there were more threads of familiarity running through them than she would have realized. Like the photo of one particular victim that she saw in the online reports.

"I knew Wendy," she said. "She was on Michigan Avenue a couple times."

***

Natasha and her son Kenny.

On her birthday in December 2018, after I had spoken to her a few times but before we met for lunch, Natasha called me, in the evening. She had seen a news report of a man arrested in Grand Rapids for killing a woman. It was a gruesome crime involving dismemberment.

"The guy who did that looks just like John Eric Armstrong," she told me excitedly. "Remember John had the red hair? I wonder if he's, like, related to him? That's why I had to call you. Because he had red hair … I thought it was like a relative to him."

I assured her this wouldn't have been a relative to Armstrong, as most of his family was out of state. Even his son wasn't the same age as this person.

"Okay, well, I wanted to tell you, because John had red hair," she repeated urgently. "Didn't he have red hair? I was just wondering if he's related …" Her voice trailed.

"He reminds me of him," she repeated. "I had to call you, Billie, because he reminded me of the red hair. But he's in prison right now, so … Is there any way you can make sure he's not out of prison or anything?"

"Oh, I definitely know, he's totally in prison," I reassured. I had visited him a couple times by then, though I didn't mention that to Natasha. She was already pretty shaken. "He'll never be released. There's no way."

"I'm freaking out."

"Oh, honey, don't worry. There's no way he could ever be released."

BREAKING HER SILENCE: ZELDA JAKUBOWSKI

As the details emerged of the Armstrong case, police learned not only of the five women killed, but of four assault survivors as well. In addition to Natasha, whose story you just heard, three others were queued up to testify at Armstrong's trials. Police always wondered how many more could be out there. They figured there had to be others, given the gaps unaccounted for in the ten or so months Armstrong lived in metro Detroit before his arrest. Years later, long after his trial and incarceration, an interesting comment would pop up on a blog post about the case, and it would lead to the following story being told here publicly for the first time.

***

The snowflakes were big and glittery that night. Like diamonds. She thought of them as "Charlie Brown snowflakes" as she stood along Vernor Highway in Southwest Detroit. It was evening in this stretch of Mexicantown.

Zelda Jakubowski had just been with a john. He was a big guy of color driving a Cadillac who had taken her to a motel east of here, then brought her back to drop her off again in her area. This was not the notorious Michigan Ave, but it was pretty close by, in another little pocket of prostitution in Detroit concentrated in a one-block stretch of Vernor between Clark and Scotten Avenues, where she now stood. She lived here. She felt safer here. Later, she would branch out to work more of the Fort Street area, which was thriving at the time in the latter '90s, before the neighborhood development and new bridge plans of more recent years would push out most of the prostitution. But for right now, Zelda stuck close to where she lived, here at Vernor. She was new to this prostitution thing. She had just quit her job at a nearby bar not too long before, unable to keep up with her drug habit. Like a lot of the women in our story, drugs are what put her out there, on the street.

Zelda is a big believer in the hereditary component of addiction because it runs strong in her family. Passed on generation after generation. Basically a generational curse. For her, the drugs dulled feelings of worthlessness rooted in her childhood in the downriver community of Taylor, just a few miles outside of Detroit. She was born in 1966, but when she was still in the womb, her mother suffered from uterine cancer and was actually advised to abort the baby. In school, Zelda was teased for having a name like a witch, causing her to use her middle name instead for a long time. And she didn't have many options growing up like other kids might. There was no discussion of college. Dead-end jobs and a get-by life seemed her destiny. The drugs helped that. At the bar, they smoked a lot of pot, so it served as a gateway for her, along with alcohol. Then came the harder stuff. By this time, she'd had a son but did not feel worthy of being his mom.

"I was just running and medicating," she recalled years later as we sat and talked at a diner in another downriver Detroit community, Monroe, in 2020. Once she had realized that she could numb her own thoughts, she ran with it, she said. "And I was the worst of the worst. I was always nice to people, but I wasn't nice to myself."

The streets were scary at times. "I was never really supposed to be there," she said with every measure of frankness. "Nobody's ever supposed to be there." And her family, who by the late '90s had mostly moved back to Kentucky where they originally were from, didn't come looking for her.

So here she was, just dropped off by a trick, thankful for the long coat someone had just given her. The coat was warm and comfy, cashmere even, going all the way down to her calves, though the night wasn't too terribly cold. But she does remember it being the first snowfall of the season. With those big, glittery flakes. She can't remember what month it was. Given Michigan's climate, you would probably assume November. There was no new snow reported in the National Weather Service's records for October or November 1999, however; the first real snowfall that winter was 1.3 inches on December 6, 1999. So for the sake of argument, we'll call it that. That would make it a few days after Monica Johnson.

But we don't know because, you see, Zelda did not file a police report—did not tell a soul about any of this for years afterward. Because she figured she deserved what happened.

And ironically, in that moment, before it happened, she was feeling thankful. Thankful for the coat.

It was just past nine o'clock, she remembered. Pretty early, still. She was standing near a Mexican restaurant on the north side of Vernor, one that still sits there as of this writing. She then crossed the street near Scotten and turned to head down the sidewalk toward Clark, the large Clark Park to her left, stretching several blocks south between Clark and Scotten on that side of Vernor. On the other side of Scotten were the schools that Rose Felt and her boyfriend Alex once attended—Amelia Earhart and Western High. This was the area where they grew up. This was also close to the railroad track scene at Military and John Kronk. And this was within a mile of Michigan Ave, which is to the north. It's all close quarters in this part of the city.

At some point in her stroll, Zelda realized there was a Jeep sitting there, parked on Vernor just in front of Clark. There was a guy in the driver's seat and he had already spotted her. He had been watching her, she felt. Was he waiting for someone? Had he just grabbed something at the liquor store, which was right there on that corner? Or maybe at the gas station just behind him? It was unclear. All she knew was that he had spotted her before she had spotted him. He'd had her on "lock," she recalled.

"And he looked at me, and I looked at him," she said. "And you know, it doesn't take words between people, when they're doing that."

After they had made eye contact, she jumped into the Jeep.

"How much?" he asked.

She told him one hundred dollars, which was higher than most charged. He didn't blink an eye and she was relieved.

She took in his reddish hair, his freckles. Her first impression: "He looks like an apple pie, the nicest guy you would ever see. Unassuming. Like the most disarming. I was thinking in my mind, 'Are you kidding me? This is going to be so easy.' I was thinking like ten steps ahead. 'This is going to be so easy; I'm going to be home quicker than I thought. It's going to be like that, it's going to be like, bam, and I'm going to get a hundred more dollars. And I'm going to be home by ten, and it's nine-thirty.'"

Though he was a big guy, well over two hundred pounds, she surmised, he was slumped down in the seat, like he was trying to make himself seem smaller. Zelda herself was at most one hundred and twenty pounds soaking wet because of the drugs. But she didn't feel afraid, due to his demeanor.

He had a pack of Newport 100s cigarettes in the Jeep, an unusual detail for this case. She remembers it because that was the kind she smoked. He was listening to classic rock, which is what she listened to. "This guy is just too easy, I was thinking—too easy."

There was minimal conversation. "He gives me a cigarette. He has the radio on. Just sitting there, you know? We're just listening to a little music."

He then drove them a few blocks down Clark Avenue. As the Jeep took off, she heard the door locks click. It gave her a little jolt. It wasn't as common an automated feature for cars back then, so she figured he might have clicked the locks himself.

After they headed down Clark, then turned onto another street, it wasn't long before he suddenly slammed on the brakes. He didn't pull over to the curb; he just slammed on the brakes in the middle of the street.

She had barely been paying attention in that moment, because there had been no further conversation between them and she was off in her own thoughts, but now she wondered what the heck was going on. This just came out of nowhere, him abruptly stopping in the street like that. Then, she saw him reach with his right hand down to the floor under his seat. When he brought his hand back up, he was holding what she described as a large buck knife. It had a wood handle with brass plate between the two halves. It was shiny, in the darkness of the car, like it was new.

"It was the biggest one that they make. So he comes up with it, and I'm looking, and I'm scarcely believing what's happening. I wasn't even scared. I just was like shocked."

He did not waste time.

"He comes at me with the knife, and he goes right here," she said, pointing to the side of her abdomen, "to stab me, and it doesn't penetrate the coat. My hand to the Lord."

It was quite astonishing to her because this guy seemed pretty big and strong. "He's a military man, and this was a very sharp knife." But she knew there was another power at work here.

She and Armstrong looked at each other, their eyes locked. Again, there were no words. Just a look.

He came at her again in the same place, and again, the knife did not go through her new cashmere coat.

She remembered him trying a third time, and that's when something in her said she had to get that knife or she just might end up dead.

She began to wrestle him for the weapon, getting cut up by it, and at one point, she held the blade of the knife down to the floor near her seat, with his hand still on the handle.

"Let go of the blade!" he demanded.

She told him to unlock the door.

It seemed a stalemate, for a second. She had the blade, and he had the handle. His face was red, his eyes were big. "I wasn't letting go. I said, 'Open the door, open the door.' He hit me, he tried to pull my hair. It was so odd. I knew if I let go of the blade, I was going to die."

It seemed like this struggle went on forever, but it wasn't that long. Adrenaline rose up within her. She doesn't know where the strength came from, other than from the Lord. She knew she couldn't afford to let that blade go.

"Let go of the blade!" he kept shouting.

She started maneuvering her body closer to the door.

He finally popped the locks and she opened the door with her other hand. She maneuvered herself out of the vehicle, letting go of the blade at last.

Zelda believes that her blood splattered all over the inside of his Jeep—all over the windshield, for one thing. He would have had to clean it up that evening before going home.

"My DNA was all over his vehicle. It was a lot of blood."

Zelda showed me the scar on her left pinkie finger where the knife cut it and the scar on the side of that hand. The tip was hanging from her pinkie finger after this incident. And she had lost some of her hair. To get stitched up, she went to a small hospital. That's the way she wanted it. And she used someone else's insurance because she didn't have her own. She left the hospital without asking for a ride from anyone, walking miles back to where she lived. She reeled from the shock for years to come, not telling anyone what happened.

"When he came up, he looked like a total different person," she recalled from that grab for the knife. "A total different person. He looked possessed."

And as disarming as this man had been when she got into the Jeep, she was convinced, after taking a breath and processing what happened, that this whole encounter was very calculated, from the moment he first saw her walking down the sidewalk toward his car.

"He was stalking me. He had already known I was a mark. He knew what I was doing, and I knew what he was doing. Without saying anything. That's just how it works."

In addition to feelings of guilt and shame of being out there in the first place, figuring she got what she deserved, another reason Zelda never reported this to police was that she thought they wouldn't take her seriously. "Not that I was scared of the police, but I knew it was a waste of time."

Years later when she got married, she did tell her husband John the story—the first person ever. John then told a longtime friend, Don, that his wife had been attacked by someone out on the streets. Don had a ministry of sorts with the prostitutes of Detroit—he would often try to help them. He also had a photographer friend who would interview the city's prostitutes on video, capturing comments however frank or crude, sort of an intriguing sociological study from his cell phone. So Don had heard a lot of things. He kept pressing Zelda for more information on her attacker. What did this guy look like? She didn't want to talk about it. Kept shutting him down. Then, finally one day fairly recently, when she, John, Don, and a friend of hers were having a bite at a ham sandwich shop on Michigan Ave, some light was shed on the attack. Don and John were in one booth, Zelda and her friend in the next booth. Don leaned over from their booth to show Zelda an image on his phone.

"Is this the guy?"

Yes. That was her Mr. Apple Pie. That unassuming guy with a very assuming buck knife.

John Eric Armstrong, convicted killer.

This was a shock to her. She actually had not seen any of the news about Armstrong years earlier. Had not even heard any chatter from anyone around Vernor or Fort Street. But after learning who this guy was, she got online and read more about the case.

Nowadays, Zelda has been freed from the grip of the drugs, by the grace of God. She has attended recovery groups and reaching out to others in need has been very helpful to her, very therapeutic. She is active at her church. She's free with her praise, free with her encouragement of others. As we sat and talked, she grabbed a young girl who was walking by, a girl who had sung at her church, and they chatted, she rather strenuously inviting the girl's whole family to come back to the church.

Zelda has waged the spiritual warfare. She feels she has been delivered from demons. "We all carry stuff," she said. A lot of people are in bondage.

"I was on a perpetual tripwire of cycles. It would come in cycles." She would go with what felt good. Up and down, with no rhyme or reason. But she was always searching for freedom. She knew forgiveness was key. So her thoughts of her attacker these days are not what you might think. The person that forgiveness frees, after all, is yourself.

"I've never asked God why. I pray for his soul. I've been able to forgive."

TO CATCH A KILLER

He's gone by the name Eric rather than John since he was a kid.

John was the name of his biological father and it's not a pleasant name to him. His father left the family when Eric was young, just over five years old, in 1979, and Eric has claimed the man was abusive toward him and even at one point said his father was responsible for the death of Eric's baby brother Michael in the crib. There are other inklings of what went on in the Armstrong household in New Bern, North Carolina, all those years ago.

Eric's mom Linda remarried in 1984, when Eric was eleven, and he gained other siblings (half- and step-) as well as a stepdad that he calls his dad to this day.

The United States Navy became Eric's career. He enlisted shortly after graduating from high school in 1992 and spent his time aboard the aircraft carrier *USS Nimitz*, traveling the world through the 1990s—Hong Kong, Singapore, Pattaya Beach in Thailand, Mina Jebel Ali in the United Arab Emirates (he visited Dubai thirteen times, he would later say), as well as spending a lot of dock time in the home port of Bremerton, Washington, near Seattle. He worked in the ship's barbershop. He met his future wife Katie aboard the *Nimitz* in 1995; they married in 1998. They had a baby son the following year, then they were discharged from the military in the spring of 1999. Shortly thereafter, they came to Michigan. It's where Katie is from, so in July, they settled in with her parents at their house in Dearborn Heights, a suburb west of the city of Detroit.

Eric found a job working security at the Detroit Medical Center in Novi, another western suburb, that first year, 1999. He worked there just a few months. That year he also got a job at the Target store on Ford Road in Dearborn Heights, then in 2000 started working for Signature Flight Support, refueling aircraft at Detroit Metro Airport in Romulus, also not too far away in the suburbs. He took some classes at Schoolcraft College in Livonia. Soon, it was learned that Katie was pregnant with their second child.

Eric didn't necessarily want to be in Michigan, but this was where life had put him, carrying on the role of a family man. He had no idea at the time that he would never live anywhere else again.

A FATAL ERROR

Detroit, of course, has developed a bit of a reputation over the years for its crime rates. It's been dubbed the Murder Capital of the US a time or three. So it's not surprising that the Motor City wasn't really fazed at the attempted murder of Natasha Olejniczak when it was reported in August 1999, or even the murder of Monica Johnson that police responded to in December. At that point, the attacker of these women was afforded the luxury of working in anonymity, and the encounter with Zelda Jakubowski only reinforced that. There could have been other incidents during these months. But with Wendy Jordan at the dawn of the year 2000, Eric Armstrong made an error that would cause things to unravel for him. Even if the Detroit police had not arrested him a few months later, Dearborn Heights police were about to.

Because Armstrong reported the body of the woman he had killed.

Did Eric secretly—perhaps subconsciously—want to get caught? Was he crying out for help, when he claimed to have discovered Wendy Jordan's body in the Rouge River? One might think. But the way then Sergeant Mike Petri of the Dearborn Heights Police Department saw it, it was Armstrong's way of trying to get out in front of this situation. One that backfired miserably. With homicide number two in Detroit, Armstrong crossed the line: He crossed from Detroit into another municipality to leave his victim in the very suburb (and the very neighborhood, really) in which he lived, and he crossed the line by calling in his own kill. Or at least having someone with a cell phone handy call it in.

He had left work at Target a bit early that day, on January 2. He had asked permission to do so, after complaining to supervisor Allison that his knee was hurting him. He seemed troubled by something, anyway, that day, she would later tell police. During the workday, Armstrong had apologized to Allison for his earlier mood, an apology she found unusual for him.

Target coworker Nancy Miller also remembered that day. "He said he wasn't feeling good. He had a stomachache. I told him to go to management, ask if you could go home."

Nancy, who was hired at Target in 1999 and had worked there several months before Eric joined the staff, knew him as a "typical Southern boy." He was very respectful, she said. There was nothing that really stood out about him. He did his work. Didn't cause any trouble. Kept to himself with most people.

"He kind of identified with me," Nancy said, "because he had just gotten out of the Navy and I had a son in the Navy. So I was kind of like, not a mother figure, but he just clicked with me. But yeah, very, very sweet and very polite."

Did Armstrong get along with his other coworkers?

"He did," Nancy said. "He did. You know. But like I said, he kind of identified with me more. I think he trusted me more than he trusted anybody."

Indeed, Armstrong did offer Nancy a couple key details from his past that he probably didn't reveal to many others, as we'll explore.

So on January 2, 2000, Armstrong, having been at Target since the morning for his day shift, left work. He was cruising in his dark bluish-gray 1998 Jeep Wrangler along Ann Arbor Trail not far from Hines Drive in Dearborn Heights between four-thirty and four-forty-five p.m., almost home, within a block or two. Ann Arbor Trail is a twisty-windy path through this western part of Metro Detroit, but at that point it's east-west. Traveling east toward his in-laws' house, he pulled his Jeep over at the bridge where he had dumped Wendy Jordan's body earlier that day, a simple concrete bridge that included a sidewalk on each side and guardrails extending out from each end for several yards. He parked on Ann Arbor Trail facing east, just west of the bridge a short distance, police would later attest.

He got out of the Jeep, walked over to the bridge, and looked over, on what was the south side of the bridge. At a house on Ann Arbor Trail just on the other side of the bridge and across the street, a couple people had casually observed this: Sarah Daros and her boyfriend, Alan Berry. They were outside at the Berry residence, and Alan was about to drive Sarah to her own house. They were chatting for a few minutes. Sarah remembered seeing the man not only look over the side of the bridge but then walk a short distance away from it and just stand for a moment. Sarah and Alan thought nothing of this guy at the bridge at first, but he was lingering there as they hopped in their car and headed in that direction, which was toward Daros' home.

As they approached the bridge, Daros would later testify, Armstrong jumped out in front of their car and told them to call 911, that there was someone in the water below the bridge. (One of the cops at the scene remembered the two saying Armstrong had told them there was a "dead prostitute" there.) Alan turned his car around, parked right in front of Armstrong's Jeep, got out and looked over the south side of the bridge himself, while Sarah stayed in the car. When Alan saw Wendy's body lying face up in the partially frozen water, he asked Sarah to go back to his house and get his dad. Sarah did so, and Alan's dad, Thomas Berry, returned with her, along with Alan's uncle, Angelo Altomonte.

It was Alan who called 911 on his cell.

"Sir, you're on 911, go ahead."

"I'm on Ann Arbor Trail, just west of Evergreen ... I'm at the Rouge River ..."

The operator interrupted, repeating the numbered address he gave.

"I'm on the Rouge River, the bridge, and there's a dead body in the river. I think she got raped. She's naked. She got her clothes ripped off."

The operator asked again about the location, and Thomas took the phone from Alan and finished the call. The men stayed there on the bridge with Armstrong, waiting for police to arrive.

Sarah waited in the car, Alan not wanting her to see the body. Thomas Berry, a cop himself, kept his eye on Armstrong, since he was the one who actually found the body. He would later testify that he wanted to assure Armstrong would be the one to talk to police, so his son would not be mixed up in any of this, just being a passerby and all. As Thomas Berry observed him, Armstrong looked at him, realizing he was being eyed, then walked a few feet away and pretended to dry heave, then made eye contact with him again. Berry pegged the supposed vomiting as "BS" at the time, he said.

Berry also said that Armstrong told them he was there in the area on vacation and visiting his "girlfriend." Evidently Armstrong really planned on this brief report being his only contact with any of these people.

Due to the time of year, it was getting dark by the time Dearborn Heights police arrived, noted as 4:52 p.m. As Officers C. Pellerito and J. Colon looked over the bridge, there was Wendy's body, lying on top of the ice and water, with one of her gold pumps lying nearby on top of the ice. There were also a cosmetics bag and a bra near her in the river. The officers contacted the station and more personnel were brought in: evidence techs and other officers, plus the Wayne County Marine Division dive team to retrieve Wendy from the river, covering her hands to preserve evidence, since her fingernails would be clipped and sent to the lab.

Officers Burt Wells, R. Poshadlo, and J. Ross would collect and document several items from the scene including the gold shoe, cosmetics bag, and bra, and some items found on the bridge itself: a black knit scarf found at about the middle of the bridge, a gold-tone ring found at the southwest bridge post, a cigarette butt, an empty cigarette pack, and a plastic zip tie.

A rape kit would be ordered for Wendy. Her leather skirt and jacket, hosiery with the feet cut out, gold pump, fingernail clippings, and hair samples would be sent to the Michigan State Police lab in Northville. The hair samples would include one hair from her tights, one from her skirt, and two from her face and mouth. A blood sample and swabs of her vagina and rectum would also be sent to the lab for a DNA test. A fingerprint card would be sent to the police station.

But first, at the scene, police naturally wanted to interview these witnesses. They collected the names and addresses of the men standing at the bridge, listened to what they had to say. After speaking with Armstrong, who told them he was driving home from work, felt sick and pulled over at the bridge to vomit, wherein he spotted the body, officers asked to take him to the station to speak more about it to Detective Sergeant Robert Stephens and Sergeant Petri.

It was at this point police felt there seemed to be a flaw in the slaw.

Gary Tomkiewicz was a detective lieutenant for Dearborn Heights Police at the time, in charge of the Major Crimes section, and he was at the station while the responding officers were at the bridge. They called in the information and right away it didn't sound right to Tomkiewicz, he recalled decades later via phone. This guy said he was sick, and he was leaning over the bridge, when the cement casting on top of that viaduct was at least two-and-a-half-, three-foot wide? "What is this guy, a contortionist or what?" he remembered thinking. And it struck him as odd that he stopped there to get sick, when he was so close to home.

The officers at the scene gave Armstrong's name and info to Tomkiewicz, and he ran a check on this guy from the station. He hit something, an incident reported with the Novi Police Department in November 1999. When Armstrong was working as a security guard at the Detroit Medical Center in Novi, he allegedly faked a break-in at the facility. He had picked up an object, either a cinder block or rock, Tomkiewicz recalled from the report, and broke a window on a door. He had evidently taken a surgical scalpel and used it to put superficial cuts on his left hand and right cheek. He had then told his coworkers at the facility that he'd fought off an attacker who was breaking in to the building. He had a staffer call 911. He filed a report of an alleged felonious assault. He later admitted the report was fabricated, according to Detective Victor Lauria of the Novi PD. A "filing a false felony report" charge was brought against Armstrong in Oakland County because of this.

But that wasn't all that Tomkiewicz, who would go on to become the chief of detectives, learned about this witness at the bridge scene. In DHPD's own records, there was a report of a suicide attempt by Armstrong following the Novi incident in '99. He read in the report the details of Armstrong leaving a note to his wife in the kitchen—a suicide note that bore the same name as the decorative license plate on Armstrong's Jeep parked at the bridge that very moment, "Baby Doll," a playful nickname between Eric and his wife. With the note were his keys and his wedding ring. "Well, you can have Baby Doll," Tomkiewicz recalled as the wording of the note, from the report's documentation. Armstrong overdosed on something—evidently medication already on hand in the house—and had to be transported to the hospital to have his stomach pumped.

So yeah, Tomkiewicz was thinking, *let's bring this guy in and talk to him further.*

Police also asked to take a look inside that Jeep Wrangler parked so unassumingly at the bridge with that Baby Doll plate. Armstrong consented. Though still fairly new, the Jeep was pretty dirty and cluttered. There was some clothing strewn about. A tin Reese's Peanut Butter Cups box next to the front driver's seat. A blue nylon gym bag on the back seat. A black three-ring binder. Crumbs and wrappers and stuff. Was that a woman's earring, or other piece of jewelry, on the back seat? A stray button. A condom wrapper. And maybe another thing or two that raised eyebrows.

Mike Petri was Tomkiewicz's lead detective at the time. Years later, at the Dearborn Heights Police Department located at Michigan Avenue and Beech Daly, graduated to captain, Petri also recalled the case.

"When we got called in, it was just called in as a female that was found in the river," he remembered. "So, you know, obviously looking over the side of the Rouge River, having been a police officer for many years, my first thought was, she looked like a prostitute. Obviously, not knowing who she was or what she was or anything like that, that's just coming from a professional observation, I guess.

"So the story that Mr. Armstrong had given us was that he was just driving along, said he was getting sick, he felt like he was going to throw up, so he stopped his car on the bridge, got out of his truck, and went over to the side of the bridge to throw up, looked down and saw a body. So in that respect, it was like, okay, here, our initial thought was, here we have a dead body, and we just have this do-gooder saying that he found a body in the river. Not knowing why she died, how she died or anything like that. She was stuck in the middle of the water and there was no way for us to get to her because she was in the middle of the river stuck in some ice.

"So looking at that from that perspective, you know, starting to question him about it, it just started seeming a little odd. One of the things that I thought was really odd was that, all right, you say that you're going to get sick, so you stop your Jeep, you jump out. My personal thought was, well, if you're going to get sick, wouldn't you just open the door and throw up? You know what I mean? I mean, from that distance to his house was literally two blocks.

"And then my second thought was, if he was going to throw up, he never did. You know, so you're going to run over, go over to the side of the bridge because you're so nauseous you have to stop two blocks from your house, get out of your Jeep, run around your Jeep, you're going to throw up over the side of the river, you look down and see a body, and that stops you from throwing up? Wouldn't you think that would make you more sick? Just from a theoretical aspect?

"So it was just kind of odd, you know, thinking that way. And then the other thing I remember is looking at the body you could see she had these like gold shoes on that had these gold flecks of—they were like the shoes that women only buy to wear to weddings, when they're a bridesmaid. I remember looking in the Jeep and seeing those, what appeared to resemble the gold specks from the shoes.

"I mean, obviously, we're always suspicious as investigators, and we don't want to accuse a person of something right off the bat. But it was just kind of like odd. And then there was a ring that was on the bridge that had nothing to do with nothing, apparently, afterwards. So we obviously set up our crime scene and got to go about investigating it. And just looking at the whole situation from a totality of circumstances point of view."

He went on: "So we asked the people, what did you see? And they basically, to synopsize, said, yeah, we were on the porch, we saw this Jeep stop, we thought it was kind of odd that a Jeep stops in the middle of a bridge, especially in that part where it narrows down. And then this guy got out, kind of looked around, and then went over to the bridge, looked down, kind of looked around for a little bit, and then flagged down a car. You know, we didn't think anything of it. Okay, 'what's going on' type thing. And then the police showed up, or the fire engines or whatever it was. I think it was me, but it might not have been. But I remember, as part of the investigation, somebody asked, well, when he got out of the car, did he look like he was going to get sick or anything? Was he holding his mouth and running to the bridge? No, he just got out and kind of looked around a little bit, and then walked over and then looked down, and then flagged down the cars. So right there, it was kind of contrary to the story he had been giving us about him. So our suspicions were alerted. But again, at this time, all we had was a female in the river. Did she get drunk and fall over and land in the river? Did she commit suicide? We don't know who she is or anything."

So when Officers Pellerito and Colon brought Armstrong to the station, Petri might have gone into the interview with this witness on limited information, but he still felt this guy was a little off. Especially learning what Tomkiewicz learned in the records. It became a mission to see just how much more information they could pry out of this guy.

"We don't know what a cause of death was," Petri said. "We don't know why she died. We don't know if it was a homicide. All we have is this individual that's saying that he found this lady. And here we are, would be accusing him of homicide, when we don't know if we even have a homicide."

And now, decades later, you have to wonder if Armstrong was expecting to look over that bridge and see the body gone, having floated down the river, but the ice made that impossible. Did he panic to see her still there, stuck in the ice? Or was he just trying to play the hero? Did he realize that a couple people at the house across the street had noticed him, and that later when the body would be found, they would give a description to the police of this guy they saw stop his Jeep at the bridge? So he better "get out in front of it," as Petri surmised? What was going through his head?

"Yeah, I mean, knowing what this case is about and what it turned into, it's easy to armchair quarterback, and I've done it a million times in investigations," Petri said. "Shoulda-woulda-coulda. Wish I had known that, wish I had done that, wish I had done *that*. Because when we were interviewing him, I felt completely confident that this guy had something to do with it. But was it one of those situations where he picked up a prostitute, she was high, died in his car, he was getting rid of her? Was he covering for the fact that, you know, he doesn't want his wife to know, so he's not going to say anything? There's a multitude of things. Is it a legitimate, 'just' disposal of a body? Did she, like I say, die of a drug overdose? At that time when we were interviewing him, we didn't know that she had been strangled. Obviously the medical examiner hadn't completed the autopsy. This was within hours after him finding it."

And so, Petri said, "we wanted him to come in, give his story, what he found, looking at it from a position of he's just a witness at this point."

At 7:09 p.m. on January 2, 2000, at the station, Armstrong gave his statement to police. Sergeant Petri conducted the interview, with Detective Sergeant James Serwatowski sitting in. Detective Sergeant Stephens assisted with paperwork and sat with Armstrong a few minutes before the interview began. In the introductions, Armstrong gave his first name as John and was called that throughout, even saying he didn't have any nicknames after police spelled out his first and middle name for the record. It was a lengthy interview, polite at first, though Petri tended to be sterner, Serwatowski more conversational. If there was a good-cop/bad-cop flavor to this interrogation, Petri was the bad cop and Serwatowski the good, soothing him as much as he could, telling him he understood that this was difficult for him. Armstrong's voice on the interview recording comes through as soft-spoken, though increasing in agitation. Petri left the room at one point (he actually was ill and had to throw up, ironically, he recalled years later—it was the flu), and Serwatowski made all kinds of small talk with Armstrong, kept him chatting about mountain bikes, Target's return policy, whatever. Armstrong kept his coat on throughout—he was cold.

"When he started talking and saying certain things," Petri remembered, "it was readily apparent in our mind that he knew at least more than this, if not he did something to her. Because just those little factors, you know. I really felt that he was somehow involved, knew something more than he was telling us, that he wasn't just the unwitting, wanting-to-be-a-good-citizen, help out, 'omigod, I found a body in the river.' Whether it was, him and his buddies went out, picked up a hooker, and she died at the house, and they got rid of her. I mean, who knows what scenario it could have been. But I wasn't buying his story that he was just a good citizen that happened to be driving by."

Why was he sick that day? police asked Armstrong.

"I was sweating real bad last night," he replied. "This morning I was feeling real sick. But as the day went on, I started getting a little bit better. Then I ate some nachos at work for lunch, which I shouldn't have. And I started getting real sick. And my stomach was turning, and just felt real yucky. And I did work and talked to a couple people; this was four-thirty, and I left."

Armstrong's Jeep was examined at the scene, then towed to DHPD for a closer look, with officers taking a variety of photos, then towed to the Michigan State Police lab for further processing a couple days later. Image: DHPD files.

Polaroid of Armstrong being interviewed at the Dearborn Heights Police Department. Image: DHPD files.

How did he feel when he first looked over the bridge and saw the body?

"I've never seen a body before in my life. We don't have nothing like that, where I come from, I've never seen. So I'm still a little shaky, and I don't know, scared, I guess. I don't know how … I didn't want to look at her." Armstrong's voice at this point was light, confident, self-assured. Helping out the police.

"Did you notice anybody around when you were driving down Ann Arbor Trail? Just coming down the road, you stopped, you were going to vomit?"

"Yeah."

Then suddenly police asked, "What made you join the Navy?"

"To get away from my hometown. We had nothing to do there."

Petri and Serwatowski tried several tactics over the course of the hour and a half or so. As they asked about the details of his life, they encouraged him. Tried to make him feel more at ease. They tried to allow for a more innocent explanation for the death of this woman found in the river. "I'm sorry that you had to become involved in a situation like this," Petri coaxed. "That we had to talk to you about it. I could tell it was weighing pretty heavily on your mind." But Armstrong wasn't giving up any info. At some point in the interview—maybe even before it began—this "witness" realized this was not just a witness statement at the station.

"His whole demeanor during the interview was very … you know, gave me the ideology that he was involved in something, somehow, some way. And I couldn't get it out of him. But I didn't have enough facts to really seriously … oh, what's the word I'm looking for? Say that 'you murdered this girl, you killed this girl,' to really go at him really hard, you know? So obviously without probable cause to make an arrest that night, we were forced to let him go, not knowing the gravity of the situation, you know, looking down the road at what we're going to do with this case."

During his questioning with DHPD, the Novi incident came up. Armstrong said that he'd lied to police when he said the break-in and assault didn't happen—it all really did happen, but he felt the police didn't believe him. He had just told them what they wanted to hear, he said to Petri. So he had tried to commit suicide because he then saw himself as a felon, he said. After that, he got counseling and still was in treatment at the time of this questioning.

Donald Riley, then a detective sergeant for the Investigative Bureau (Detective Bureau) of the Dearborn Heights Police Department, was the officer in charge of the Jordan case. He started out as a cadet with DHPD in the 1980s and worked his way up, later going on to the Special Operations Bureau. He remembered the red flags going up in officers' minds as they questioned Armstrong that day.

"All right. So he's on his way home, allegedly, and felt nauseous. So he stopped alongside the road to vomit, throw up, or whatever. He looked over the bridge, and lo and behold, there's a body there," Riley said glibly via phone in 2017, having moved on to become the chief of police in Scottville, a city on the western side of Michigan. "So naturally, we get called out. And, well, first thing—there's no vomit anywhere, okay? So right off the get go, there's a problem with his story because he didn't throw up. I don't remember if we interviewed him right then or there, right then or not. But did some checking, and he had filed a report in Novi where some guy came in to a nursing home where he worked or something, and was going to get people, and he saved the day, and he got cut with a knife, and the guy fled into the woods, and all that stuff. So we reached out to Novi PD and we talked to one of the guys over there, who basically said, 'Yup, that story was bullshit, and he's a liar. And he's probably lying to you guys too.' So we interviewed him. Myself and Detective Sergeant Stephens. And he was lying, okay? I don't remember all the particulars. But he was being deceitful. We knew it."

As questioning continued, Armstrong was feeling increasingly uneasy about all this. So many personal questions. When he met his wife, how long he was in the Navy, how old his son was. He became more defensive in his answers. Sometimes sarcastic.

"You seem like a nice guy," Petri told him. "You're getting your life back together. You know, after this incident right here?" No doubt pointing at the November documentation sitting in front of him.

"Trying to," Armstrong said.

"And that's what we want. We want to help you out. You know, we want to make sure—you know, people see TV; they look, 'omigod, I found a body, that automatically makes me connected. Everybody's going to think I killed her.'"

"That's how I feel right now!"

Petri explained to Armstrong what they would be looking for at the scene, that they would check Wendy for evidence, such as DNA. "Obviously, we've got a whole team of investigators out there looking at the body. Are we going to find anything from you on that woman?"

"No, sir."

Petri said maybe he's trying to hide from his wife the fact that he frequents hookers. Armstrong denied that, only admitting to being with a hooker before he met his wife, in the Navy overseas. Not after he met her, he said.

"It's illegal, but who cares," Petri reassured. "You know what I'm saying? It happens every day, day in and day out. And if you're with somebody, you're with somebody; if you're not, you're not. It doesn't matter. We don't care about that. We want to find out who this girl is. If she was with you, she passed out, she OD'd, she jumped off the bridge, anything like that. We're not going to tell your wife that. We want to find out who she is. We're not saying that you did anything to her. We're not saying that you killed her. We're not saying that you did anything. We want to know who she is. We want to know where she came from."

"Right."

"And like I said, I don't want to find out something later that's going to jam you up later and make you a suspect in a murder."

As things wore on, Armstrong said this was upsetting him. He wanted to go home. Serwatowski, stepped into the conversation to try a different tactic, giving him a new opportunity to reveal more: "Okay, my concern was that maybe you didn't have anything to do with it but somebody you know might have had something to do with it. So you stopped to look over the edge to see if this body that somebody told you about was really there, or is it still there. Or something of that nature."

"I don't have any friends that are here," Armstrong replied.

During the questioning, police had already seen a condom wrapper in Armstrong's Jeep. When asked about that: "My wife doesn't want to get pregnant right now. I bought some rubbers, and I wanted to see how it felt, because I've really never used a rubber. So I put it on at work and I masturbated at work."

He purchased the condoms yesterday at a Mobil on Warren Avenue and Southfield Road, he said. That brought police a little closer to the truth because what was a Dearborn Heights boy, still fairly new in town, doing driving around in the 'hood?

"I got off work about ten-thirty last night. Drove around because I couldn't sleep. Midnight, I would assume. About midnight. That's when I finally came home."

"Where did you drive around at?"

"Just looking around. Because I'm not really familiar, and I was trying to get lost so I can find my way back home. Because that's what my wife wants me to do."

"To get lost and find your way back home so you get familiar with the area?"

"Right."

"Not a great idea in the city of Detroit."

"That's what she tells me, but she tells me not to go into Detroit, I guess. Um ... especially like on Ford Road, she wants me to get lost on Ford Road. Take some back streets, learn how to get to where. Like if there's an accident on Ford Road, how to get around it. Just different things like that, that she wants me to learn. Since I'm not really familiar."

After Petri left the room and Serwatowski kept Armstrong talking, kept trying to soothe him, it was apparent that Armstrong was quietly getting emotional. Maybe crying. They discussed the fact that his wife had spent the day in Ohio and was due home this evening, and there was a long pause, after which Serwatowski softly said, "It's okay ... If you were in our shoes, John, what would you do? Do you agree that we should talk to you and ask you these tough questions?"

"Yes. Just talk to me about the situation. Don't—"

"Don't what?"

"Don't keep saying that do you know her, or do you know her by her work or whatever. I didn't know her."

Petri was taking an awfully long time coming back.

"I know you want to go home," Serwatowski said. "I'm sure that's what Sergeant Petri is probably talking with the boss about now, and they're probably going over some things and deciding if there's anything else we need to do with you. I know you're telling me that you didn't know anything about this, that it happened the way you said it did, that you went over there, to vomit over the side, and you happened to see her. But let me ask you this, for the heck of it: if for some reason you did in fact know more about this, are you the type of guy that would tell us?"

"If I knew more about it, yes, I would, but I don't."

"Okay. Do you think most people, if they knew something about it or had anything to do with it, would tell us? Or do you think they would just deny everything?"

"I think they would tell."

"You think it would be easy for someone to tell us? Or do you think it would be difficult?"

"Probably difficult."

"You wouldn't expect somebody right off the bat just to start blabbing about it, would you?"

"If they had a burden about it, they would."

"And you don't have any burden?"

"Nope."

While Armstrong was at the station, Detective Sergeant Stephens went to his in-laws' house to let them know he was there. He knocked at the door on Fairview Drive but received no answer. He left his business card and departed. The family later called, wondering what was going on. Then Stephens returned to Armstrong's house to tell them in person. Katie's mother Diane answered the door that time.

Armstrong's family then had a lawyer come to the station. His name was Thomas Cardinal and he arrived around nine p.m. Cardinal also was asked about the vehicle search and okayed it.

Donald Riley recalled his overall impressions upon meeting Armstrong that day, as well as the lawyer who was called in.

"*Ah* … I wouldn't say cold," he said of Armstrong. "You know what I mean? I wouldn't say cold. I think—just meeting him on the street—maybe just different. He was just different, you know? My style of interviewing is a little bit more lackadaisical than like Bob Stephens, for instance. So I'll let people go on and on and let them talk. Later on, I'll say they're bullshitting, you know? Bob was a little bit more 'less patient' than I was, where he would maybe call them out a little bit more. But like I said, he got defensive, and the next thing you know, he had this family attorney who was like—I'm not going to knock the guy or nothing—but they just said, hey, if you're going to talk to these cops any more, you better take this attorney with you. He's a family friend, you know. Well, he wasn't an 'attorney' attorney. You know what I mean? Not like a homicide defense attorney or something."

And their "witness" from the bridge left Tomkiewicz, in his own contact with him that night at the station, with an impression of being meek, mild, mannerly. Soft spoken. "A guy that you wouldn't feel threatened or intimidated by," he said.

The North Carolina-plated Jeep was towed to the station around ten, ten-thirty p.m., and photographed and searched. Serwatowski, who aided in the search of the Jeep, would later testify to what they found in the vehicle: a condom wrapper with a hair or fiber, an Old Timer pocket knife, a box cutter, two earrings, some pieces of paper with names and phone numbers, and a button that appeared to be from women's clothing. DHPD records show the papers found included two sheets from the Hegira Health mental health and substance abuse treatment center located in the western suburbs of Detroit.

There was a handwritten note from a therapist, addressed to whom it may concern:

> *John Armstrong is currently receiving counseling to address his feelings of anxiety, distrust, depression and poor communication skills. He began receiving treatment effective Nov. 16, 1999 and meets weekly with his therapist. For additional questions, feel free to contact me.*

After the interview with Armstrong, Tomkiewicz went to the bridge scene, where officers were still processing evidence. The dive team had lucked out with the position of their victim in the river, with the time of year it was, and maybe with whatever awkward way Armstrong had thrown her over.

"The position she landed in was her legs were spread up on an ice jam," Tomkiewicz said. "Water is flowing on the Rouge River. And the way she hit that ice, she came up with her legs up over the ice, and that preserved the semen. Because it's water soluble, and otherwise, it would have washed away."

In his own survey of the bridge scene, Tomkiewicz saw something else that convinced him even more that this guy had something to do with this. The ring—it appeared to be a wedding ring—sitting right on top of one of the bridge posts.

"Grab that ring," he told an evidence tech. He was thinking about the incident report of the suicide attempt.

"The ring is significant, in my mind," Tomkiewicz later recalled, "that when something was going bad in his life, he leaves the ring, or a note, or whatever."

It was something that did not pan out, was determined to not be connected to their suspect, but that night it still served a purpose to spur on Tomkiewicz and others in their pursuit of Armstrong.

After Armstrong left the DHPD that night, which was late—he'd been there for several hours—he returned to the bridge scene with Katie, a witness said. Perhaps, though it was not made terribly clear, this was to show her what the fuss had been about, why he was at the station for so long.

Petri said, "In thinking back, I wish I had had just ten, twenty percent more information, because I really felt like I was getting close to breaking him when we were doing the interview. If you didn't do anything wrong, your natural response is, 'Hey, hey, hey, whoa! I was just driving down the street, and I looked over a bridge! I didn't do anything! I don't even know what you're talking about! I'm just trying to do the right thing! I called *you guys*!' 'What's going on here,' you know? And even if you do have that, 'I'm not giving *you* my blood; I don't know what you guys are trying to do.' You know, you watch a TV show and some bad cops did something, whatever. But he was just kind of—he never really looked at me and said, 'I didn't kill her.' I should say, he might have said things like that, but it was like, at the end, I was talking pretty close to him, and it just wasn't a natural—you can't really sit there, and I'm telling you that I think you killed this girl, or if you killed her, and it's like, you've got your head down, you're looking at the floor. Maybe your head's bobbing up and down, saying yes, but you're saying no. I mean, it's like I said, it's been so long ago, but I walked out of there, and like I said, I got sick. I mean, like, literally."

The police let Armstrong go, but they were not about to let this go. They dug in. They spoke to employees at the Mobil gas station on Warren that Armstrong mentioned. The station only carried Trojan condoms—the wrapper in Armstrong's Jeep was a LifeStyles brand. The employees had been seeing Wendy around the area for a couple years. Police talked to employees at the Sunoco on Warren and Evergreen; they'd seen Armstrong's Jeep around, and an employee remembered seeing Wendy in the store the early morning of her death. He estimated it was four-thirty a.m. Another police officer saw her at three a.m. at Warren and Heyden. One man who had seen Wendy working the area said he had also seen Armstrong hanging around Chick's Bar on Warren between Southfield and Evergreen Roads. Police talked to a jogger who had happened by the bridge scene that night and to neighbors of Armstrong's family on Fairview. One person at the house next door remembered hearing a car start up then leave the driveway at Armstrong's in-laws' house in the early morning hours of January 2. The man sleeping in the bed next to her heard a car running in the driveway at about five a.m.

On January 3, the autopsy on Wendy found the cause of death to be strangulation and the rape kit was done, with samples taken for the lab. Her clothing had been put in a locked area to dry, then hair was processed from it. Her fingerprints provided her identity in the Automated Fingerprint Identification System (AFIS).

DHPD wanted to take another look at that Jeep. Riley recalled the feeling among the officers that they just hadn't seen everything there was to see about that vehicle. "We weren't convinced that there wasn't more stuff in there," he said. This time, they wanted to send the Jeep to the Michigan State Police crime lab. On January 4, they returned to the house on Fairview with a search warrant for the Jeep. It was photographed again by DHPD, then towed to the MSP lab in Northville on January 5, placed in the evidence garage, and processed for a few days, with the lab report completed on January 11.

DHPD felt the results of the Jeep examination could clinch their case. At least get the guy formally arrested. "So now we get the search warrant for his Jeep," Riley said. "We take it to the state police crime lab. They're going to do a thorough investigation on this thing, you know? And the prosecutor's office basically told us, if you put her in that Jeep, we're going to issue on this. Okay. No problem."

The crime lab fingerprinted the Jeep but found no usable prints. Tape lifts were done from the front passenger and front driver seats and the front passenger-side floor. The evidence analysis included known seat fibers and known carpet fibers, and other hairs and fibers recovered from a pair of boxer shorts, a white shirt, the passenger seat, and a condom wrapper.

The Dearborn Heights investigation traveled further onto the streets of Detroit to delve into the prostitution scene where Wendy had sometimes been. Serwatowski took along Wendy's photo to find out where else she was seen.

Riley also recalled talking to other prostitutes about Wendy or anything strange they had seen or heard around town.

Police meanwhile asked Cardinal to accompany Armstrong to be interviewed by police from the nearby suburb of Westland for a polygraph test. They requested Cardinal accompany Armstrong to have blood drawn. Cooperation continued to ensue in all of this, as the DHPD pressed further and further into this story of "discovering" Wendy Jordan's body.

Investigator David Heater of the Westland Police Department administered the polygraph test in January. Armstrong's story remained that he purchased condoms at the Mobil station at Warren and Southfield, one of which he had masturbated into while on break working at Target. He had only stopped at the bridge because he was going to vomit, Armstrong said, and then he saw the body in the river. He waved someone down, had them call police, the police arrived, asked him questions about it, took him to the police station. In reference to the death of the victim, it was Heater's opinion that Armstrong was not being truthful during the polygraph. Deception was indicated.

On January 17, Sergeant Riley went to the Garden City Hospital to meet Armstrong and Cardinal for the blood sample from Armstrong, along with the samples of head and pubic hair also named in a search warrant. In a detail that would be remembered by several people connected to the case (including the victim's sister, Bonnie, as it came up later), Armstrong showed up to the hospital with his pubic hair gone.

Riley remembered that one well. "Now he's cooperating with his attorney because he's innocent—he didn't do anything," the former DHPD sergeant explained with a touch of facetiousness. "So he came in. And I don't remember if this was all in one day or not. But he came in whatever day he was scheduled to and we fingerprinted him, did what we did, took him to the hospital where he was going to get his blood draw and hair samples and stuff. And he goes into the examination room, and a little while later, the male nurse comes out. He says, 'Hey, I just wanted to tell you guys something. He is completely shaved. He shaved everything.'"

The registered nurse, Gary Fazio, told police for their records that the pubic hair had been cut close to the skin with "possibly a pair of barber clippers." It was approximately 1/16 of an inch long. Armstrong told Fazio that he cut it because his wife "likes it that way."

Riley continued, "Okay. Well, anyway, they were able to get pubic hair off his scrotum or something. I don't remember. But they got what they needed. And when he had been interviewed again, he's, like, well, you know, my wife likes it that way. 'Cuz it was a question—what the hell is this all about, pal? You know, this guy's our suspect at this point."

Gary Tomkiewicz recalled this incident as a point where he knew this guy was playing cat and mouse with the DHPD. The lieutenant had actually objected to what was called "rough shadowing" of the guy, as the idea was raised among detectives working the case. Armstrong had been cooperating with them, Tomkiewicz argued. He hadn't really lawyered up, other than Cardinal. So the lieutenant wanted to play nice with this mouse. At least for the moment.

The hair and blood samples from Armstrong became part of the evidence the Michigan State Police were examining, along with the blood sample, vaginal swabs, and rectal swabs from the victim. The samples arrived at the lab in Northville on January 3 and 18, but DNA results would not be determined for months. The process for DNA analysis had only been developed in the mid-1980s, and the technology of it had not advanced enough by 2000 for results to come back quickly. A window of several months was pretty typical for the time.

So it was a waiting game. Aoun Cruz, neighbor to Armstrong and his family on Fairview, would later tell *The Detroit News* that police instructed him to call if he saw Armstrong leaving his house with a lot of luggage. And Aoun's fiancée, Catherine, the one who had heard a car start up and leave Armstrong's driveway on the morning of the murder, understandably couldn't sleep.

From the perspective of Armstrong himself, in those weeks following the discovery of Wendy Jordan's body, he could certainly feel the heat of the authorities, though he could do little about it. He confided in Nancy Miller at work about how police seemed to find him suspicious from the very first conversation:

"I think they did," she recalled. "It makes sense. Because I think they did question him. He told me that the police were questioning him, and there's no way that he could have done it. And then all of a sudden, his Jeep was impounded. And so once the Jeep was impounded, then things kinda started falling apart, I think, for him. Because he told me that—he would come in to work and he would tell me that, you know, unfortunately they had to take pubic hair for testing, they had to take hair off his head. I would say that all the things you would normally not tell a person, he's telling me. And I'm like, *ooo*kay … That's wonderful!" Nancy sorta grimly laughed in relaying this so many years later. "And I said, 'Well, you know, they can tell a lot of different things by those tests.' So I think eventually he knew that he was going to be caught."

She added, reflecting her perspective of the case and what she knew of her work friend, years later, "But his wife had no idea. He would work, he would get off at about eleven o'clock, he would go home, talk to his wife for a little bit, say that he had to go out, and then he would go out and have sex with a prostitute and kill her, and then he'd come back home."

Armstrong had another coworker at Target at the time with whom he confided just as much, perhaps even more so, than Nancy Miller. Her name was Jennifer, last name now Westberg, and she was young, only sixteen when she began working at the store in 1998. It was a part-time job for her, mostly evenings and weekends like Eric. She struck up a friendship with him. Spent a lot of time talking to him. She had a rapport with him. They even talked, at one point, about moving into a rental with their significant others. The four of them would be living together, sharing expenses, they envisioned. Five, counting Armstrong's toddler son, and it would have become six before too long.

Jennifer's connection to this case is rather unique, however, beyond just the friendly chord she struck with her coworker. Jennifer had the distinct displeasure of later realizing that she had been sitting in the very seat where her friend was having sex with, assaulting, and murdering other women. Jennifer got rides to and from work with Eric in his Jeep. She even got a ride to work from him on January 2, just a few hours after Wendy Jordan had sat in that same seat. It's a thought that will send chills down Jennifer's spine for the rest of her life.

"I was already working there before he was hired in," she explained via email in August 2017. "In fact, I was one of the folks who trained him when he came in. Ie: I told him how we zoned at night and showed him some best practices to get out as soon as possible every night."

She went on, "I was still underage and did not have any interest in getting my driver's license before my eighteenth birthday. And I lived only a couple miles from the store so I would ride my bike to and from work so my parents didn't have to drive me. Sometimes I would get a ride into work and my boyfriend (now husband) would come up and we'd ride bikes or walk home together. He didn't have a license either. One day my boyfriend came up to the store to visit me. I introduced him to Eric since we were both working that night. We were supposed to walk home together that night but Eric offered to drive us both home instead. After that he would give me rides when the weather was bad and we were both working the same shifts. It probably happened less than a handful of times before he got the job at the airport and we were working less hours together at Target."

So what kinds of things did Jennifer remember talking about on the way to or from work? What seemed most important to her friend Eric, at the time?

"In general, a lot of our conversations were about our parents," she said. "As [I was] an angst-filled teenager with mommy issues, we were a great pair. We talked about why he goes by Eric and not John. He told me about how his mom was never very supportive and how he hated her growing up. He would also tell me about his wife who he met while in service. He also disliked her mother, who they lived with in either Dearborn or Dearborn Heights. I don't remember. But he loved his wife. He would tell me what a great mother she is. And one day he came in on his day off and I was working. I got to meet her and their son. He was getting a pregnancy test, which I helped pick out. I believe it was EPT because I would always recommend EPT when someone would ask. Of course, she ended up being pregnant, which I was immensely happy for. I mean, who wouldn't be happy that their friend is having more babies.

"After finding out that she was pregnant, Eric started talking about needing to get his own space for him and his family. He said he couldn't afford to get a place on his own, outside of his mother-in-law's house. I said, you should get roommates. Then we casually tossed around the idea of my boyfriend and I moving in with them after graduation. The arrangement would be sharing living expenses and us helping with the kids when he and his wife were working. Although I don't remember if she actually worked or not. I would get to move out of my parents' place and he would have someone under his roof who's trained in child care. It would be a winning situation for everyone involved.

"Then he found the body on Hines and all of our conversations changed gear. It was no longer about family. It was about him being victimized by the police ... He came into work and told us he had found a body near Hines Drive. He said he suffers from insomnia, which he had previously mentioned in passing. But everyone who has a little trouble sleeping thinks they are an insomniac so I thought very little of it. So he said he suffers from insomnia and often goes on drives to help him. He said he was feeling sick and got out of the car to be sick on the side of the road instead of in the Jeep. And that's when he saw the body. So he called the police and instead of hailing him a hero for finding her, they began picking his story apart. At this point he'd already been deemed as sketchy by the local police after the false police report ... So the police 'stole his trash cans' (his words). So he thought he was really clever and said he called the police to report his missing trash cans."

On January 6, Armstrong's mother-in-law Diane filed a report with DHPD of "larceny of garbage cans." Three metal garbage cans and one plastic one (with wheels) were stolen from the front of her residence on January 5 or 6, the report said.

"I'm sure we took his trash," Petri concurred years later. "That was a normal protocol, to see if there was any evidence in it. And it's completely legal. You don't need a warrant to do it, as long as it's put out by the curb. You just grab it and see what's in it, and go through it, to see if there's anything that you can use as evidence or whatever. I know we were following him around for a little. I know he had a surveillance group. I don't know what depth there was, that we were surveilling him, but there was nothing really that he was doing that really, you know—if I remember correctly, he curtailed his travelings to see hookers and stuff like that. He wasn't going anywhere."

Jennifer went on, "And they also impounded his Jeep so there went my rides. He said the police told him they would only need his car for a short period of time but I don't remember if he ever got it back. I remember he was saying these things right at the electronics counter with other employees and customers around. One of the other employees, Nancy, actually made a call to the police herself to share what was going on at work. Unlike myself, she didn't trust him for a minute. But I was blinded by friendship, the promise of a new place outside my parents' house, and a total lack of life experience with liars."

When Jennifer and Nancy discussed it later, Nancy—though she'd had such a rapport with Eric—confided that something about Eric's story just seemed a little "off" to her, that he shouldn't have been talking about it that way at work, in front of customers. He shouldn't have been, essentially, bragging about this police attention he was getting.

Regarding the story of the false police report at his other job, Jennifer remembered, "He came into work with a bandage on his face. Told us that some crazy guy cut his face with a knife. He got tons of sympathy from everyone at work, especially when he said the police kept trying to poke holes in his story. I mean, what kind of crazy person would cut themselves and make up a story like that?"

Still, Jennifer seemed to echo Nancy's thoughts of the "Southern gentleman" they worked with: "Everyone liked him. He was a kind man, he did good work, and customers seemed charmed by him."

It was not long after Wendy's body was found that Armstrong stopped working at Target. Whether he quit his job, or Target decided it wasn't a good idea for him to continue on there, is unclear.

"Once he found the body, I got no more rides," Jennifer said. "And the last time I remember seeing him was the day he was telling me about the stolen trash cans."

Armstrong did find new employment during this time at Detroit Metro Airport, working as a refueler for Signature Flight Support, having filled out an application there in late January. He got along fine with coworkers there, his trainer would later tell police. He would talk about his time in the Navy, his other job at Target, even troubles with his wife. He also told coworkers he wanted to move back home to the South.

While police were in their holding pattern for DNA results, a few weeks after Wendy was found, some other lab results came in. Both animal hair and human hair were recovered from Wendy's body, and both animal hair and human hair were found in the tape lifts from the Jeep. Examination found the animal hair from the two different places to be similar in visual appearance. And as far as the carpet fibers from the Jeep, they were found to be consistent in color, diameter, cross-sectional shape, type, and chemical composition with the fibers from the tape lift of Wendy's hosiery.

The tape lifts from the passenger-side floor of Armstrong's Jeep revealed what Mike Petri remembered having raised his suspicion that night of January 2—the gold flecks from Wendy's shoes. Gold particles from the floor of the Jeep were also consistent in appearance and chemical and elemental composition with the gold substance from the lining of Wendy's shoes.

"So it wasn't too long later," Donald Riley said, "the crime lab—and again, I don't remember how long—the crime lab said, okay, we've got her hair, and we've got other stuff that … She was in that Jeep, you know? So the prosecutor's office said, well, now that there's DNA involved, we're going to hold off until this DNA comes back."

An arrest warrant would not be issued.

Petri said, "You have to remember this was 2000. Back then I think you still needed a substantial amount of evidence

for them to be able to do DNA and it took quite a while …
And that was probably a rush job at that time."

It was a bitter pill to swallow for Petri, Riley, and team,
and one that forever changed the lives of several more
people, some who survived and some who didn't.

THE ASSAULTS CONTINUE

The watchful eye of the Dearborn Heights PD as they
anxiously awaited the DNA test results may have been
enough to keep Armstrong on the straight and narrow for
a couple months. He knew he was a suspect. His blood had
been drawn, his hair tested. He may not have known just
what a good case they were amassing against him, but he
could imagine something along those lines. What could he
do now, other than keep on living his life? He continued
on with his job. He took a trip back to North Carolina to
see family in March, even paying a visit to the grave of his
deceased baby brother.

But he certainly did hunt again. And as the weeks wore
on, he escalated. He sped up his timeframes, and those
timeframes do become a bit murky, possibly with multiple
assaults on the same night, as events led up to his arrest.

The next death after Wendy Jordan, assumed to be around
mid-March, was Rose Felt, left on the secluded stretch of
railroad tracks where she had suggested Armstrong take her
for their own encounter.

Then, a woman named Wilhemina Drane was walking
along Michigan Avenue between 51st and 52nd Streets at
around ten-thirty p.m. on Sunday, April 2, 2000, thinking
about catching the bus, when she met Armstrong. It was a
cold night and she was wearing a scarf.

Armstrong pulled up to the curb in his Jeep.

"What are you doing?"

"What does it look like I'm doing?" Wilhemina quipped.

He asked Wilhemina if she needed a ride, she later told police. Armstrong evidently saw something about the forty-two-year-old Detroit resident that seemed prostitute-like, though there is no indication that Wilhemina, who died several years later in December 2012, was doing anything but simply catching a bus. One news story online reported that she had described herself as a one-time prostitute but the case files simply state that she told police she once worked on Michigan.

Wilhemina told police that she asked this stranger if he was crazy or some killer. "No, I'm not like that," he told her.

Once inside the Jeep, she asked Armstrong to take her to Joy Road and Livernois. That's where she lived and it was quite a hike from where she was on Michigan, many blocks. Waiting for the bus was taking too long, she told him.

"He didn't say a whole lot," she would later tell *The Detroit News*. "I was doing most of the talking. He really didn't seem weird at all. He seemed pretty normal at first. I noticed he had on work clothes, and I saw a tattoo on his arm of a lion."

She asked him if he lived in the suburbs. He said yes. She asked if he had a girlfriend. He said no. He seemed like a nice guy, she told police. Seemed educated. She merely pegged him as a Good Samaritan. At least at first.

Armstrong was heading east on Michigan and she directed him to turn left on Livernois. Then they were going north, toward Joy, but when he got part of the way up, around Warren Avenue, "he pulled down an abandoned street, and I knew something was funny. I got scared."

Armstrong stopped the Jeep and said he needed his coat. He reached behind the seat. Wilhemina was looking away, out the window. Then she felt him grab her neck. They fought. "I was lucky I had on a scarf; that saved me. He got my scarf instead of my neck."

She knocked Armstrong's glasses off in the struggle. "I had a can of mace in my pocket, and I was trying to get it.

But by then, his fingers were around my windpipe. I finally got to the mace and sprayed him. Then I jumped out of the car."

She threw bottles at his Jeep as he drove away, she told police.

Several days later, when she heard about the three bodies found at the railroad tracks, she felt she should file a report with the police.

And she vowed never to accept a ride from a stranger again.

Just a few days after the attack on Wilhemina, still in the early days of April, a prostitute who went by Devin Marus was working Michigan Avenue between Wesson and Campbell when picked up by Armstrong. Marus also lived to tell the tale, a tale that was key to actually arresting Armstrong a few days after that.

Marus was born a man but reportedly was in the process of a drug therapy to help transition to female at the time of this case, dressing as a female while working Michigan Ave (though by all accounts did not have the surgery in subsequent years). Reported by local media to be a "transvestite," Marus self-described to authorities as a "pre-operative transsexual." Devin's name was recorded different ways in police reports, court transcripts, and the media: Devin, Devon, Marus, Marcus. Here, we'll go with how it was signed. Those names would end up being only a couple variations of the several names used through the years, however, as Devin, with a real name we'll leave off since she could not be reached for this book, has had trouble with the law more recently, charged with armed robbery and felonious assault and incarcerated a time or two. Since Devin identified as female at the time, we'll use "she/her" references for the most part.

Devin was convincing enough that Armstrong may have assumed this was a woman he saw, yet she was strong enough to fight off Armstrong's attack. Devin was twenty-two at the time, five-foot-eight and around one hundred and forty to one hundred and fifty pounds. She generally worked Michigan between Livernois and Junction, she would later testify, and she estimated it was around eleven p.m. when Armstrong pulled up on the curb.

This guy in a Jeep, no doubt innocent-looking despite the multiple tattoos here and there, asked if Devin was a cop. She replied no and asked if Armstrong was a cop. No. So okay, that was out of the way.

"Then I got in his Jeep," Devin told police, "and I asked him what can I do for you, and he said how about a blowjob." They agreed on a price of forty dollars. With this, you have to wonder if perhaps Armstrong knew all along that Devin was transgender and it was never about a sex act.

Armstrong took them to Joe Street near Michigan, parking midblock. Devin was intrigued by Armstrong's tattoos and commented on them, she would later say in court. Armstrong fished around in his vehicle for the money. In the initial account to police, Devin did not state that a sex act was performed, but stated it later in court, saying that afterward Armstrong squeezed both hands around her throat, uttering that he hated "fucking prostitutes."

As the choking continued, "I wrestled away from him and was able to break free of him," Devin said, "and got the passenger door open and jumped out." Her purse was still in the car, though. She wanted it back.

"Give me my purse."

"Come in and get it" was the reply.

"No way."

Armstrong drove off and Devin walked toward home. When she got up to Michigan, she saw Armstrong turn off Wesson onto Michigan, then head toward Livernois. He was going home as well. Maybe.

Devin later remembered the "Eric" she'd seen on her attacker's work shirt. She also remembered the spare tire on the back of his vehicle, with JEEP written on the tire cover. And other descriptive details.

The murder of Kelly Hood likely came right after that, in April, although we cannot be sure of the timeframe. It's possible it was the same night or the next night. Or it might have happened the night before Devin's attack, which is given as April 7 in some reports, April 4 in others.

But Armstrong was not done yet.

Like Devin, another young assault survivor of Armstrong was known by a few different names—Cynthia Marie Smith, the street name of Jasmine, and a real name of Avon with a last name we'll again leave off for privacy. She opted not to do an interview when contacted for this book and has worked hard to put her Detroit days behind her. In court documents, she is referred to as Cynthia Smith, so we'll use that name here. She was twenty at the time. Her encounter with Armstrong was likely Saturday, April 8, or Sunday, April 9 (she remembered it as Sunday night/ Monday morning in at least one police report). Cynthia, clad in a short black leather jacket, cheetah-print blouse with black tank top underneath, and blue jeans and boots, was on foot on Michigan Avenue near Weir, near a Marathon gas station, when Armstrong pulled up next to her, asking her if she needed a ride. She remembered it as between three-thirty and three-forty-five a.m.

Armstrong would later recall for police that she wore a black leather jacket and had long black hair. He estimated her at about five-foot-seven, one hundred and twenty pounds (correct on the weight, but five inches over on the height). She asked if he was a cop; he asked the same. He told her he worked at the airport. She would later tell police she didn't believe Armstrong wasn't a cop and asked him to prove it by showing his privates. They then talked price and he took her to a gas station at Michigan and Wyoming so he could withdraw the agreed-upon one hundred dollars from the ATM. He would remember it, as he needed to buy condoms because she said she didn't have any. She had just gotten out there that night, she told him.

They then left the gas station. He said she directed him to a place he couldn't recall for police. Cynthia herself told police they parked on Western south of Michigan, and that yes, she had directed him there. She gave police the address of the building they parked in front of on Western.

There are conflicting reports of what happened next. Cynthia initially told police (from an investigator's report at the time of Armstrong's arrest) that once they parked, Armstrong demanded she remove her coat and give him her purse. "I refused to do these things," she said, "and told him I was going to get out of the car, and he couldn't do anything about it."

She tried to exit the vehicle, she said, but the passenger door was locked, and then things went sideways. Armstrong produced a metal object in his hand. "I think it might have been a knife. He reached toward me, holding this object between his thumb and palm with his other four fingers extending straight outward."

He then grabbed her with both hands, pushing her against the passenger door as he started to choke her. He repeatedly said he hated prostitutes. He put the metal object in his mouth as he then used both hands to strangle her. She said that after about forty-five seconds she blacked out and when she woke up, she was lying in front of some house and he was gone.

In Armstrong's confession to police, however, he said that once they parked, Cynthia took one leg out of her pants. He pulled his pants down and business proceeded. As the act was wrapping up, Armstrong said, "that's when I saw my father's face and that's when I strangled her."

Cynthia's account changed a bit when she testified in court in 2001. She said they had sex, then she promptly told him to get off her. He had leaned back in the Jeep, but then he leaned forward and started choking her. "I hate prostitutes!

I hate prostitutes!" were the words he uttered. Both of his hands were around her neck, squeezing. She blacked out.

In his confession, Armstrong said he realized what he was doing and stopped. He drove about a block away, took Cynthia out of the Jeep, and placed her on the side of the curb. Then he left. Unlike with Natasha, when he evidently figured he was leaving her for dead, he appears to have made the conscious effort to stop what he was doing.

A couple of hours later, Cynthia woke up on a lawn in front of a house at Michigan and Addison, not far from Weir Street (in the McGraw area, she initially told police). She said she knew where she was because she looked over and saw "Michigan" on the street sign. There were tractor trailers parked nearby. Missing was her black imitation-leather purse with a blue butterfly design on it (Armstrong remembered this as a backpack he said he threw out somewhere on Ford Road). Her three hundred dollars in twenties was all gone, along with the other items in her purse: makeup, water, sunflower seeds, peanuts, a pack of Kool cigarettes. Her clothing was ripped. That had to have occurred after he choked her because she didn't recall him ripping her clothing during the incident. She had red marks and bruises on her neck and near her collarbone. She would also discover she had a cut that went across her abdomen, about ten inches long, and she had no idea how she got it. She walked back to the gas station at Weir and Michigan, she told police, where one of the other girls there asked what happened. She got a cab from the gas station, which she took home. Her sister paid the cab.

Armstrong, meanwhile, had gone home and taken a "very long" shower, he later told police.

"Did you know that what you did was wrong?" police later asked him.

"Yes."

After the encounter with Cynthia, it would have been Nicole Young, on the night of Sunday, April 9. It's possible that Armstrong attacked Nicole the night before Cynthia, or on the same night. In his confession, he said he encountered Cynthia on Monday, April 10, and that's what she remembered. That would seem to indicate she was attacked right after Armstrong's final known kill.

Whatever the timeframe, the night after her own attack, Cynthia was picked up at Michigan and Lawndale by another john. At their motel room, Cynthia told this other john about the assault. She showed him the big scar on her abdomen. Her bruises. She told him this guy drove a Jeep and she thought he was wearing an aviator mechanic's uniform.

Cynthia had no idea that her attacker was about to be caught, and right on the very heavily trafficked street on which he had picked her up. The notorious Michigan Ave. She also had no idea what had been happening at the railroad tracks.

A DISCOVERY AT THE TRACKS

Monday, April 10, 2000. It was about forty degrees in the inner city that morning, with no precipitation. Clear and cool, it was noted on one police report. Winter was gradually giving way to spring in the blustery state of Michigan, as three women lay dead at the railroad tracks near Military and John Kronk in Southwest Detroit.

At the time, Conrail, a major freight hauler, was a switching and terminal railroad operating about twelve hundred miles of track in three regional areas. Conrail's Detroit line, covering about three hundred and fifty-nine miles, focused along the corridor connecting Trenton, Detroit, and Sterling Heights/Utica, and covered Macomb, Monroe, and Wayne counties, according to Conrail.com. The hub was Livernois Yard in Detroit, located at Livernois and John Kronk, just a street over from Military. Conrail still does business there, around Detroit, though names and ownership have changed a bit over the years.

Denis Kupser was working as a conductor for Conrail at the time, and he was on his shift from eleven p.m. on April 9 to seven a.m. the next morning. In his fifties then, he lived in Lincoln Park in the downriver area of metro Detroit, where a lot of his Conrail coworkers tended to live as it was close by. Via phone in 2017, Kupser recalled how things worked.

"Well, Livernois was a situation where, at that time that I was working there, a train would come in from another location. Let's just say, for example, Toledo. And then they would bring the train into the yard, and it had a mixture of rail cars in it. And that mixture of rail cars would then have to be separated and sent to other yard locations. So cars going like—mainly, basically, automobile parts were the things that the railroad [carried], as far as freight were concerned. It was like eighty percent or ninety percent actually automobile parts and things to do with automobiles. Tires, alternators, mufflers, whatever. So as a result of it, there were various plants in Detroit, you know, like a Chrysler plant or a General Motors plant or whatever, where they would have certain cars that would be designated for their locations. And then there were industries along the way or in the general area where you would separate the rail cars, and this train that came in from, let's say, Toledo, and you would separate it into tracks that had to go like from Livernois to North Yard, because there were certain cars in that train that had to go to that location. But then there were other rail cars and there were like scrap cars that had to go to various scrapyards or steel that had to go to the Ford Motor Company, at Zug Island, and different locations. River Rouge. You had to separate them out of the train in order to get them to be headed in the correct direction. Since they came in in one unit, they had to be separated in order to get those rail cars to go to various locations, in order to have them placed in the industry and have them serviced."

On the morning of April 10, just as it was getting to be light outside, Ed Mannix was at his post as a conductor on a train that would have been traveling from the Livernois Yard to the North Yard, which is several miles northeast. Also in his fifties and living downriver in the town of Gibraltar, Mannix was on the shift after Kupser, starting work between seven and eight a.m.

"We were coming east with an engine," Mannix would later tell police, "and we stopped just east of Military to flip the switch. And when I got out to flip the switch, I saw the dead woman just north of the tracks." This was around eight a.m.

Dale Lemieux, who worked a lot with Mannix and had just come in for a twelve-hour shift at around seven to serve as his engineer, heard that he'd found the body and then walked over there himself to check it out, coming within ten feet of her, he told police.

Russell Walls, a switch inspector for Conrail at the time, also went over to check out the discovery.

"I felt sick," he said via phone in 2018. "I mean, I knew when I drove up the hill and I saw her, and her legs were propped up—she was laying on her back, and her legs were propped up and apart. And I thought, this is sick. And I kind of walked over, onto the track where I know nobody would have probably been, up on the ties—you wouldn't have seen anything over there anyway, up on the rocks and stuff. And the rest of the road was like cinder. So that would leave footprints or car prints or whatever else. So I just kind of stayed up, and I stayed twenty feet back. I didn't get anywhere close to it."

At this time, neither Walls nor anybody else saw the other two women lying just a few yards away. The multiple sets of train tracks side by side were lined by a gravel service drive and a row of scattered trees and brush with a wire fence on the north, and some trees and a graffitied short block wall on the south, forming a border with glimpses of

Detroit's industry and lower-end neighborhoods beyond. The other two women were obscured by brush, weeds, a few broken or fallen tree limbs.

Mannix had been there at the same time the morning before and had not seen the body. The night before the discovery, at around eleven, Conrail police officer Barry Linsey had been checking the area for trespassers and had driven right over where the body was later discovered and not noticed a thing, he told police. So with that we can certainly pinpoint when Nicole was left there.

Tom DeSimpelaere, who worked as an engineer for Conrail at the time, actually commuting from a nearby slice of Ohio, said it was pretty common to see a homeless person sleeping near the tracks, so that might be what goes through a rail worker's mind at first if confronted with a body lying near the tracks. Also, the railroad workers would typically see people coming and going in this area, often engaging in various questionable acts because of its secluded nature. This part of the tracks, heavily littered with brush and trees, is accessible by the single-lane gravel service drive going up from a small parking lot of a business off John Kronk, at one time the Michigan Dry Ice Company. The body they discovered was technically lying on what was considered this service drive running alongside the tracks, though it looks simply like a gravel shoulder of the railroad's line to this day.

"It wasn't strange, in effect, to see lovers alongside the track in various locations, because nine times out of ten it was dark," Kupser said. "There's no streetlights on the track, you know, or nothing like that. So they would make use of a dark area, a shaded area, in order to carry out nature."

And this wasn't the first time a Conrail worker had discovered someone deceased at railroad tracks in Detroit.

"There have been occasions where people have been murdered or killed or whatever, and for some reason, they seem to think that if they do drop the body off near a railroad track that it has less chance of being found," Kupser said. "In my railroad career, there's probably been two or three different situations where they found the body near the railroad tracks. One—I didn't find it, but it was somebody else in the railroad, but it was over just off of Mack Avenue near the Chrysler Jefferson plant in Detroit. It was off of Mack Avenue in the Mack Yard. They call it Mack Yard. And it's since been redone and reworked and revamped, so that particular spot and location now is different. And then it's been brought to my attention where there was, on the railroad there were two people that were murdered, execution-style, over near the area of … oh, what would it be? It would be Schaefer and Pleasant Street, in that general area of where the railroad tracks are. It would be north. The tracks are north of Schaefer and Pleasant Street. In that general area."

Walls recalled another incident. "Over at Davison Yard one time, we were walking through there inspecting. We were going to get rid of some tracks in that yard and everything. We had just taken over the Terminal East and Terminal West Railroads. There's kind of a lot of brush and stuff in there, where it hadn't been used for a while. Just high grass and stuff. And there was a guy who was tied to the telephone pole, and his penis was cut off and shoved in his mouth and set on fire. That would have been back in the … well, let's see … probably right around the beginning of the '80s."

A story for another book, evidently.

"I've seen 'em killed at crossings and different things like that," said Walls, who put in thirty-four years with Conrail, retiring just after 9-11. "But you never get used to it."

Conrail protocol in a situation like this was to first call in the Conrail police. Walls saw the Conrail officer arrive while he was still at the scene. Then the Detroit police were notified, with Mannix telling them he initially thought the woman had been stabbed to death in the chest, perhaps because she was wearing red.

With the discovery, DeSimpelaere remembered something. In a statement stamped two a.m. on April 11, he told police that just a couple hours after he had come on duty the night of April 2, when he was in charge of switching moves of the trains, he had seen a vehicle with its headlights on right at the place where Nicole's body was later left. It was between one and one-thirty.

"The vehicle, what I think was like a Jeep Cherokee, was parked," he told police. "I observed the driver's side door open and then saw an unknown male, kinda tall, get out and walk toward the bushy area. I don't remember him carrying anything nor do I remember him actually going into the brush. I was always able to see him. I do not remember the color of the car."

He continued, "I then saw the man return to his car and get back into the driver's seat. I believe this all happened within five minutes. I saw the car back up and at that time I pulled away on the train. I wasn't able to see if the car actually left the area at that time."

About ten or fifteen minutes later, DeSimpelaere had returned to make another train switch and the vehicle was gone.

MORE THAN THEY BARGAINED FOR

Detroit Police logged the time the call came in as nine a.m., with the first officers arriving on the scene at the railroad tracks east of Military Street and south of John Kronk at nine-fifteen and securing the scene at nine-twenty-five. That was Derek Watkins and Angela Simms of the Fourth Precinct. Other officers then arrived, including Eugene Fitzhugh and Constance Williams of DPD's Evidence Tech Unit, who met Sergeant Arlie Lovier of the Homicide Section in charge of the scene.

What was discovered first was the body of the woman who would be identified as Robin Brown/Nicole Young, noted in Fitzhugh's report as "a young black female lying on the ground face up with her head facing south and her feet facing north." Her legs were spread in vulgar fashion, knees bent. Her arms were splayed out on each side, parallel with her thighs. She lay on the north side of the tracks, on the gravel service drive, described in the report as a berm about twenty or thirty feet wide that provided access to the tracks for repair and maintenance.

Nicole Young on the north side of the tracks at Military and John Kronk, spotted first by a Conrail worker. The trees are still bare on this April day. Image: DPD files.

Nicole was nude from the waist down except for a pair of ankle-length white socks. She wore a shiny plastic-looking black waist-length jacket, open, and a shiny plastic-looking red waist-length jacket underneath it, closed. Under the red jacket were a gray T-shirt and lavender bra; the shirt had been pulled up to above her breasts, underneath the red jacket. Her mouth was open, teeth visible. Her eyes were open too, seeming to gaze off in the distance. Her short, reddish-tinted hair appeared to be brushed back. And around her neck was a light-colored nylon stocking, possibly used to strangle her, the evidence tech surmised. He also noticed a white substance on both inner thighs. There was no sign of decomposition, Fitzhugh noted. She had *just* been left. The night before, they figured.

"It is my opinion the complainant was positioned as a display," Fitzhugh wrote. "Not only is the complainant nude from the waist down, her legs are spread apart and bent slightly at the knees completely exposing her inner thighs and vagina. She was on a cold surface of dirt, gravel and very little grass."

She was pronounced dead at 10:18 a.m. by Dr. Leigh Hlavaty, noted as Unknown Female No. 19. A rape kit and investigation of her fingernails and clothing were ordered. Trauma to her neck was noted. She was wearing pearl-colored fake fingernails, some of which were missing, police saw. One fingernail was found nearby, assumed to be hers.

Soon after they arrived at the railroad track scene, however, police also spotted Rose Marie Felt, discovered second but later determined to be dumped first due to her more advanced composition. She lay a couple yards northeast of Young, just below the crown of a small, rocky ravine on the north side of the tracks. Head facing west, feet facing east. Her face was blackened considerably from the decomposition, crime scene photos show. Her blond curls were also darkened, but still showing as lighter in parts. She had on a black bra, still fastened but pulled up above her breasts, her whole chest and torso gaping out gruesomely. Her arms were bent upward, her hands near her head, almost as if she had been defending herself but more like they had been moved out of the way. She was wearing a pair of shiny plastic-looking black pants (which seems to be a cop's term, again, from the report) over a pair of black stretch-type pants. The shiny outer pants were pulled down to midway on the thigh. The crotch of the stretchy inner pants was cut out, exposing her privates—exactly what her killer later noted to police when describing their encounter. "What further made it possible to see the complainant's exposed crotch," Fitzhugh's report said, "was the fact the right leg of the complainant was at a thirty-degree angle to the left leg and bent at the knee." Also posed, cops would later testify in court.

Near Rose's head were two coats. One was shiny black like her outer pants. The other was a black fur-lined coat with a couple prescription bottles in its pockets: Paxil, 20mg. Zyprexa, 10mg. Prescribed to a man named Anthony.

Logged as Unknown Female No. 20, she was pronounced dead at 1:53 p.m. by Hlavaty, and a rape kit and hair and nail sample analysis ordered. Ligature marks were noted on her neck.

Then, at the bottom of the hill in the small, tree-filled ravine, Kelly Jean Hood. Head facing northeast, feet facing southwest. Nestled into some brush, not as visible. Not so posed. Elbows bent, hands tucked almost neatly near her throat. She wore a soft pink sweater, described as a blouse in the report but showing in the photos as a pullover sweater like something out of the 1980s that stays in fashion because it's a classic. She might have worn something a lot like it in high school.

As with Young, she was nude from the waist down, but without socks. The back of her neck rested against a tree trunk and showed bruising, her head tilted up. Her waist and hips were at a lower position than her chest and her legs, her legs bent at the knee, laid over fallen tree limbs and spread apart, exposing her genitals. "It appears complainant landed in this position with great force," the report noted. The branches and wood debris under her had caused indentations in her back and thighs.

Near Kelly was a tan trench coat and another black fur-lined coat.

She was pronounced dead at 1:59 p.m. by Hlavaty. Unknown Female No. 21. Rape kit, nails and hair analysis ordered, as well, and ligature marks noted on her neck too.

So, there was a lot of work to be done here. Fitzhugh requested the help of several more personnel to photograph, sketch, and otherwise process the scene.

All in all, it was not quite what these officers wanted to find. Not quite what they wanted to radio back to the office. There was something very cat and mouse about the whole thing, sort of like this killer was saying "catch me if you can," one officer was later quoted as saying. What the DPD didn't know that day was that they were inheriting a case their brethren in Dearborn Heights had started, and that same cat-and-mouse feeling had occurred to them too. But no worries. DPD was pretty well-versed in this whole homicide thing.

Gerald Cliff, former commanding officer of the city's Violent Crime Task Force and now retired, remembered that day well. He was sitting in a meeting that morning with the homicide inspector and others on the force, members of the Violent Crimes Section, Homicide Section, Special Investigations. It was a meeting that kept getting interrupted.

"We're all sitting around the conference table for a Monday morning briefing with the commander," Cliff recalled. "And we're talking about what's going on in our various sections. The CO of Homicide got a call. He said, 'I'm sorry, I've got to take this call.' Because we had pagers at the time. He says, 'I'm sorry, I've got to interrupt the meeting. I've got to take this phone call.' So he gets up and he goes over to Doc's [Commander Dennis Richardson's] desk, and he picks it up. He calls his front desk, and they tell him what's going on. He goes, 'Okay, well, keep me apprised.' And he comes back, and he says, 'We've got a body up in the Fourth Precinct.' They say Okay. So we go back to what we're doing. That wasn't that unusual, that it would require the head of the Homicide Division to leave the meeting and go out to the scene. He had investigative teams to do that. Well, then he gets another call a few minutes later. And he goes, 'I've got to take this.' So he gets up, he takes that call, and he comes back and says, 'Now there's two.' Doc kind of looks up and he goes, 'Two?' And he goes, 'Yeah,' and he said, 'One's older than the other one. One's fresh and one's been there a while.' And that's when the mood in the room got kind of tense. So he informs his detectives, all right, I'll be down there in a minute, or something to that effect, meaning he was probably going to have to leave immediately and go out to the scene. And at that point then he gets another message. And that's when he says, 'There's more than two' or something to that effect. At that point, Doc just adjourned the meeting and the majority of us went out to the scene."

Cliff himself did not go to the railroad scene that day but he did work the case as it unraveled in the next several days and weeks. He was the officer in charge of the Violent Crimes Section at the time, having obtained a bachelor of science degree in criminal justice at Michigan State and a master's in criminal justice administration from University of Detroit Mercy, then earning a second master's in labor and industrial relations and a Ph.D in political science at Wayne State. Born and raised in Battle Creek, the son of a Battle Creek cop, Cliff graduated from the Detroit Police Academy in January 1974. He would later leave Detroit to become the chief of police eighty-five miles north, in Saginaw, then would become a research director at the National White-Collar Crime Center. Cliff spent more than thirty-one years with the DPD, though, even a year working the notorious Cass Corridor, and the Armstrong case left an indelible impression on him. In fact, he always figured it would make a good book, and he was the one responsible for kickstarting this whole project.

Dennis Richardson, who was Cliff's boss at DPD at the time, did go to the railroad track scene that day. Nicknamed Doc, Richardson was quite the character in the department. "If you ever watch *Chicago PD* or *NCIS*," Cliff said, "and you can visualize a personality comprised of the best of Sergeant Hank Voight and Leroy Jethro Gibbs, you can imagine how warm and fuzzy this guy is, and he's not acting, he's the real thing. He was that way before these fictitious characters even existed. The members of his team who were married used to joke about their spouses joining 'WAR' (Wives Against Richardson) after the hubby was assigned to the task force. Working for the guy, you either loved him or you hated him passionately. It was not at all unusual to go to work on a Monday morning and not get home 'til sometime Wednesday night. Once on the trail of a bad guy, Doc never let up on us. All he would say is, every minute we weren't on the trail of this guy, he could be victimizing another person. Doc hated what he called 'telephone detectives' and coined the acronym GOYAKOD, which he posted on the wall of the conference room. It stood for 'Get Off Your Ass and Knock On Doors!'"

Richardson would go on, after his retirement, to serve as police chief in Brownstown Township, a community south of Detroit, and deputy chief of the Criminal Investigations Division of the Wayne County Sheriff's Department.

Richardson was joined at the railroad track scene by the homicide inspector and the deputy chief of the Major Crimes Division. Sergeant Dave Babcock, an evidence tech, arrived at the scene by lunchtime to supervise the collection of evidence, from Fitzhugh's request, along with Officer Steven Baylor to photograph several tire impressions and shoe impressions found there. Officer Frank Horan made a sketch of the scene, what they were finding from where. Officer Steven Yakimovich also assisted. Everything was carefully documented. All kinds of cigarette butts were bagged, for instance, each one meticulously noted for origin, using the railway's nearby gray electric box as a point of reference. There was a yellow rope two feet seven inches long. A clear plastic juice bottle. A Kit Kat wrapper. A McDonald's cup. Empty Marlboro boxes. Used condoms, of course—but would they be related to this case or just a sign that this secluded spot was well used? Seeing that these victims appeared to be prostitutes and knowing what he knew about the area, Richardson insisted that every condom be collected from the scene. Not a pretty task but it had to be done.

Styrofoam cups. A yellow butter dish. A Diet Pepsi bottle. Anything could have DNA on it from a killer. A hooded jacket. A blue seat cover. A tan jacket. One white sock. A Kleenex with suspected blood on it, which got evidence tag 544437. A white blouse. Brown tights. Lots of clothing items left around these railroad tracks, for whatever reason. But the pair of panties, size 9, Anne Marie brand, in a pink bubble pattern, evidence tag 544440, found twenty-four feet north of the first railroad track and one hundred and forty-five feet east from the railroad power box, would prove significant. The panties would be connected to Kelly Hood.

Oddly enough, there was a dead cat lying fifteen feet from Nicole, decomposing. Hair was collected from the cat at Richardson's request. The wadded-up tissue material near Nicole's feet was collected. Along with a white plastic straw lying close by.

Back at the station, Detroit Police received a fax of Conrail work schedules from the Conrail Police Department. Statements were taken from all the Conrail guys that were there, working the night before, working the morning of, working the past few days, actually. DPD officers asked if they had noticed cars coming and going from the tracks. If they had seen anything else suspicious.

And as the day wore on, additional officers were called in to hold the scene. Word was bound to get out soon, even if this was long before Facebook Live. There were already people near the scene, hanging around, trying to see what was going on. Officer Ira Todd and others photographed them and their vehicles.

George Hunter was on his way to work that day at *The Detroit News* (where this author was also working at the time) when he was called to the scene. The police-beat reporter wasn't sure what he was driving into but soon after he got there, he knew it had to be a pretty good story.

"That was the first day that all that went down. There were cops there," Hunter later recalled, and by cops, he also meant his sister, who worked for the Detroit Police then. "And [Police Chief] Benny Napoleon was up there too. The whole brass. We didn't know what it was. We knew it was something big because, you know, the police chief doesn't really show up to these. And then rumors started coming, that it was [a] body. Then it was like, no, it was a couple bodies. And I was fairly new on the police beat. This was before cell phones, or before everyone had one. I didn't have one at the time. So it wasn't like you could just call your sources and find out what the heck was going on. So we got called there because there was a body found, but we didn't know the extent of it until much later. And we knew something was big because if it was just a body, you wouldn't have the police chief and all his brass up there."

Richardson wanted the benefit of an FBI profiler at the scene, and he dialed up his contact in the Detroit FBI field office while he was still at the tracks. They couldn't send a profiler for a while, he was told, at least many hours and possibly a few days. Richardson offered to hold the scene, but that was going to be nearly impossible. So that night, Richardson sat in the office of John Bell, special agent in charge of the Detroit office of the FBI, who was a good friend of his, and on speakerphone, they called the Behavioral Analysis Unit in Quantico—the "BAU" made well-known in many media such as *The Silence of the Lambs* and *Criminal Minds*.

Richardson conveyed the magnitude of the day's discovery, along with his gut feeling that this killer was escalating. "If we don't catch this fucker," he pressed, "next week, there'll be a chair in the middle of the tracks with a dead prostitute in it. He's just a killing machine."

The BAU agent gave him a pivotal thought: "You're focusing far too much on his successes. What you need to do is focus on his failures."

So in other words, find someone who survived. And they certainly would.

Everett Monroe worked the case for DPD and would go on to earn a Ph.D and eventually trade the harsh Michigan winter for the warmer clime of Georgia, becoming a police captain in the town of Elberton. He remembered this day vividly when reached via phone for this book project. "I was a police officer assigned to a specialized federal unit called the Violent Crime Task Force. And we dealt with all high-profile investigations, serials, rapes, robberies, murders, kidnapping, drug investigations. We were designed to handle all high-profile investigations … Well, we were called to the scene. A body was located. We went out there, and there—it's a like mini hump yard. There are many tracks through there. And the train really goes through there pretty fast. And she was probably about, oh, twenty, twenty-five feet from the tracks. Her legs were spread and propped open, and you could see her distinctively from the railroad tracks."

He went on, "We then set up a perimeter and started to check for evidence. Dave Babcock, who is one of the best evidence techs that I had the opportunity to work with, and probably one of the best evidence techs the police department had, was called out to the scene because of his expertise. And he was taking pictures. And he called us over and says, hey, guys, we've got more bodies. And we were like, oh shit, you know. So now we go over there, and these bodies, you could tell, had been there a while."

Monroe remembered a particular detail that didn't seem to be reported and that didn't come up during the later court proceedings. A very intriguing detail, from a psychological perspective: "It appeared that Mr. Armstrong had visited the area on several occasions. And he was taking clothing off of one body and putting it on another body and switching the clothing around." Was this just one officer's impression? File that one away for later.

"So now our crime scene has expanded even larger," Monroe said. "We must have stayed out there six, seven hours, maybe, processing the crime scene. And assisting. And I went to interview the engineer, and some other train personnel." Monroe remembered Mannix talking about finding the body, that it was partially nude, that there was a stocking around her neck. Vivid details that don't fade in a couple decades.

There was reportedly a fourth body found at the railroad dump site tracks that day, determined to be unrelated to this case. Monroe remembered that too.

"Yeah. If I remember correctly, I want to say it was undetermined whether it would have been an—because people used to get into the train cars. I know someone had mentioned it was a possibility that they might have been killed playing around on the tracks or something. But I don't remember that too much. I was mainly focused on the situation we had, which was all those bodies."

THE HUNT FOR A SERIAL

THREE WOMEN FOUND SLAIN read the headline of George Hunter's story on the Metro page of the April 11 edition of *The Detroit News*. He interviewed residents of the neighborhood, one saying this was normally a quiet place, another commenting that hookers frequented the secluded area near the tracks. It "used to be a nice neighborhood," he told Hunter. Like so much of Detroit.

Police canvassed the area around the tracks, knocking on doors, interviewing residents about what they may have seen recently on this stretch. "I see cars go there all the time to take care of their sex stuff," Maria on Military said. "It's not just at night. It's all day." She had often seen an older-model Ford pickup truck, green and rusty, drive up there, with a white male driver in his thirties. Most of the men who went up there for sex were white, she said. And she would sometimes see a newer model white Chevy, like a Caprice.

Maria's neighbor Charles would walk through the area to pick up his wife from work between ten and eleven a.m. and remembered seeing a lot of clothing strewn around the tracks. Tanya on Hammond Street would see a white car like the one Maria saw, and she described two young white men she would see inside.

Sherry on Military told police she would see a man in an older gray Ford Bronco drive up to the tracks with a prostitute several times a week, almost every day. This was in the afternoon, between three-thirty and four. One time the man had a white blond female with him, but she later saw the female walk back down from the tracks and pass by her house. She knew her as a prostitute she had seen on Livernois.

Another neighbor on Military, George, saw a small blue vehicle drive up onto the tracks the Thursday before. The driver was a white man, about twenty-five to thirty years old, with a young white woman in the vehicle.

And Sandra on Military said she was threatened by a strange guy in an older blue car while she was walking home from work around four-twenty p.m. the day before. The guy drove off, but then as she got closer to home, he returned, this time on a ten-speed bike, and rode up to her and put his hand on her butt, she told police. "I'll be back for you," he said, having called her a bitch several times. She kept walking, eventually reaching home safely. (Ah, my beloved Detroit, where you never know what you're going to encounter. One day on my own walk to work downtown, I saw a big trash dumpster moving on its own down a sidewalk. Another day, there was a guy passed out at the wheel of his old beater car, speeding backward down Washington Boulevard. *Anyway, let's not digress too much …*)

During the police search of the tracks, which ended up spanning about twelve hours for all personnel, a few distraught parents stopped by the scene to ask for descriptions of the victims—because their daughters were missing. None matched.

Police checked in on registered sex offenders and various other parolees. It was already apparent on that day at the tracks that the three women had been killed at different times. A chilling thought. A dumping ground for a single killer. It was not apparent at that point, however, just how many other victims this serial had—in, or even outside, of Detroit. Perhaps there were other bodies dumped elsewhere they did not yet know about. As Everett Monroe recalled, a key element was that this case involved different jurisdictions in the metro area, each doing its own thing, so on that day at the tracks the DPD had no idea that Dearborn Heights had already had dealings with the perp.

From his perspective as a police officer back in 2000, was it uncommon or common to find a dead "lady of the evening"?

"It wasn't uncommon," said Monroe, who started with DPD in 1985 and served there more than twenty-five years. "The problem was that investigators never really took the time to see if the incidents were connected. It was just that, you know, we had a victim here. Let's just try to find out who it is. A lot of times we would be called to scenes, we didn't even know who the victim was, let alone who had committed the crime. So let's just try to find out who it is, who did it, why they did it, and bring them to justice. Well, in the first investigation that I worked in, serial investigation, it was a long time before they admitted we had a serial killer. That was Benjamin Atkins. And he killed, I want to say, twelve or thirteen."

Benjamin Atkins, also known as the Woodward Corridor Killer, earned himself eleven life sentences for raping, torturing, and strangling women in 1991 and 1992, most of them in Highland Park, a suburb tucked inside the middle of the city of Detroit. Many of the women were known to be prostitutes. The similarities with the Atkins case were haunting officers like Monroe after the discovery at the railroad tracks.

"Benjamin Atkins was in the '90s. And we were finding victims, and there were a lot of similarities to the crime scenes, but the upper management did not want to admit we had a serial killer."

A serial, of course, creates a panic. "You've got a problem. So it wasn't until it just became where we found all these girls in one location that they said, okay, we have a serial killer. And the same thing was with John Armstrong. You know, you had a body over here, body over here. Okay, fine, let's find out who it is, who did it, bring them to justice. Uh oh, we have three bodies over here; okay, we got a problem. Okay, now let's start conducting our investigation toward a serial pattern."

Even though Atkins had been arrested, tried, convicted, and then incarcerated at one of the correctional facilities in Jackson, Michigan, for his 1990s serial killings in Detroit, and even though it was known he had died with an HIV infection in 1997, the discovery on April 10 was so unsettling, Detroit Police actually contacted the prison and confirmed he was gone. Just to be sure.

At the time of the Armstrong case, the Detroit Police Department was comprised of thirteen precincts plus a vice squad, gang squad, narcotics division, crime lab, evidence tech unit, motor traffic unit, aviation unit, harbormaster, mayor's security unit, even fleet control to handle maintenance of the four hundred-plus vehicles the department coordinated. And within all of this, there was a very wide array of specialized parts of the units, sections, and divisions.

Each precinct had its own investigations section to deal with the day-to-day stuff that came up: burglaries, street robberies, vandalized vehicles and auto stripping, non-lethal assaults, and so on. But for the higher-profile crimes—serial killings and the like—there was the Headquarters Bureau (later called the Criminal Investigations Division) and its specialized investigative units.

Centered at what was back then DPD headquarters on Beaubien Street downtown, things were structured like this:

HEADQUARTERS BUREAU

Commander: Dennis "Doc" Richardson

- Violent Crimes Section: Each of the three teams was run by a lieutenant, all of whom reported to an inspector, who at the time was Gerald Cliff, who reported to Dennis Richardson, who in turn reported to a deputy chief, then the assistant chief, the chief, and then, technically, the mayor. (The rank of inspector at DPD at the time was the equivalent to captain in other places: one rank above lieutenant, one rank below commander. It wasn't like, for instance, the old Dirty Harry movies where the term inspector was equivalent to detective.) This Violent Crimes Section numbered close to 150 detectives on all three teams, plus about a dozen or more civilian personnel to handle administrative tasks.
  - Violent Crime Task Force: located on the fifth floor of DPD headquarters, across from the Homicide Section.
  - Fugitive Apprehension Team: located at the Federal Center in the FBI offices. They technically came

under the purview of the commanding officer of the Violent Crimes Section but were supervised by FBI personnel.

- Crime Analysis Unit: located on the fifth floor of DPD headquarters, across from the Homicide Section, along with the VCTF.

- Homicide Section: located on the west side of the fifth floor. Had 62 personnel.

- Special Investigations Section: the largest section within the division, taking up all of the seventh floor of headquarters, plus three other locations throughout the city. This section had well over two hundred personnel.
  - Armed Robbery
  - Sex Crimes
  - Domestic Violence: had offices on Cass, north of Myrtle.
  - Child Abuse: located in Eastern Market.
  - ICAC (Internet Crimes Against Children) Task Force: comprised of Michigan State Police and DPD personnel under the direction of an assistant state attorney general. Located in the western suburbs at a Michigan State Police facility.
  - Financial Crimes
  - Cyber Crimes
  - Commercial Auto Theft (existing for a short period): located on the far west side near Vernor and Central.

In total, the Headquarters Bureau comprised several hundred specialized investigative personnel. In recent years, the DPD has downsized considerably, at this writing, numbering perhaps half of what it was at the time of the Armstrong case.

And so, amid this organizational structure, it was the Violent Crime Task Force that was mobilized to handle this gruesome discovery at the tracks. In 2000, it was a relatively new unit founded a few years before when Isaiah "Ike" McKinnon was police chief and Benny Napoleon served as deputy chief. The concept was a multi-agency task force, basically without borders due to the presence of state, county, and federal officers—not just the DPD but also the Michigan State Police, the FBI. Its membership was diverse, whereas you might have a Detroit beat cop working alongside an FBI agent like Paul Sorce, the former Western Michigan University football player who appeared in the 1993 movie *Rudy*, starring Sean Astin.

Richardson hatched the idea for the task force in February 1994, proposing to then Deputy Chief Napoleon an expansion of the Repeat Offenders Program, which at the time consisted of a sergeant, a couple investigators, and a few officers. Repeat Offenders, which had worked a couple big armed robbery and rape cases the year before, had been short a couple officers. The squad was otherwise stretched from the court caseloads that resulted from its work—precious time spent away from its primary job. This second squad of the Repeat Offenders Program, as Richardson envisioned it, would work with the Detroit FBI and possibly other agencies on specialized cases from the Major Crimes Division—serial rapists, career criminals, high-profile homicides. Investigators from other areas of Major Crimes would be temporarily assigned to run a case with the task force. Members would be chosen by merit and expertise. Federal programs would help with overtime expenses. Response times would be quick—no "wait until morning" mentality. The quick mobility of the task force would allow it to be proactive rather than reactive, Richardson argued, and all of this would certainly be good PR for the department.

Leadership okayed the idea, and in the ensuing weeks Richardson met with representatives from the FBI and Michigan State Police to further pitch this multijurisdictional task force concept. The FBI pledged four full-time agents to the cause. MSP committed two to four officers. DPD would provide seven to nine officers. Richardson asked around to a couple other agencies, but they were not interested. He made the point, and reinforced it, that the task force needed to be housed in spirit and in physicality with the Detroit Police Department in order to be effective. He didn't want any feelings of elitism or aloofness. He requested space on the fifth floor of HQ on Beaubien Street. He requested "take-home" cars for the officers to assist in the rapid-response nature of the team, day or night. MSP offered to donate some desks and other office equipment. The FBI agreed to supply pagers. Arrangements were made for the task force to have its own radio communications for surveillance, a separate channel from the DPD patrol (and this would come into play later, in the Armstrong case). Richardson also arranged for each member of the task force to have a DPD ID badge regardless of his or her agency affiliation; this would help clear the way for more effective work on the scene of an incident or when obtaining records. Things were coming together—General Motors even loaned several new vehicles to the officers for the effort. The 3M Corp. donated billboards for a media campaign to receive crime tips.

One particular case that marked the early years of the task force, occurring just before the Armstrong case, was an effort to apprehend a gang of violent armed home invaders dressed as police, conducting supposed "raids" throughout the city.

"They were raping people. They were robbing people. They assaulted a couple people," recalled Benny Napoleon, who in his career also worked cases like Young Boys Inc., or YBI, a gang prolific in the '70s and '80s and known for using minors to traffic heroin. He worked the assault on figure skater Nancy Kerrigan at Cobo Arena. A graduate of Cass Tech High School, Napoleon truly worked his way up, joining the DPD at age nineteen in 1975 and going from a beat in the Second Precinct to sergeant in 1983, lieutenant in '85, inspector in '87, commander in '93, deputy chief in '94, assistant chief in '95, then chief under Mayor Dennis Archer from 1998 to 2001. For Napoleon, serving as Wayne County Sheriff decades later as he spoke via phone for this book, the home invasion case was the biggest he ever worked, involving a large volume of law enforcement resources and methods—wiretapping, surveillance by plane, even— and many individual lives affected by the band of about a dozen perps. "The number of cases that they had was in the hundreds, and it spanned, I know, Michigan and Ohio and I believe Indiana. And they were posing as the police and they were robbing what they thought were drug houses, and some of them turned out to be former drug houses. Very dangerous people. And we had several shootouts with them. It was nuts. It was the craziest thing I'd ever seen in my career."

The home invaders case ended with one particular blazing gun battle between the bad guys and the real police, involving a high-speed chase with multiple shots fired. "The chase ran for quite a distance," recalled Gerald Cliff, "right past the front door of the 10th Precinct station, exchanging shots the entire distance." This blazing battle made front-page news and involved the ramming of multiple police vehicles and lots of shots fired from both sides one late night in November 1994.

One unique aspect of the Violent Crime Task Force was that it was an exempt unit: to get into it, you were hand-picked, as opposed to the normal seniority-based transfer process. It was something a talented detective from a precinct might aspire to. Normally, the department's union structure required a member to submit a transfer request to move from one assignment to another. Regardless of qualifications, according to union contract, seniority on the department was the determining factor governing if and when you got transferred. If you wanted to go to traffic, bomb squad, harbormaster, aviation, whatever, you submitted your transfer request and waited for an opening to happen. If you were at the top of the list (senior) when an opening became available, you got transferred.

The VCTF was one of a few exempt units within the department wherein you applied for transfer into the unit, then your productivity, quality of work, case closure rate were all considered. You got interviewed not just by the command staff but by members of the unit with whom you would be working. If you passed all that, it didn't matter how much time you had on the job; if you were able to stand out based on your achievements, your quality of work and what you would bring to the team, you were in. You stayed until you failed to produce or you asked to leave, which some did due to the high-speed nature of the job or the stress on their families.

"Doc tended to select his supervisory staff the same way," Cliff recalled. "I got noticed because as a lieutenant, I had been asked to establish and run the home invasion task force, something new to the department. In '96-98, the city had experienced an average of fourteen thousand home invasions per year. The task force I developed and came to command was successful enough that it reduced the incidence of home invasions by nearly thirty percent in just over two years. The resultant drop in the Uniform Crime Index for 1999 had the city near the bottom of the list of ten most violent cities in the nation, after nearly a decade at or near the number one slot on that list. (That's what had earned us the title 'Murder City.') This is what got me noticed and promoted to inspector. When notified that I was promoted, I was given a choice of where I wanted to be assigned (something else that rarely happened in the department). I said I wanted to work for Doc."

The members of the task force shared a bond and a camaraderie that transcended the work schedule. Once a month, for instance, they would get together and go to an inner-city neighborhood to spray over graffiti. It was a way to show the neighborhood, often in fear of the rampant gang activity, that yes, police were present. There was definitely an in-your-face approach against gangs in particular. After covering the graffiti, they would often leave their own symbol behind—a small "VCTF." Sometimes the folks in the neighborhood would bring out doughnuts for them on those painting days (of course, right?). And these guys would go to the funerals of each other's family members, no matter how far they had to travel.

"We were truly a family," Doc Richardson recalled.

The members of the task force would surprise him. They would propose a crazy solution for a case. Richardson joked that it was almost like they would plan to "rappel off the side of the Renaissance Center and see if they could spot the suspect on the way down," and somehow it would work. They solved a lot of cases that looked impossible. One particular VCTF member, Del Christian of the Michigan State Police, had a motto he called MEALS—if it was Moral, Ethical, Affordable, Legal, and Safe, then let's do it. Christian was with the MSP for thirty-two years—sixteen of those on the VCTF. "If we didn't have a love for Doc and a love for the work, we wouldn't do it," he said years later.

The Violent Crime Task Force quickly evolved from its creation in the mid-1990s, and the discovery at the railroad tracks really kicked this team into gear. Cliff explained: "When we discovered the bodies was the first we knew that we had a serial killer working the city. In a high-profile case such as this, the team went into motion in a highly coordinated multifaceted process of turning up information and acting on it in as close to a simultaneous method as possible. One of the earmarks of the team was what Doc often referred to as the 'sense of urgency' that was required to obtain the kind of results VCTF became known for."

Richardson affirmed: "When cases like this come in, we immediately split into twelve-hour shifts. Twelve on, twelve off. But it's really that you're working about sixteen on and eight off."

Cliff said, "Doc mobilized the unit, assigning several detectives who canvassed the entire area. That often meant, as it did in this case, that the Fugitive Apprehension Team could be pulled from their routine duties and tasked with assisting the VCTF itself, lending manpower, surveillance teams from the Headquarters Surveillance Unit or whatever else might be needed. Crime Analysis would be searching for reports of attempted abductions of hookers, found bodies that, although investigated by Homicide, may not have been recognized as one of this killer's victims. In the event that more manpower might be needed to accomplish all the canvassing, interviewing, etc., that might be needed, we could have called on any or all of the other specialized investigative units within the Headquarters Bureau to assist. As it turned out, we utilized the personnel from Violent Crimes Section from the outset, and teams of our detectives were sent out to canvass the area looking for information, witnesses, potential victims who may have escaped, etc., while other teams were assigned to work the scene, gathering and analyzing information that the evidence techs were turning up while the scene processing was in progress.

"They put together bits and pieces of information from potential witnesses, located a survivor, analyzed the information being developed from processing the crime scene, and ultimately turned up a description of the perpetrator and what he was likely driving. To the greatest degree possible, a profile of his territory, how he worked, who he was likely to target, how he was likely to treat them, etc., was all being put together. Based on the location of the bodies, the identity of his victims, their backgrounds, and whatever information we could turn up through victimology, we were able to get a sense of where he was likely to be operating, who his preferred victims were likely to be, his methodology as to how he was likely to rape and kill and any other pertinent information that might be useful in finding and apprehending him. From that point forward, a preliminary description was provided to the patrol force in the Fourth Precinct through briefings at roll calls so as to have as many eyes on the street looking for this guy as possible, but that was not the end of the process."

Some of those eyes on the street belonged to Officer Rodney Durham and his partner Bradford Bullock of the Fourth Precinct, based at the now defunct old station at Fort and Green. They were still pretty new—Durham, at that point, a couple of years on the force, and Bullock maybe a little over three. They had been at the roll call; they had heard all about the railroad track scene. They knew a serial killer was out there. They had also been told to stay away from the Michigan Avenue area; the task force had already set up surveillance there, just as they had been surveilling the area of the tracks. The VCTF suspected Michigan Ave as a likely place their perp was finding victims. They didn't want any marked units coming in there, unless there was a patrol run or it was an emergency, or to back up another officer. But Durham and Bullock, not knowing anything else about the maneuvers of the surveillance units, kind of had to go through that area to get where they were going in their patrol duties. They were a north-end car, working the northern part of the precinct. Dispatch would yell at them, telling them to stay off Michigan, but what could they do?

At that particular time, the two patrolmen were on the midnight shift together, Durham recalled via phone years later. And when the big news hit of the railroad track discovery, he remembered, his partner Bullock had a crazy idea.

"He's like, 'Hey, man, let's go out and find this serial killer guy.' And I chuckled and laughed, and I was like, 'Yeah, man, let's do it, but that's almost like winning the lottery.' A needle in the haystack, you know?"

Indeed.

So that night, on their overnight shift driving through the area just before three-thirty a.m. on April 11, less than twenty-four hours after the discovery at the tracks, they spotted a prostitute on a corner near Michigan and Junction Street. They decided to stop and see if they could find anything out.

It just happened to be Devin Marus.

Have you heard about the three girls found at the railroad tracks? they asked. Have you seen anything weird going on? Caught any scuttlebutt?

"Oh yeah, I heard about it," Devin replied. "I don't know nothing." Straightforward. Not wanting to say anything else. What prostitute wants to be seen standing there talking to a couple of cops anyway?

But the officers pressed on. "We're not here to arrest you. We don't care what you're doing. We just want to know what you know."

"Well, I've got a little bit of information about a certain incident that happened to me, but I'm not really wanting to talk about it."

Well, that's interesting.

It took some convincing on the part of Durham and Bullock. And it helped that some of these missing girls were Devin's friends, she would later testify in court. Finally, with a twenty-dollar bill out of the pocket of each of the officers and during a quiet ride in the squad car, Devin spilled the story about the darkish-colored Jeep with JEEP written on the back tire cover. It was a stick shift, she said. There was paper currency in the ashtray, as well as trash on the floor. She told them about the work shirt with "Eric" on it. She gave them the description of a white male, late twenties or early thirties, stocky, tall, with reddish-blond hair, glasses. She described a tan work shirt with brown trim, with the name on the right and other writing on the left. The rest of his clothes were dark blue, she said.

It was the key information police needed, and it would be credited with leading to Armstrong's arrest.

"It gave us something very tangible to look for," fellow officer Everett Monroe remembered, then unknowingly echoing Durham's thoughts: "It's like trying to find a needle in a haystack. Okay, we know it's there, but where? Now we know that his area is Michigan Avenue. We know that he drives a Jeep now. So our scope has now narrowed. And we could direct our resources to something that's tangible. And so that bit of investigation just blew the case open for us. It was just a matter of locating him. Trying to find him before we had another victim."

Police meanwhile continued to surveil the area of John Kronk and Military all day on April 11. They noted vehicles coming and going, stopped a few motorists for questions. A Channel 4 news truck was parked nearby that evening. There were a few area residents simply checking out the scene after catching it on the news. One guy walking his dog into the crime scene was questioned by police and made it into the case files.

Not far from the area surveilled that day, a man was seen trying to approach teenage girls in a white Oldsmobile Cutlass, a 911 caller said. Police arrived at the location, near Buchanan Street, and spotted the vehicle. The man spotted them back and sped off. Police chased him down and finally pulled him over, then seeing what appeared to be blood smeared on the rear of the car, near the trunk. There was a hammer sticking out from under the front passenger seat of the car. He had a fresh quarter-inch cut on his left hand. He smelled like alcohol. Pretty suspicious, the officers felt. They arrested him. He was a white male, though older, in his mid-fifties. He consented to a blood sample. He, of course, was determined not to be our unsub.

The man whose prescription bottles were found at the railroad track scene, first name Anthony, was brought in for questioning at the headquarters at Beaubien around midday April 11. He could not give a reasonable explanation for why his pills had ended up with a victim. He did consent to a polygraph and blood sample. Police learned that Anthony had threatened his cousin Andre with a gun in March, so they took a closer look at that record. His cousin had told police at the time that Anthony was drunk and "in a rage." Anthony didn't have a permit or registration for the .25-caliber Barretta semi-automatic gun he had.

As the investigation proceeded, the police department in Flint, a little over an hour north of Detroit up Interstate 75, contacted Detroit police about cases that they had of prostitute homicides, for any possible connection. They offered access to DNA samples of semen from the victims.

A forty-one-year-old prostitute named Debra visited DPD headquarters on Beaubien Street within an hour of having a suspicious encounter with a john on the evening of April 11. She was the one mentioned earlier who knew the three girls found at the railroad tracks; she had noticed them missing in recent days. She was staying in a room on Michigan Ave and was the mother of four children living in Florida at the time. Whether motivated by fear for her own safety or just the need to do the right thing, she decided to report a white male driving a pickup truck who had approached her on Michigan near Joe Street. He insisted on taking her to the railroad tracks, she said, and told her he had just been there three days earlier. "He was acting quiet," she told Ira Todd of the VCTF, "like he was far away somewhere." She had her hand on the door handle as she watched him.

He also insisted that Debra take off her shoes, socks, and pants. "Normally the johns want you just to take off your top," she explained.

Did she take off all of those items? "Hell no, I refused to take them off."

Then some undercover police came by where the two were parked at Military and Buchanan. They flashed badges and took the guy's information. He took off; she reported what had happened. This guy was older, though, in his forties, with blond hair almost to his shoulders. And his pickup truck was white.

Other tips were coming in to police of missing girls in the area, and of "Arab men" picking up girls on Michigan and taking them back to their houses, then girls running out of the houses with no clothes on. People were calling police to turn in their friends and acquaintances. "He definitely did it," one caller said of a guy named Randy, who evidently dealt with "crackheads and prostitutes." People were also calling to ask if any of the as-yet-unidentified girls found at the railroad tracks had a certain tattoo or other markings, like one caller who asked if any of the deceased had the tattoo of a cross with the word BABY in it, another mentioning old telltale gunshot wounds to the right leg.

Wilhemina Drane, having seen the news about the three bodies, called police at ten-twenty-five p.m. on April 11 to tell them of her attack earlier in the month, and her story sure hit some familiar notes. Lieutenant Marilyn Hall-Beard of VCTF, who had been at the railroad tracks the day before, took the call. Drane told her about this white male in his late twenties or early thirties, with a round face and possible bumps, along with short, bushy-type reddish or brown hair and wire-rimmed glasses. She recalled his work-type uniform with blue pants and a white shirt with black or blue stripe and green writing on each side, and black work boots. She said he wore a watch with a silver band. And she remembered his tattoos, one in particular being of a lion or tiger on his right forearm, she told the officer. There was also one on his left shoulder, but she couldn't make out the design. She remembered the Jeep as silver or gray.

So now police had two survivor descriptions of what seemed like the same guy. What seemed like *their* guy. Hall-Beard, herself a seasoned cop who started in the 12th Precinct in May 1977, radioed out Drane's description to the VCTF officers who were out watching Michigan Ave that night.

The first of the three railroad track victims to be identified was Kelly Jean Hood, from fingerprints on arrest records. She had been arrested in July 1988 for disorderly conduct and "flagging." The files also showed arrests in May 1998, November 1999, February 15, 2000, and even on March 20, 2000, shortly before her death. She was going by her maiden name and listed her address as in Muskegon, saying she'd been there thirteen years. Kelly's body was also identified at the morgue by her ex-husband Tony and a member of his family.

When Rose Felt was ID'd, the DPD contacted the Grand Rapids Police Department for information on her. They received back a fax indicating a trespassing/loitering charge from March 8, right before her death. The report said she had been hanging around the parking lot of a closed business, a window treatment place on South Division Avenue in Grand Rapids, in the early morning hours. A note in police files indicates that Roes's mother, living in the western Detroit suburb of Livonia at the time, had been contacted and would be identifying her daughter's body in the morgue on April 14, joined by Rose's sister of Dearborn Heights.

Police had less luck tracking down family members of the third victim, Nicole Young. Chicago police were contacted, and they went to the address she had given when she'd been arrested, but a knock on the door produced no one who would claim knowing her. The prosecutor's office at one point managed to get a relative on the phone. Not a mom, but an aunt. And she had barely a passing interest in the girl's death. The conversation was along the lines of, "Okay, well, thanks for letting me know." A photo of Nicole was later requested for use at trial, to show that this was indeed a human being who should not have lost her life. What the prosecutor's office received in the mail was a tiny school picture of when Nicole was eight or nine years old.

Kelly's sister Shannon remembered this about the case's youngest victim, from the talk in the ensuing months leading up to the trial: "When the police department tried to contact her family in Chicago, they basically wanted nothing to do with her. They were just, like, you do what you gotta do. Take care of her, bury her, whatever. Her family didn't want to claim her. They didn't want nothing. She was a teenage runaway. From Chicago. I remember that. Because I was just like, that's heartbreaking. What kind of dysfunctional family are you raised up in that they don't even want to claim you, you know?"

Shannon's family, however, was faced with the painful task of mourning Kelly's death. It wasn't easy, after her ID was made public. "I remember at the time," Shannon said, "the news media was just in a complete frenzy about it. Because my poor brother-in-law, they couldn't even leave their own house. Even when we had Kelly's funeral, you know, the funeral director there in Detroit did what he could do, but everybody was camped out across the street. And then when we did the procession to the cemetery, we had to have a police escort. To keep the news media out of the cemetery."

Meanwhile, the pieces of this case were coming together, and armed with the reports of Marus and Drane, police were about to catch their man.

A MISSION ON MICHIGAN

It's unclear whether or not Armstrong himself had seen the news reports of the discovery at the railroad tracks. You would think he had—it was blasted all over the place. But some of the officers of the VCTF who worked the case really didn't think he had because he was right back out there, on Michigan Avenue, the night of April 11. And there's nothing to indicate he wasn't out there the night of the 10th as well. Uninterrupted. Like he was getting away with murder.

A bit of irony came into play that it was Officers Rodney Durham and Bradford Bullock of the Fourth Precinct who were also back on Michigan Ave that next night after they had talked to Devin Marus. Yeah, maybe there was a bit of an attitude of screw-HQ-and-the-lack-of-information-they're-giving-patrol-about-this-huge-case going on. But they had just gotten a police run into that warned-off area. They were there legit. And when it came right down to it, whatever politics went on in this workplace like so many others, the DPD really did get this guy off the streets as one unit. Everybody had the horror at the railroad tracks foremost on their minds that week, along with the knowledge that their prey could be looking for his own new prey right that very minute. Durham, for one, had grown up in Southwest Detroit—born and raised there, lived there all his life. His dad had been a cop, as well as his uncle. Whatever its quirks or crimes, he loved his town.

So with his partner Bullock, he had just gotten on his shift at midnight on the night of April 11/morning of April 12. It was between midnight and twelve-thirty.

"I remember it was right off the ramp," Durham said. "We got a police run to Addison and McGraw on a vehicle accident. And I was driving; Brad was in the passenger seat. And we went up to Addison and McGraw like we were dispatched to. And we got there and there was no accident there. There was nothing there. So I came up Addison, which goes over I-94, and the next main street is Michigan Avenue. So I made a left-hand turn onto Michigan Avenue going east, and going west was this dark Jeep, just kinda cruising by himself."

The Jeep looked almost black in the streetlights.

"And I looked at Brad; Brad looked at me. I said, 'What do you think, man?'"

"Let's get behind him and see," Bullock told him.

By that point, the VCTF surveillance units had spotted this patrol car in their area. They had also spotted the Jeep. Back at the office, Doc Richardson and Del Christian were getting updates. The task force was communicating on a different radio channel, so the patrol car didn't realize they were right there with their eye on this stretch of Michigan. The VCTF wasn't happy about seeing the patrol officers there, but they decided to just let them take the Jeep.

Durham did a U-turn and got behind the Jeep. There was the word JEEP on the back spare tire. He then pulled up next to the vehicle and drove parallel for a good thirty seconds.

"And I'm looking at the guy, and I'm like, oh man—white guy, glasses," he recalled.

Durham fell back and turned the lights on. The Jeep stopped at Western Street and Michigan, and they pulled up behind it. The vehicle had a North Carolina plate, the officers noticed.

Durham got out and approached the Jeep. "How you doing?" he asked Armstrong.

"Oh, I'm doing great."

"You got a license and registration?"

"Yeah, I sure do."

Durham asked him to turn the vehicle off, and he did. "Where you coming from? Where you headed?" Durham asked.

"I'm coming from work."

"Oh. Where you work at?"

"Well, I work at the airport, out in Romulus. I'm an airplane fueler. I fill up airplanes."

Hmm, Durham pondered. *Romulus is the way you were headed.* "So right away his story didn't make any sense," he recalled. "And I kinda knew he was a little bit jumpy, like a little bit nervous."

Durham asked him to step out of the vehicle. He frisked him for weapons. Armstrong was perfectly compliant. Durham told him he wasn't under arrest or anything—he just wanted to check him out a bit. Then he could be on his way.

Durham walked back to the squad car and told Bullock to run the guy's name.

But when Durham walked back to the Jeep and started writing down the VIN, he saw some stuff that raised his hackles. Stuff shoved under the seat, stuff in the backseat. Gloves. Condoms. Some panties or hosiery? Oddball things, he recalled.

"Right away in my head I'm thinking, man, this could be our guy? You know, as ironic as it may sound, this might be this person."

Durham walked back over to the squad car and relayed to Bullock what he had seen. "I said, 'Look, man, you go look at this Jeep inside.' Because we didn't touch anything. 'Just go look at it and tell me what you see, just so I'm not seeing things.' And he's like, 'Yeah, yeah, yeah, no problem.'"

While Bullock did that, Durham re-engaged Armstrong in conversation.

"Where do you live?"

Dearborn Heights.

"How long you work at the airport?"

Couple months.

"Well, why are you coming up Michigan Avenue, if I may ask?"

"My wife told me to take this new way home and I was coming up Michigan Avenue. I got lost or something."

Shades of his conversation with Dearborn Heights PD.

You're a long ways from Kansas, Dorothy, Durham thought. *You're way out of your comfort zone.*

It was about this time, maybe fifteen minutes into the stop, Durham estimated, that a minivan pulled up. It was David Wasmund, formerly a patrolman but now working with the Violent Crime Task Force, joined by some others from the plainclothes unit.

What you got? they asked the patrolmen.

A whole lot, it turned out.

Bullock had to be glad for the assist; he later testified that he wasn't quite sure what they should do with Armstrong.

Wasmund instructed the officers to take this guy down to the station and have the Jeep impounded.

Armstrong was placed in the back of the patrol car, then while they waited for the tow of his Jeep to the evidence tech impound, along comes someone else on this dark, seedy stretch.

She was on foot. It was Avon, aka Jasmine, aka Cynthia Smith.

She had spotted the man in the Jeep Wrangler on Michigan a bit earlier that night. Here it was, only two or three days after her own attack, and this guy was back there again, driving around. "I was trying to get a glimpse at him," she would later testify about seeing him drive up and down Michigan Avenue, "but he was putting his head down."

So now she sees his Jeep parked at the curb next to a police car.

"The cops had him pulled over," she later recalled. "I don't know why, but they had him pulled over. So I was being nosy, and I walked over there to see if this was the guy who tried to kill me a couple of nights before. And then I looked in the back seat of the squad car and I noticed it was him, and I just totally went off the deep end and started yelling at him or whatever."

Later in court, Bullock remembered her exact words pretty well: "That's the motherfucker that tried to kill me!"

Reporter George Hunter also remembered this quote years later: *It's a small world, that Michigan Avenue.*

"And the cops pulled me back," Cynthia went on during her later testimony, "and said, who are you and where did you come from?"

Bullock remembered this gal as higher class than the prostitutes usually encountered on Michigan Ave. She looked better, not like some who were addicted to narcotics.

As Durham and Bullock rolled up Michigan Ave toward headquarters with their quarry in the back, Armstrong began to mumble.

"I'm glad this is over, I'm glad this is over," Durham remembered him saying.

"Eric, what are you glad that's over?" Durham asked him.

He didn't really elaborate. "Well, I'm just glad that this is all over. I'm just glad."

Durham asked, "Look, man, have you ever had any run-ins with the law? Have you ever had any trouble with the police or anything like that? Have you ever been arrested or anything?"

"No, no, actually I haven't. I'm a good citizen." Armstrong went on to illustrate what a good citizen he was, that he had talked to Dearborn Heights police two or three months ago about a body he found in the river.

That's interesting, Durham thought. He asked again, "What are you glad that's over? If you want to, you know, reiterate what you're trying to tell me, what are you glad that's over?"

Durham remembered Armstrong then saying he was glad they caught him. "So at that point, right then and there," Durham recalled, "I was creeped right out. I said, you know what, I better read this guy his Miranda rights, and just cut it off here for now. So I read him his rights. I told him, I said, 'Eric, you don't have to say another word. You have the right to remain silent. Anything you say can and will be used against you.' I went through the whole thing. And he says, 'I understand my rights.' At that time, we were already at headquarters. We had pulled up. And we took him in through the back way. Up to Violent Crimes, is where we ended up taking him first. And that's where Doc Richardson was, the commander. And he said, 'Yeah, we're going to interrogate him,' we're going to do this, and we're going to do that. I need you guys to do your reports on this incident, what happened, and all this other stuff. And he goes, 'And I need you guys to go find this Devin. I need you guys to go find her. Like right now. You're out of service; just go get her.'"

Richardson told them not to say a word about the arrest to anyone. "And I mean, we were in trouble," Durham said, "because our radio dispatch had been calling us all night long and we weren't responding to them. We actually had officers out looking for us."

So Durham and Bullock went back out.

"Devin had given me an address over in the 10th Precinct, but it was a vacant house. So me and Brad go over to the 10th Precinct. Now mind you, we're in uniform, it's dark, we're over there in areas like total—it looks like a bomb went off in it. And we're going up and down the street looking for this person. And you know, people aren't going to talk to me. They're like, what the hell does the police want with her? So finally, we find her in a dope house. Believe it or not. And I mean, this is like eight o'clock in the morning, nine o'clock in the morning. So we actually find her, and we took her back downtown and dropped her off."

Chief Benny Napoleon took the officers' paperwork and told them to go home for a few days and to not talk about this to anyone. If anybody had a problem with it, they were to call him.

Then Durham and Bullock returned to the station at the Fourth Precinct. "Our supervisors are pissed because they're like, 'Where the hell have you guys been all night? We've been trying to call you on the radio, we've got officers out looking for you! We were worried you guys were shot up somewhere dead.' It was a big mess. I go, 'Look, man, I'm going home. I'm tired. I don't really want to argue about this. It's been a long night. I was told to tell you if you have a problem with something to call the chief. Bye.' And I went home."

For this patrolman, it was the end of his work on the case, though his partner went on to testify at Armstrong's second trial. Sergeant Donald Pace, who had been the first patrol supervisor on the scene at the railroad tracks discovery, nominated Bullock and Durham for the 2001 National Association of Police Organizations' eighth annual Top Cops Award. They received an honorable mention. Durham would later leave the Fourth Precinct and work undercover himself in the Eighth.

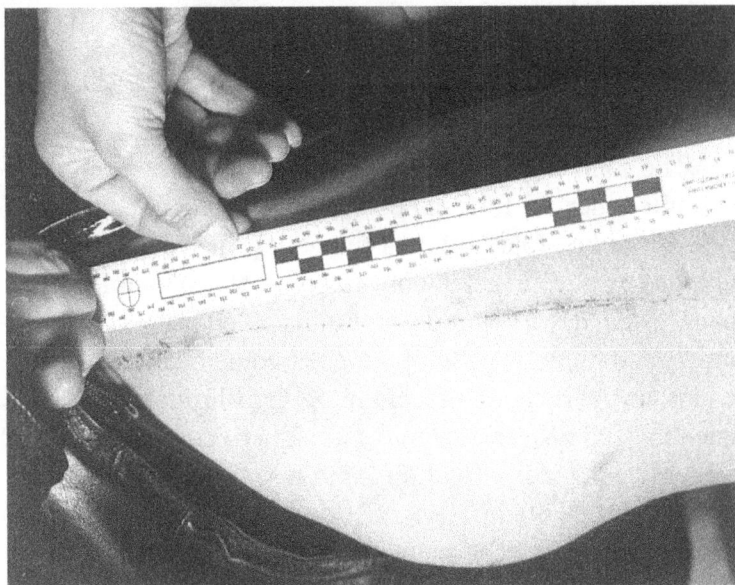

Cynthia Smith with the scar on her abdomen. Image: DPD files.

Cynthia Smith gave her statement to David Wasmund down at headquarters on Beaubien an hour or so after Armstrong's arrest, at one-thirty a.m. An officer photographed her and the mysterious scar on her abdomen. One officer who worked the case speculated the scar was caused by her body being caught on something like a metal handle or latch on the Jeep door as she was pushed out, not by the knife her attacker evidently had.

Cynthia's account was a bonus the police hadn't planned on but one they certainly welcomed. "I don't know how important this is," she added, "but he told me that a couple of days ago he picked up this Black girl, who took him to some apartment. When he got inside, there were two Black guys there. 'They beat me up and took my money, then they threw me out,'" she quoted him as saying. There's no way of knowing how true that story was, as it has a certain similar flavor to Armstrong's tale of his place of employment being broken into in Novi. Was it a way for him to get a little sympathy from this girl he had just picked up? Or did he really get in over his head that time in his roamings on Michigan Ave?

The john Cynthia was with the night after Armstrong assaulted her, a forty-nine-year-old man named Ronald whom she had told all about the attack, also came forward and gave police a statement. This was at 1:05 a.m. He had caught the news reports on the discovery at the railroad tracks and figured Cynthia's attacker could be the guy, so he had gone out earlier on the night of April 11 looking for her, back to Michigan Ave, with the thought of convincing her to tell police her story. He didn't find her, so he went to police himself, ironically just as Armstrong was being arrested and Cynthia questioned about her attack.

Ronald estimated he had encountered Cynthia on April 7, however. He remembered it as a Friday. And he remembered her saying Armstrong picked her up between eleven and eleven-thirty that night, not the later time she gave police. She also had told Ronald that she'd had sex with this creepy john before the assault, which she only later admitted in court.

"She was a very nice person, and I expressed some concern for her welfare," Ronald said, "but didn't ask for any more details because at that time I hadn't heard any news about the three female victims found in the area."

The arrest of Armstrong marked the end of a quick but intense effort for DPD to nab this guy, Gerald Cliff recalled.

"We moved quickly to put surveillance crews on the street," he said, "armed with the preliminary information we were able to obtain, at the same time being fed more information as it was being developed from interviews and the canvass that were still ongoing. Ultimately, we were quite fortunate in that he was never aware that we had discovered the bodies and were on the lookout for him. When he went out looking for another victim and was spotted by both Fourth Precinct uniform patrol and the surveillance crews at the same time, even the uniformed officers from the precinct stated that they were quite surprised to see what seemed like an 'army' of plainclothes officers descend on them when they made the investigatory stop. Even they never knew the full extent of the mobilization that had taken place."

Not every murder case has such a short timeframe from body discovery to arrest. "Some cases do require a lengthy, complex investigation before a perpetrator can be identified and arrested, no question," Cliff said. "Examples of such investigations were the East Side School Girl rapist(s) that we worked for weeks before we had an arrest. These cases took place after the Armstrong case and involved mobilizing two precincts of uniforms, the Gang Squad, Tactical Mobile Unit, all of whom had their hours changed to cover the times the rapists were operating. The sense of urgency in these cases is every bit as high, but in the Armstrong case, things just happened to come together quickly in that we caught the perp within hours of discovering his dirty work."

Though the arrest meant a burden off their shoulders, the work of these special investigators was far from done.

"One of the trademarks of the VCTF was that when we had a hot case going, no one went home until the investigation either produced an arrest or all the available leads were exhausted," Cliff said. "It was constantly stressed to everyone in the unit that if we didn't work it that way, it could cost another victim being raped or killed or both. It was that philosophy and work ethic of the members of the unit that ultimately led to quick arrests and quick case closures. Once he was in custody, we could all take a few hours to get some sleep, grab a snack and a shower, collect our thoughts, and then put together the best investigation possible so as to assure a conviction. This is when the bulk of information is compiled, organized, analyzed, and put before a prosecutor to build the information necessary to bind the accused over at the preliminary examination. Once he was securely in our custody and we knew we could hold the perpetrator, we had time to begin to fill in all the blanks, answer all the unanswered questions (sometimes develop more questions), conduct more in-depth interviews, confirm facts, cross-check dates, etc., so as to make sure we had the right guy and put together an 'airtight' case for a successful prosecution. All that work would not have mattered if the investigation that we put together wasn't sufficient to send him to and keep him in prison."

And there was the irony of two police departments working separately on the same case. "We have no clue that the bodies are piling up in Detroit," Donald Riley of Dearborn Heights PD said of those weeks between the murders. "Detroit didn't know we were investigating a homicide."

Then alas, for the DHPD, the final DNA results they had been awaiting finally arrived, issued by the Michigan State Police lab on April 12, faxed from Northville at four-thirty-five p.m. A preliminary report had arrived in later March, but the instructions were to wait on the final report and now it was here.

The report's conclusions:

1. The DNA profile generated from the vaginal swabs match Wendy Jordan.
2. The DNA types generated from the male fraction of the rectal swabs indicate a mixture of DNA from Wendy Jordan and an additional donor.
3. The DNA types detected from the additional donor match John Armstrong.

Gary Tomkiewicz, the DHPD detective lieutenant on the Jordan case who was in charge of Major Crimes, was the one who received the call from the MSP crime lab. He recalled the delays with the DNA report and that at one point, they even had what was considered the final report, but it still needed one last detail—the stats that give the probability of another match in this case. Without that one last bit, the prosecutor's office would not consider the DNA report completely "final" and would not issue the warrant.

But their wait was about to end anyway. DHPD got a surprise on the same day the fax arrived.

Tomkiewicz would be on the phone daily with the guys he knew over at DPD, sharing information. Relaying what was going on right then at the station.

"We'd solved many crimes together," Tomkiewicz said, "just hooking up and talking to each other. And I'd make personal visits there and they'd make personal visits to our department. And it's just camaraderie."

The camaraderie, in this case, connected the dots. Turns out, the two departments were working on the same guy, he learned. Armstrong was in custody.

For Tomkiewicz, the information he'd gleaned from his DPD buddies on that morning's call struck an eerie chord. He had grown up in that area of Michigan Avenue.

THE HORRORS REVEALED

After his arrest between twelve-thirty and one a.m. on April 12, John Eric Armstrong was interviewed on the seventh floor at police headquarters on Beaubien, a location chosen because it was quiet, devoid of personnel at that time. He was not handcuffed as he sat and talked to police, they would later attest. He was fed—pretty well, by all accounts, as the hours wore on and he started making his confessions. For breaks he was taken up to a ninth-floor cell to rest. You would have to wonder what was going through his mind.

Here he was, being interviewed again by police, much like a few months earlier, but this time it was a tad more serious. For one thing, that chick he'd tried to kill a few days ago had walked up and identified him while he was sitting in the back of a squad car. Getting his trash stolen was now the least of his concerns.

Detroit Police Officer Donald Johnson and Wayne County Sheriff's Detective James Hines, both members of the Violent Crime Task Force, were sent in to have the first go at Armstrong right after he was arrested, and they were sternly told not to mess it up. Johnson had started out with the Detroit Police just a few years before, in 1994, having studied criminal justice and law enforcement administration at Western Michigan University. He was still pretty new to this whole thing. "Totally surprised me," he said of the decision to send him and Hines into the interview room, given all the more senior officers around the force at the time.

It was a bit of a tug of war that resulted in the decision. Del Christian, the MSP officer on the VCTF who was in charge of this case, wanted to send in Johnson and Hines. Doc Richardson, commander of the Headquarters Bureau, wanted to send in Ira Todd—nicknamed "Bond" and whom he knew as a skilled interrogator. Christian knew Bond had already worked all day. He insisted, to Richardson, "You put me in charge of this case; now let me make this decision."

For his part, Hines had been on the task force for three or four years. He had six years under his belt as a detective and had worked internal affairs, felony warrants, and the road patrol. He had some years on Johnson, had been around the block a bit more. But he felt the heat with this one too.

"There was an extremely intense level of pressure, with the significance of the case," Hines recalled by phone in 2020. "The main focus was to remain calm, keep my emotions in check. I'm sure the same was for DJ. We maintained our composure. But the main focus is to extract an admission or confession." He knew they would have to make a connection with this guy. Establish a rapport.

"We started off the interview with him," Johnson said, "myself and James Hines, and here it is, I have this six-foot-four, two hundred and fifty-plus-pound guy, sitting across from me, that's cuddling a jacket," Johnson recalled, also via phone in 2020. "I didn't know what to say. My partner didn't know what to say. All we knew was we couldn't mess it up. Because there was a lot of pressure on us to get the confession, by them sending myself and James Hines into the room to talk to him. So I saw a tattoo on John's arm. He had a tiger tattoo. I just started talking to him in regular conversation about the tattoo. Because you've got to figure out a way to break the ice. So that's how I was able to break the ice with him, to start talking to him about his tattoo. And I can tell you, I talked to John about everything from Frosted Flakes cereal to hockey. And at that time, I didn't know anything about hockey. Absolutely nothing.

"And so, when I started talking to him, we just went over like his family history, where he's from, his wife, all those types of things. And he shared a lot of good information with us in reference to his family and stuff like that. And so when I talked to him about his family, he told me about his wife, and how his wife treated him. And I was just like in awe listening to this guy talk about all these things that have happened in his life. And so we're talking to him, talking to him, talking to him, and I'm sharing a lot of stuff with him, stuff about me. And I think one of the reasons they sent me in there with him, because John and I were around the same age at the time. And so I can kind of relate a little bit better with him, you know?"

There was no two-way mirror in this room. No fancy monitoring equipment. It was just a room. At one point, Del Christian pressed his ear against the other side of the door. He heard something about Frosted Flakes cereal, and he thought to himself, *these guys are on the right track. They're doing fine.*

"In my conversation with him," Johnson continued, "I was able to build a rapport. And as I build this rapport with him, John starts to break down a little bit, in reference to just being more open about things that had transpired in his life and stuff like that. And so we were talking to him. We talked to him for about two and a half hours. Two and a half to three hours is the amount of time we had been talking to John about various stuff and everything other than the case. And not one time did we mention the case to him. We just talked about everything else. Like I said, we talked about Frosted Flakes cereal. We talked about hockey … And as I'm talking to him, he was opening up and starting to become more relaxed. And as he became more relaxed, it finally got to a point where he just felt very, very comfortable with me. We had built a relationship with him while we were in there talking with him."

Hines let Johnson lead the conversation and he observed. He didn't interrupt; he just let them talk. Let his partner do his thing. Armstrong struck him as soft, the kind of guy who could be easily intimidated. But he was a big guy too and Hines could imagine him being able to easily overpower the petite women whose bodies he had seen at the railroad tracks a couple days earlier.

Hines felt like this guy thought the two cops were stupid. For one thing, he didn't really seem to mind having this conversation, contrary to what Hines had come to know from suspects who actually are innocent. If they were innocent, he had learned, they would be more agitated—like, "Why am I here talking about all this crap? Can I leave?" But their chatter with Armstrong went on and on.

"He looked across the table at us," Hines said, "and figured he was smarter than us, we didn't know nothing and probably had nothing for him to fear. He was very passive. He was willing to sit there and hold this senseless conversation with us, talking about his tattoos and his Navy time, and this and that, and just going on with a boring—a really boring—conversation."

To Hines, Armstrong seemed to be almost boastful about his education, the fact that he had attended college. He figured he had the edge, was Hines' impression. The upper hand. But things were about to take a turn from this nice chatter. Johnson brought the details of the case into the conversation. The women at the tracks. There were denials on Armstrong's part. Then, between two and three hours in to the small talk, Johnson asked Hines if he had any questions for Armstrong.

"Don had him on the edge," Hines recalled. "He had him on the edge, but then we got to the point of 'you did,' 'I didn't,' 'you did,' 'I didn't.' But all the time he's interviewing him, I'm watching him, I'm watching his mannerism, I'm watching his response, I'm watching how he's responding. And at some points, he's kind of like, head tucked to the side, kind of cocky with his response. Other times he's looking like a little passive. And it seemed like he wanted to present himself as this super-nice guy, that 'I couldn't do it, I couldn't do anything like that.'"

So when Johnson asked if Hines had any questions, Hines looked at Armstrong and said, "Man, you went to college, right?"

"Yeah."

"You know, you seem like you're a pretty intelligent guy. You understand DNA, don't you?"

"Yeah."

"Do you realize ..." Hines said as he leaned over and rubbed the back of his hand against Armstrong's hand, "when I just did that, I left a little of me on you, a little of you on me."

Pause.

"You left a lot of you on those victims."

What came next was a minor explosion that has stuck in the memory banks of both Johnson and Hines.

"'I killed 'em! I killed 'em, I killed 'em, I killed 'em!'" Johnson recalled Armstrong blurting. It was astonishing, coming from a guy he had witnessed cuddling his jacket and speaking in a soft, squeaky voice.

"And I'm thinking like, holy cow! And then my partner, he jumps up and runs out of the interrogation room. And says, go up and tell our bosses that John just blurted out, utterly excited, that he killed the young ladies."

"We got him," Hines remembered telling the officers outside of the room. And even though he had again leaned toward Armstrong, this time putting his hand reassuringly on his back, telling him he was doing the right thing, in his mind he was doing somersaults.

It was time to get real.

"And I'm sitting there," Johnson said, "and here it is, a fresh new investigator, and I've got to be calm, and all these things. I'm like, holy shit. This guy just confessed that he did it! So now we have to kinda like stop everything, because now we have to read him his constitutional rights, even though we have his excited utterance that he killed them. So now we read him his rights, and he signed off on the Miranda and everything like that. And so once he signed off on it, he walked me through each one of the cases. Each one of the murders that he had committed. He walked me through each one. And I tell you, it was something that I will remember the rest of my life, like yesterday. I can tell you, like it was yesterday."

As Johnson and Hines kicked into gear, a certain gentleness was evident in their handling of this big guy who had been cuddling his jacket. "Tell me what happened with the girl that was found at the bottom of the hill by the railroad tracks off of John Kronk and Military" begins the very first signed confessional statement for Armstrong, noted as three a.m. Then, a little while later, "Eric, you said there was a second female that we need to talk about. Is that OK with you, Eric?" And on and on. And on.

Donald Johnson already had some pictures in his mind, in studying the case and in seeing the scene at the railroad tracks. But hearing the words of the perp now, the descriptions he gave of what he did, how the victims looked, what happened afterward, brought it all into a certain Technicolor. A sort of HD clarity.

"We went through the first one, because what happened prior to that, prior to us getting him in custody, I went through the scene where they found three bodies at the railroad tracks. And so, we saw how he had positioned the young ladies out on the railroad tracks, how he would go back to the railroad tracks where he had put the bodies. And so when we were talking about them, I could actually visualize those young ladies on the tracks as he's walking me through each one of the homicides. He's giving me detailed description about how he picked them up, how he had sex with them, how he strangled them while he was having sex with them because he was envisioning his father's face, and at the point of ejaculation. And so he took me through each one of the homicides, and I tell you, that stuff is forever embedded in my head, 'til the day I die."

With every detail, Johnson and Hines were drawn deeper and deeper into the mind of a killer. And Johnson remembered picking up on the energy—albeit negative energy—and running with it, keeping the conversation flowing, trying to understand where he was coming from. "I would just sit there and listen to all of this and there were some things I was hearing I just didn't believe," Johnson said.

They had to keep Armstrong talking, but they were only human. They could only go so long with this. After many hours of questioning, about ten to twelve hours, Johnson recalled, they needed to be relieved. The two officers had taken Armstrong's statements through the early-morning hours of April 12 and all the way to lunchtime, with breaks for all parties, and then Ira Todd of the VCTF joined in at noon. Johnson continued on with Armstrong for a little while as Todd sat in for a smoother handoff. Agent Gregory Geider of the VCTF-ATF was working an afternoon shift that day and spent some time assisting with monitoring Armstrong while still working on his own investigative reports. By that evening, Armstrong was in DPD's (long-term) squad bay, and just before midnight, Geider stepped in to assist with the confessions, along with Everett Monroe, also with the VCTF at the time, who helped take statements that evening and into the early-morning hours of April 13.

As this newly apprehended perp kept talking, Detroit police got more than they bargained for, much like they had at the railroad tracks. They learned not just about the murders that happened in their own town, the three they knew of, but a couple more they didn't. What Armstrong told them stretched out far and wide—across the country, across the world. Johnson remembered leaving the station for a while then coming back to learn that this guy had killed a lot more people than he had imagined.

And as he kept talking, they kept writing. Each of his confessions got a fresh cover sheet outlining Armstrong's rights that was initialed and signed by him, and after officers transcribed the conversations, Armstrong initialed each of the responses written down for him and signed the bottom of each page. Armstrong asserted that he was given the chance to review the statements and make corrections if needed. He initialed the part of the statement that said he had not been denied food, water, or sleep, that he had not been coerced in any way, that he was not under the influence of drugs or alcohol. Detroit police were not going to let this one slip out of their grasp.

Everett Monroe remembered it well: "It was our policy that we would give him Miranda, and make sure he understood Miranda, and if he waived his rights, then proceed to focus in on one particular victim," he said. "Once we concluded with that victim, we then Mirandized him again and focused in on another victim. And on and on and on. Well, Miranda was still in effect from the very first one, but just to make sure that we would not lose this case on a technicality, or people thinking that we're abusing him or violating his rights, we made sure that we Mirandized him on each one of the cases that we focused on. We made sure that we allowed him time to go to the restroom. Allowed him time to get something to eat. To have a break. You know, to just chitchat about whatever. And then we would focus back in on the investigation and we would Mirandize him again. And start focusing in on another victim."

Ira Todd was well practiced as an interrogator at the time. Holding a bachelor's degree in criminal justice and corrections from Concordia University and a master's in interdisciplinary technology from Eastern Michigan University, Todd has spent a long career in law enforcement and nowadays has quite a few stories to tell. He's even thought about writing his own book—if he can find a ghostwriter, he joked via phone in 2017 for this project (he has since found one). At that point, he'd already been in law enforcement for more than thirty-five years. In 2013, AMC aired a gritty, edgy police drama shot and set in Detroit called *Low Winter Sun*. It was all of ten episodes in a single season but was rather stunning in how true to life it depicted the city and the cops who serve it. Ira worked as a technical advisor for the series. He has also worked as a consultant and advisor for other series.

Gregory Geider came into the picture from the Department of Justice and the Bureau of Alcohol, Tobacco, Firearms and Explosives (ATF). Schooled at Western Michigan with a bachelor's in criminal justice/police science, he was on assignment to the VCTF at the time. Years later, Geider talked about his work as a special agent/criminal investigator back then: "I had been 'on the job' for about twelve years and at VCTF for two years," he recalled. "To me, the VCTF was the epitome of Detroit police work. VCTF was divided into long-term and short-term squads. Generally speaking, long-term focused on historical conspiracy cases. For the most part, I was working Chaldean organized crime with my FBI partner, Tony Hartman. I always felt that VCTF was the triage unit of Detroit law enforcement. Whatever the crisis of the week was, kidnappings, police officers being shot, assorted homicides or assaults, VCTF would be requested to respond. Long-term would often be called in to augment the response to any given situation."

In the Armstrong case, Geider had been somewhat aware of a suspected serial killer investigation that week but had no vested interest in it. That was until Armstrong was arrested. He recalled how VCTF and DPD Homicide were both housed on the fifth floor of the old DPD headquarters. For the April 12, 2000, entry, at 13:00, Geider's diary indicates that he was involved with "Initial Security on Armstrong."

"My recollection is that he had been interviewed by other Homicide/VCTF investigators since his arrest early that morning," Geider said. "On the evening of April 12, I remember Armstrong being detained in the long-term squad room, where my desk was located. Armstrong was interviewed by DPD's Ira Todd and Everett Monroe. Armstrong was confessing to numerous homicides that he claimed to have committed while in the Navy. At some point that night I remember escorting Armstrong to the men's room down the hall from our office. I believe that I had him cuffed to the front. He was a big boy but appeared to be physically 'soft.' Being alone with him I was on my guard as I believed that he was likely a real lunatic. As he used the urinal, I remember standing behind him and telling him that he was doing the right thing by talking to us."

Geider said of assisting in taking statements from Armstrong: "Seemed like he was wearing out the available interviewers so we tag-teamed him."

And during those several hours after his arrest, Donald Johnson in particular got close to this perp, closer than perhaps anyone else working the case. He heard things he didn't necessarily want to hear, but that he had to hear, to work it, to have a successful outcome that would assure no one else got killed. For one thing, Armstrong told Johnson that his biological father sexually abused him as a child and even tried to abuse his baby brother at the time. Armstrong said he saw himself as his brother's defender, telling Johnson he even offered to his father to take the abuse instead of the baby. That's how Johnson remembers it. And he told Johnson that his natural father was abusive toward his mom as well. But at the same time, Armstrong took a protective stance for his biological dad. "He loved his dad, even though his dad was doing all these bad things to him," the officer recalled. It would seem this killer had a very complicated upbringing. Or could this be a jumble of elements tumbling out of the mouth of a newly arrested perp in fear for his life?

"As a young investigator—I'm in my twenties at the time—and as a young investigator, I'm taking all this stuff in," recalled Johnson, who from his bachelor's degree in criminal justice would go on to earn a master's in organizational leadership and management. Johnson also went on to serve as the commanding officer of the Homeland Security office in Detroit. "I'm like, oh my God, you know. And so just from a psychological standpoint, you're getting all this, and the deeper we get into the conversation about the various homicides that he committed, I'm just like, wow. But I'm happy at the same time that we got this guy in custody, off the street, all those things. But you know, to bring closure to those families as well. But yeah, it was very, very, very interesting, a very interesting case for me, for my partner at the time, James Hines. We talked to him; it was like literally I lived with him, with this guy. And so every step of the way, I just really, really got to know him."

So many years later, this former officer speaks matter of factly, but almost with an edge of sympathy, about the perp. There's a totally nonjudgmental quality to the tone of his voice. Johnson has also worked in the security field, starting his own protective measures consulting firm. But the Armstrong case still stands out in his mind as one of the biggest he worked on. "I remember that case like yesterday. I lived it."

And so, those first couple days on Beaubien, Armstrong's confessions flowed in this order, covering the three victims at the railroad tracks first, then branching out from there to other victims in other locales:

WEDNESDAY, APRIL 12, 2000

3 a.m.	Rose Marie Felt
4:35 a.m.	Kelly Jean Hood
6:40 a.m.	Robin Brown/Nicole Young
8:40 a.m.	Cynthia Smith/Jasmine/Avon (survivor)
Noon	White female—Newport News/Norfolk, Virginia
1:36 p.m.	Asian female (transgender)—Thailand, victim one
3:45 p.m.	Wendy Jordan
4:45 p.m.	Monica Johnson
6:15 p.m.	White female—Seattle, Washington
8:09 p.m.	Black male—Seattle, Washington
9:48 p.m.	White female—Waikiki, Hawaii, victim one
11:15 p.m.	White female—Waikiki, Hawaii, victim two
11:50 p.m.	Asian female—Hong Kong, victim one

THURSDAY, APRIL 13, 2000

12:50 a.m.	Asian female—Thailand, victim two
1:20 a.m.	Asian female—Singapore, Southeast Asia
1:35 a.m.	Asian female—Hong Kong, victim two

The confession spree did not include the assaults of Natasha Olejniczak, Wilhemina Drane, Devin Marus, or Zelda Jakubowski.

Through the confessions, the officers would typically ask questions such as if he had been denied food or drink or threatened in any way, and so Armstrong would reaffirm this verbally in addition to acknowledging it on the signed statement. He cooperated through the whole process. He had orange juice, he said in one of the Hong Kong confessions, and had eaten the hamburger and fries officers had given him. "I had some eggs and hashbrowns this morning," he added. "I had some Tootsie Rolls candy that you gave me." This was not him being facetious. Armstrong was talking— and talking a lot. Later, in court, his defense attorney would try to allege he was being treated unfairly by Detroit police but it wouldn't go anywhere.

During one confession on the afternoon of April 12, Armstrong estimated that his total kill count was nine. Hours later, though, after telling officers how he killed the second person in Hong Kong, Armstrong estimated the total number of people he'd killed as fifteen. This was around two a.m. on April 13. He added a handwritten note to the bottom of this confession:

> *I might have possible [sic] done at least 3 more. I stopped counting at around 8. I tried the best I could to remember. I can try at a later date to remember how many more people I killed. I would like to apologize for all the people I have killed, and all the families that have suffered because of me. I hope I can be forgiven of my crimes. But I would like to seek help for my problems. I do remember having sex with some of the bodies after dieing [sic], such as Seattle, Hawaii and Detroit.*

Around one-twenty a.m. on the 13th, just before that above confession on the Hong Kong killing, Armstrong related to police an incident with a woman in Singapore. At the end of this confession, police asked him if, as he was killing these women during shore leave off the *USS Nimitz*, he ever got close to getting caught. "No," he replied.

"Why do you think you never got caught?" they asked.

"I don't know."

"Do you know how you got caught?" they pressed.

"No."

He wasn't evading this line of questioning quite that easily: "How do you think?"

"Keeping that one female alive," Armstrong said.

Except that it wasn't one female. Four people would be scheduled to testify against Armstrong about surviving an attack by him, to supplement and support the five women who had lost their lives. And that was just in Detroit.

The word choice of "keeping" was interesting in that statement, as opposed to "leaving." As if to indicate a decision, not a mistake.

Things weren't always peaceful during Armstrong's interrogations. Officers found out where the sensitive areas were in Armstrong's background, as Monroe recalled: "He had a dual personality. To sit down and talk to him about any of the crimes, any of the victims, locations, et cetera, et cetera, he was very forthcoming. But when you started to probe into his personal life, that's when he began to change. He became very hostile. He was angered about his father. He had this like deep hatred for his dad. He didn't want to talk much about his father. He didn't want to talk much about his younger life, but he had no problems talking about the cases. And he was very remorseful about the victims. But he led you to believe that his internal problems became the motivation to commit these crimes. The most unique fact about it is his dual personality."

How would Monroe have described him to somebody, apart from any of the facts of the case?

"A gentle giant. I mean, he didn't speak loud. He seemed to be very humble. You know, he didn't seem like he would be a serial killer at all."

How truthful did he seem at the time?

"He seemed to be very truthful," Monroe said. "I mean, you could ask him about a particular situation, and he would just tell you. It would be a matter of him trying to remember. He remembered well. And he would give you intimate details about it to let you know, pretty much, he knows what he's talking about. So if you asked him the right question, he would give you the answer and then some. But it was just a matter of keeping away from his personal issues because once you started probing into his personal issues, it was going to disrupt your investigation. Because he was going to change. His personality was going to change. He was going to start shutting down. You needed to let him cool out and gather himself. And then you could go back to asking questions about the investigation."

Ira Todd found that out. He remembered his own impressions of this perp: "Yeah, he was really interesting. I remember when I was interrogating him, and I was really pushing some buttons. And I remember at one point, he jumped up. And there was a full file cabinet—full. That thing had to weigh maybe a couple hundred pounds. An old metal file cabinet. And he punched this file cabinet. And I'm not exaggerating—he probably moved that file cabinet about a couple inches."

Armstrong was, of course, a big guy at the time. As Donald Johnson had noted, more than six foot and something like two hundred and fifty pounds.

"Yeah. But you can break him down like a baby," Todd said. "All I had to do was pretend I was his father, you know, like an authority figure over him. And I would say, 'You want to tell me something else, or I'm going to tear these other confessions up,' you know, that kind of thing. And he would go ahead and confess to another one."

He added, "He was passive, but if you hit the right button, he would turn into a monster, right in front of you. Right in front of you."

Another thing Detroit police found intriguing about Armstrong, those first couple days he was in custody, as noted by Johnson, were his tattoos. Evidence tech Sergeant Dave Babcock, who had faithfully worked the horrors of the railroad track scene, remembered the tattoos well and photographed them and Armstrong himself for DPD records. A Jesus Christ on his left arm, a tiger and tiger cubs on his left forearm, a tiger on his right upper forearm, a tiger on his right forearm, a tiger on his right calf, a sun at his nipple. (Interestingly enough, Armstrong would go on in 2004 to write a woman from prison that he had only five tattoos, four tigers and one sun, for which he said, "I lost a bet with a friend of mine.")

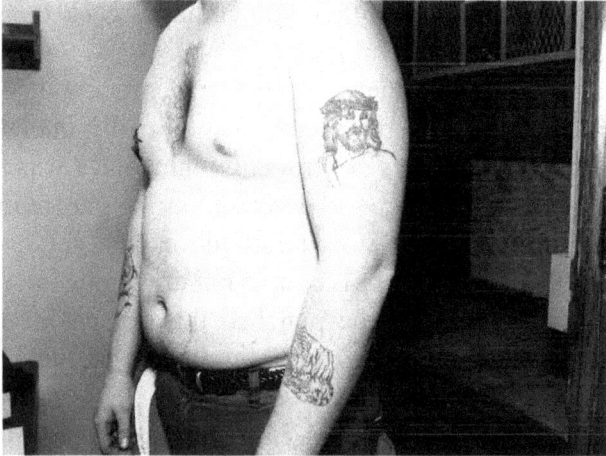

A DPD evidence tech photographed Armstrong, in particular his interesting tattoos. Images: DPD files.

"There were some magnificent tattoos on this guy," Babcock recalled years later. "He was quite proud of them. And it just really brought him up, just talking freely. Nothing about the crimes, but about the tattoos and the different countries he went. Going all the time. He knew exactly where every one came from, on the body. He was quite interesting. He spoke very fluently for me. He's not a dummy, by any means."

So now, Detroit police had their man in custody. And it happened pretty quickly after the discovery at the railroad tracks. Gerald Cliff of the VCTF recalled how well that played for the public announcements the DPD was making. Informing the public of homicide cases can be tricky business, but not so much this time. Chief Benny Napoleon had called a press conference about the railroad track discovery, Cliff remembered, to announce that there was a serial killer operating in the city. Now a day later, the chief called another press conference. But from the press perspective, it had to be like, for what? It wasn't clear. Could be an update on this situation, maybe another victim. Could be an update on some other situation. Maybe something else was happening in the city. Could be something, could be nothing. Who knows. But when you're the media, you show up to find out. Just in case. There was a serial killer on the loose, after all. The public wanted to know how the investigation was going. If this guy was going to be caught. Or if they had to continue on in fear every time they went out. Perhaps with many wondering if this person had a taste that extended beyond prostitutes.

"When the press began to file into the headquarters conference room," Cliff said, "I recall a reporter ask the question in passing as he entered the room, 'So, Chief, are we getting daily briefings on this thing?' Benny smiled and replied, 'Nope, this will be it,' and just kept walking, leaving the reporter with a puzzled look on his face."

But then, when the chief called the meeting to order, he introduced the two uniformed officers from the Fourth Precinct who had made the stop and arrest of John Eric

Armstrong. He informed the assembled press that the suspected killer was in custody.

Oh. Okay.

Napoleon had to laugh about that one, years later.

"We had a pretty good relationship with most of the press that followed the crime situation in Detroit," the former chief said. "There were a lot of pretty hot cases—I mean, I was involved intimately in the Nancy Kerrigan case and a bunch of other stuff. So I had a pretty good and long relationship from back in my younger days when I was commander of the gang squad. We knew all the press people very closely. So when they asked the question, 'Are we going to get this daily update?' When we had the Kerrigan incident, we were doing daily briefings. So something as serious as this, they wanted to be updated every day as to where we are. So when they walked in and they asked, 'Are we going to get daily briefings,' I figured I'd joke with them, say, 'Nah, I don't think I'm going to do that.'"

The chief then went on to recount for the assembled press the massive efforts to apprehend Armstrong, Cliff remembered, including informing the patrol force of the description of his vehicle. "He then explained how the surveillance crews had spotted his vehicle and just as they were positioning to make the stop, a uniformed crew from the Fourth Precinct spotted the vehicle, made the stop and were somewhat surprised at the mass of plainclothes officers that suddenly appeared to assist. The chief spent considerable time giving credit to the two officers for being aware and attentive to their duties, to the information they had been provided and for attempting the arrest of a multiple murder suspect on their own."

At the time this story broke, it was opening day for Comerica Field downtown and the sparkling new home of the Detroit Tigers was engulfing the news cycle. NEW HOME, NEW HOPE blasted across the front page of *The Detroit News* on Wednesday, April 12. It was a frigid opening day on

Tuesday, but excitement was high. There were rave reviews of this new stadium constructed with much anticipation right there in the heart of downtown, its presence making a bold proclamation that, indeed, this city was rising from the ashes of its riots decades earlier. Opening day included some glitches—long waits at the concession stand or running out of coffee or whatever—in the paper's coverage led by this author's late best friend, longtime writer Mark Puls. But those small things weren't about to ruin this day for the city.

The next day, though, the case of the bodies at the tracks, still in people's minds from earlier in the week, reappeared on *The News'* front page, April 13, in a story by George Hunter: 3 KILLED AFTER SUSPECT RELEASED. Armstrong had been arrested and it was discovered, as reporters dug, that the Dearborn Heights PD had him pegged, had him DNA tested, had other lab results, but he had still been free to attack again. It would be a sickening thought for a few sets of family members, especially looking back decades later, now that DNA technology has advanced so much and the timeframe for results is so much shorter.

"In the final analysis, I could say, 'Geez, if they had gone forward, maybe some people would be alive,'" defended Richard Padzieski, chief of operations for the Wayne County Prosecutor's Office, on the wait for a warrant. "We wanted the final DNA findings before we went ahead." The warrant wasn't denied, just delayed, he told the media. And that's what he had been told, he asserted—that the final DNA report was needed for the warrant. This was a recent change in policy, he said, driven by a couple cases where things went wrong when the final report wasn't there for the preliminary exam, which must be held within fourteen days of a suspect's arraignment after the arrest. The goal is to have enough evidence in hand to bind the suspect over for trial. What the prosecutor's office was saying, essentially, is that they were trying to make absolutely sure they could hold this suspect after the arrest.

It meant multiple delays for this case in those crucial months following Wendy Jordan's murder. The lab results had already placed Wendy in Armstrong's Jeep via the hair, carpet fibers, and gold flecks from her shoes. But the decision was made to wait on the warrant since DNA was involved. Then a preliminary DNA report had come through at the end of March, confirming a match to Armstrong, but the prosecutor's office felt at that point that if they had gone by the preliminary report, it was explained in an Associated Press story, a defense attorney could have argued to release Armstrong until the final report was available. And the prosecutor's office wanted to wait for the probability stats to be placed in the final DNA report before they would issue the warrant, despite DHPD objections.

You might wonder why the prosecutor's office felt they needed to bring a gun to a knife fight, since the standard of proof for a preliminary exam in Michigan is only probable cause. Not guilt beyond a reasonable doubt, as in the actual trial, but probable cause. Even hearsay can be used for probable cause at a preliminary hearing. There was more than adequate probable cause in the Jordan case, the DHPD argued at the time, and the DNA report wasn't needed. They'd still be able to keep their suspect off the streets. The argument fell on deaf ears.

The news of Armstrong's many confessions spilled out in the media coverage. "This guy has created terror around the world," *The News* quoted Police Chief Benny Napoleon. "He's a serial killer. He's a sick person."

Police had now realized, with Armstrong's confessions and recent case files, that Monica Johnson was his first Detroit fatality back in December. Also, on April 13, just a few miles down Michigan Avenue, Detective William Sullivan of Dearborn Police saw the news story, pulled the reports on his case, and realized this guy might have been the one who attacked Natasha Olejniczak. Natasha then saw the report in the newspaper and called Sullivan and crew.

Sullivan then contacted both Detective Wasmund of Detroit Police and Detective Lieutenant Tomkiewicz of Dearborn Heights. Three different jurisdictions working on the same perp.

Decades later, former Police Chief Benny Napoleon explained the process of connecting the dots: "The advantage of having a centralized homicide and sex crimes section is to make sure that all of those serious crimes like that go into a central point, so that investigators can get briefed when new cases come in and recall, 'Oh, I had a case like that,' or you know. In homicide cases, they go to squads if they have a similar pattern. So these folks talk to each other and the head of Homicide would go over cases every morning with the squad leaders. And so they would talk about the details so that at that point that something was similar, then the squad leaders were like, 'That's similar to this case,' and then you start putting the puzzle together. That's how we can tell it's truly a serial killer because generally, they will have a pattern, with something that they do unique. And we don't really make all of those things public. Because people will come in—believe it or not—and confess to a crime. So the only way we can determine whether that person is serious or not is that they know intricate details that clearly gave us the indication that it was the same person. And that definitely aroused our suspicion … And so, any of that evidence that's left at the scene, once we get it back, will tie folks together. So that's kind of how we do it between the briefings that the squad leaders have every day by the person in charge of Homicide, and then when they start seeing similarities. The same goes with robberies and sex crimes. The person in charge of the unit every day should go over those kinds of details with the squad leader."

Monica's mother Beatrice, age fifty-two at the time, told *The News*: "My heart is hurting. I feel sorry for all of their kids and mothers too. I feel better he was caught but I don't know why he did what he did."

Back in Dearborn Heights, Armstrong's former Target coworker Nancy Miller was shocked to hear about the arrest. "I was getting ready to go to Target, to work," she recalled, "and the news came on and said that they had arrested him for intentionally killing prostitutes. And I threw up all over my kitchen." As the words of the news report sunk in: "It was after the fact, after he was arrested, then you start thinking, wow, did I ... When he was arrested like, oh, maybe, within a week, I went and talked to the detectives in the Dearborn Heights Police Department, and I said, wow, was I a bad judge of character! He goes, oh, no, no, no, don't think that, because he is a typical Southern boy. And serial killers can just surprise everybody. You would never, ever think in a million years—there was no indication that he did anything. And seriously, there was no indication that he was doing this after work. None whatsoever."

She said, "And I thought, well, should I have been worried? And he goes, no. He would have never, ever harmed you because he identified with you." Nancy thought about her coworker Jennifer, getting rides to work from Eric. "And I said, well, would he have hurt her? And he goes, no. He was only after prostitutes. And I said, well, that's good to know! Because my judge of character just ... And he goes, oh, no, no, no. No, no, no. They can just surprise you to no end. You would have never even known that he was doing the things that he was doing."

And of course, this motherly figure realized Eric had not really been sick that day in January.

"No, he was not, he was really not, but he just said he was." And given what Nancy learned, that Eric had attacked others even before the one he left in Dearborn Heights, she saw the Rouge River as a turning point too: "This was I think like the catalyst. I think he realized that something had to be done. That's when they started investigating him."

An even greater shock was felt by Jennifer Westberg, to whom he was closer. The one with whom he shared stories of his childhood, stories of how the Dearborn Heights police were harassing him, stealing his trash.

"I was getting ready for school one morning and watching Channel 4 news," Jennifer remembered, "when the newscaster said they'd arrested someone in connection to the deaths of the women found in Detroit. My first instinct was, 'Thank God, now they can leave Eric alone.' But I looked at the TV and there he was. It was the picture of him with both his arms opened like he was welcoming the hug of an old friend. For the first and only time in my life, my knees buckled under me and I collapsed on the floor in my room, sobbing."

What was it about Eric that had made Jennifer believe, during those weeks he was telling her about the Dearborn Heights police following him around, that he couldn't have done what the police were suspecting him of?

"Blind trust," she said. "He'd always been kind and went out of his way for me. He talked to me like a real person and treated me with respect. How could someone who loves his wife and family and is willing to work two jobs just to get them a roof over their heads. ... How could that be the same man who strangles prostitutes? Plus, I was 'at that very same time' studying serial killers and mental illness in my high school psychology class. I thought serial killers fit into a mold and were antisocial freaks. Eric was anything but antisocial. He seemingly enjoyed being around others. And yes, we did discuss Eric in class many times before and after he was arrested. One kid in our class mentioned that his grandma lived a few houses down from Eric's mother-in-law's house and that he would often see him mowing his lawn. He said Eric gave him the creeps. I think he was just trying to feel related to the story. I, on the other hand, didn't want anyone at school to know. My boyfriend knew but that was it. I skipped the second half of school the day Eric was arrested. I spent the day reading every news article about him and crying my eyes out. I felt like the man/friend

I knew had died and was replaced by some monster. And all I wanted to do was defend him."

Unlike her coworker Nancy, Jennifer did not speak with police about Armstrong. "The managers at Target did call me at home the day after he was arrested. Told me it was okay to take the day off if I needed it. And also asked if I needed anything from them. They were aware of our bond and were concerned at how the news would affect me."

Later, on the morning of Armstrong's arrest, at eight-fifty a.m., Detroit police were already at the modest brick home on Fairview in Dearborn Heights where Armstrong lived with his family. A handful of Dearborn Heights police stood by at the house while it was searched, including Sergeants Riley and Serwatowski. Police had to secure three large dogs at the residence until the search was concluded.

Among the items showing up in the evidence tech report that day were a short-sleeved Signature Flight Support uniform shirt bearing the name "Eric" with suspected blood on it found in the upstairs bathroom. There were also Trojan and Lifestyles condom boxes and wrappers and unused condoms found in three bedrooms, porn magazines in two bedrooms and one bathroom, and a videotape of John Leslie's *Drop Sex* found in a bedroom. A black pair of pants was found in the trash can in the driveway. There were also a camera and lots of rolls of film, both exposed and unexposed, in multiple rooms.

A warrant was issued for new samples of Armstrong's hair and blood.

Police searched Armstrong's Jeep with a warrant on Wednesday evening, April 12. They noted the condition of the Jeep, a few stains on the front passenger seat. They took the items from the glovebox, including paperwork such as repair bills for the vehicle and a book of blank checks. A Trojan condom wrapper was found between the dashboard and the windshield on the right side. There was a road atlas, in which would be discovered a key bloodstain. The vehicle seats were vacuumed, the vehicle itself dusted for fingerprints. Any stains were noted, along with their color. Carpet samples were taken. A strand of hair was processed from in between the blank checks and another from the rear bench seat. The clasp of a necklace was discovered and sent to the lab with the other items on April 14. A tube of eyeliner. A black hair net. Some chewed gum. A couple pairs of gloves, including rubber gloves. Some socks. A hairbrush. A couple towels. And interestingly, a utility knife was found in the vehicle. DHPD, in their own search of the Jeep, had found a box cutter, along with an Old Timer pocket knife.

Three different assault survivors noted that Armstrong had a knife—Natasha, Zelda, and Cynthia. Natasha and Zelda remembered it being a big knife—bigger than a pocket knife—while Cynthia wasn't sure. It could have been a box cutter or a pocket knife Cynthia saw, based on how she described it and how Armstrong held onto it in his mouth. Then there was whatever Armstrong used in the presumedly faked Novi work incident (said to be a scalpel), plus a knife that he reportedly had as a teen when he locked himself in the bathroom threatening suicide (noted later in a bit more detail). Armstrong certainly had different knives in his possession at different times.

Police went to his workplace, Signature Flight Support, with a search warrant dated April 12 for the work locker or storage area assigned to Armstrong. Nothing was taken from that search. They obtained employment records such as his badge application and background check, employment verification, Department of Justice employment documents, and W-4 form. Police requested a printout of his work hours from March 15 through April 11.

DPD received a strange tip from a local resident in the late afternoon on Wednesday that a Black female who went by "D" had, months earlier, been forced into a blue Jeep, which then headed onto the Jeffries Freeway. She was then found dead in Detroit's Rouge Park in December or January, the resident recalled. Could this have been confusion of the details of Wendy Jordan's murder or another incident?

Wilhemina Drane gave another statement to police on the afternoon of April 12.

"Were you in fear for your life on April 2?" she was asked.

"Yeah!" she replied. "But I knew it wasn't time for me to go."

Drane was then called in to the police station on Beaubien at seven p.m. on Thursday, April 13, to identify Armstrong in a lineup. The six men she saw were all seated, all white males in their twenties or thirties, three of them over six feet tall, a couple five-foot-eleven, all over two hundred pounds. Drane made a positive ID of Armstrong "within 15 seconds," police noted on the report. But an attorney present for the lineup noted that Armstrong's photo had been shown on the six o'clock news. It was unclear whether or not Drane had seen the news report.

Pittsburgh police called about their own recent unsolved homicides of prostitutes, six to twelve of them, all found partially nude. Detroit PD also connected with law enforcement in Raleigh, North Carolina, and the cold case squad in New York City.

On Friday of that eventful week, the story led *The Detroit News'* front page (captured in microfilm below), in its prime real estate above the fold: CONFESSION A TALE OF HORROR, complete with the photo that had previously been used of Armstrong and a shot of the front of his Jeep bearing the BABY DOLL license plate.

The coverage, by a team of reporters from *The News*, focused on the confessions.

"This guy will go down as one of the big ones," it quoted Sergeant Donald Riley.

It was then that details emerged publicly about Armstrong alleging his father was abusive toward him, along with the idea that his hatred for prostitutes stemmed from his being shunned by a high school girlfriend for a classmate who gave her gifts.

It was also reported that police found a fourth body at the railroad tracks scene that day but it was determined to be unrelated to the Armstrong case.

Novi Police Chief Doug Shaefer was quoted in the paper with the account of Armstrong's claim of fighting off the November work break-in. "Apparently he just wanted to attract attention to himself; something sensational, which seems to be part of his make up," Shaefer said.

Also on Friday, Armstrong was arraigned in Detroit, delayed from the day before because of the volume of confessions he had been making. "He's still talking, and we didn't want to interrupt him," Assistant Detroit Police Chief Marvin Winkler was quoted as saying.

Armstrong being led to his arraignment, his arm held by Donald Johnson to his left. Behind them in the beige suit is James Hines, in the foreground in a black coat is Ira Todd, to Armstrong's right in the white shirt is Arlie Lovier, and on the other side next to Johnson in black is John Morrell. Image courtesy of Ira Todd.

Gregory Geider recalled a sunny day for this walk to the courthouse. "On 14 Apr 2000, my diary indicates that we escorted Armstrong from DPD to the 36th District Court for an initial appearance," Geider said. "I remember this as being a classic 'perp walk' on a beautiful sunny day. The first opportunity for the media scrum to get a look at the suspected serial killer. We wanted the media to see Armstrong in DPD custody but at the same time went to great lengths to also protect Armstrong."

The Detroit Free Press reported that Armstrong was wearing gray pants and a gray shirt, black work boots, and a blue baseball cap with POLICE on it. He attempted to cover his face with a jacket.

Right before he took the perp walk, Armstrong had made an unusual request.

"I just remember," Ira Todd said, "when we informed him that, you know, you've got to take him over to jail, get him processed, and there's cameras going to be out there, we can't avoid that. You know, we kind of prepared him for it and still tried to stay friendly with him. And I remember he asked me for a teddy bear. And I knew that was one of those things, that he wanted publicly to be walking out with a teddy bear because I think he was creating a defense for mental illness or something like that. And he wanted a teddy bear, and I remember I talked to Doc, who was our boss at the time. I was like, 'Doc, he wants a teddy bear.' Doc is like, 'Hell no, he ain't walkin' out there with no teddy bear!'"

Investigator Donald Johnson, having gotten so far inside the mind of this killer during the interrogations, had his own memory of the day of arraignment: "I tell you, one of the craziest things was, I was sitting in the cell with him, in the holding cell at 36th District Court when he was arraigned. And he looks over at me, he says, 'Thank you.' I said, 'Thank you? Thank you for what?' He tells me, 'Thank you for being my best friend.' I'm like, wow. That blew me away. But I was thinking, I was like that psychologist for him, so to speak, because he shared so much with me. He shared with me about how he was sexually assaulted by his dad, by his biological father when his mom would leave for work. And so, the various things that his dad would do to him, and how he protected his little brother from these sexual encounters. Because he would tell his dad, 'No, don't do anything to him; do it to me. I'll do it.' And so he just, I mean, he just talked about all these things with me. Talked about the relationship with his wife, how his wife would reject him."

Armstrong stood mute for all the charges brought against him, not just first-degree premeditated murder charges on the four women in this jurisdiction but also a collection of assault charges for the victims who survived. The Associated Press reported that he "hung his head and fought back tears" in the Detroit courtroom. Several television cameras were positioned in the court and Armstrong tried to avoid them, the AP report said. District Court Magistrate Irma Chenevert-Bragg entered pleas of not guilty for him. He was ordered held without bond pending an April 28 preliminary examination.

Armstrong pressed a jacket to his face while being led to a waiting car, next taken to 20th District Court in Dearborn Heights to be arraigned for their single murder charge. He was asked how he felt and he whispered, "So bad," the AP said. Anything else he had to say? "Sorry." An innocent plea was entered for him by Judge Leo Foran in Dearborn Heights in a proceeding that lasted just a few minutes, then he was taken to the Wayne County Jail.

The Free Press noted that Armstrong was on suicide watch, that he had even been reported to have thoughts of "death by cop," of grabbing a gun in the hopes that police would shoot him. The story also noted investigators said that since his arrest Armstrong had been having dreams of killing other people.

One person who watched the arraignment was a friend of Kelly Jean Hood named Isabella Ramirez. "He didn't look like a killer. He looks so pitiful," she told *The Detroit News.*

The Free Press also reached Armstrong's mom, Linda, in New Bern, North Carolina. "I'm really going through a lot," she was quoted by reporter Jennifer Dixon. "It is just not a good time for me." Armstrong had visited her with his wife and son just weeks earlier. One of Linda's neighbors noted that Armstrong had seemed really happy during the visit. He was jumping on a neighbor's trampoline with his younger brother. Was even thinking about getting another tattoo since this neighbor was a tattoo artist, but he didn't have enough time on this trip. This was part of the *Free Press'* April 15 coverage of the case. Paperwork that DPD found in Armstrong's Jeep indicated he and Katie had the vehicle serviced at the Meineke Muffler shop while in New Bern and had a vehicle inspection done. This was on March 6 and 7.

Also on Saturday, April 15, Armstrong's father-in-law Bob issued a statement expressing condolences to the family members of the victims.

The next day, April 16, in a story headlined, SUSPECT CAST AS JEKYLL AND HYDE, *The News* reported more details of Armstrong's background, including the idea that he had been traumatized by the death of his little brother as a child, and that a short time after the baby's death, the young Armstrong deliberately rode his bicycle out into heavy traffic. His baby brother had only been two months old when he died, and Armstrong reportedly was crushed by his death. Armstrong's mother told *The News*, "He said he wanted to be with his baby brother."

Armstrong's stepfather Ron, who with mom Linda continues to regularly visit Armstrong in prison as of this writing, told *The News* at the time, "We're having a real problem reconciling all of this."

By the Monday after Armstrong's arrest, Ron and Linda had arrived in Detroit to see him, a teen boy in tow who likely was their son, Armstrong's half-brother. Del Christian, the VCTF member from the Michigan State Police in charge of the case at the time, remembered talking with Linda and the boy at the station. The officers even gave a Red Wings jacket to the teen, who had the same reddish hair as Armstrong, Christian remembered.

It was then, upon talking with police, that Linda and Ron learned what Armstrong had said about his biological father, his claim that the man had sexually abused him as a child. It was news to them, Officer Donald Johnson recalled, who talked with the couple multiple times during his work on the case. "I was the one who shared that information with them," said Johnson, having spent so many intense hours with Armstrong after his arrest.

As the facts were revealed and the case against Armstrong crystalized, the timeline became clearer of this killer's encounters in Detroit, which began not long after he moved to Michigan with his wife and son in the summer of 1999:

Natasha Olejniczak	August 15, 1999
Monica Johnson	December 3, 1999
Zelda Jakubowski	December 6, 1999 (probably)
Wendy Jordan	January 1, 2000
Rose Marie Felt	mid-March 2000
Wilhemina Drane	April 2, 2000
Kelly Jean Hood	April 4-7, 2000
Devin Marus	April 4-7, 2000
Cynthia Smith	April 8-10, 2000
Nicole Young	April 9, 2000

The timeframe for Rose Felt's murder is based on her movements in Grand Rapids shortly before, as well as Armstrong's trip out of state and his estimate that he killed her three or four weeks before his arrest. Kelly Hood's timeframe is probably the murkiest here, though her sister Shannon remembers her disappearing on April 7.

Cynthia Smith and Nicole Young could have been attacked on the night of Sunday, April 9, except that in Armstrong's confessions for both, he said the next thing he did was go home and take a long shower, which would indicate that they were attacked on separate nights. Or is it possible he went back out? He told police he encountered Cynthia on Monday, April 10. She remembered it as Sunday night/Monday morning, about three-forty-five a.m. Combined with Cynthia's own report and that of her other john from around that same time, her assault happened somewhere in the April 8 to 10 timeframe.

Federal investigators, meanwhile, were working the other, non-Michigan confessions by the end of the very busy week of Armstrong's arrest. Interestingly enough, Geider recalled: "Some weeks later, a subject came up to the VCTF office and implied that he was an investigator with NCIS. This investigator was working on the suspected homicide of a USN officer's wife on the East Coast. Further vetting determined that the investigator was actually working for a defense attorney representing the Navy officer that was accused of murdering his wife. Armstrong must have appeared to be a good fall guy for that case."

All in all, the first half of April 2000 had been one for the record books. The discovery at the railroad tracks at Military and John Kronk had touched off a sequence of events bringing everything in this case together at that same time, much like a freight train speeding down the tracks:

APRIL 10

8 a.m.: One body spotted, then two additional bodies found, at the railroad tracks at Military and John Kronk.

10 a.m. (approx.): The discovery hits the news; police process the scene and investigate all day.

APRIL 11

3:30 a.m.: During their overnight patrol, Officers Rodney Durham and Bradford Bullock interview assault survivor Devin Marus and get a description of the suspect and his vehicle.

10:25 p.m.: Assault survivor Wilhemina Drane calls police and tells them about her incident.

APRIL 12

12:30—1 a.m.: Police apprehend Armstrong on Michigan Ave; he is ID'd by another assault survivor, Cynthia Smith, while in the squad car.

1:30 a.m.: Cynthia Smith gives her statement to police at the station.

3 a.m.: Armstrong begins making statements, continuing all day.

8—9 a.m.: Assault survivor Devin Marus is brought to the station to give a statement.

10—11 a.m.: Dearborn Heights PD is planning to arrest Armstrong and learn he's in custody in Detroit. They assist as Detroit PD executes a search warrant on Armstrong's house, 10:58 a.m.

2 p.m.: Wilhemina Drane comes to the police station and gives her statement.

4:35 p.m.: Final DNA report arrives in Dearborn Heights linking Armstrong to the Wendy Jordan murder.

6:35 p.m.: Police search Armstrong's Jeep on a warrant.

APRIL 13

4:30 p.m.: Detective William Sullivan of Dearborn PD sees the news report on Armstrong and suspects he assaulted Natasha Olejniczak.

7 p.m.: Wilhemina Drane IDs Armstrong from a lineup at the police station on Beaubien.

APRIL 14

Early afternoon: Armstrong is arraigned on four murder charges and three assaults in Detroit.

3 p.m.: Dearborn Heights PD transports Armstrong from the 36th District Court in Detroit to DHPD to execute their own official arrest of him for the murder of Wendy Jordan. They take him to 20th District Court to be arraigned, then take him back to Detroit custody at the Wayne County Jail.

Naval Criminal Investigative Service (NCIS) arrives to investigate the non-Detroit confessions.

Though Wendy Jordan had been picked up and murdered in the City of Detroit, Dearborn Heights kept that case. Donald Riley explained further the crossing of jurisdictions, particularly with the Jordan murder: "Through his confession I think he had admitted that he killed her behind a funeral home on Warren Avenue, which was in Detroit. And our position and the prosecutor's position at the time was, well, okay, that's what he said, everything's cool. We can't prove she was dead in Detroit behind that funeral home. But we can prove that she's dead in Dearborn Heights in the river. So we handled that homicide case because the proof was that she was dead in our city, even though he said he killed her in Detroit."

"A significant amount of the investigation in this case took place after the apprehension," Gerald Cliff recalled. "Although he was ultimately persuaded to confess, everything had to be confirmed and validated against information we already had, and were constantly in the process of gathering through the FBI backtracking his naval career. Dates, times the ship was in ports, when he had shore leave, reports of missing persons during those times, unexplained discovered bodies, etc., all had to be obtained, coordinated and reconciled against what he was telling our interviewers. Once we knew he had been discharged from the Navy in Norfolk, and whether he admitted to one murder or not, a check had to be made for similar murders matching the profile of our cases in that general area. He admitted to one in Norfolk during the interview process, but there could well have been others. We had to verify that if there were others, they either did or didn't match his profile. This was going on from the moment of his arrest and first comments to our detectives.

"The arrest isn't always at the end of the investigation; it can actually mark the beginning in some situations pretty much as it did in this occasion. We had to 'make the case' and we had to do it right, otherwise the prosecution might have failed. We had seventy-two hours to make the case to a judge that a crime was committed, it was committed in our jurisdiction and that there was probable cause to believe that he committed it. We then had twelve days to put together a sufficient amount of evidence to bind him over from trial on the charges."

On April 19, back at the Dearborn PD, Detective Sergeant Allan Ruprecht retrieved out of the property room the silver-tone belt buckle found in Natasha Olejniczak's hotel room and had it processed for prints. Nothing was found.

The next day, April 20, it was determined that a blood sample from Armstrong would be delayed until after the DNA work was done to avoid any allegations of contamination.

Robert F. Mitchell would serve as his defense attorney, court-appointed. Mitchell was well known in Detroit, a criminal defense lawyer for many years, getting his start in the 1950s and rising up through years of racial strife that discriminated against lawyers of color like himself. When he died in September 2016 at age ninety-one, the *Free Press* described him as "a colorful character known to generations of lawyers as 'the Chief.'" He had a gravelly voice, it said, as well as colorful suits and a trademark cigar. He would typically work humor into his courtroom presentations. A *Detroit News* editor who'd known Mitchell for years described him at his death as "courtly and a gentleman." "Nobody could command respect like him," a local judge said.

Mitchell had defended other rather notorious clients, like Lowell "Ed" Amos in 1996, convicted and sentenced to life for injecting his wife full of cocaine, then suffocating her.

Prosecutor Elizabeth Walker, meanwhile, was assembling a case against Armstrong in the months following his arrest. She grew up in the city of Detroit and she taught in the Detroit public schools before deciding to pursue a law degree. With a heart keenly tuned to matters of justice, she had become dismayed at what she saw in the school system. One school would have one set of workbooks for three sets of classes, requiring kids to share workbooks in class and not be able to take them home to study. Another school, meanwhile, would have stacks of extra workbooks. It was frustrating.

"I said, okay, I'm done with this. I've had enough," Walker said years later, reached for this book project via phone during the coronavirus pandemic in 2020.

A friend who was in law school urged her to look into that field but Walker was skeptical. "My mother had always wanted me to be a lawyer; I thought she was nuts. I thought law was boring. But she was right; it was great."

She took the LSAT and went to law school, continuing her teaching job for the first two years, then getting a scholarship for the third. With some other financial aid, she made it work. And she spent all of her law career in the city where she grew up, with ten months in the EEOC office, then as assistant dean at Wayne State University's law school for three and a half years. "While I was doing that, I had a small private practice. So I did criminal defense, and I did a little bit of dabbling, what new lawyers do. Whatever someone with money comes to them and asks them to do, if they can figure it out. And that's the point at which they're willing to try to figure it out."

In her first summer at law school, a particularly horrifying rape case helped her figure it out. The perp was convicted of the rape, but there were flaws in the case and his confession was ruled inadmissible. "So as a brand-new, just-been-in-law-school-two-weeks, it was like, what?" Walker said. "He did it, he said he did it, and they still let him go? I was like, what? And I could see there was something wrong—the police had done something wrong or the prosecutor had done something they shouldn't have. And I knew at that point I wanted to be a prosecutor. It seemed to me the victim got screwed.

"I did not know then that, well, look, that conviction got overturned, but we can go back and start again. They do have the option of trying them again. And seeing now as a prosecutor I later learned and that's not always so successful. The second time ten years later doesn't always work. Sometimes it does. I had one that did. I've had a couple that did. But I understood the miracle of that. So that was why I wanted to be a prosecutor because I felt like, you do it right, you respect the rules and the defendants' rights, and you don't lie, cheat, or steal, if you get him convicted, he stays convicted."

The Armstrong case was larger than a lot of the other cases the now retired Walker tried in her law career, though she also tried a couple years later another high-profile Michigan case, that of Jeffrey Gorton, convicted in 2003 for the murders of a university professor in Flint and a flight attendant at a hotel near Detroit Metro Airport. But with the Armstrong case, there were so many details to juggle, so many witnesses to look after, and these witnesses were not your standard witnesses.

Devin Marus, in particular, was a challenge: "I felt so bad for him," Walker said. "I remember I had to keep him in the jail because I was worried. He had a drug problem, and I was worried that he would be dead before the trial. An overdose or some other misadventure, because you know, serial killers are sort of—or homicidal idiots—are sort of a risk of doing that kind of business, so I learned. And I just didn't want anything to happen to him. So I kept him in the jail, and I kept telling him, you're going to get paid for all this time, you're going to get paid for all this time. And I did—I managed to eke out a check for him. It was almost seven hundred dollars, which was unheard of. But I think once he had testified and once it was over, I don't remember if I could ever find him again and give him the check. Once he got out, he was like gone."

And so, witnesses secured and evidence coming together, Betty Walker set herself to square off against John Eric Armstrong, perhaps with a shiver or two down her spine: she lived in the same city as he did, Dearborn Heights, and she even shopped at the Target store where he had worked.

She also had to prepare to square off against Robert Mitchell, whom she had faced in the courtroom for other trials, who actually was one of the senior attorneys in Detroit when she first started to practice. In Walker's experience, there were defense attorneys you had to keep an eye on, but

Mitchell was one you had to keep both eyes on. He had a few tricks up his sleeve and wasn't afraid to use them. On top of keeping track of her witnesses during the proceedings, as well as the court officers who are bringing them in and lining them up to testify, then tracking how the proceedings are flowing in general, Walker had to carefully watch this guy. The guy they called "The Chief."

"Mitchell was just a master," Walker said, thinking back on the various times she had encountered him on the other side of a case. "He would do things; like, one day he came to court, he was in trial, and he had on one black shoe and one brown shoe. Now, Bob Mitchell knew what he was doing. It was only in my case that he would do these bizarre things. In his case, he looked like F. Lee Bailey ... So he's got one very obviously brown shoe. We're not talking like burgundy, like men's shoes would be. *No, no, no, no, no.* We're talking tan. *Light* brown. Light brown! Why was that? Because then when he's sitting down with his legs all stretched out, instead of paying attention to my witnesses, the jury's looking at his shoes! Because 'What? He's got on one black and one brown!' Keep 'em focused on that. He would do stuff like that! Oh heck ya! Anything to distract!"

She recalled another time, which may or may not have been during the Armstrong case; Walker didn't recall exactly when it was. "He was sitting at the table—now, you know the layout of a courtroom. The prosecutor's always sitting closest to the jury. Then there's the podium. And then the defendant and the defendant's attorney is sitting on the other side of the podium. Usually the podium is in between the two tables. So they're sitting farther away from the jury. They're at an angle, but they're farther away from the jury. In our court, in the Wayne County court, the defendant, if he's in custody, and usually even if he isn't, he sits on the inside part of the table. Like there's a table there, the defendant's attorney is on the outside, the defendant is on the inside. And that's so that the officers have better control.

You know, we've had folks try to make a break for it. So it's easier to control them; there's one more hurdle. They've got to get around that table."

She continued, "So the Chief was sitting at the table. And I can't remember what he was looking for. He wasn't looking for anything, really. He was supposedly going through the transcripts. Right? And it could be some exam transcripts. It probably wasn't even the transcripts of this case. But he needed like a page marker or a book marker, right? So he takes his yellow legal pad and he tears these *loooong* strips of paper. You know how loud a sound that is? And it's a long legal size. And of course he's not tearing the short end. He's tearing the long way. *Riiiiiippppp* .... Now, he's not looking at you; he's not looking at the witness. He's *riiiippppping* his paper. Then he puts it in there. Then turns a page or two more. Very quietly does he turn the pages. Then he *rrrriiiiiipppps* another strip of paper."

Walker laughed. "He's doing stuff like that while you're trying to question a witness and make a point here! And you're not just trying to fill the air with sound—it's to make a point! So he's distracting, right? He pulled the attention away from them. You've got to find a way to combat that. So I remembered that in that case, while he was doing that, I kept asking my questions, and I walked around my table, up to the court clerk. I reached over her bench and grabbed her box of paper clips and kept on questioning my witness and went back to his table and turned the box upside down and slammed it down on the table: 'Here! Here's your paper clips!' He was, 'Thank you! Thank you very much, Ms. Walker! Thank you very much.' So he would do things like that, in a trial."

But Mitchell's skills went far beyond those courtroom antics. "He was one of the best writers," Walker recalled. "His writing was masterful. He really could write well. It is truly a lost art on some folks. If he filed a motion, it was really well written. He could turn a phrase. He had excellent vocabulary. He was such a good writer. But he was a character!"

And, she said, he was a very nice man. "He was delightful. He had a rich sense of humor. He was a character! I mean, he was not a buffoon, now. He knew the law. He knew how to spot a legal issue. He knew how to work it. He knew people. All of that distraction? That was intentional. That wasn't no accident! He knew what he was doing. He was not just clumsy or inartful. Oh no, he was very skilled."

On Wednesday, April 26, Robert Mitchell requested that his client undergo psychological testing for the Jordan case. A preliminary exam/hearing had been scheduled for that murder, and the attorney wanted it delayed until it was determined that Armstrong was competent to stand trial. An order was issued for a competency evaluation. Likewise, the defense (with an attorney standing in for Mitchell) requested a competency hearing for the Detroit cases on April 28, with the motion granted and a hearing scheduled for June 5.

Mitchell was already working an insanity angle. "This man is very distraught and has strong emotional problems that emanated many, many years ago," he told the media. He also tipped his hand on another approach he might use: He promised to produce witnesses that would attest Wendy was alive when Armstrong left her.

On May 18, Dearborn PD made a warrant request for Armstrong for the Natasha Olejniczak assault. Walker approved it the next day. He was arraigned on May 25 by Judge Runco for assault with intent to murder. The fourteen-day rule for preliminary exam was waived, pending a forensic exam requested by Mitchell, there in court with him that day. Katie was also there. She asserted that her husband was innocent and said that he was out of state at the time of the incident. The next day, Detective William Sullivan called her up, asked her if she could prove where Armstrong was when Natasha was assaulted. She told him she believed her husband was in North Carolina then, taking an exam to become a police officer. She was going to check the exact dates, though.

Dearborn PD also learned a little more about that belt buckle found in Natasha's room. They learned the company Armstrong was working for in 1999 was called Initial Security. They examined the logo and wording on the buckle, which matched the company logo, and reached out to Initial on June 6. The company provided them with a similar belt buckle, along with examples of the logo on patches and letterhead. And police planned to take a look at Armstrong's employment files there.

Lab results arrived in May from many items processed at the railroad tracks, such as potato chip wrappers, candy wrappers, empty drink bottles, cigarette boxes, condom wrappers, jackets, and slacks. Some were dusted with powder, some treated with Superglue fuming and Rhodamine 6G dye, and examined with an alternate light source to try to detect latent fingerprints. Results were negative.

DNA from an oral swab of Monica Johnson was analyzed in July against several items found, though the report does not specify where they were found: paper napkins, cigarette butts, used condoms. Monica's DNA profile was not consistent with most items but could not be excluded as a contributor to one of the condoms.

The exam for Natasha's assault was on July 28 in front of Judge Sobotka. Mitchell was there and Walker represented the People. Natasha testified and Armstrong was bound over to Circuit Court. Bond was set for fifty thousand dollars on that charge, though not a factor since he was being held without bond in the murder cases.

Police also took a look at other unsolved strangulation homicides in Detroit going back a couple years, with the idea that he may have traveled to Michigan with Katie to visit family while still in the Navy. None of the unsolved strangulations matched with any timeframe he would not have been on the *USS Nimitz*.

All in all, for what had been assembled with the five first-degree murder charges and four assault charges against Armstrong, Walker would later say in her interview for ID's *Very Bad Men* episode, "We had a prosecutor's dream—or a prosecutor's nightmare. With all the evidence that we had, we could still lose because you never know what a jury will do."

And they were well aware it was possible there were still others out there, other assault survivors or even casualties of Armstrong that they did not yet know of. Riley of the DHPD explained of the January investigation into Armstrong: "We interviewed other prostitutes on Warren Avenue ... Some of them, a couple of them had pulled me aside and said—because we showed them pictures of the Jeep. We had the Jeep; it was either in our custody or it was in the state police custody. But we heard: 'I don't want to say much, but you find that Jeep. I'm telling you right now, you find that Jeep.' So they were saying that this guy was out there doing shit. They didn't really want to say too much, but like I said, when nobody was listening, they would say, 'You've got to find that Jeep. I'm telling you, you've got to find that Jeep.' Well, we already had the Jeep. They didn't know it. You know what I mean? So there were more people out there that may have been assaulted or whatever."

After the June competency hearing, at the rescheduled preliminary exam on Friday, July 21, for the Wendy Jordan murder, Armstrong was ordered to stand trial. Judge Mark J. Plawecki ruled he was mentally competent. He was arraigned for the Jordan murder on August 4, an "arraignment on information" (versus the arraignment on warrant that occurred on April 14). Then, for the Detroit charges, on August 15, at the 36th District Court before Judge Maria Oxholm, Armstrong was bound over for trial: four counts of first-degree murder, one count of assault with intent to murder, one count of assault with intent to do great bodily harm, and two counts of unarmed robbery.

Another arraignment on information occurred on September 5, where Armstrong also stood mute on all charges, with the Court entering a plea of not guilty for him.

At that August hearing, one charge against Armstrong was dismissed—the assault with intent to murder for Wilhemina Drane. She would not enter the courtroom because of the media coverage, police notes said. But Walker, who had done a lot of care and feeding of these four assault survivors as she prepared her case, had her misgivings about this particular witness anyway. "I don't think Wilhemina Drane was even one of his victims," she said years later. There were parts of Drane's story that seemed a little squirrelly to her. For one thing, Wilhemina evidently wasn't out there doing any prostitution when Armstrong spotted her—she denied any involvement in that. Walker firmly believed that this perp was only targeting prostitutes, not women in their forties simply getting a ride instead of waiting for the bus.

Drane did call police with a pretty accurate description of her attacker hours before his arrest on the night of April 11, a description that included his trademark tattoos, and she ID'd him from a lineup in just seconds.

But that wasn't what was giving Walker uneasy feelings. "She had been particularly uncooperative, even with police, in terms of coming in and giving a statement," Walker said. "Other witnesses, the other victims, they were cooperative." When Drane didn't show up for the preliminary exam, it made things easier for this prosecutor. "I didn't complain about it. I didn't make a fuss about it. I just dismissed that one."

The warrant for a blood sample from Armstrong to compare with DNA evidence in the four Detroit homicides was signed on January 18, 2001. Armstrong was identified as Wayne County Jail Inmate No. 2000-38381.

Evidentiary hearings were held in January and February 2001, with witnesses from law enforcement testifying, as well as a couple psychology experts who had interviewed Armstrong.

A lot of details were coming together, and for the prosecution, it was showtime. First up was justice for Wendy Jordan, the strongest case, involving multiple police departments and quite a lot of evidence.

"They went with our case first," Riley said, "because, well, I'm not knocking DPD; I'm just saying we had the best case. We had the best case. We had her in the Jeep. We had him in her. We had the best DNA, the best trace evidence. We had the best case."

Gary Tomkiewicz echoed that sentiment, explaining Dearborn Heights' unique geographic shape and position and how that affected the business of solving crimes. Ironically, much of the geography centered around the avenue where this case started, an avenue that essentially splits this suburb in two.

"Michigan Avenue is the border between south Dearborn Heights and north Dearborn Heights," Tomkiewicz said. "So Dearborn Heights, we border Allen Park, Lincoln Park, Taylor, Romulus, Westland, Garden City, Livonia, Detroit, Dearborn. Look at a map and see how many cities we border. And Inkster, on top of it. And Redford. From Michigan Avenue north, we are in mutual aid with western Wayne County. From Michigan Avenue south, Dearborn Heights is affiliated with Downriver, which would be Taylor, and I mean, Allen Park, Lincoln Park, Romulus and all that. So our SWAT teams, we had an alliance that anything south of Michigan Avenue, Downriver, we were in mutual aid with them. Anything north of Michigan Avenue, we were aligned with western Wayne County. Very, very unique city for about twelve square miles. But on this particular case, Detroit stepped up to the plate and then the FBI stepped up to the plate. It was our case all the way. You know, we had the goods on him. We had the best case and everything else. That's why they took him to trial with us. But in my position as a lieutenant at that time, I have to deal with these agencies on a daily basis and respect their assistance. I'm not concerned about being in front of the media. I just want the case solved."

HIS DAY IN COURT

On Monday, February 26, 2001, coming up on a year since his arrest, the trial proceedings began for Case No. 00-008526-01-FC, the People of the State of Michigan versus John Eric Armstrong for the murder of Wendy Zelane Jordan. It would last eight court days.

Judge Mary Waterstone presided. In her early sixties at the time, she had been appointed judge of the 36th District Court in 1991, then in 1997 was appointed to Wayne County Circuit Court. Before that, as her 2014 obituary read, she was "a pioneering woman lawyer for Michigan Bell," which evolved into Ameritech and then AT&T. Schooled at the University of Michigan and at one time an adjunct associate professor at Wayne State University Law School, she was an animal rescuer and an accomplished athlete, running marathons and climbing mountains (even Mount Everest) up to a year before her death.

The first day and a half of the first trial were spent with *voir dire*—questioning and selection of the jurors. Absent that first day were not only the media, which surprised Elizabeth Walker a bit but was pleasing to her nonetheless, but also Armstrong's wife, Katie. Mitchell told the Court that Katie wasn't there because she was afraid of Walker. Armstrong's wife did share some information with him the previous week, however, Mitchell said, that should help establish his whereabouts elsewhere while this crime was being committed.

Just before the potential jurors were interviewed, the two lawyers haggled over which witnesses would be testifying and what information Mitchell claimed he did or didn't have. Armstrong's Target coworker Nancy Miller was subpoenaed and she was on the list of witnesses stated for the defense on day one, but she ended up not being called. Mitchell had originally planned to make an argument that Armstrong couldn't lift a body like Wendy's because of bad knees, Miller said.

Mitchell entered a plea of not guilty for Armstrong on that first day, adding, "Now I like for you to caution Ms. Walker that we're just trying *this* case," he said. "We're not talking about Norfolk and Seattle and Hong Kong."

Walker said she planned to call a polygraph examiner from Westland, but only from the perspective of an "interview" he conducted with Armstrong—it wasn't an actual polygraph test, but it was noteworthy because in it, Armstrong gave contradictory information. What information was that? The idea that he didn't know Wendy Jordan and had never met her. How is that contradictory, defense insisted. From the DNA found in her rectum, that's how, Walker stated bluntly. This was not going to be a nicey-nicey affair in court between these two attorneys.

One item the defense was intending to use was an alleged tip received by police that "three Black men," with possibly one of them actually being a Black female, inferring Wendy herself, were spotted on the bridge on Ann Arbor Trail before Armstrong reported the body and before the police ever came. This was going to present reasonable doubt. Mitchell, in this trial, was willing to give up the fact that Armstrong had sex with Wendy (especially after that tidbit above), but he was asserting his client did not kill the woman. Mitchell, it was clear from the first day, would also maneuver some kind of insanity defense.

"Usually with the insanity defense," Walker said when interviewed years later, "you're admitting that you did it but you're saying, I didn't have the mental capacity to do it in the way the law says I have to have intended it, in order to be criminally responsible. In fact, that's why we call it lack of criminal responsibility. Not that he didn't do the act, but that he didn't have the mental state that's required to make that act a crime."

With that insanity idea, the defendant does not understand the difference between right and wrong. "And/ or they can't conform their conduct to the requirements of the law," Walker said. "Their behavior—they can't control that. 'I couldn't help it; the devil made me do it.' That kind of thing."

But okay—was Mitchell saying Armstrong did it but was insane, or that he didn't do it and these other guys on the bridge had something to do with it? Isn't that sort of a confusing strategy? Shouldn't it be one or the other? Shouldn't it be consistent? Not necessarily, Walker explained. In a case like this, the defense attorney only has to make one juror doubt he did it, by whatever means he can employ, even if it's by multiple means. Sometimes, they throw a few different things at the board to see if one will work.

"Something might stick," she said. "And you only have to get it to stick with one person. You don't have to convince all twelve. You just have to unsettle one."

Jurors were grilled in the morning and all through the afternoon on day one. Were they ever victims of a violent crime. Did they know anyone who was the victim of a violent crime. How did they feel about prostitutes. Did they or anyone they know suffer from mental illness. Did they ever serve in the military. All the stuff you would expect for a trial like this, all aspects of their lives: work, school, family, whatever. Jurors were sternly instructed not to watch the news on this case, nor to discuss it with anyone. It was something Walker was particularly concerned about. A few jurors were excused amid the questioning.

In jury selection, Walker would tend to avoid women, especially in a case with a sexual component. Here, her victim was a prostitute. Women are judgmental, she had found in other cases. A female juror might pass judgment on her victim—why was she out on the streets in the first place? If she wasn't out there living a high-risk lifestyle, she wouldn't have gotten killed. And since Walker would have to have at least a couple women on the jury, she looked for younger women, maybe in their thirties, with some life experience, preferably from the city, and hopefully having some kind of urban struggles in their background.

Voir dire continued on day two, February 27, with more excusals. Walker expressed concern, at two p.m. after a break, about a magazine article she'd just learned of: Details magazine and writer Kevin Gray had just done a story on Armstrong and the case. Armstrong had been interviewed for it, and he had sent a thirty-page letter to Gray. Walker wanted to know what was in that letter. Mitchell said he wouldn't oppose it being entered into proceedings. In the story, published March 2001 and still posted on Gray's website years later, Gray described the thirty pages as "history of his childhood, his time in the Navy, and his own account of what happened on the streets of Detroit during his self-confessed reign of terror last spring." Since so many months had passed since his arrest as he was about to go to trial, one can imagine there were quite a few differences between the letter and his confessions.

Walker and Mitchell gave their opening statements on day two, after eight men and four women were settled into the jury. Walker went first, discussing some of the specific points she would present to the jury, such as the fact Armstrong gave permission for the Dearborn Heights police to search his Jeep the day of the body's discovery, that he had willingly been interviewed but then stopped the interview on his own at one point, that he'd hired a lawyer, Tom Cardinal (who would testify), who okayed the Jeep search as well, and that Armstrong consented to a blood sample. Fibers from Wendy's gold shoes were found in the Jeep, Walker noted, and hair from her face proved similar to hair found in the Jeep. Hair in her black tights proved similar to hair found in the Jeep.

"Ladies and gentlemen," Walker said, "the evidence at the end of this case is going to convince you that John Eric Armstrong was not mentally ill and he was not legally insane; he wasn't drunk. He knew exactly what he was doing. He hated prostitutes but he engaged Wendy Jordan's services and ultimately killed her."

It was an unremarkable defendant who sat before her in the courtroom. Quiet. Appearing to be unassuming. Perhaps even appearing to be innocent.

"Armstrong looked like a big ole baby boy," she recalled, "I mean, curly blondish hair, you know. He was not a bad-looking—he was a nice-looking young guy. You just would not think, to look at him, that he was capable of that kind of evil."

The fact that he worked at her local Target store was a bit of irony because she likened him to any guy you would see at the supermarket or Home Depot, maybe the mechanic who's fixing your car. "He just was very ordinary. The boy next door."

For his own opening statement, Mitchell worked an angle of the cops treating Armstrong badly, both in Dearborn Heights and Detroit. The police spoon-fed him information during his confessions in Detroit, Mitchell said. He brought up Armstrong's claim that he pulled over to the bridge to vomit, defending the idea that there was no vomit at the bridge (which would be discussed at great length during the trial). He said it was not possible for Armstrong to lift a one-hundred-and-forty-pound woman and throw her over the bridge. That allegation had to draw snickers from the prosecution, you would imagine—the estimate of Wendy's weight was close (she weighed one hundred and thirty-five pounds), but Armstrong was quite huge, any "bad knees" notwithstanding.

The first witness called for the prosecution was Sarah Daros, who testified that she was at her boyfriend's house near the bridge when she saw Armstrong's Jeep pull over and park, and Armstrong get out, walk to the side of the bridge, and look over. Next to testify was her boyfriend, Alan Berry, adding his own perspective of the scene and his call to 911. Mitchell did not cross-examine either witness.

Thomas Berry, Alan's dad, took the stand next, relating the story of Armstrong pretending to dry heave at the bridge while they were waiting for police to arrive. Mitchell jumped on that in cross, accusing Thomas of intimidating Armstrong to remain at the bridge so that his own son wouldn't be in "danger" from police.

Court adjourned at four-twenty that second afternoon. Wendy's sisters Bonnie and Judy had watched the proceedings, as they would every day, and Armstrong's mom Linda and stepdad Ron were there as well, holding hands stoically, as noted by *Detroit News* reporter Shawn D. Lewis.

Walker also recalled Armstrong's parents. "I remember seeing the mother and the stepfather sitting in the courtroom throughout the trial. And the mother was very quiet. And of course, I wouldn't have any interaction with them. I couldn't. I mean, what could I say? Nothing. And she sat holding her husband's hand, you know, in her lap or down next to her. Almost every time I saw them, that's what I saw. And I felt really bad for them."

The News story quoted Judy: "They keep saying our sister was a prostitute, but she had three children and was working at a Subway restaurant in St. Clair Shores and at a gas station in Royal Oak. If she was a prostitute, we didn't know."

Bonnie told *The News*, "Our mother died when we were young, and my father is too devastated to come to court."

At the same time, Bonnie was becoming dismayed at the press coverage of the event, even from national outlets miles away. "It was sad," she said years later, "because at the end of the day, it was never about any of the girls. It was always about this sailor. It was always about him. They didn't care about those girls."

Bonnie and Judy were two of only a handful of victim family members present for the court proceedings. Kelly Hood's family—and members of her ex-husband's family—were there. But that's about it. Bonnie's remembrance of the trials: "I just thought it was pitiful that this was about a killer. If he would've been a Navy Seal, it would have never been mentioned, period. That's the thing about it. It was never about my sister, period. Just wasn't. It was about who he was."

And one other thing has stayed with Bonnie, in the years hence, something that Elizabeth Walker said that struck her deeply. "She taught me something. I said, Miss Walker, 'What's taking you so long to pick this jury?' And she said, 'I'm being real careful because women are hard on women.' Just with any little thing. You know, those women would have let him go free and he had been killing people since he was eighteen off the boat."

Day three, February 28, began at nine-forty-five a.m., and the next witness called was Jeffery Munroe, who responded to the bridge scene. Like the other witnesses, he helped establish that there was no vomit at the scene, despite the fact that Armstrong claimed he had pulled over to throw up. Munroe also said he returned to the bridge scene later that night, between eleven and eleven-twenty, he estimated. At that time, he saw Armstrong back at the bridge too. Now, however, Armstrong and his wife were walking by. On Mitchell's cross-examination, Munroe said Armstrong introduced him to his wife.

Timothy Olszewski, a member of the dive team that retrieved Wendy's body from the river, testified next. Here, the first items were entered into evidence, several photos from the crime scene, the first one of Wendy's body in the water and ice. Her hands were bagged before she was moved out of the water to preserve evidence, Walker had Olszewski explain. On cross, Mitchell tried to dig at that removal procedure to poke any holes he could, also questioning the weight of the body.

Next up was Carl Schmidt, MD, deputy chief medical examiner for Wayne County. He testified to Wendy's injuries, told how he could determine she had been manually strangled, rather than by a ligature. Walker discussed with him how long it takes to die in that manner, discussed the rape kit, the morphine in her blood indicating heroin use. The toxicology report was entered as evidence.

James Serwatowski of the Dearborn Heights Police Department was next on the stand, and, along with other cops at this trial, took the most beating in the witness box by far. Hours of it, frankly, as the lawyers volleyed back and forth on various points. Serwatowski talked about where Armstrong's Jeep was parked, about why Armstrong's story was suspicious to police and why he was questioned at length that day. This was an area in which Mitchell would grill him very strenuously. Serwatowski told how Armstrong consented to his Jeep being searched, that it was towed to the station that day so they could check it out there. Serwatowski had assisted in the Jeep search, and he mentioned several items they found. Armstrong remained at the station during this search and was at the station four or five hours altogether, Serwatowski estimated, out of there by midnight or before, with his Jeep (and also with his lawyer, the next witness). Walker had to dance carefully with this stated departure timeframe, since one of her prior witnesses had put Armstrong back at the bridge scene that evening in a close timeframe, if not quite exact.

On his cross-examination, Mitchell went after the vomit issue, asking Serwatowski about times when he, himself, was feeling sick and about to vomit. "And you are going to penalize him," Mitchell asserted to the cop, "because he tried to vomit and couldn't vomit, so that's peculiar too, when you try to vomit and don't vomit? That is peculiar?"

Mitchell attacked the police's decision to question Armstrong further that day. He pointed to the interview transcript where Armstrong had said (rather facetiously, truth be told, if you actually listen to the recording), "Just let me go home, God ..." On the recording, it's a frustrated, impatient, why-all-these-questions type of muttering, and many people would not consider it an actual request, but Mitchell did what he could with it. At issue, of course (and in a big way), was whether Armstrong really felt he was free to leave the station that day. You could read it either way— was he really being accommodating and polite or was he feeling pressured? It was a blurry line and Mitchell pushed it as much as he could.

The next witness was Thomas Cardinal, the lawyer contacted by Armstrong's family to meet him at the police station that night. He said he arrived there around eight-thirty or nine p.m., and he and Armstrong were out of there, with the Jeep, between eleven-thirty and midnight. He discussed being contacted the next day about further questioning, plus the hair and saliva samples requested from Armstrong. When Mitchell cross-examined, he questioned why Cardinal wasn't called when Armstrong was arrested in April.

The condom wrapper found at the scene was among the other items entered into evidence that day. Armstrong was noted by *The Detroit News*' Lewis to have taken "copious notes on yellow legal pad paper while his mother and stepfather sat in the first row." Court adjourned at four-thirty.

The following day the prosecution continued making its case. Investigator David Heater was called to the stand, discussing the details of Armstrong's written statement prior to the polygraph examination: points like the condom purchase at the Mobil, the "finding" of Wendy's body, the reason he had the condoms, and his opinion of Armstrong's answers.

On day five, which was Friday, March 2, Robert Stephens was called. He was sharing an office with Serwatowski at DHPD and had sat with Armstrong a few minutes before the interview. He also had been the one to start the tape recording of Armstrong's interview, which was explored a bit because it was (evidently inadvertently) taping over a previous interview for another, unrelated, case. Mitchell cross-examined Stephens on his arrival to the bridge as one of the responding officers to the 911 call. He asked Stephens about his two visits to the home of Armstrong's family that day to let them know where Armstrong was. He pressed Stephens about the police showing up to the house again the next day with a warrant to search the Jeep—again.

"You take away his freedom, now you take away his car?" Mitchell inquired.

"Objection," Walker said.

"Sustained."

During Stephens' testimony, Mitchell also argued whether the gold shoe retrieved at the crime scene actually fit Wendy Jordan.

Next up was Mike Petri, and like Serwatowski and later Donald Johnson, he was a cop grilled rather ferociously on the stand. The fact that Petri left the interview room during Armstrong's questioning became an issue he had to answer for. He was genuinely feeling sick that day, he testified. This was not some kind of cop trick (it had, after all, left Serwatowski in the room to make idle chitchat with Armstrong during his absence while the tape was still rolling). During the course of Armstrong's visit to the station, however, Petri had also received the report on a recent suicide attempt that Gary Tomkiewicz of DHPD had discovered while doing a bit of a check on this interesting guy they were questioning. That was brought up during Petri's testimony but not fully explored. Just touched on. At least one photo of the ring found at the bridge scene was entered into evidence and it was made reasonably clear the ring could have something to do with this apparent suicide attempt by Armstrong, but not really explained. Nevertheless, Walker and Mitchell took several turns on Petri, relentless going at each other. Again, the issue of whether Armstrong was being detained by DHPD was vigorously contended. The tape of Armstrong's interview was entered as evidence.

Petri wasn't done on day five as Court again adjourned at four-thirty—he was back on the stand on the morning of day six, the following Monday, at nine-fifty. There was a discussion of the Jeep being dusted for fingerprints at the Michigan State Police crime lab but no usable prints being found.

When Petri was at last released, it was time to hear from a family member. Bonnie Jordan, closest sister of the victim, took the stand. Her testimony was brief, mostly to establish that the gold shoe found at the crime scene did belong to Wendy. She also talked about receiving the call to identify Wendy's body. Mitchell did not cross-examine.

Next in the hot seat was Officer Donald Johnson and it was indeed very hot for this Detroit cop. At contention here was exactly what Detroit police knew about any link of Armstrong to the Dearborn Heights case when they arrested him in Detroit on the tip of an assault survivor. Just when, in the string of confessions with Armstrong that morning and throughout the next day, did the information about Wendy spill out? What did Johnson and the other officers know, and what did they act on, when they garnered all these signed confessions? The waters could seem a bit murky, despite the heavy-duty efforts of Detroit police at the time to have everything fully Mirandized and signed, their suspect fully fed and comfortable. Both lawyers worked strenuously with Johnson to try to clear up those waters in their favor.

Johnson described Armstrong as sometimes sad, often calm during the questioning. He seemed like just an average, everyday guy, the cop said. He read Armstrong's confession regarding Wendy Jordan for the Court. He said he learned from Armstrong's mother that her son had been in counseling at a young age. When Mitchell cross-examined Johnson, he grabbed on to this, wanting Johnson to admit that Armstrong was "sick." Mitchell alleged that Johnson threatened to hurt Armstrong's toddler son and his wife.

The trial continued the next two days, with Mitchell presenting his defense—a shorter affair, no doubt because he had used his cross-exams in the prosecution's case so earnestly. Dr. Calmeze Dudley Jr. took the stand for the defense on day seven, Tuesday, asserting that Armstrong was mentally ill, stricken with a condition called intermittent explosive disorder. And here was where the idea was raised that Armstrong had allegedly been sexually abused by his father at age five.

"He has been haunted by nightmares of his father's abuse for more than twenty years," Dudley was quoted by David Shepardson of *The Detroit News*. "This is a substantial disorder." Dudley also said Armstrong blamed himself for the death of his baby brother. The psychiatrist said he believed Armstrong suffered from alcoholism and depression.

When cross-examined, Dudley said this intermittent explosive disorder is associated with seizures but there was no indication Armstrong ever had seizures.

Armstrong's wife Katie also took the stand on Tuesday. She shed light on the suicide attempt a few months before Armstrong's arrest. He left a note and his wedding ring at home. A lethal dose of cold medicine was what he was planning, Katie testified. She said her husband was innocent of this crime and had dreamed of becoming a law enforcement officer himself, applying for police jobs.

Her demeanor on the stand left a big impression on Bonnie Jordan, as well as on the prosecuting attorney. "I still can see her sitting on the witness chair," Walker said years later. "It was like she had a rod up her spine. Just rigid and knees close together. I mean, she had a military background too."

Both Wendy's sister and the prosecutor said when interviewed that they felt that Katie's behavior was demeaning toward her husband. Walker found herself wondering if there were aspects of their marriage that could have contributed to Armstrong's crimes. "I'm not a psychologist," she said. "Didn't take psych in school. Nothing. None of that. That's just my little dime-store belief."

On day eight, Wednesday, Johnson was back on the stand, noting just how many times Armstrong had been read his rights during questioning. His dramatic testimony of the confessions brought a hush in the courtroom, *The News'* Lewis reported. Johnson talked about how he had begun the interviews with Armstrong with small talk about hobbies and the Navy before moving on to the crimes. How their suspect had taken naps in between the confessions.

A forensic psychologist testified that Armstrong seemed to be pretending to be mentally ill, a response to Mitchell's play at an insanity defense that also included two alleged suicide attempts by Armstrong. Walker called other rebuttal witnesses, including a couple fellow sailors once serving on the *USS Nimitz* with Armstrong. They said the defendant did not handle stress well and argued often with his wife.

Nurse Ronald Mathis, who had spoken with Armstrong at the Wayne County Jail after his arrest in Detroit, testified that he had asked Armstrong at the time how he felt. "I feel sad because I hurt those women" was the reply.

Clinical psychologist Jennifer Balay testified that Armstrong told her he saw the face of his father on the prostitutes he killed.

In her closing arguments, Walker dramatically held up her hand and timed out the thirty seconds that she said it likely took Wendy Jordan to die, as silence draped the courtroom. "And you can imagine that she was not just laying there waiting," Walker said, "wondering how long it would take to die. She probably struggled for her life."

For his own turn, Mitchell portrayed Armstrong as a small-town Southern boy, naïve to the ways of the world, and making a mistake by reporting the body he found at the river. He used the fact that Armstrong consented to the vehicle search by Dearborn Heights PD that day to indicate the defendant was not sane. But Armstrong was not insane, the prosecution asserted—just a murderous liar who hated prostitutes.

The matter was turned over to the jury and it took the jurors just two hours on the afternoon of Thursday, March 8, to find Armstrong guilty of murder in the first degree. *The Detroit News* reported that the defendant showed no emotion and the paper's lead art stretching across more than half of the Metro page depicted Armstrong sitting in court, head bowed, with his mother and stepfather seated behind him. The two parents cried as the verdict was announced.

Wendy's sisters cried as well, with Bonnie embracing and thanking Walker for her work on the case. Armstrong's wife was not present.

"My sister would have been forty-one on Easter Sunday," Bonnie Jordan was quoted by *The News'* Lewis. "Our family has waited a very long time for this day, and I am so happy. I feel justice has been done. He can never do this again."

Armstrong returned to court for sentencing on April 3, 2001. Mandatory life in prison without parole.

The two sisters who had been there in court during the trial returned as well, this time each giving an impact statement. Bonnie went first as another sister, Ina, looked on, along with a cousin, Joyce.

"You have no remorse for what you have done," she told Armstrong as part of her sharp, succinct statement. "You had the nerve to put your grubby paws around my sister's neck and choke her until she couldn't breathe. She was a helpless one hundred pounds and you had to kill her. You are a predator much worse than an animal. An animal kills to live."

Decades later, Bonnie remembered that moment.

"It was so quiet in there; oh my God," she said. "He didn't want to cry. I said, I'm going to make him—everybody always told me, Bonnie, there's something about you; you can make somebody cry. Well, I used my power that day."

Her younger sister Judy was next with a statement, explaining at first that she was the middle sister—with two older, two younger—in the Jordan family. "Who are you that you should change my life?" she demanded. Her big sister Wendy would never get to see her twins again, Judy said, and she would never see her again either, hinting at a relationship the sisters had needed to work on. Though her time speaking was shorter, Judy's words were more condemning: "I hope you have nightmares that wake you up shaking and crying because we do. I pray you have no peace for the remainder of your life, John Eric Armstrong."

Walker had no statement of her own. The sisters had spoken for her, she told the Court.

Mitchell gave some words for his turn, reiterating issues brought up at trial.

Then Armstrong had a chance to speak. He used the time to request another attorney. He was unhappy with Mitchell's performance on his behalf. He asked that Mitchell either step down or be removed by the Court. He cited several reasons in a rather lengthy statement:

- Michell did not retrieve Armstrong's medical records from the Navy at Armstrong's request. Katie, he said, had to try to get the records on her own and it was harder for her to do this than it would be for his lawyer.

- There were three witnesses who did not testify but should have.
- Armstrong received an incomplete discovery package for the trial and later than he should have, shortly before the trial started.
- The hair found on the body and on the condom wrapper—whose was it? This issue wasn't explored, he said.
- Depositions from people who knew him in his hometown in North Carolina could have helped.
- Mitchell fell asleep at least twice during the court proceedings.
- Armstrong only got the chance to see Mitchell four times while in jail.

Walker interjected that Mitchell did, indeed, have Armstrong's medical records from the Navy. She also defended Mitchell on the sleeping issue, saying she knew him and he wasn't actually sleeping. Mitchell himself was quoted by *The Detroit News* in the hallway as defending his forty years of legal experience, saying he listens better with his eyes closed but only sleeps at home.

Armstrong received his sentence, and so ended the trial for the murder of Wendy Jordan. And for these two attorneys, this particular sparring match was over; they would still be friendly to each other outside of the courtroom, still stop and chat when they saw each other in the hallway downtown. It was that way with lawyers, at least sensible ones. Like UFC fighters, they might tear each other apart in the octagon, but when the horn sounds and it's over, they're hugging like friends.

"You really can't take this stuff personally," Walker said. "You shouldn't. If you do, you're going to burn out. You'll burn out."

A motion for Robert Mitchell to withdraw as Armstrong's defense attorney was filed the same day as the sentencing, April 3. The motion was granted.

One case down, several more to go, from that vantage point. The prosecution geared up for Round 2, Kelly Jean Hood. This trial, however, would last only four court days. Case No. 00-009350-01-FC, the People of the State of Michigan versus John Eric Armstrong for the murder of Kelly Jean Hood, began on June 4, 2001, again before Judge Mary Waterstone of the Wayne County Third Circuit Court. Ira Harris took over for Mitchell in defending Armstrong. Virginia Trzaskoma assisted Walker during proceedings. There would be a different approach for the prosecution in this trial. For one thing, three of Armstrong's known assault survivors would testify, no doubt making a powerful impact.

Shannon Wilson attended the court proceedings to see justice for her sister. She was struck by the assault victims she saw at the various dates in court. Those surviving victims couldn't really tell you why they survived, she recalled. One she described as simply a "heavyset grandma," presumedly Wilhemina Drane, who'd dropped out of the process earlier on. One she recalled as a male transitioning to a female, Devin Marus, describing herself to the prosecution as a "pre-operative transsexual." Another, Wilson remembered, took her assault experience as a wakeup call and got off the street. That would be Natasha Olejniczak. Then there was Avon, aka Cynthia Smith, the other survivor queued up for this trial. Though Shannon didn't remember this part, Cynthia was the one who skipped town.

Despite the pain of the trial, there was a saving grace in it, for Shannon. "Miss Walker was the prosecutor. And she was a really honest woman. And you know, she was very open with us through the whole thing, which I was thankful for."

And how would Shannon describe the demeanor of the defendant, as she attended the trial and observed everything?

"Just quiet. Wouldn't make eye contact with anybody … He was just really non-emotion. Because I'm not in with knowing what the charges and things like that are. Because I had asked Miss Walker—I knew from Wendy Jordan, he was trying to get away with the insanity plea during that trial, which failed for him. He was found with first-degree murder. Well, then when Kell's trial come up, he tried going with criminally insane. And that's when I asked Miss Walker, I'm like, you need to explain the difference to me on this. You know, you're either trying to go with the insanity plea, or you 're not. Because basically with Wendy Jordan's trial, I know he pretty much threw his family under the bus. But he didn't have a bad family life."

It was clear on day one of Kelly's trial that Walker set out to prove Armstrong intended to kill Kelly, he was not mentally ill, he knew the difference between right and wrong, and chose to do wrong. Harris, for his turn, would try to show that Armstrong was indeed insane. The defense's approach was to admit Armstrong committed the murder (not wanting to argue the DNA evidence) but to show that he was not mentally or emotionally responsible for his actions. And really, just as one of the public defenders for serial killer Edmund Kemper once said, the only thing you can do with someone who has confessed everything is to try to prove him not guilty by reason of insanity. Certainly, Harris had this same unenviable task after Mitchell's failed approach, especially given how neat and tidy Detroit police had wrapped up those confessions, complete with hamburgers.

Dr. Dudley had stated in the evidentiary hearing and in the first trial that Armstrong suffered from intermittent explosive disorder, which was explained now as "several discrete episodes of failure to resist aggressive impulses that result in serious assaultive acts or destruction of property." So that was one card on the table, and it was Walker's task to poke holes in it or throw it out altogether.

Early on, Walker argued that Armstrong's behavior was purposeful and goal-directed, not at all insane. "Purposeful, goal-directed behavior is sane," she told the Court. Armstrong hated prostitutes and set out to kill them.

The judge excluded from the trial some information on Rose Marie Felt, who, like Kelly, had DNA in her body linked to Armstrong. Judge Waterstone did allow the testimony of the three assault survivors, though, to show a common scheme and plan on Armstrong's part.

Mixed into this on the first day was the highly annoying disappearance of Cynthia Smith. Walker had requested the FBI keep track of her but she had given them the slip. They had allowed her to go to Arizona and from there she was in the wind, with no one at the address she gave being willing to offer any help. The last sighting of her was a couple weeks before this trial, in Denver. She had testified at the preliminary exam, however, and Walker was willing to add her testimony by way of that transcript if need be.

Voir dire took up the rest of the day and the approved members were seated, then Court adjourned at four-twenty-five.

The jury returned at nine-thirty on June 5 to hear Walker's opening statement. "It's going to be for you to decide, ladies and gentlemen," she said. "The proof is going to be fairly clear. It's not going to be a comfortable decision for you, it's not going to be earth-shattering, it's not going to take a whole lot of soul-searching. It's going to be pretty clear."

Harris skipped an opening statement, reserving the right.

Up first on the witness stand was Edward Mannix, Conrail conductor, who said he was going back to throw a switch when he saw the first body at the railroad tracks, later identified as Robin Brown/Nicole Young. He recalled the body as on the west side of the tracks, about thirty feet from the engine where the train stopped. She was a Black female wearing shiny red on top but nothing on the lower part of

234   B.R. BATES

her body, and she had something around her neck. He could affirm that the body wasn't there the day before, when the train came through the same way. He estimated he spotted her around eight a.m. on April 10, and the first thing he did was radio his yardmaster.

The next to testify was Sergeant Arlie Lovier, who responded to the call for DPD and arrived at the tracks to investigate. He recalled the body as being on the north side of the tracks. She, and the other two women, were identified via fingerprints because they all had been arrested before for prostitution.

Lovier described Nicole's body as "clean," meaning he surmised she hadn't been killed there on the tracks because there wasn't really any soil on her. When Rose was found, he said, it looked like she had been there a couple weeks. Both Rose and Nicole had been posed, he noted, though Kelly's body seemed not to be, as it was partially concealed under brush. Her arrest record showed that she had been working the area of Michigan Avenue and Livernois/Junction.

With these discoveries, Lovier immediately called the office for help, he said during Walker's questioning. It was clear this was a serial. Officers hit the street in the area of Michigan and Central, near Livernois, to question other prostitutes who knew Kelly. The girls hadn't seen her in a couple weeks, they had told police.

Lovier also discussed the evidence found at the scene. When it was Harris' turn to cross-examine, he only asked Lovier if there seemed to be any attempt to conceal the three bodies. He said not with the first two.

The next witness was Eugene Fitzhugh, evidence tech on the scene. His long report was entered as Exhibit 1, with Exhibit 2 being a blow-up of the sketch from his report, and Exhibits 3-14 being photos from the crime scene. Fitzhugh told Walker more about the positioning of the bodies. Harris had no questions for him.

Next was Bradford Bullock, one of the arresting officers, who told of being on patrol on Michigan Avenue with his partner Rodney Durham on April 12, then pulling over Armstrong, with David Wasmund of the VCTF arriving, before Cynthia Smith walked up to so colorfully ID this perp. Cynthia was a bit higher class of call girl, Bullock told the Court. She looked better, dressed better. He contrasted her with Devin Marus, telling the Court you could tell the difference between the two because Devin was a narcotics addict.

Harris' only cross for Bullock was the idea of whether or not prostitutes who use fake names could really be trustworthy sources.

Next, David Wasmund took the stand to reinforce Bullock's testimony of the night of Armstrong's arrest.

Kelly's ex-husband Antonio then testified to identifying her body at the morgue. The last time he had talked to her was the last week in March, probably on a Thursday or Friday. He told the Court his ex-wife was five-foot-six and one hundred and ten pounds at the time. Antonio's mother Rosa was also on the witness list but ended up not being called to the stand.

Then Devin Marus took the stand. She told the grisly tale of her own assault. When she mentioned commenting to Armstrong about his tattoos, Walker asked the defendant to roll up his sleeves to reveal the tattoos to the Court.

Armstrong said he hated prostitutes as he was choking her, Devin testified.

Harris had no questions.

The next witness was Michael Choukourian, an officer who executed the search warrant on the home of Armstrong's in-laws in Dearborn Heights. They were primarily looking for articles of clothing, he said. His report became Exhibit 15, detailing the condoms, camera film, sex video, and porn mags they took from the home, along with the gray shirt and work pants that would be revealed as Armstrong's

Signature Flight Support uniform. The shirt appeared to have a bloodstain on it, Choukourian said.

Harris only asked him if he went through the whole house or just part of it, and how many people lived there at the time: four adults and a child.

Jeffrey Rolands, a forensic serologist who collected samples at the railroad tracks, next explained the process for DNA. The jury was excused while counsel and the judge discussed what would be used from his report. After the jury returned around two-thirty the second afternoon, Rolands continued to explain the DNA process and told of the bloodstain found on a page of a road atlas in Armstrong's Jeep. It was shown to be Kelly's blood. Kelly had been wearing the Anne Marie brand pink panties found at the railroad track scene, panties from which stains were tested. When a rape kit was done on her, Rolands testified, the DNA profile on the rectal swab matched Armstrong. There it was, the inarguable evidence. Harris had no questions for this witness either.

Forensic pathologist Yung Chung followed on the stand. She did the autopsy. Kelly had quite a few scratches and marks on her body. She was wearing a pink sweater but nude from the waist down. Chung mentioned the rose tattoo near her left breast, the heart tattoo on her right upper back. She had been dead at least a couple days, Chung said, and she discussed cause of death. Her reports were entered as evidence, and Harris had no questions for cross.

Evidence tech Frank Horan, talking about his search of the Jeep and the finds of condoms and the atlas, rounded out the flurry of witnesses on that second day. The prosecution had covered a lot of ground. The jury was excused at four p.m.

Day three turned up Cynthia Smith. She was located in Colorado and was being brought to Detroit, with testimony hopefully later that afternoon. Meanwhile, the first witness on the stand that day was Samuel Fluker, Armstrong's trainer at Signature Flight Support, who only knew the defendant a month or a month and a half. He offered little insight besides the fact that Armstrong typically worked from two to ten or eleven p.m., and that he got off work at about ten-thirty on April 11. Harris asked what Armstrong was like at work and got little but a standard answer that he didn't cause any problems.

Detective James Hines, partner of Donald Johnson in first interviewing Armstrong after his arrest, next discussed the process for that questioning. Armstrong had a calm demeanor for the most part, Hines remembered, maybe a little agitated at times. Armstrong's entire confession on Kelly Jean Hood was read for the Court and entered into evidence. Harris had no questions.

Next was nurse Ronald Mathis, who also testified at the first trial. He relayed the incident of talking with Armstrong when he had been crying, and noted that Armstrong was kept in the mental health ward for three weeks, pretty standard procedure for a case like this. For his cross, Harris attempted to probe the angle that Armstrong was considered suicidal.

Then Natasha Olejniczak took the stand. Her tale was far grislier than Marus' account. She offered all the horrid details—the knife, how she was slammed down on her back, the knees on her shoulders, the phone cord wrapped around her neck, wrapped so tight that when she came to "I was biting my tongue, saying my kids' names."

Interestingly enough, she told the Court that the name Armstrong gave her that night was John. Not Eric. John, as she repeated years later when interviewed for this book. The name of his father.

Harris had no questions for Natasha.

And with that, the prosecution rested, with the provision that Walker still intended to bring Cynthia Smith to the stand when she arrived.

So it was the defense's turn. Harris' approach was simple—one psychiatric expert to state that Armstrong was bona fide crazy. After the Court recessed for lunch that third day, he gave his opening statement, then put Dr. Dudley on the stand.

The psychiatrist had examined Armstrong over a certain period and learned that his infant brother had died when Eric was only five, and that his biological father had reportedly sexually and physically abused him. All of this meant intense anger and rage, Dudley testified, rage that was misplaced. Armstrong's marriage did not help matters for him, due to a lack of intimacy between them. Girlfriends when Armstrong was a teen had only worsened things. The defendant was suicidal, unstable, often with feelings of emptiness, the doctor said. He mentioned the November suicide attempt.

Walker went on the attack for her cross and stayed there the rest of the day and into the next day, probing whether Armstrong really met the definition of mentally ill, questioning whether he knew right from wrong. She asked if Dudley examined Armstrong's Navy records, if he interviewed folks from his former workplaces, if he talked to his wife or his mother or his stepfather. Was Armstrong really truthful and consistent with Dudley, she challenged. What about his hearing voices when he was drinking? And how heavy a drinker was he? When he applied for a job as a Virginia State Trooper, they did a background check and found no evidence of heavy drinking from those who knew Armstrong. So what about that?

What about the auditory and visual hallucinations Armstrong talked about? Dudley said he didn't connect those with Armstrong's diagnosis of intermittent explosive disorder.

Armstrong had a couple girlfriends as a teen, it was stated. One of them he avoided having sex with by claiming he had AIDS. He had trouble with intimacy in general, the doctor said. Another girlfriend wrote him a Dear John letter while he was in the Navy.

It was an intense grilling that day, with a break only when Harris asked to approach the bench and the jury was briefly excused.

Court adjourned for the day at four-fifteen p.m.

Day four, June 7, then picked up where day three left off, with Dudley back on the stand. His statement the day before that he had not talked to Armstrong's wife and stepfather was amended to be yes, he did talk to them.

Armstrong's interaction with prostitutes, the psychiatrist testified, served as the "pivotal feature, pivotal precipitant to causing his underlying anger to come out."

With the conclusion of Dudley's testimony, the defense rested.

Next, the prosecution picked up again, calling Dr. Jennifer Balay, another witness from the first trial. With Walker's questioning, the forensic psychologist basically refuted Dudley's claim of mental illness for the defendant. She did not believe Armstrong had intermittent explosive disorder. She talked about the defendant's accusations of abuse at his father's hands, which he said continued for about a six-month period before his father left the family. Armstrong believed his father killed his baby brother. Balay discussed the process of evaluating Armstrong along with a few of her colleagues. During questioning, for instance, they applied a little trick that is sometimes done in a case like this to see if the patient is being truthful. When discussing a condition, they throw in a spare symptom or two not really found with the condition, just to see if the patient will say *yes, I've experienced that.* Armstrong did.

Harris cross-examined Balay rather extensively to try to regain his ground, then Walker jumped right back in for a redirect as the two hotly contended whether or not Armstrong was really insane.

Alas, the final person to take the stand for the second trial was Cynthia Smith, to tell one last horrifying tale of assault and survival. Details poured forth of Armstrong picking her up, going to the ATM, parking elsewhere, having sex with her, choking her, then her waking up somewhere else a couple hours later. Then she talked about seeing him driving back and forth on Michigan Avenue a couple days later, his being pulled over by police. Of her walking up to the squad car. Of her seeing, once again, the face of her assailant. "That's the motherfucker that tried to kill me!"

The police took her to the station for a statement and photographs, she testified, particularly of that big cut on her midsection she didn't know how she got. The photos of her were entered into evidence.

The prosecution rested. For good this time.

Walker gave her closing argument, then Harris.

"Ladies and gentlemen," Harris addressed the jury, "I think I can sum up a lot of my closing argument in seven words: Sane people don't do things like this."

Walker took the opportunity to do a rebuttal argument after Harris' statement. She wasn't about to lose this second trial either.

The jury were given their instructions, then excused at one-forty p.m. on day four.

They returned at three-thirty-five. Guilty of murder in the first degree. Every jury member was polled and concurred.

On June 18, 2001, Armstrong was sentenced to mandatory life with no parole for the murder of Kelly Jean Hood. Alma Olds, Kelly's sister-in-law, spoke on behalf of Kelly's three kids. "I don't have hatred toward you," she told Armstrong. "I have pity because you are a person with personal problems and you take out your anger on innocent people."

Kelly's mother, Jonell, whose oldest daughter bore her own maiden name, said, "You took a part of me that can never be replaced and there is no describing the pain

I feel inside, and it will be with me the rest of my life. My daughter's death will be with me forever." Jonell passed away in 2017.

Armstrong's only statement that day was short and simple.

"I'm sorry."

SENTENCES

John Eric Armstrong had to know after the Kelly Hood trial that his goose was cooked. Prosecutor Betty Walker offered a deal.

Kelly's sister Shannon remembered it well: "Oh yeah, we were there for the whole trial," she said, "and we went back for his sentencing. Because it was at the end of Kelly's trial, because he was actually only tried for the two, Wendy Jordan and my sister. And then it was at the end of my sister's that (was) his sentencing. And at end of Kell's trial, Miss Walker, the prosecutor, told us that she was putting the big plea deal out on the table for him to take. Because they didn't want to try everything."

And Armstrong accepted.

"When we went back for the sentencing on Kell," Shannon recalled, "he had agreed with Miss Walker's deal of pleading out to all the other charges. Because I mean, there was not only the other girls who were murdered, but the attempted murder on the survivors, just a slew of other charges."

It was logged on June 18, 2001, that Armstrong had pled guilty to second-degree murder for Monica Johnson, Rose Felt, and Nicole Young. He also pled guilty to assault with intent to do great bodily harm for Cynthia Smith and Natasha Olejniczak. The charge against him for the assault on Devin Marus was dismissed at the request of Elizabeth Walker.

And so the job was made a bit easier for Walker, who had assembled a witness list for the Monica Johnson case that included her boyfriend Cliff, who had driven her to Michigan Ave that night, and her mother Beatrice, who had ID'd her at the morgue. Among the Fourth Precinct responding officers that night was Nathaniel Womack, also queued for possible testimony, who had been only a few days out of the academy for this, his very first homicide scene. No testimony would be needed from him or any others lined up for these remaining cases: evidence techs, coroners, witnesses at the scene.

In April 2002, Armstrong filed an appeal on his convictions for the Wendy Jordan and Kelly Hood murders, as well as the other murders he pled out. "Defendant maintains that his confessions were coerced by intimidating police tactics, and that because of his mental health status, his confessions were not knowing or intelligent," the Court's opinion statement said. But it was a firm *no* on that. The appellate court affirmed the lower court's decisions for all convictions in August 2003.

Ultimately, here's how the court proceedings ended up for Armstrong and what he is now serving, beginning with the two jury trials and followed by the plea deals:

SENTENCE 1—KELLY JEAN HOOD

HOMICIDE—MURDER, FIRST DEGREE
MINIMUM SENTENCE: LIFE
MAXIMUM SENTENCE: LIFE
DATE OF OFFENSE: 04/01/2000
DATE OF SENTENCE: 06/18/2001
CONVICTION TYPE: Jury

SENTENCE 2—WENDY JORDAN

HOMICIDE—MURDER, FIRST DEGREE, PREMEDITATED
MINIMUM SENTENCE: LIFE

MAXIMUM SENTENCE: LIFE
DATE OF OFFENSE: 01/02/2000
DATE OF SENTENCE: 04/03/2001
CONVICTION TYPE: Jury

SENTENCE 3—MONICA JOHNSON

HOMICIDE—MURDER, SECOND DEGREE
MINIMUM SENTENCE: 31 years 0 months 0 days
MAXIMUM SENTENCE: 70 years 0 months
DATE OF OFFENSE: 12/03/1999
DATE OF SENTENCE: 08/21/2003
CONVICTION TYPE: Plea

SENTENCE 4—NICOLE YOUNG

HOMICIDE—MURDER, SECOND DEGREE
MINIMUM SENTENCE: 31 years 0 months 0 days
MAXIMUM SENTENCE: 70 years 0 months
DATE OF OFFENSE: 04/10/2000
DATE OF SENTENCE: 08/21/2003
CONVICTION TYPE: Plea

SENTENCE 5—ROSE MARIE FELT

HOMICIDE—MURDER, SECOND DEGREE
MINIMUM SENTENCE: 31 years 0 months 0 days
MAXIMUM SENTENCE: 70 years 0 months
DATE OF OFFENSE: 03/27/2000
DATE OF SENTENCE: 08/21/2003
CONVICTION TYPE: Plea

SENTENCES LISTED AS INACTIVE

SENTENCE 1—CYNTHIA SMITH

ASSAULT WITH INTENT TO DO GREAT BODILY HARM LESS
THAN MURDER

MINIMUM SENTENCE: 4 years 9 months 0 days
MAXIMUM SENTENCE: 10 years 0 months
DATE OF OFFENSE: 04/09/2000
DATE OF SENTENCE: 07/03/2001
CONVICTION TYPE: Plea
DISCHARGE DATE: 04/10/2010
DISCHARGE REASON:: Order Terminated, Continued on Additional Order(s)

SENTENCE 2—NATASHA OLEJNICZAK

ASSAULT WITH INTENT TO DO GREAT BODILY HARM LESS THAN MURDER
MINIMUM SENTENCE: 4 years 9 months 0 days
MAXIMUM SENTENCE: 10 years 0 months
DATE OF OFFENSE: 08/15/1999
DATE OF SENTENCE: 07/03/2001
CONVICTION TYPE: Nolo Contendere
DISCHARGE DATE: 04/10/2010
DISCHARGE REASON: Order Terminated, Continued on Additional Order(s)

ASSAULT WITH INTENT TO MURDER—WILHEMINA DRANE
Dismissed, 08/15/2000

ASSAULT WITH INTENT TO MURDER—DEVIN MARUS
ROBBERY—UNARMED—DEVIN MARUS
Dismissed as part of the plea bargain, 07/03/2001

In the years since he received his life sentences, Armstrong has bounced around a bit in the Michigan Department of Corrections system. He was in the Earnest C. Brooks Correctional Facility/West Shoreline Correctional Facility in Muskegon Heights, the Michigan Reformatory (RMI) in Ionia, and the Standish Maximum Correctional Facility, the last of which closed in 2009. As of this writing, he is at the G. Robert Cotton Correctional Facility in the Jackson, Michigan, prison system. He was classified as Level 5 for security when he was first incarcerated, until his case died down a bit (as he put it when I spoke with him), the publicity wore off, then he was downgraded to the less restrictive Level 2, which he is at now.

Besides the episode ("Psycho Sailor," season two, episode four) of *Very Bad Men* that aired on the ID channel, it was discussed in an episode of *History's Mysteries* on the History Channel, *Twisted Killers* ("The Dead Don't Say No," season one, episode two) on Oxygen, and *World's Most Evil Killers* (season eight, episode three) by the UK's Woodcut Media. The case has also been the subject of quite a few podcasts and blog posts.

Some believe the Port-to-Port Killer in season eight of *NCIS* was based on, or inspired by, Armstrong, though there are some big differences between that character and Armstrong. A closer match is a 2001 episode of *The District*, a crime drama based in Washington, DC, and starring Craig T. Nelson. In the season one episode "The D.C. Strangler," a sailor stationed aboard a US Navy ship kills several prostitutes in different parts of the country as he goes from port to port, including Norfolk, Virginia. He's a white guy in his twenties—and he has red hair as an added kicker. His M.O. is strangulation, though he does torture—the girls have bite marks and cigarette burns—and he even records some of the torture. Sometimes he dumps the body elsewhere, sometimes he leaves the girl where she is, such as in a motel room. He escalates his crimes right before he is caught, just like Armstrong and so many other killers. He is an active serviceman, however, not discharged. A major theme of the episode is the humanization of the victims despite their line of work, as emphasized through Nelson's lead character and a supporting character who took the opposing view that these were only throwaway women. The episode aired nine months after Armstrong's arrest made national news.

Decades later, even though Armstrong has multiple life sentences, Bonnie Jordan doesn't think it was enough. She wishes the other charges would not have been pled out. "They should've went ahead with them," she said. "I wouldn't care if they made it seem like, oh, gosh, he's never going to get out. Who cares?! He should have thought about that. He should have thought about getting out before he did all those crazy killings. Just out killing people. Like, I mean, not thinking twice about it. You know, okay, they be out there selling their bodies for their drug addictions. Okay. If you don't want to be buying from them, then don't buy. Just keep going. You know?"

It's a sentiment echoed by Rose Felt's one-time boyfriend Alex: "That's the sad thing, that they didn't kill the bastard. That's what they really need to do with him. He's a sick motherfucker. Excuse my language. He's a very sick man."

From another perspective, prosecutor Betty Walker prefers for Armstrong to still be alive and serving prison time, relieved that another jurisdiction outside of Detroit didn't pursue Armstrong for murder with a potential death penalty.

"I'm glad they didn't come get him," she said. "I never wanted to do anything with the death penalty. I am very, very strongly opposed to the death penalty. Even for these guys!"

THE UNKNOWN AND UNCONFIRMED

Once Armstrong was in custody in April 2000, he was singing like a bird, as the cliché goes. And soon, Detroit police realized they might have a bigger case on their hands than a few victims in Detroit. Armstrong speedily began making other confessions—confessions to killings while he was a sailor aboard the USS Nimitz, which was between 1993 and 1999. He skipped around in the timeframe as he remembered incidents across the country and globe, talking with Donald Johnson, James Hines, Everett Monroe, Ira Todd, and Gregory Geider of the Violent Crime Task Force. These confessions to other murders during the Navy period are presented here in the order in which he said they occurred, though they were not confessed to in this order (see the confession timeframe listing in the subchapter "The Horrors Revealed").

Beyond the confessions below and the Detroit crimes, Armstrong indicated to police that he had committed an additional three murders but needed more time to remember the details. He said those three occurred in Virginia. He also said he might be responsible for three murders in North Carolina.

There are conflicting reports of what would have been Armstrong's first kill. Police have suspected it was in North Carolina in 1992, shortly after he enlisted in the Navy but before he reported to the boat. Several days after his arrest in 2000, however, it was reported in the media that Armstrong told police it all began in North Carolina in 1991, before he graduated from high school, at the age of seventeen. There's even a month attached to that alleged incident in some reports: June. Police said they could not find an unsolved homicide in the area of his hometown that would match for the timeframe he gave. Then, on a blog post about the case where so many people who knew Armstrong have commented, there is a comment from an "Elizabeth" claiming to have been his teenage girlfriend. Several details in the comment match what is known about Armstrong, which we'll discuss in more detail later: that he tried to commit suicide as a teen, that the death of his baby brother in the crib had a deep effect on him, that at the time of his arrest he and his wife had a young son with another child on the way. Elizabeth claimed that Eric's first kill was in October 1989, just months after his suicide attempt, which followed her breaking up with him. Her comment gives no other details about this alleged first kill, or how she would know about it.

A story in the *New Bern Sun Journal* after Armstrong's arrest said the Craven County district attorney was looking at him as a possibility in the disappearance of a convenience store clerk in New Bern in the early 1990s. The female clerk of the store on Neuse Boulevard disappeared at Christmastime in 1990 or 1991, the DA was remembering, then her bones were later found in a nearby area, Bridgeton. Nothing came of it, however.

What follows are details from Armstrong's confessions to murders outside of Detroit. As many details as possible are included here, with the chance that these incidents did actually occur much like Armstrong described them. At the point where law enforcement stopped back in 2000, you can call this crowdsourcing. We are a much more connected world now than we were in the 1990s, after all.

WHITE FEMALE: SEATTLE, WASHINGTON

1993, probably mid-August

Armstrong said his first murder while in the Navy occurred not far from where the *USS Nimitz* was stationed in Bremerton, Washington, during his initial year on the ship.

He was quite detailed to Officers Johnson and Hines about his first time visiting Seattle: "I just started walking around because I had never been to a big city before. I caught a cab up to Capitol Hill, just looking around seeing what I can see, and this woman approached me. She offered to have sex with me for a couple hundred dollars. I kept telling her to leave me alone and she kept calling me a Navy boy. Then I started walking through an alley and she kept following me. I asked her to quit following me and she wouldn't so I hit her in the face twice. I pushed her against the wall and I started strangling her until she passed out. Then I raped her and I left and I went back to the ferry and then went back to the ship."

Armstrong described this woman as white and in her mid-twenties to early thirties, five-foot-eight and one hundred and thirty pounds, medium to slim build, and wearing stonewashed jeans. He said he removed her jeans when she passed out, placing them on the side of her, and he wore a condom as he raped her. He said she wasn't breathing. This happened behind a big green or brown dumpster, he said, which he then placed her inside. No one else was around. He remembered the time as about seven p.m.

"What color panties did she have on?" the officers asked.

"I don't remember the panties."

"What color shoes did she have on?" the officers pressed.

"White tennis shoes."

"Why did you rape her after you killed her?"

"Because that's the only way I could have got the pussy."

Armstrong said the woman had gone into the alley of her own free will, that he told her he had the money but really didn't. Then the details of the struggle seemed to change somewhat. The woman tried to flee, he said, and that's when he hit her. It caused her to bleed from the nose and mouth, he said. He got some of the blood on his hands.

"Why did you kill her?" police asked.

"Because she looked like my ex-fiancée a little bit."

Armstrong said the woman had made him angry: "The way she talked to me like I was retarded, because back then I had my accent real bad."

Johnson asked if there was anything else Armstrong wanted to add to this statement.

"I'm sorry for killing her and raping her."

BLACK MALE: SEATTLE, WASHINGTON

November 21, 1996

Armstrong's next confessed killing was also in Seattle, under seemingly similar circumstances, though this one appeared to have different motivation.

"I was walking down Pioneer Square," he told Officers Todd and Monroe, referring to a historic neighborhood in the city, "and this Black male just kept asking me for money. I kept walking and the Black male kept following me. I walked down the alley and found a pipe. I hit the Black male with the pipe across the shoulder, then across the head. He fell down so I just kept beating him with the pipe. I then ran back into one of the bars and had a beer."

Officers asked if the man was dead and Armstrong said he didn't know, that he didn't look back. He had been bleeding, however, in the head where he was hit, from his nose and mouth. Armstrong remembers this one as happening a couple days before his birthday. He wasn't absolutely sure about the year but believed it to be 1996.

"How did you feel when you were beating him?" officers asked.

"I got a rush. Just hitting somebody, just losing control was a little exciting to me."

"Why?"

"I never really attack—attacked—somebody like that. It was different."

"How did you feel afterwards?"

"Afraid."

Armstrong said he threw the pipe, which was steel and silver, a little heavy, and about two-and-a-half-feet long, into a green trash dumpster.

"How did it sound when you were crushing his skull with this metal pipe?" officers asked.

It sounded like something breaking, like bones breaking, he told them.

Blood from the victim splattered on him, he said, and he described the beating as "pretty bad."

Armstrong said he did not know the man's name, did not beat him because of his color, and did not have sex with him. The guy was not a hooker, as far as he knew. He said he also did not position his body in any way or take anything from him. The bar, he said, was right on the corner, not remembering the street but remembering that it was the very last bar on Pioneer Square. He told no one about the incident.

At first, during this series of confessions, Armstrong had thought this was his first kill. But then he remembered the female prostitute from 1993. So this man was the second person he ever killed, he told the officers.

"Do you like killing?" they asked.

"No."

"Why do you kill?"

"I like to be in control."

"Why do you like being in control?"

"Because my father was in control of everything."

More on this particular conversation later.

After this apparent November 1996 murder of the Seattle man, several others followed pretty quickly, as Armstrong described to police, all labeled in these statements as Asian females overseas. The first in the timeline Detroit police were trying to piece together was actually transgender, the file marked as number one for 1996/1997.

ASIAN FEMALE (TRANSGENDER): THAILAND

1996/1997

It was the end of 1996 or the beginning of 1997, Armstrong said, when he went to a bar in Thailand and took a hooker to his hotel room. When he saw her "standing up peeing" there in the room, he said, he made threats and "wanted 'it' to get out." He described the individual as a transvestite or transsexual, saying the person did indeed have a penis, and it "was bigger than mine."

Armstrong threw the hooker out the window. Then, he said, nothing happened. "Nobody investigated. They just picked up her body and left."

He described the prostitute as very small with black hair, a large Adam's apple, and wearing a blue or gray dress. He couldn't remember the name of the hotel but said it was "off the main drag" with a mall nearby. Though he couldn't remember the exact timeframe of the incident, he said the weather was hot, as it always is in Thailand. The *Nimitz* was in the bay of Thailand, a place called Pattaya Beach.

He told no one about the incident, and he did not have sex with or take anything from the prostitute.

"Which murder was this?" Todd and Hines asked.

Armstrong said it was the third.

"How many have you killed total?" they asked at that point, which was just after one-thirty p.m. on April 12, early on in this long confessional spree.

Nine, he replied.

"What do you do to most of your victims that's common?" they asked.

"I leave their legs spread open," he said, though this was not the case for the second and third non-Detroit killings he described, and perhaps not even for the first, though it would be a mode police would recognize in the Detroit murders.

Police asked why he left the legs this way. "Actually, I don't know. That's just the way I set them down."

This was the first international killing Armstrong confessed to and police asked him to start from the beginning—what year did all this start? He then listed off the first two killings described above, jumbling their order, as well as the ones that follow. Since this was earlier in the day on April 12, it was a key moment that gave police the cues to very carefully document each confession, in whatever order he was offering it, Mirandizing him completely before each statement. Lots of information was coming out of this perp. Armstrong maintained, during this particular statement, that he didn't want a lawyer and that he had not been threatened by police.

Are you sure there were no murders between 1993 and 1996? police double-checked.

"Yes, sir."

"Why?"

"I was very busy with the Navy. We had sea trials."

"Is this the truth?" they asserted.

"Yes."

This incident of the transgender prostitute, with the detail of the victim being thrown out the window, has often been recalled later by those discussing the details of the Armstrong case. One police officer who worked the Armstrong case had heard a rumor that this person was located and determined to have survived the attack. We may never know.

ASIAN FEMALE: THAILAND

1996/1997

It was only a day after the first murder in Thailand that Armstrong chose to kill there again, he told police. Again it was at a hotel near Pattaya Beach. This person was also a prostitute and he said he met her as she was walking the streets. He described her as a petite Asian female with long black hair, five-foot-six, one hundred and twenty pounds, wearing cutoff blue jeans, a T-shirt, and sandals.

"I had her follow me into my room," Armstrong told Todd, Geider, and Monroe. "I paid her thirty dollars." As if he had learned from the experience the day before, he added that she took off all of her clothes first, then he took off his own clothes.

He said they had straight sex in the bed of his hotel room, which was registered in his name. This lasted about a half hour before he strangled her with his "hands only." It was a matter-of-fact explanation this time, no indication of triggers or emotion.

After Armstrong killed her, he said, he went down to the hotel desk and got himself another room, again in his name, and left the body of the woman up in the first room where it was.

Police asked if he got his money back. It was unclear if that was from the first room at the hotel or from the victim herself. Either way, the answer was no. And he did not have sex with the woman after she died, Armstrong said.

Years later, it was this particular confession that stood out for Gregory Geider of the Violent Crime Task Force, who assisted with the statements. "I found it particularly chilling that he would leave the women's body in one room and casually get another room in the same establishment."

ASIAN FEMALE: SINGAPORE, SOUTHEAST ASIA

March 1997

Armstrong estimated the timeframe of this next incident as March 1997. In Singapore, he was approached by this woman, who asked if he wanted to have sex.

"She took me back to her apartment down on Orchard Street," he told Officers Todd, Geider, and Monroe. "We get to her apartment and she charges me fifty bucks. I paid her. She took all her clothing off. I took all my clothing off and we got into her bed. We (had) straight sex and then I killed her."

Again, Armstrong said, he strangled her with his bare hands. He then left the apartment, with the woman still on the bed, and did not tell anyone about the incident. He didn't take anything from the woman, did not have sex with the woman's body after he killed her, and did not position the body, he said.

"How long did it take her to die?" police asked.

About ten minutes, he replied.

There was no description for this female included in the confession other than that she was Asian.

"Why do you kill hookers?" officers asked.

"I dislike them."

"Why?"

"I don't know why."

ASIAN FEMALE: HONG KONG

Around March 31, 1997

The next victim was in Hong Kong, Armstrong said, and he recalled it being March 30 to April 3, 1997, that the *Nimitz* was docked there (which was incorrect according to *Nimitz* records). On the first night the ship was there, he went to shore with his then fiancée Katie. The next night, he went alone.

"I went to a bar where I met a girl," he told Todd and Geider. "The girls in the bar were prostitutes. She took me to a room in the hotel next to the bar." This was on a strip of bars and hotels just a block or two from the boat landing, he said.

He described this female as "real short," five-foot-six and one hundred pounds, with long black hair. She was in her late thirties and wearing a red skirt with a white top. She was Asian.

When they got to the hotel room, she asked Armstrong to take a shower. When he got out of the shower, she was going through his wallet, a wad of his money in her hand. She went for the door, he said, and he grabbed her from behind by the throat and put her face down on the floor. At that, point he choked her with his hands, his confession says.

"How long did you choke her?" police asked.

"For about ten minutes and then I realized I was choking her and I left."

"Why did you stop choking her?"

"I realized I was choking her?" as if he was asking the question himself.

"Was she dead at that point?"

"I don't know. I could not see if she was breathing. I assumed she was dead."

"Why did you assume she was dead?"

"She was not moving."

"What did you do then?"

"I ran. I went back to the ship."

When he got back to the ship, he took another shower. He had retrieved the money the woman had taken out of his wallet, he said. He did not remove any of her clothing, and he did not tell anyone what had happened. When police asked if he had been afraid that something like this might happen when he left the ship, he said yes.

In his own hand, at the end of the printed confession, is this note from Armstrong.

I'm sorry for killing this female. I felt very angry that she would steal my money. If I had to tell her family member that I killed her, I would say that I was very sorry, but she shouldn't have taken my money. And I hope that they could forgive me.

ASIAN FEMALE: HONG KONG

Around April 2, 1997

Just a couple nights later in Hong Kong, Armstrong killed again, he told police.

"I went down the road from the last bar. I went on the second road that have *[sic]* all the bars. I'm not familiar with the streets over there."

Monroe, Geider, and Todd coaxed him to continue.

"I saw her walking. She walked up to me and grabbed my hand. She told me to walk with her. She asked for thirty bucks American. We had straight sex."

Armstrong described this female as Asian, about five-foot-six, one hundred and twenty pounds, with shoulder-length black hair. He thought she was wearing black pants and a blue short-sleeved shirt but wasn't sure.

The woman took him to "her place, that was right around the corner next to a bar." They had sex in her bed, then he choked and strangled her to death, he said. Armstrong said he left her lying in her bed, naked from the waist down. He did not position her body in any way.

"Did she feel cold?" officers asked.

"I didn't touch her after she was dead."

Again, the officers went over the typical questions, asking if he had been denied food or drink or threatened in any way. Armstrong continued to be very cooperative. He said he'd had sleep as well.

At the end of this confession, however, after telling officers he killed two people in Hong Kong, Armstrong estimated the total number of people he'd killed as fifteen, rather than the nine he gave earlier. This was after around two a.m. on April 13.

WHITE FEMALE: WAIKIKI / HONOLULU, HAWAII

May 1997

The next few incidents would be back in the United States and 1997 seemed to be a very active year for Armstrong.

The *Nimitz* was stationed at Pearl Harbor in May, he said. He and Katie left the ship and took a bus to the area of Waikiki in Honolulu. He told police he went to a hotel called the Outrigger.

Armstrong explained the incident to police this way: "Me and my wife got a hotel room. We got into an argument. She left the room. Me and a buddy of mine went and got two hookers. We had sex with them. The next night, I went out alone and I got the same hooker from the night before. I went to the hooker's apartment and had sex with her on her couch."

Todd and Monroe asked what color the couch was and he said black.

After they had sex, Armstrong said, he strangled the woman. At one point he used one of the woman's own stockings to strangle her. He told police, when asked, that the stockings were tan.

It took about twenty minutes for this woman to die. He choked her for a long time, he said. "I was out of control." At first, he said, he choked her with his hands until she passed out. Then he put the stocking around her neck. Police asked if he tied any special kind of knot and he said no.

"Did she fight you off?" they asked Armstrong.

"Yes."

"Did she scratch you?"

"No."

"Did she beg for her life?"

"No."

"What was going through your head while you were killing this hooker?"

"Getting back at my wife." Reminiscent of prosecutor Elizabeth Walker's impression in the courtroom.

He told police he left the woman face up on the floor of her apartment. They'd had sex twice but, he told police, he did nothing with the body after he killed her. Armstrong had used condoms for this encounter and flushed them down the toilet.

At that point, Armstrong said this was his only killing in Hawaii, though a few minutes later, he remembered another victim. Another confession would follow. He said he left Hawaii a couple days later. The *Nimitz* was in Hawaii for four days as he recalled.

He described this first victim as blond, five-foot-seven, "real skinny," a white female in her early thirties, with an accent. She wasn't from Hawaii, he said; her accent sounded German.

Police asked if he had planned on choking her. "No, but I was afraid that it might happen," he admitted.

He was never questioned by police in Hawaii at the time about this murder, he said, just like all the preceding killings. But, he told the Detroit officers, he did want to get caught, at least in some way. "So I could get help," he explained, though he said he didn't do anything specific to get caught.

Armstrong was a little confused about details toward the end of this confession. He remembered his other Hawaii victim, a redhead killed that next night, but then he remembered the Hong Kong victim who tried to take his money as happening after these Hawaii incidents, in April 1997. Perhaps it was the way the question was worded: "After the redhead, did you kill anyone else in 1997?" He replied yes, in Hong Kong. Perhaps he was not meaning the Hong Kong killing literally happened after Hawaii, but that he was going to confess it after, which he did (Hong Kong eleven-fifty p.m. versus this Hawaii confession at nine-forty-eight p.m.). Or the timeframes of these killings got a little jumbled and perhaps when he said these Hawaii killings happened in May, he really meant March. We can see Armstrong did get dates and times at least a bit confused because in this confession he at first said Katie was his wife-to-be, then he had the "to be" struck from the statement, indicating they were married at the time. He told Dearborn Heights police during his questioning there that he and Katie married in fall 1998.

At any rate, many of the dates of these non-Detroit confessions don't quite mesh with the schedule for the *Nimitz* provided by the Navy to investigators, a chart which follows these confessional details. For one thing, you'll see that for the months in 1997 when Armstrong said a lot of these Asian killings occurred, the *Nimitz* was in the United States.

WHITE FEMALE: WAIKIKI / HONOLULU, HAWAII

May 1997

For the other incident in Hawaii, occurring the next night, Armstrong told Monroe and Todd that the victim was a redhead about five-foot-six and one hundred and twenty pounds. She was wearing a short black skirt, white top, and sandals. He met her outside near a mall he couldn't remember the name of at Waikiki Beach.

"We walk back to her place," he said. "She lived around the corner. I asked her how much she wanted; she said one hundred and fifty bucks. That was for straight sex. We went into her place, and I gave her the one hundred and fifty bucks. We had sex. I used a condom. All I know is that I started strangling her after the sex." Once he had choked her, he ran out of the apartment. "I went back to my hotel and got into the shower."

He used only his hands for this strangulation, he said, and he left her face down in the bedroom. He took nothing from the apartment—not even the money he paid her, since he didn't know what she did with it when she disappeared into the bedroom when they first got there.

Police asked if he closed the door behind him when he left. He said yes. Was it locked? "I don't know; I didn't check it." He did not return to the apartment and he didn't know when the woman was ever discovered. As with the other incidents, he told no one about this.

"How did you feel about this murder?" he was asked.

"Upset after I left the apartment."

"How did you feel during the murder?"

"I really didn't feel anything."

Police asked if during his shower at the hotel, he thought about this girl.

Yes, he said.

What were his thoughts?

"I started crying. I was very upset that I had did it [sic]. That I was sorry that I had did it."

If you were so sorry, they wondered, why didn't you confess it to police there?

"I was too scared to."

"What were you scared of?"

"Going to prison?" Again with a question mark.

He said the *Nimitz* left the port at eight the next morning with him on it.

WHITE FEMALE: NEWPORT NEWS/NORFOLK, VIRGINIA

July or August 1998

The *Nimitz* arrived in the dock at Norfolk on the first of March 1998, and at this point, Armstrong and his wife settled in for a longer stay, getting an apartment nearby. It was here that this confessed killer remained for many months before he was discharged from the Navy, and it was here he said he encountered his last victim before heading to Michigan.

Armstrong described this female as white, five-foot-six or -seven, one hundred and forty pounds, wearing blue jeans and a T-shirt. It was summertime in Virginia in 1998, he said, either July or August.

They parked at some road off Jefferson Avenue, he told Johnson, Todd, and Hines. "We had straight sex. I gave her fifty dollars. I dropped her off, then called the police." Why, he was asked. "I called my wife and told her I got robbed because the fifty dollars was supposed to go to something for my son."

His son, however, would not be born until the following year, and Armstrong and his wife would not be married until fall 1998. The only explanation for this anomaly would be, again, a jumbling of timeframes on his part or perhaps the idea that he and Katie were already planning their family at that point. In August, they likely knew Katie was pregnant.

Though this incident is late in the timeframe of his confessed killings while in the Navy, it was early in the confession period in Detroit, noon on April 12, 2000. When asked if he killed this woman, Armstrong at first said *yes*, then corrected it to *no*, initialing that correction in the paper copy of the statement. He did not kill the woman or even hear later that she was dead, he said.

He remembered her name starting with an *S*, like Susan or maybe Susie. Before he blacked out, Armstrong said, his hands were on her waist in his Jeep and he started crying. Why was he crying? "Because I was cheating on my wife."

Next, he said, he threw the woman out of his Jeep. "I kicked her out."

"Then what happened?" police pressed.

He pulled away and "felt a little bump."

"On which side of the vehicle did you feel it?"

"On the right side." The victim was behind the right rear tire, he said.

"Did you hear any hollering and screaming?"

"Before I left and when I was driving away."

Armstrong said he threw the condom he had used into the toilet back aboard the *Nimitz*. Again, a jumbling—why was he driving what he referred to as his Jeep, implying the new 1998 Jeep Wrangler plated in North Carolina that he and Katie would later take to Michigan—if he was going right back to the boat? Or did he, stranger yet, squirrel away the condom for a while to dispose of later on the boat?

He said the encounter with this prostitute occurred at about ten p.m. Armstrong's whole statement for this one is confusing in other regards. It is repetitive but not very consistent, if that makes sense. At first, he seemed to say he just had sex with her, dropped her off, then left. Then a few questions later, he said he had his hands around her waist, was crying, blacked out, then threw her out of the Jeep and hit her with the car as he was leaving. A few questions later, he elaborated more on what happened inside the Jeep, only then mentioning the strangulation.

During this confession Armstrong gave an important detail, also included in his confession to assaulting Cynthia Smith in Detroit. This detail would pop up in court testimony and even be reported in the media, and it accompanied the other contradicting or at least confusing details about just how the woman got out of the Jeep.

"I had sex with her, then I saw my father's face on her, then I started strangling her, then I stopped. I took her out of the Jeep. I had to take her out because she was limp at that time and I put her on the ground, but before I drove off, she started to move and sounded like she was coughing. She was laying on her back with her legs closed."

"Why did you strangle her?" the officers asked.

"Because I saw my father's face."

And then to confirm, police asked, "Eric, did you hit her with your Jeep?"

"Yes, I put her on the ground and the next thing I know was I felt a bump."

"Did you put her behind your Jeep?"

"No, I put her to the side and I had to back out and that is how I hit her."

After this, he said he drove off and had a beer at "one of the taverns." Again, perhaps conflicting what he said earlier—he did not go back to the boat and throw away the condom, at least not right then.

At this point, when police asked why he killed this woman, he said, "I didn't mean to; it was an accident."

This Virginia account is interesting for a variety of reasons. But one thing different about the incident is that Armstrong had been with this prostitute before. With the exception of the woman in Hawaii he said he was with two nights in a row, this really hadn't happened, where he picked up the same prostitute another time. He told police he had been with this Virginia victim a couple of times before, but he said there was nothing different about this particular time when she ended up dead.

"Why are you telling me about this incident now?" one of the Detroit officers asked, since he said he had told no one about it up to this point.

"Because it's been on my mind every [sic] since, and I felt guilty about it."

At the end of this confession, when asked if there was anything else he wanted to add, Armstrong said, "That I'm sorry for killing her, I didn't mean to, I need some help." He also added that thought in his own handwriting at the bottom of the paper copy of the statement.

This last incident during Armstrong's naval years was the only one of these non-Detroit confessions that investigators were able to pair to a real murder.

THE INVESTIGATION LOOKS OUTWARD

The Friday after Armstrong's arrest, April 14, 2000, officials with the Naval Criminal Investigative Service, the primary law enforcement agency of the US Department of the Navy, arrived on the scene. They began to piece together the details Armstrong had offered in his string of confessions to murders around the country and world. Armstrong's confessions were holding some weight with law enforcement because the details from the Detroit confessions matched up pretty well with how the bodies were found. The Violent Crime Task Force had already received the itinerary of the *USS Nimitz* for Armstrong's time aboard via fax and they had requested a copy of his entire personnel package from the US Navy. Special agents from the Detroit office of the FBI also engaged in the investigation and they conducted their own interviews with Armstrong.

In that busy week after Armstrong's arrest, calls were coming in to DPD from law enforcement all over the country, wanting more information.

Some local law enforcement agencies were adopting a wait-and-see approach. "We have to get some facts of when this guy was here before we start opening files," a spokesman for the Seattle Police Department told the media. "Just because he's saying it, it doesn't mean that's the case."

A week or two later, a detective with the Seattle force told the media, "We haven't found anything yet that matches what he said. Eventually, after we get a timeline, we will put together what we think are some cases and then interview him."

Detroit police completed a check of Armstrong's activities and were contacting officials at places where he claimed to have killed, *The Detroit News* reported on Tuesday, April 18. "His timeline is off on some things," Assistant Chief Marvin Winkler was quoted. "It may be that he didn't remember right or something like that. Some things jibe and some things don't. It will take time to check this out."

For the alleged first kill in North Carolina, authorities were rather quick to dismiss. "All of our prostitute murders have been solved," said one from the Onslow County

Sheriff's Department, the next county over from New Bern. A few other nearby counties also reported no similar unsolved crimes.

The keen among you may say, wait—did Armstrong actually say that first murder in North Carolina was a prostitute? You certainly have to wonder that. There was the convenience store clerk mentioned in the New Bern newspaper for instance. It's possible that first crossing of the line wasn't a prostitute. Who knows. Can we be sure everything was checked thoroughly? Maybe the body from whatever was his first kill was never found. Or perhaps there had been such advanced decomposition that it became only skeletal remains and no identification or evidence of homicide could be determined.

So many details to sift through. So many angles to consider. For the DPD, it was important to continue to pay attention to the investigation of the non-Detroit confessions, to assist as necessary. To be intently engaged. This perp had confessed to the crimes—a lot of crimes—but a batch of confessions does not a case make.

"While none of this had any bearing on what we needed to establish in Wayne County courts," Gerald Cliff of the VCTF explained, "it was still pertinent in consideration of a number of issues such as the potential for bail, the likelihood that other jurisdictions might want to bring him up on charges, that extradition might play into the process, etc. Validation of all this information pertaining to the murders he committed in Detroit was part and parcel to his being so forthcoming with more and more information. The more we were able to learn and validate with evidence or witnesses, the more likely the perpetrator is to realize we have enough on them that lying or trying to be deceptive is a waste of effort and time. Again, this requires a speedy and efficient collection of accurate information. If the perpetrator begins to suspect that the interviewing detective doesn't know what they did, or is just exploring (fishing) for information, the suspect may feel free to try to deceive, minimize and deny, thereby confusing the facts enough to cast doubt on his guilt. We have to have enough information to convince them that we literally 'know everything' and we are just trying to get their side, confirm a few minor details, etc. This takes a massive amount of very quick yet skillful detective work."

In late April 2000, though, as investigators were still knee deep in the details, Armstrong's lawyer was on the case, nudging things in the other direction.

"That is probably part of his persona if he, in fact, made these up," Robert Mitchell said of the varied non-Detroit confessions, having just requested a delay in Armstrong's preliminary hearing to do a competency evaluation. "I can tell you that the trail is cold. There is nothing there at all."

The March 2001 story on the case by Kevin Gray in *Details* magazine said that during the investigation, an FBI agent learned that Armstrong returned to the *Nimitz* late one night in Thailand with his face cut up and bleeding. A senior officer filed a report on it, the magazine said.

Below is the list of port calls for the *USS Nimitz* during Armstrong's time in the Navy, as faxed to Detroit police during the investigation. The *Nimitz* was homeported in Bremerton, Washington, before making a WestPac (West Pacific) deployment, then coming to Norfolk, Virginia, for an overhaul shortly before Armstrong's discharge.

1993

February 4	North Island, California
February 26—March 2	Hong Kong
March 6-10	Singapore
April 10-14	Mina Jebel Ali, U.A.E.
May 8-12	Mina Jebel Ali, U.A.E.
June 6-11	Mina Jebel Ali, U.A.E.

July 1-7	Pattaya Beach, Thailand
July 20-22	Pearl Harbor, Hawaii
July 29	North Island, California
August 1—September 20 Bremerton, Washington	Puget Sound Naval Shipyard,
September 26-29	Indian Island, California
October 21-28	North Island, California
(Indian Island on some reports)	
November 6-28 Bremerton, Washington	Puget Sound Naval Shipyard,
December 2	North Island, California
December 7	North Island, California
Dec 12, 1993—Jan 28, 1995 Bremerton, Washington	Puget Sound Naval Shipyard,

1995

February 2-17 Bremerton, Washington	Puget Sound Naval Shipyard,
February 21—March 9 Bremerton, Washington	Puget Sound Naval Shipyard,
April 3-28 Bremerton, Washington	Puget Sound Naval Shipyard,
May 11-21, 1995 Bremerton, Washington	Puget Sound Naval Shipyard,
June 12-15, 1995	Point Loma, California
December 21-25, 1995	Hong Kong
Dec30, 1996—Jan 3, 1996	Singapore

1996

February 3-6	Mina Jebel Ali, U.A.E.
February 24-27	Mina Jebel Ali, U.A.E.
April 18-24	Pattaya Beach, Thailand
May 7-10	Pearl Harbor, Hawaii
May 16	North Island, California
May 20, 1996—Jan21, 1997 Bremerton, Washington	Puget Sound Naval Shipyard,

1997

January 23-24	Port Hadlock, Washington
January 30-31	North Island, California
February 15-17	North Island, California
March 5—April 10 Bremerton, Washington	Puget Sound Naval Shipyard,
May 9-12	North Island, California
May 25—June 17 Bremerton, Washington	Puget Sound Naval Shipyard,
July 4-13	North Island, California
July 30—August 31	North Island, California
September 3-5	San Diego, California
September 21-22	Yokosuka, Japan
September 28—October 1	Hong Kong
November 26—December 3	Mina Jebel Ali, U.A.E.
Dec 27, 1997—Jan 1, 1998	Mina Jebel Ali, U.A.E.

1998

January 10-14	Mina Jebel Ali, U.A.E.

| Jan 30—Feb 3 | Mina Jebel Ali, U.A.E. |
| March 1 | Norfolk, Virginia |

NCIS records show these leave periods for Armstrong:

1993

December 13-27

1994

February 13-27

December 16-26

1996/1997

August 3, 1996

December 29, 1996—January 9, 1997

May 27—June 3, 1997

1998

March 16-30

April 21—May 1

November 18

December 24, 1998—January 3, 1999

1999

January 14-18

January 23-27

February 3-14

April 23-30, then discharged on April 30

Strangely enough, though Armstrong was said to have gotten married in Michigan in September 1998, there is no leave noted for that time period. The only fall 1998 leave was just one day, November 18. It's possible Eric and Katie actually married in the spring 1998 leave period or the records erred.

VIRGINIA POSSIBILITY: LINETTE HILLIG

At around seven a.m. on March 5, 1998, a cleaning lady spotted a woman's body in a parking lot behind a building on East Little Creek Road in Norfolk, Virginia. Norfolk police responded to the call, generating a report at 7:21 a.m. The woman was identified by her fingerprints as Linette Ann Hillig, a white female, age thirty-four. The building where she was found held a bingo parlor at the time but in more recent years has been a thrift store. A manager at the thrift store, when reached via phone for this book, said that the thirty-two thousand-square-foot building on three acres has been a few things over the years—including a school— and bordered a neighborhood that was pretty sketchy back then. The building was dark, then, too—not too many lights at night. Just the kind of environment for Armstrong's M.O. of engaging a prostitute, then leaving her. The *Nimitz* had arrived in Norfolk just a few days before Linette's murder.

Linette, purported to be working as a prostitute in the Ocean View area of Norfolk, had been last seen at 10th Bay and East Ocean View Avenue in the early-morning hours of March 5, police records said. Her address was listed as an apartment on East Ocean View Ave.

Beyond the case files, however, Linette was so much more to those who knew her. And like most of the other women in our story, her start in life was what anyone would call normal. Good, even.

Born in October 1963 and raised in Fairport, a city not far from Rochester in the western half of the state of New

York, Linette had two older twin sisters, two parents who loved her, and a stable home.

"She was an incredibly happy baby," said Linette's sister, Kathleen Fitzmaurice-Ward, by phone in 2020. She is one of the twins and three years older than Linette. "My mother having given birth to twins, when Linette was born, she was such a good baby that my mother thought something was wrong with her and took her to the doctor's office, because she was just a happy baby. And she was always very happy, growing up."

And as far as the dynamics in this family: "Linette and I were the closest," Kathleen said. "My sister Doreen wanted to go the mommy route and that was pretty evident early on. And Linette and I were a little more like my dad, where we would challenge things. We liked to get into mischief and that sort of thing." But Linette was "always extremely good-natured. Her personality was always a sunny personality."

Kathleen said, "She was my parents' baby, and I know that you're not supposed to favor children, but I would have to say that my mom's favorites were Linette and Doreen, and my dad favored Linette and myself. He used to call her Linny Bell all the time, so she had a special place in his heart."

Growing up, the family belonged to various clubs, like golf clubs and swimming clubs, spending summers in those activities in their area of New York. Linette swam on a country club swim team. She was a great swimmer, her sister said. She played tennis. "She was just a normal kid, you know? Just a very normal child."

The neighborhood where these girls grew up was very typical. "You'd play tag and softball in somebody's yard because the yards were big. You know, half-acre yards. We'd go pool-hopping, and put dog poop in bags and light it on fire, and the neighbors would come out and step on it." Kathleen laughed. "So we had a blast. Our childhood was great. Loving parents and they stayed together, and we didn't come from a split family. Very normal family. We were middle class. I mean, we had a good upbringing. We were able to afford to go to a country club. My mother was a stay-at-home mom. We were fortunate. Dad provided well for us and we had everything we could need."

But life was not without its rough spots for Linette.

"She struggled a little bit in school," Kathleen said. "She had a bad experience with a couple of teachers when she was young, who were very cruel to her. And that kind of set her along a path of not feeling very confident about herself. So she started losing weight and became anorexic, prior to the Karen Carpenter issues and news that had come out about her. So kind of an unknown thing, but it was one thing that she had control over."

Though she didn't have a lot of close friends in school, people still loved her. She could light up a room, her sister attested. But growing up, things started to change for Linette when she became anorexic. "But that didn't change her personality. We know now that it was a control thing. And they really just didn't know how to treat it at that point in time and thought that my parents were starving her and things like that."

Linette worked through it, made progress to get past it, taking jobs here and there, such as at a grocery store or a drugstore. At one point she lived with Kathleen at her apartment in an old historic building in Rochester, New York. And here is where Kathleen saw her sister's giving side on a daily basis.

"Linette had a tendency as we were growing up to always root for the underdog. And when she lived with me—and she did live with me for a while—I would come home and Linette would be feeding the homeless in my penthouse apartment. It was a 1920s building. It was a grand old building. And there were a lot of people that had lived there from the '30s and '40s, and were elderly. And I would find Linette cleaning for them, or we would cook—Linette liked to cook all the time—and she would cook a twenty-four-pound turkey, and the next day it would be gone because she would be feeding the elderly. That was just who she was. I mean, that was her in a nutshell. She liked to give to people. And that never changed, from day one. She would always take the smaller piece of candy if she were sharing with a friend. That's just who she was."

In Florida, Linette met a man named Jeff, who was in the Navy. He and Linette went on to get married. They then had a little girl, in the mid-'80s, naming her Sarah, and this event changed Linette's life dramatically.

"Sarah was her world. She loved being a mother."

But for this young couple, it was a bumpy road. "Jeff and Linette both had issues with alcohol," Kathleen said.

The pair went to Victor, New York, where Linette's parents were living at the time, and Sarah stayed with the family while Jeff and Linette sought addiction treatment. Then Sarah went to live with Jeff's side of the family in another state. Jeff then shipped out for Desert Storm.

And then, Kathleen said, there was cheating involved in the marriage, and that was the end for the pair. Jeff went to Tennessee, taking his little girl with him, but Linette did not know where they were. Losing contact with her child, just five years old at the time, was very difficult. "That really turned Linette upside down and that's when she started smoking marijuana and drinking probably more than she had been. And she wanted to die. Just wanted to die. Every time we would speak and it was very often, it was all about Sarah and finding Sarah. She wanted to find Sarah."

It was a heartbreak Linette never recovered from. "It destroyed her," Kathleen said. "It destroyed her. That was the downward spiral. You know, growing up, happy, happy-go-lucky. And she was still a happy person. But this actually broke her. Broke her. When she died, the only thing she had in her wallet were photos of the family and a prayer card. At least that's all we received. No license, nothing like that. And Linette was very faithful. We were raised Catholic. And she believed in God. And that was just part of our upbringing. So she always gave things over to God and God to help guide her. And she was misguided in some ways. Men were very attracted to her. So were women. She was just outgoing and friendly. No pretentions. She wasn't pretentious. She was approachable. And I think that's what got her into trouble. Linette trusted too much. She trusted everybody."

Linette at her family's home in Fairport, New York. Image courtesy of the family.

It was determined from Linette's autopsy, a case summary noted, that she died from being struck by a car and the bloodstains at the scene told the tale.

The lot where Linette was found, her apartment, and the area where she was last seen are all just a few miles to the east of the Norfolk Naval Station and piers.

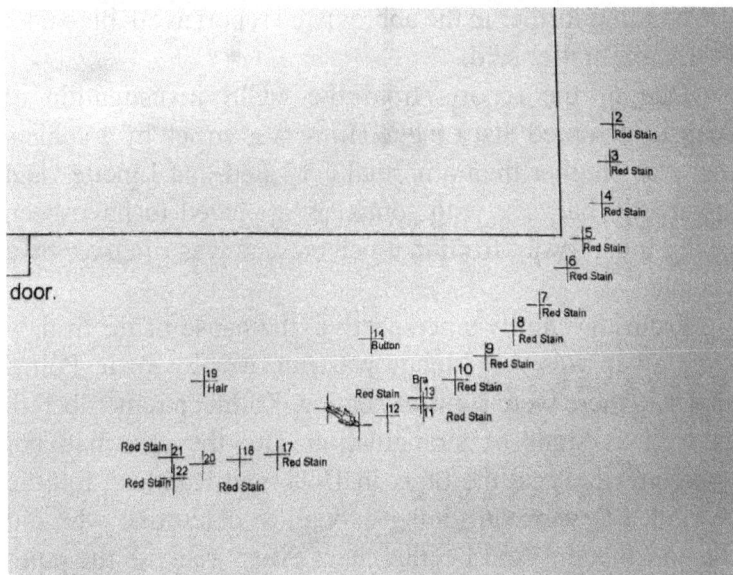

"I put her to the side and I had to back out and that is how I hit her," Armstrong said in his Virginia confession. The police sketch shows the bloodstains on the parking lot where Linette Hillig's body was found, with the rectangle representing the building. Hair, a bra, a barrette and a white button also were part of the physical evidence processed from the scene. Image: DPD files / Norfolk PD files.

A couple decades after the incident, Norfolk police could not release any other details under the Freedom of Information Act (FOIA) besides the fact that the police report stated Linette's death was from an undetermined cause, and that the case became inactive and remains unsolved. A call to Virginia's Office of the Chief Medical Examiner, Tidewater District produced the detail that Linette's death was determined a homicide due to "severe, acute, blunt force head, chest and abdominal trauma." Any signs of strangulation, I asked, and was it determined for sure she was run over by a vehicle?

Nothing further in the abbreviated report available under FOIA, the staffer said.

One of the reports from the NCIS investigation of Armstrong noted that Linette Hillig was struck by a vehicle that was "higher than a normal car," and that Linette "had apparently had sex with someone, appeared to have been trying to get away from that person, and was run over by a vehicle."

From the family's perspective, the cause of death they were given was that Linette was run over by a car. Police also said there were signs of beating, Kathleen remembered, as well as signs of strangulation. But the case had not gone anywhere, at the time, in 1998, and Kathleen felt the Norfolk PD were not doing enough to determine who did this to Linette. "And I called them every week, to the point where they would no longer take my calls."

In fact, she had a very bad experience with one particular officer. "He said, 'We don't waste our time on prostitutes. Our time is much better spent …' And he came right out and said, 'These are nothing people. Nobody cares about them.' And he got frustrated with me and said things I'm sure he didn't mean to say."

Linette's murder didn't occur in the summer timeframe Armstrong remembered for his Virginia confession, but it was just three or four days after the *Nimitz* arrived in Norfolk after a six-month deployment that had been sidetracked to the Arabian Gulf to support UN initiatives, a spokesperson from the Norfolk Police Department told *The Detroit News* in 2000. And if it was his dark bluish-gray 1998 Jeep Wrangler that Armstrong was referring to in his Virginia confession, a vehicle that would sit "higher" than a standard car, the assumption here would be that as soon as the *Nimitz* docked in Virginia on March 1, 1998, and Eric and Katie were aware they'd be staying in the area for a while and went out to rent an apartment, they also right away purchased the car, brand-new. And for whatever reason, Armstrong had it plated in his home state. Perhaps they took a quick trip there to purchase the car and plate it, then returned to Virginia by March 4. Maybe he didn't plate it until the second half of March, when he had a leave period and could have made a trip home. A lot of speculation, of course, but it is possible. Or perhaps it was another vehicle Armstrong was driving that night. Maybe a borrowed vehicle or even a rental. We know Armstrong did jumble details of that Virginia confession, such as the timeframe in relation to when his son was born.

When DPD searched the Jeep Wrangler in 2000, among the items found were the Jeep's manual with a thirty-day temporary receipt, no date noted in the DPD report, plus a business card from a car dealership in New Bern. So this would indicate the Jeep was purchased in North Carolina, not Virginia. There was also a North Carolina taxpayer receipt for the vehicle, dated June 10, 1999. So either he originally bought and plated it in that timeframe, summer 1999, right before moving to Michigan, or he had already owned it a year and just paid the yearly plate fees then. A call to the dealership in New Bern, now doing business under a different name, could produce no sales records dating back that far, but one shipmate of Armstrong did remember that he owned the Jeep as of late 1998, confirming that he bought it that year and not the next.

And certainly, to determine if Armstrong killed Linette, DNA evidence would be key. Armstrong's DNA would have to be matched with any DNA that might have been found at the scene in Norfolk. There is no indication in the police reports that DNA samples were taken at the scene, though one would assume a rape kit was done. On the other side, Linette's DNA would have to be found on that Jeep.

What became of the Jeep? Unclear.

DPD cops who worked the case said it would have been towed to a yard, kept there until the case was fully resolved and every appeal exhausted, then there would be an attempt to return it to the family. A call to the company that towed and stored the vehicle in 2000 found no records of it by VIN. So many years later, it's doubtful the vehicle still exists. And it would have gone through a few car washes over the years, for sure.

Whatever the case, when Armstrong was arrested and began making all of his confessions, and other jurisdictions were contacted, Linette's name became associated with his case. Police contacted Kathleen's family to tell them about Armstrong. And the family felt a certain amount of relief.

For Kathleen, who had been brought to her knees sobbing upon first learning of her sister's death, it was another measure of heartbreak amid the relief and she then had the chore of informing her father about Armstrong. The father who had been so close to his baby girl. The father who had actually had a sort of premonition about Linette years earlier and who so badly needed closure.

"My father, who was very intuitive—I don't know how but he had told me on a number of occasions that Linette was going to die an early death. I kind of have that level of perception myself. And that's just what he thought, partly because she liked to go out and party and drink. When we were, I guess, drinking age, we would go out and dance. And we would have drinks. It was nothing really excessive. But just to have fun. But I don't know why he felt that. But he did say it."

Linette's death marked only the second time Kathleen had ever seen her father, whom she described as a stoic Roman Catholic, cry. "When she passed away, when we were sitting down with Father Joe, my dad was at the head of the table, and he said, 'Now I know what it's like to die of a broken heart.'"

And when Armstrong was arrested and Kathleen told her father the news: "My father had asked if he had been arrested for Linette's murder, and I said no, he had admitted it. And he kind of took that at face value. I'm sure he did research; that was just my dad. And I'm sure he kept up with it until the day he died. I remember him sitting in my living room when he came to visit—my mom and dad came to visit me after Linette's passing. It had to be a year later. And I saw him just kind of staring off into space. I knew what he was thinking. I knew exactly what he was thinking. He lost his girl. He used to call us the girls: 'C'mon, girls!' You know, he had a female dog, he had his wife, and us three girls. And it was like, 'C'mon, girls!' You know? We were close growing up."

Linette's name is listed, along with the five Detroit women, as one of Armstrong's victims in an FBI memo dated April 13, 2000. She's also included in DPD files. And in Kevin Gray's 2001 story on the case for *Details* magazine, an FBI agent speaking on condition of anonymity said that Virginia law enforcement was preparing to file charges against Armstrong.

It was noted in NCIS case files at the time that Norfolk police had another unsolved homicide of a prostitute, this one in April 1999, that could fit the timeframe for when Armstrong lived there, as he was honorably discharged from the Navy on the last day of April that year. This other case involved a Black female strangled and left in a Norfolk residence. The Newport News and Hampton police departments were also queried but did not find any viable unsolved homicides. The Virginia Beach police department did have one unsolved death of a suspected prostitute but from 1991—a female found in a green duffle bag near the Marine Science Museum.

But that's about as far as it went. An unofficial answer to a case that's still officially showing as unsolved. Linette's family accepted Armstrong as the probable murderer. Years later, Sarah posted on an online message board that Armstrong killed her mother. There are parts of her childhood she doesn't remember clearly, and certainly parts she doesn't understand. But she does want to know the truth about her mother's killer. She does want to know for sure who committed this act.

"I know that she loved me," Sarah said via phone for this book, "and I know that losing me was devastating."

Beyond the fact that Linette's case best fits Armstrong's Virginia confession, especially since she was struck by a car, this particular confession proves interesting in another way: It may have been a motivating factor for Armstrong to recant all of these non-Detroit confessions (and all confessions, essentially), even though he had so freely confessed upon his arrest, as one cop who worked the case and was interviewed for this book postulated. At the time, the Commonwealth of Virginia had the death penalty (it was abolished by the state in 2021). In fact, Virginia had a short time on average, compared to other states, between death sentence and execution (less than eight years), according to Wikipedia, and it did a high rate of executions compared to other states. That's not true for Hawaii and definitely not true for Michigan. Washington State has had the death penalty but also a governor's moratorium on it. So, perhaps, had Armstrong not changed his tune between his confession spree and his proclaimed innocence for the trials, and/or had investigators actually moved forward with charges in the Hillig case, it could have meant his death.

Kathleen, who had gotten online and read whatever she could on Armstrong when the police first told her about him, takes comfort in the fact that the likely killer of Linette is behind bars with no possibility for parole. It provided one of two big things she had wanted for Linette: their father could die knowing who killed his daughter. The other thing was a duty Kathleen took upon herself: she found Linette's own daughter Sarah, at age sixteen, after hiring a private investigator. Sarah had been about eleven when Linette was killed, and time had continued to march on without anyone in Linette's family knowing where she was.

"I promised Linette I would find her. That was a promise I made to Linette. I'll find her."

And so Sarah—who at that point did not even know her mother had died years earlier—began a new relationship with her mother's side of the family. "She's asked a ton of questions and we've been honest and forthright. She knows her mother suffered and had some issues and as a result, Sarah was taken away and raised by her father. So we talk all the time. We're family."

Amid Sarah's own mixed feelings, she understands as an adult that her mom was troubled. "If there was one thing I could say to her, it would be to let her know that I forgive her."

The dichotomy of their two lives was striking to Sarah. While speaking for this book, her mom's birthday was about to happen in October 2020, and a couple months later, Sarah was about to be the same age as Linette was when she was killed.

"I've tried to put in perspective her life compared to my life. I will outlive her. And when you're sixteen, you think thirty-four is so old. But years later, you're like, here I am—I'm doing great in my career, I have a great husband, we're working on building our second home. I have two beautiful boys, and at the same age she was that I am now, she was doing all that, and I just can't imagine … I have to remember that she had a disease. This is a disease that just controls everything … It's probably going to be a rough day for me … She's still my mom."

Linette's father died a couple years after Linette did and her mother is gone now too. Her death has caused all range of emotions for her family, including regret on her father's part—the feeling that there was something he could have done to protect his baby girl, as unrealistic as that was.

And even though great memories remain, Kathleen said: "I know a piece of all of our hearts was gone when Linette was killed. And you never get over that."

HAWAII POSSIBILITY: LISA FRACASSI

Another name popped up in the investigation of the non-Detroit confessions, that of Lisa Ann Fracassi, a New York native who had been living in Hawaii when she was killed. The thirty-seven-year-old had been a registered nurse and a certified lifeguard who had been working as an exotic dancer just before she was found strangled to death in the hotel room where she was living in Waikiki on November 3, 1994. Years later, Lisa is still listed as one of Armstrong's victims on a few websites, but he was never charged with her murder and it doesn't fit for a couple reasons.

The biggest issue is the timeframe. Armstrong placed his two Hawaii confessions in May 1997, years after Lisa died. Of course, the *Nimitz* schedule says that the ship wasn't in Hawaii in May 1997—it was in California and Washington. The schedule says the two times it was in Hawaii for Armstrong's 1990s time aboard were July 20-22, 1993, and May 7-10, 1996. Since Armstrong remembered the first Hawaii killing happening on a night he got into an argument with his wife, with whom he had traveled from the ship to a hotel, it would seem the two back-to-back Hawaii incidents happened during the May 1996 timeframe when the boat was at Pearl Harbor.

He had met his wife in 1995. Though they weren't married in 1996, he could certainly still refer to her as his wife in a general sense when recalling these details. So the May 1996 port of call for the *Nimitz* makes sense for the two Hawaii confessions, especially given the fact that he was confusing the timeframe with his Hong Kong confessions as well. That would place the Hawaii murders at May 8 and 9, 1996, with Armstrong noting that the ship was leaving the morning after the second one, which would mean May 10. He remembered the ship as being in Hawaii for four days. At any rate, whether the Hawaii murders happened during the 1993 or 1996 port of call, it still doesn't work for the murder of Lisa Fracassi, unless for some reason Armstrong was on leave and in Hawaii in late October or early November 1994. (His leave record says he was not.) Or if the schedule of the *Nimitz* varied from what was on record.

But the two Hawaii confessions also do not match Lisa Fracassi in appearance. Victim 1 he remembered as a white blond female, really thin, five-foot-seven, in her early thirties, with a German accent. Victim 2 he described as a white redhead, five-foot-six, one hundred and twenty pounds. Lisa Fracassi had dark hair, her mother said when reached via phone in 2019. And Lisa was petite like her mom.

"She was five-foot-three," her mother said. "She was tiny. Of course, she wasn't as short as I was. I'm only four-foot-eleven. My children are, like, five-foot-three, my two girls."

Decades after Lisa's death, the pain was still evident in the voice of this brokenhearted mom, in her nineties and still without closure. She was barely even contacted by law enforcement, really only to tell her that Lisa had been found in her apartment. She has never learned who was responsible for the strangulation of Lisa. There seemed to be very little effort to do that.

Born in 1957, Lisa was an honor student at Niagara Falls High School before moving to Florida, earning her nursing degree from Broward College, and working as a registered nurse in University Hospital and Medical Center in Fort Lauderdale, Florida. She moved to Hawaii in 1990, very much missed by her mom at that point.

"We begged her and begged her to come home," her mother said. "I mean, she was educated. She was beautiful. Not because she was my daughter. She had everything going for her and she just wouldn't come home."

She went on, somberly, "She got mixed up with the wrong people. She had everything going for her, everything, everything. Then this happened."

Lisa was living at the Honolulu Prince Hotel for several months leading up to her death and was working as a dancer at a club called Exotic Paradise. Before that, she had danced at another club, Pure Platinum. Her body was discovered at the hotel by a maid delivering linen.

Compounding this mom's grief is the fact that it's not even clear when her daughter died.

"They found her and we couldn't bury her—we had to have a closed coffin. She was just … just not there." With difficulty, she continued: "She was—I hate to say the words … she was just rotted away."

Lisa had been lying in her apartment for an undetermined period of time.

"And they had her shipped home and we buried her with a closed coffin."

Her mother recalls no follow-up from law enforcement whatsoever regarding her daughter's murder. She also had never heard the name John Eric Armstrong when I talked with her in 2019. When news of Armstrong's many worldwide confessions hit the media, the Honolulu police started looking at cases from the timeframe of the *Nimitz*'s visits to Pearl Harbor. The *Star-Bulletin* reported on Friday, April 14, 2000, that Honolulu police had looked into any unsolved murders for both 1993 and 1996. "But none match the profile of Armstrong's victims," the paper reported. "The only local case with a similar victim profile was that a stripper who was found dead in her Waikiki apartment in November 1994, police said." That's when Lisa's name popped up.

But back in Niagara Falls, New York, mom heard nothing. She did, however, receive one phone call just a few years after Lisa's death. A very strange phone call that is as much a mystery as who killed Lisa.

"Some fella did call and say that they know who did it, and he was a friend of theirs, and we didn't get any names or anything. And then we got that one phone call; we waited and waited and nothing came of it."

The caller was male, her mother said. He told her he was a friend of Lisa's killer. She didn't get the man's information and he never called again. She didn't recall exactly when this was but she knows it was before the death of her husband, Lisa's father Ernest, which was in 2003.

"He never called back," she said of the mysterious man. "I guess I—I don't know what I did over the phone with him. I must have frightened him. I don't know. I should have written everything down, but I was so…

"It was closer to when it happened, you know."

As I was doing research for this book, I emailed back and forth with a man who claimed that his friend killed Lisa Fracassi. I surmise it's the same man who called Lisa's mom. He talked about the fact that though his friend would never go to police and confess, the incident has destroyed his life. The emailer confirmed that, indeed, this friend of his, the alleged perp, is not John Eric Armstrong.

WHAT BECAME OF THE INVESTIGATION?

At first, there was no indication in the Detroit case files or from anyone who was talking just why and when the investigation of Armstrong's non-Detroit confessions stalled.

"After we got through with our portion of the investigation," former Detroit cop Everett Monroe said, "everything was pretty much handed over to the government for their investigation of it. I don't know exactly what came of that, because we weren't filled in on it. It was a very involved investigation. It was very trying."

Gerald Cliff of the Violent Crime Task Force recalled: "The criminal investigations division of the DPD handled the Armstrong investigation as well as any professional law enforcement agency in the world would have. Our Violent Crimes Section contained FBI agents, Michigan State Police detectives, Wayne County investigators, investigators from the State Attorney General's office as well as the 'best of the best' detectives in the DPD, all handpicked with the approval of the chief. During the Investigation we worked hand in hand with the US State Department, the real NCIS, and a number of foreign law enforcement agencies trying to corroborate Armstrong's admissions to murders of women all over the world."

Cliff himself shared an office with an NCIS investigator who was working from Detroit—an early, rather impressive web-connected laptop in tow—to solve the mystery of the non-Detroit confessions.

In a snapshot of the two sections above, the only other victim names associated with Armstrong's case besides our five female victims in Detroit (and the several Detroit assault survivors) shake out like this:

LINETTE HILLIG

FITS:

- Location: Newport News/Norfolk, Virginia, area
- Ethnicity: white
- Gender: female
- Age range (possibly—age wasn't specified in confession)
- Timeframe: matches the *Nimitz*'s arrival in Norfolk (discounting Armstrong's own recollection of what month it occurred)
- Manner of death: run over by a car
- Victim a known prostitute

DOESN'T FIT:

- Site of the murder and drop: Armstrong said he took her to a spot off Jefferson Avenue in Newport News, but Linette was killed on East Little Creek Road in Norfolk

LISA FRACASSI

FITS:

- Location: Hawaii
- Ethnicity: white
- Gender: female
- Age range (probably)
- Manner of death: strangulation
- Site: victim's apartment

DOESN'T FIT:

- Timeframe (the biggest factor)
- Physical description of victim
- Lesser point: No solid indication Lisa was working as a prostitute, though she was stated to be an exotic dancer

So one seems to fit; the other doesn't. But how did investigators see it at the time?

In the course of the research for this book, quite a few Freedom of Information Act—FOIA—requests were made of law enforcement or other agencies. A lot of very useful, actually crucial documents were obtained from this. Many agencies were great to work with. FOIA is the law and they were dutifully compliant. FOIA requests were made of the FBI, for its Detroit office's work on the case, as well as NCIS, to try to shed light on just how far the investigation went into Armstrong's Navy-era confessions, and when and why it was dropped. These two FOIAs were made in March 2020, and within only a week of the FBI request being made, it was deftly answered. And closed.

"You have requested records on one or more third party individuals," the March 13 letter read. "Please be advised the FBI will neither confirm nor deny the existence of such records pursuant to FOIA exemptions (b)(6) and (b) (7)(C), 5 U.S.C. § § 552 (b)(6) and (b)(7)(C). The mere acknowledgement of the existence of FBI records on third party individuals could reasonably be expected to constitute an unwarranted invasion of personal privacy. This is our standard response to such requests and should not be taken to mean that records do, or do not, exist. As a result, your request has been closed."

Well, okay then.

NCIS also quickly sent an acknowledgment of the request, but instead of swiftly closing the matter, said it would take several months to locate and assess the files. This was amid the coronavirus pandemic—COVID-19 had just hit the US full force. So hey, I emailed back that I was good with that. And thanks. Stay safe and all that. Then surprisingly, in the first week of April, I received a long PDF document of the files with personal information redacted due to the privacy exemptions above. But still with some good information intact.

NCIS closed the case on Armstrong on October 12, 2000, so it was open for six months. It was categorized as an investigative effort in support of the Violent Crime Task Force in Detroit, at the VCTF's request.

Throughout the NCIS investigation, agents pursued information along various avenues. They obtained the ship logs of the *Nimitz* to determine Armstrong's whereabouts throughout the time period of his confessions. They looked through his processed travel claims and leave slips. They dug into his earning records, even the eligible dependents he had on file. They went through his medical records, learning he was diagnosed with "mild adjustment disorder" in July 1994. They checked his naval reserve records and found he did not drill or do any naval activity after his active-duty discharge in April 1999. They contacted law enforcement in Armstrong's hometown of New Bern, North Carolina, and had them do some poking around. The NCIS agent currently assigned to the *Nimitz* was tasked with locating Armstrong's service record and the ship schedule, plus any associates of his that were still on board. And numerous interviews were conducted with officers still on board who knew him. According to NCIS records, the interviews happened on April 14 and 17, 2000. Though disciplinary records, retained for two years, didn't reveal anything for Armstrong, one former shipmate interviewed recalled a period of time in late 1997 during Far East port visits that Armstrong was on restricted status due to an unauthorized absence.

Notes were made of NCIS' contacts with law enforcement in the locations of Armstrong's various 1990s confessions:

In April 2000, as the investigation was beginning, the NCIS office in the *Nimitz*'s one-time home port in Bremerton, Washington, said that they had an unsolved homicide in the records: the bones of a female were discovered on the riverbanks near a bridge on a road between Bremerton and Tacoma. The surmised timeframe of her death was not noted in the report.

A special agent in North Carolina reported that there was an unsolved case of three years earlier in the city of Wilmington. This involved a Black female who was strangled with a ligature. In another North Carolina town, Jacksonville, a Black male had been beaten to death but it was determined to not fit the Armstrong case.

Contacts were made with law enforcement in several Virginia cities. Newport News and Hampton reported no unsolved homicides that would fit for Armstrong. Norfolk reported the Linette Hillig case as well as another prostitute found in April 1999. Virginia Beach reported an unsolved murder of s suspected prostitute from 1991.

On May 2, 2000, the Singapore Police Force Intelligence Division was contacted. The inspector there said a review of files showed no unsolved homicides or suspicious deaths in the timeframes the *Nimitz* was there: March 1993 and December 1995 to January 1996.

At that point in May, the Royal Thai Police had also been contacted, in coordination with FBI in Bangkok. They had no record of unsolved or suspicious deaths in Pattaya Beach during the July 1993 and April 1996 timeframes the *Nimitz* was there.

Also in May 2000, the FBI in Seattle was contacted and replied that they didn't need the NCIS' help with this, that the Seattle Police Department had already determined there were no unsolved homicides for the time period in question.

By the end of May, the FBI Legal Liaison Office in Hong Kong had been working with law enforcement there to try to identify any possible victims in the timeframe of Armstrong's confessions, but nothing had been found.

As in the Detroit police files, Linette Hillig's name is listed with the five Detroit victims as known victims of Armstrong throughout the NCIS case reports.

One interesting tidbit that came up in a report summary dated July 2000: NCIS was attempting to find a Navy officer once assigned to an F-14 squadron aboard the *Nimitz* during its 1996-97 deployment but was unable to do so. A May 1996 timeframe was indicated in particular in trying to find this squadron member, who would have been part of a group called the Strike Fighter Squadron 211 (VFA-211), nicknamed the "Fighting Checkmates." The VCTF had identified this individual as a potential witness to one of the Honolulu murders Armstrong confessed to. (NCIS had evidently concluded that Armstrong's recalled timeframe of May 1997 for the Honolulu murders was a mistake; they were surmising that the *Nimitz*'s actual May 1996 port visit to Hawaii was more likely than the 1993 one for those two killings.)

It's unclear how the (redacted) name of this potential witness came up—during DPD's various interviews with Armstrong (or possibly during the FBI's own questioning of him, which FOIA could not reach?) or from someone else, perhaps one of his *Nimitz* shipmates? Maybe it was a phone tip? NCIS pursued this lead of a possible witness with the Enlisted Personnel Management Center and other entities but nothing came of it.

During his confessions, Armstrong mentioned going to get hookers in Hawaii with a buddy, so was this buddy the mysterious person NCIS tried to locate? Or was this just a red herring Armstrong threw out there for investigators?

Along with an FBI special agent, the NCIS investigation was conducted by agents of theirs based in Norfolk, Virginia; Pensacola, Florida; Cleveland, Ohio; New Orleans, Louisiana; St. Louis, Missouri; Memphis, Tennessee; and Washington, DC.

The bottom line: no additional charges for Armstrong based on the non-Detroit murder confessions.

Armstrong's prosecutor in Detroit, Elizabeth Walker, offered her thoughts and they were right along the lines of Kathleen Fitzmaurice-Ward's understanding of why charges were not brought against Armstrong for Linette Hillig's murder: "No one ever explained it to me, but here's what my guess would be," she said. "They got him in Michigan for five homicides. He's not getting out. Let them feed him. Why should we spend the money?"

To depart from the discussion of the 2000 investigation and explore the possibilities a little further, let's take Hawaii first. The state has only a few homicides on record for the two time periods the *Nimitz* was at port there. Hawaii is not a state that has a lot of homicides. In 1993, for instance, the state showed a population of 1,172,000 and recorded forty-five murders. In 1996, the population had risen to 1,184,000 but the murders were at forty. For July 1993, there were four incidents on record, only one of which was unsolved. That was related to an attempted robbery outside a bar or nightclub, and the victim was a fifty-three-year-old man. Since the *Nimitz* was in Hawaii in latter July, is it possible the body or bodies could have been discovered later and counted for August? August 1993 logged six homicides, only one of which was unsolved, and the victim was male.

For May 1996, there were two homicides on the books, one with a male victim and one with a female. The female victim was forty-six and her murder is unsolved. The weapon listed is a rock thrown through a windshield, however. And on the off chance it was not logged until the following month, all five of those homicides, only two of which were female, were solved.

The Honolulu PD's cold case division lists a few unsolved homicides from the '90s on its website, but none fit the profile/timeframe for Armstrong's confessions. Of course, it's possible there were a couple homicides—of prostitutes—that were never reported. And it's possible there were some cases of missing persons that fit the profile and remain missing to this day.

MJA Investigations Inc., specializing in missing persons and John and Jane Does, posted on its website in 2017 a report of three missing women and one Jane Doe in Hawaii from the '90s. The three missing women were from the mid- to late 1990s, though their timeframes of disappearance do not fit either of the two times the *Nimitz* was in Hawaii. The Jane Doe, however, does. She was found in July 1993. She was in her late twenties to early thirties and had a petite build. She was an Asian female, not fitting the description Armstrong gave for his two Hawaii confessions, but where she was found is compelling: in the bushes near 1000 Nimitz Highway in Honolulu. If you look at a map, you can't get any closer to where the ship was and still be on dry land.

If this Jane Doe was one of Armstrong's victims, it means he scrambled or fabricated many of the details of these Hawaii accounts since he said he left both Hawaii victims in their homes and that they were white females. But the idea that he committed a bunch of murders in these locales outside of the Detroit and just confused the details, or threw up a bunch of lies about them off the top of his head, remains a possibility.

Exploration of DoeNetwork.org for the state of Hawaii reveals another Jane Doe found in Honolulu in the 1990s. She was ironically discovered on April 30, 1996, just *before* the *Nimitz* docked for that second visit during Armstrong's time on the ship. But she had decomposed to just bones and there was no indication in the report of how long she had been there. It could have been years, perhaps even since 1993. Only a skull and thigh bone were found, actually, during a cleanup of brush by grounds crews at a part of the National Memorial Cemetery of the Pacific that had been undisturbed for ten to twenty years. It was determined the bones had not been a part of one of the cemetery's graves. The cemetery is just over a mile from where the *Nimitz* docked. This female was white and estimated to be five-foot-one and forty to sixty years old.

Still another Jane Doe was found in Honolulu County in October 1998, again just bones and having been there an undetermined length of time. She was an Asian female, estimated age thirty to forty. Her skull and some bones were found a half mile from Camp Erdman, in a brushy area on the side of Farrington Highway, near a well-used hunting and hiking trail. This is on the other side of the island, however, and several miles from where the ship docked.

The *Nimitz* spent a lot more time in Washington State, since Bremerton was its home port at the time. There were large amounts of time in August, September, November, and December 1993 that the ship was there, then all of 1994, then on and off through May 1995. The ship went overseas, then returned to Washington in May 1996, staying there through the rest of the year and most of January 1997. This means the timeframes Armstrong remembered for the two Seattle incidents fit the times the ship was there. Then there were periods during March, April, May, and June 1997 that the *Nimitz* was there. Bremerton is in Kitsap County, so if we take just the county into consideration, it showed three murders in 1993, and two arrests for murder. No info is given as to victim demographics or method of death. Kitsap County recorded ten murders the following year, 1994, with eleven murder arrests. For 1995, it was seven murders and three murder arrests. For 1996, it was five murders and six murder arrests. And 1997 had five murders and two murder arrests. The arrests, of course, could occur in one year but pertain to a killing in another year, perhaps even several years earlier. And the arrests, like reported crimes, are recorded here in a hierarchical fashion where only the most serious crime is counted, the Washington Association of Sheriffs and Police Chiefs says. Therefore, while a person arrested more than once is counted each time, each arrest is counted only once regardless of the number of crimes that may have been committed. So it's a little dicey to read through these stats to determine how many of these crimes were unsolved.

The Kitsap Sun ran a list of the county's unsolved murders on its website. Matthew Evans, age twenty, was found dead in August 1993, having been hit in the head with an unidentified object. He was white, however, but was found very close to where the ship would have been.

Seattle, where Armstrong said the murders took place, is in King County. The 1960-2010 King County cold case files from the sheriff's office note a young Hispanic male killed in January 1995, a twenty-six-year-old Black male shot to death in November 1995, a thirty-year-old white male killed in March 1997, and a young white female who fits the confession but was killed while the *Nimitz* was in Singapore in January 1996. For the year 1993, King County had one hundred and four murders and sixty-five murder arrests, for 1994 it was one hundred and five murders and eighty-one arrests, for 1995 it was seventy-nine murders and fifty-eight arrests, for 1996 it was seventy murders and forty-six arrests, and for 1997 it was eighty-five murders and thirty-seven arrests.

Snohomish County is right next to Kitsap and Seattle and reported on its website that the sheriff's office has over the years investigated sixty-five unsolved murders and missing persons occurring since 1962. The Snohomish County Sheriff's Office Cold Case Unit cleverly created a deck of playing cards depicting the victims and distributed them to local inmates. *The Everett Herald* published a story about each cold case featured on the cards. Armstrong claimed to have killed a white female in August 1993 and a Black male in November 1996. Of the sixty-five Snohomish cold cases, a handful of white males were killed or went missing in 1995, fitting the *Nimitz*'s schedule but not the race or method of death in Armstrong's confession. An unidentified white or mixed-race male in his twenties was found in a lake in June 1994, having been shot and left in the water for several months to a year. A thirty-two-year-old white female named Kathleen Stewart was last seen at the lounge in the New World Chinese Restaurant in Ballard, a waterfront neighborhood of Seattle, in July 1995. The *Nimitz* was at sea then. Since the cold-case campaign was published by the county sheriff, an arrest was made for the May 1995 murder of twenty-two-year-old Tracey Brazzel, last seen at Kodiak Ron's Pub. If the person arrested is not the perp, Tracey is a possibility. Then there was twenty-six-year-old white female Patti Berry, who worked as a dancer at a local club, last seen at the end of July 1995. Here, the *Nimitz* was again at sea. None of the other cold-case files in Snohomish fit for the Armstrong case.

Tacoma, Washington, and its Pierce County are not far from Bremerton and Seattle, about twenty to thirty miles from each. The website of the Crime Stoppers of Tacoma/ Pierce County has listed unsolved homicides dating back to the 1990s. The bones of an unidentified female were found in October 1997, estimated to have been killed between

September 1994 and October 1997. She was thirty to fifty years old, blond, slender, wearing a sweatshirt and pants. She also shows up on the DoeNetwork.org site, with greater detail. The pants she was wearing were jeans, fitting Armstrong's recall, and she was also wearing white Reeboks (he said the victim was wearing white tennis shoes). Her age, build, and race fit. She's a decent candidate, with the caveat that she was discovered in a remote location, miles from where the *Nimitz* would have been. She is also likely the person mentioned for Washington in the NCIS files.

Another female, a white woman named Linda Thompson, was found dead in an alley in April 1995 but from gunshot wounds. A Black male named Steven Polite was found beaten to death with an unidentified object in January 1995, though he was found near a school. Polite, known to be involved in narcotics, was killed sometime between midnight and eight a.m.

Another Jane Doe turned up who could fit the profile, though on the lower tip of Washington State, which would have likely meant an outing for Armstrong on a stretch of days off the ship. She also was wearing pants and white tennis shoes. She was a white female, age thirty-five to forty-five, about one hundred and thirty pounds, and five-foot-three, brown hair and brown eyes. She was found in March 1998 and could have been killed any time before. Skeletal remains of a few other Jane Does have been found closer to Seattle and Tacoma in the past couple decades with an undetermined time of death.

Turning to North Carolina, site of Armstrong's alleged first kill, mentioned only vaguely in case records but evidently part of the discussion when police interviewed him shortly after his arrest, several Jane Does show up. A young, white, petite female strangled to death in September 1990 in Hillsborough, found along Interstate 40. A young Native American female, still small at five-foot-four, discovered as skeletal remains by horseback riders adjacent to the banks of the Yadkin River in Lewisville in July 1993, undetermined how long she'd been there. A Black female whose skull was found in a creek bed off of a railroad track embankment near South Road in Randolph County in May 1997. Others. All are in various parts of North Carolina a considerable drive from Armstrong's hometown, but of course he and his family didn't spend all of their time at home.

Near Fayetteville, a couple hours from New Bern, thirty-two-year-old Shelby Williams was found strangled to death in June 1990. Wilmington is a little closer to New Bern, and there, a twenty-four-year-old math teacher named Charlene Thigpen was found on the side of a highway in spring 1992.

None of the unidentified but unsolved homicides on the North Carolina State Bureau of Investigation's Cold Case list fit for Armstrong's details.

And in Virginia, where Armstrong said he had committed other murders besides the specific confession for the victim he ran over, there are Jane Does who have turned up that could have been killed in the 1998-1999 timeframe he lived there.

SO DID HE ACTUALLY COMMIT THESE OTHER MURDERS?

It's a question with no clear answer. Armstrong was arrested in Detroit, convicted in Detroit despite his defense's approach of claiming innocence (or insanity), and his confessions to other murders outside of Detroit fell by the wayside, with his lawyer claiming he had made them up.

Various people who worked the case or covered the case have their own opinions on whether Armstrong actually committed these killings.

"I think he did," said former Detroit cop Everett Monroe, adding that, in terms of the FBI/NCIS investigation, "Mr. Armstrong was an individual that, you really had to cultivate him during the interview. I think they probably went in a little abrasive and caused him to shut down. But that's just my personal opinion. Now, could he have been fabricating it? It's a possibility. What would he glean from lying and fabricating when he said all this other stuff? It just didn't make sense, but you know, stranger things have happened. I've had people confess to murders that they really didn't commit because of the intensity of the interrogation."

Is it possible Armstrong recanted his confessions later because he thought it might reduce his sentence or his case?

"I have no idea, to be honest with you," Monroe said. "He knew pretty much that he had reached the point of no return. So it wasn't like he was going to be able to get out in fifteen, twenty years or something like that, so. I don't know. I mean, anything is possible. I've been doing police work long enough to say that there's nothing on here that occurs crime wise that surprises me. It doesn't surprise me because it's just that the inhumane acts of man cause strange things to happen. So I mean, like I said, we've had people confess to murders that they did not do. We've had people claim to be innocent but were guilty as all-out. You never know. And his mind was—it was very interesting."

Mike Petri of the Dearborn Heights Police Department said, "You know—for him to go off on a tangent and make all that stuff up seems kind of odd."

Another officer who questioned Armstrong, Donald Johnson of DPD, feels very strongly that the confession of the murder of the transgender prostitute in Thailand, the person he said he threw out the window, is true because of the level of detail. Johnson's gut impression of the rest is that there's a "very strong possibility" they really did happen.

"With a lot of the countries," he said, "when they were going to the various ports, think about it—it's very easy to do. Because you're in and you're out. You're right back on the ship. And so he went and handled his business and came back to the ship like nothing ever happened."

Johnson's interview partner James Hines thought much the same thing of whether or not Armstrong did those other crimes: "I think he did. Maybe not as many, but I don't think it was an exaggeration. Because you know, you get off the boat, you do your dirt, you get on the boat, nobody knows it. There's no trace. They're probably not rushing to an investigation. It's probably something that happened all the time to prostitutes. Maybe those different countries just didn't value their deaths."

And with the jumbling of details: "It could be just that he's so busy he can't remember. Or he may have been high at the time of the incident, so therefore he doesn't recall where he was, or what port or what date or what time. He's trying to remember, so he's throwing dates out there. And only he knows the answers to all of that."

Rodney Durham, from his time spent with Armstrong at the arrest as well as that interesting ride to headquarters in the squad car, believes he had to have committed the non-Detroit murders. "With today's technology, with DNA and all this stuff, I wouldn't be surprised if you could match him up with umpteen more killings elsewhere. You know. It wouldn't be a surprise." Particularly in North Carolina and Virginia, Durham said, where Armstrong spent so much time.

Gregory Geider, former member of Detroit's VCTF, had this recollection: "In retrospect, what stands out to me was the nonchalant callousness of Armstrong's confessions. He did not appear inherently evil due to his resigned demeanor but certainly seemed to be by his actions that he described to us. I have always wondered about the veracity of many of Armstrong's claims. I certainly think that it is possible that Armstrong believed that he killed some of his victims that may have in fact survived. After thirty-plus years in law enforcement, I've become rather jaded to the human condition so the whole episode seemed like just another bump in the road."

That idea of Armstrong strangling but then leaving his intended victim alive is an interesting one, as we know that he did do this several times—Natasha Olejniczak, Cynthia Smith, Monica Johnson, even Kelly Jean Hood, according to his confession. He may have figured each of these women were dead, assumed that they had to be. Or he may have purposely stopped himself from going any further, as he claimed, and left the scene. And this pattern of leaving some alive may have extended beyond the women in Detroit.

"I did hear, and I don't know if it's true or not, that they did find a victim—he claimed he killed a guy in Thailand," said one cop who worked the case and was a little leery of being quoted for this rumor. "Picked up a prostitute or whatever. And found out that it was a guy, not a girl. Said that he threw her out the window and killed her. I heard through the grapevine—I don't know if it's true or not—that they did find that report. And the guy didn't die. A guy did get thrown out a window, and he landed or whatever, and got up and took off. They corroborated that. But again, that was Naval intelligence, and I don't know if that's true or not."

There was unfortunately no evidence of this in the NCIS files obtained via FOIA.

Detroit News reporter George Hunter admitted it all seems a mystery, why the NCIS investigation stalled, or what degree of effort they put into the investigation outside of Detroit. "Well, you never know," he said. "And if it was hookers, you know, you're talking about a hooker in Singapore. Maybe that murder or disappearance isn't going to show up on anybody's radar. You're talking about an underground economy and in a lot of places, people that live off the grid. So definitively, to say these didn't happen, I don't think you can do that. Even if they didn't die with what's in their record, I'm sure there's people in Singapore who get killed and if the body's never recovered, then they'll never know they were killed, because they were off the grid. Especially that long ago. So it's hard to really get a gauge on it. We know for a fact he did the ones around here."

Dr. Lawrence J. Simon has studied serial killers for years and wrote the books *Murder by Numbers: Perspectives on Serial Sexual Violence* and *Mortal Desire: Origins of Sexual Violence*. He works as a consultant and trainer in the law enforcement community. He points out a few different aspects to the question of whether or not Armstrong committed the other murders.

"These serial killers—I've seen it before—they do like to boast," said Simon, who was born in Detroit and got his undergrad degree in psychology from Eastern Michigan University. "So they'll actually increase their number. What you'd obviously want to do to prove that is have these guys draw a map. To map something out, or where was this done, to try to get more specifics out."

And as you know from the confession details earlier, we've got a lot of specifics from Armstrong. Place names. Physical descriptions of the victims. What they were wearing. Things that they said to him. Even the timeframes of the incidents, albeit a bit scrambled.

But in a case like this, details get scrambled anyway. How tall was Nicole Young? A Chicago police report from the July before her death said five-foot-two. The Wayne County medical examiner said five-foot-six. Her killer said five-foot-six. How about her weight? Chicago police records said one hundred and twenty, the medical examiner said one hundred and thirty-four, the killer said one hundred to one hundred and ten. Weight may vary over time, but we have to assume Nicole had a fixed height(!). How can it vary so much, from three different sources in the same general timeframe, even considering the fact that she was only seventeen when killed? And don't forget her true name, or her true age, both of which had conflicting information. This illustrates how details can get scrambled and can vary quite a lot, but certain basic truths arise from them. So if Armstrong mistakes the date, or what a certain victim was wearing, it doesn't necessarily mean he didn't kill that person. The Detroit murders were all very recent to him, so it was easier to recall the correct timeframes, but years earlier would get a bit fuzzier.

There is only one of Armstrong's confessions for which we have another side of the story to compare it to, the other person's perspective, to perhaps see how truthful he was being. That is the assault of Cynthia Smith. How does his account of the assault stack up to hers? How truthful was he when relaying this one to police during his confessional spree? Well, acknowledging the fact that he knew she had ID'd him that night in the squad car and would be telling her story to police too, here's how their accounts compare:

MATCH:
- Timeframe: around April 10
- Her physical description: Black female with black hair
- Her clothing: black leather jacket, pants
- Pickup location: near the Marathon gas station on Michigan
- Sequence of events: she got into the Jeep, then asked him if he was a cop
- Negotiation: one hundred dollars for straight sex
- Parking location: she directed him to the place where they parked
- They had sex (she at first told police they didn't, then later said they did)
- He started to strangle her
- Drop location: he placed her outside of the Jeep on another street
- Robbery: he took her purse/backpack

WHAT HE SAYS AND SHE DOESN'T (THOUGH THESE ITEMS STILL COULD HAVE HAPPENED):
- He also asked her if she was a cop

- He went to the store to buy condoms
- They had sex in the back seat (this was fairly unusual, as most of Armstrong's encounters occurred in the front passenger seat)
- When he left her, she was half-nude from the waist down

WHAT SHE SAYS AND HE DOESN'T (AGAIN, STILL COULD HAVE HAPPENED):
- He demanded her coat and purse right after stopping the car on the secluded street
- He had a metallic object she believed was a knife
- He yelled, "I hate prostitutes!"
- She was bruised and scarred from the incident

Without actually sitting down with Armstrong and talking to him, Dr. Simon is hesitant to say for sure if Armstrong's non-Detroit confessions are true, especially due to the perp's later defense of "making up" the confessions.

"Let's say that you say, 'Well, Doc, I'm up late at night, I urinate frequently in the evening, I have cold sweats, I get tired often.' A medical doctor is not going to know that you're diabetic until they draw some blood. See? So it's the same thing with me, that I would have to sit down. He could present all the symptoms at the end of the day, but at the end of the day, what is the motivation for recanting?"

There's always a possibility Armstrong could change his tune—again—from prison and provide more details of the possible non-Detroit murders.

"Each individual, in my experience, has recanted before, but also has produced bodies because they were given something. Whether it's running around and getting fresh air for three or four hours, or mapping something out, which is important. Then you give them something. And I don't think there's anything wrong with that; you've just got to make sure—it's just like a little chess or checkers match. To me, to find the body is, you know, you want that. So if you're going to go ahead and get five Big Macs in exchange for a body, I mean, hell yes. You know what I mean? Or you're going to get a slice of pizza, a pizza pie. Or you're going to take them out, what have you, so you could deliver the body. But before you do all that, they have to give you something."

So could Armstrong have been thinking a lot of this through at the outset, cooking up a premeditated bargaining chip to be used later from prison? Saying he killed a bunch more people, then later saying he didn't?

Katherine Ramsland, Ph.D, wrote in *Psychology Today* that based on her studies, there are three popular reasons perps tend to inflate their kill numbers: 1) they delight in duping law enforcement, 2) they want to be famous, 3) they want to be infamous, "the world's worst."

"The reason I'm bringing this is up," Dr. Simon continued, "is that's what I do; I consult with detectives on this very aspect, where sometimes they'll get into these little pickles to where these guys are saying that they're going to give them something, 'Hey, I've got another body for you.' But at the end of the day, they're just giving a wild goose chase. But they'll be down about ten or eleven Big Macs, and now they want fries. What I'm saying is, there's all kinds of motivations Armstrong could be having for recanting that. However, though, I will tell you this, because you're looking for something. I'll tell you this right off the bat that I'm a stat guy. I'm going to lean more toward that yeah, he probably did kill abroad. And the reason I say that is, once you have that desire and opportunity that you've killed, if presented an opportunity elsewhere—whether it's in Zimbabwe or whether it's in Hawaii or whether it's in Japan—there's no doubt that he's going to go kill again. So there's very little doubt on that.

"So I would probably lean more toward, if it was me, I would lean more toward that yes, he's probably killed abroad."

Blake Hempstead of Montana served aboard the *USS Nimitz* with Armstrong. When he arrived on the ship in later 1993, Armstrong had been there for several months. Hempstead, who went to barber school, worked with Armstrong in the barbershop of the *Nimitz*. He saw him on a day-to-day basis. Journalism has been Hempstead's career in more recent years, from a longtime interest since his high school days, and aboard the *Nimitz*, he owned video cameras. He took a video camera everywhere he went. And some of the things he liked to videotape were the shore leave excursions he and his shipmates would enjoy when the *Nimitz* dropped anchor. And therein lies the reason why he absolutely believes Armstrong could have committed these 1990s murders.

"You've got to realize," Hempstead said via phone in 2020, "that you work so many hours with these people when you're in your divisions or your different work spaces. You build friendships. And those are really the only friendships you have. You don't have any friends when you're coming onto the ship. You only know the people who you work with, because you only get to see them day after day after day. So when we were going out, and I can remember—we were on an aircraft carrier, so you're not able to dock like a boat coming in to shore. So with the aircraft carrier, you're taking 'liberty' boats, and you're docked out in the harbor. So when you're going to Hong Kong and you're going to Singapore, you're docked out in the harbor. And when you leave to go on liberty, you have only planned to go with the people who can go. Those are the only people that you go with. In essence, you plan trips with your friends and the people who you are working with. So you all leave at the same time."

So the guys would all take the liberty boat together to shore at whatever exotic port they found themselves. There would be eight to ten people and it always tended to be the same ones making these planned trips together. Hempstead would capture the moments on video when they would hang out, cutting loose, having some fun.

"And I have looked through all my videos," he said. "I remember looking back through all that stuff. I believe he was on one of them. But then he just wasn't there. So no matter what, he was never around when we did all that stuff. Either he was there initially, but he was never there when all the fun parts of the videos came up, when we were partying in the hotel rooms or enjoying other things. He was just never there. He just disappeared. He would just go and do his own thing."

Armstrong also would not take the same boat back to the ship as the rest of the guys. "We never saw him" on the return trip, Hempstead said.

It's circumstantial, certainly, but you would have to wonder if that perspective would have made it into a prosecutor's case files if charges had been pursued from the non-Detroit confessions. If Hempstead's name might accidentally have popped up on a witness list.

Hempstead was never questioned by authorities after Armstrong's arrest. He didn't even know his former shipmate had been arrested at the time. He only heard about it later. An injury prevented Hempstead from remaining on the *Nimitz* for the next tour anyway; he got an early discharge in August 1997.

Another shipmate, Tony Palmer, was a friend of Armstrong and defended him to the media after his arrest. "I never saw him in trouble at all," Palmer told the *Kitsap Sun*. "He worked hard. You asked him to do something he got to it right away. About 90 percent of the time, he had a smile on his face, cracking jokes, just an all-around good guy."

Palmer, who was contacted for this book but did not do an interview, told the media at the time, "He would basically just talk about how he would head over to Seattle with a couple of friends to go to a couple of bars. He'd be back the next morning and working, like everybody else."

THE QUESTIONS OF WHY

There are a lot of questions that arise in a case like this. Let's first tackle an interesting one that is bound to arise, from a sociological perspective, then after that we'll look at the million-dollar question.

WHY PROSTITUTES?

When John Eric Armstrong was making one of those many confessions to James Hines and Donald Johnson at the then headquarters of Detroit police at 1300 Beaubien at four-thirty-five a.m. on April 12, 2000, this time talking about Kelly Jean Hood, he was asked how he felt about women who prostitute themselves. "I dislike them because women shouldn't be doing that," he said. "I get angry and hostile. I lose control."

Many hours later, that night, he told police about killing a prostitute in Honolulu, Hawaii, while his boat was docked at Pearl Harbor.

"Why do you choose hookers to kill?" he was asked.

"Because I can control them."

A simple statement.

But you might argue it's a bit more complex than that.

US serial murder cases with prostitute victims accounted for 32 percent of all US serial murder cases involving female victims only from 1970 to 2009, according to a study by Kenna Quinet of Indiana University-Purdue University

Indianapolis. That equated to about 22 percent of all serial killer victims, male or female. But that number rose to 43 percent in the decade after, said writer Adam Janos in a story for the A&E website. Prostitutes represent only about 0.3 percent of the US population, the story continued. Killers of prostitutes amass a greater average number of victims than killers of non-prostitutes, Quinet argued, and when analyzed by decade, those who kill primarily sex workers, kill for slightly longer periods of time.

"Being a prostitute increases your chance of being murdered by 200 times," said Eric Hickey, a social psychologist and author of *Serial Murderers and Their Victims*.

Indulge me a bit, and forgive me a lot, as I get a little personal. For me, as I researched the Armstrong case, the question of "why prostitutes?" became just as much a question of why on earth were these women out there on the streets in the first place, putting themselves at risk? I am the same age most of them would be now and I felt very strongly as I dug into the details that it could have been a matter of a wrong turn somewhere in their lives that put them where they were. But that they had once started out just like me, in a regular family, living a regular childhood. My own life has had a wrong turn or two; I am an addict myself, though many years in recovery. So what was it about their lives that made them go in this direction while I did not? The question haunted me. I wanted to learn more about each one of the five deceased women in Detroit. That was something striking a chord for me at the beginning of this project—I really set out to take each of those five "bodies" found, five names in a news report, and put a life around it. Show that each one of those women had a life worth living, a life just like mine and yours. Show that each one had a label other than "prostitute": a label like daughter, niece, sister, mom ... dreamer, tennis player, rock collector, cat lover, whatever!

But alas, it really didn't happen that way. The more I researched, the more I tried to contact family members or friends, the less I seemed to come up with. A few very kind people (thank you!) told me about the lives of four of the five. But it was incredibly challenging to get to them. Many, many phone numbers now disconnected. Emails sent and ignored. Facebook messages (quite a lot) sent and ignored. LinkedIn invitations sent and ignored. Cards with my phone number left at physical addresses around Detroit I had tracked down online. No response. I know I found quite a few of the family members. I can be sure of it because the Internet does still yield *some* information, after all these years, even for women that lived off the grid at the time. And for a couple people I contacted who evidently weren't actually related, I got a polite response right away. But for the rest, no response, over and over. Not even an acknowledgment that they had received my inquiry.

I worded every ardent appeal a little differently, and for some, I sent a chaser message a few months later, just to make sure my contact was being received.

"I'd like to know more about her, what she was like growing up, what her interests were, what her hobbies were."

"The public only knows one thing about her—I want to show she had a life worth living."

"I want to do right by your sister."

"I would be happy to have you review the text before publication, to make sure it says just what you want it to say."

In so many cases, nothing, nothing, and more nothing.

Of the five women to research for our story, the most challenging one for the longest time was Rose Marie Felt. There was no photo of her published in the media at the time of her death. No family members were interviewed. No family members attended the trials, by all accounts. No one posted later on Internet message boards saying they knew her. Her autopsy, death certificate, scant arrest records provided little insight.

Along with the other women, she was killed near the beginning of the Internet Age, but even a couple decades later, when our lives are continually documented online, Rose was but a vapor. Exhaustive Internet searches turned up a birthdate in October 1967 and a few previous addresses. Visits in 2018 to those five previous addresses, all in the inner city, revealed that three of them had become simply three more of Detroit's many empty lots. At the other two addresses, they hadn't heard of her. Neighbors didn't know her. There seemed to be no family members to hunt down. "Felt" families across the state were called (that is, if they had a phone number to be had—so many people have unlisted numbers). Nothing. There were girls who knew her at the time she was on the street, but they were nowhere to be found. According to an employee at a local cemetery, she could have been disposed of with many other unclaimed bodies in a mass cremation. No obituary, not even a death notice in the paper.

Of course, all of this would lead one to believe that Rose Marie Felt was not this girl's real name. Maybe the age, the previous addresses, maybe even the birthdate, were just fake info she gave to police when arrested, as in the case of Nicole Young. I began to wonder if it was actually a phantom profile I was searching online. And that certainly didn't help the search.

She was the most frustrating and heartbreaking of the five female lives in Detroit I sought to give a life to in this book. After many months of searching, it was finally a single court record, the name of just one certain individual associated with her, that led me on another long string of searches and phone calls (even more disconnected numbers!), until finally, at long last, I got a person on the phone who actually knew Rose. And I could confirm she was a real person, not a ghost. And that Rose Felt actually was her name.

So since I had finally found someone to speak for Rose (three people and then a fourth, as it turned out), this moved Nicole Young into the number one position as most elusive prostitute to research. I could reach not a single family member or friend of hers. Just a landlady of the address she used, the mom of a friend of her former boyfriend. A woman who, yes, had laid eyes on her once or twice.

Therein lies a blatant clue as to the nature of sex work and its effects on family and friends. And it speaks to the mystery of "why" for these five women. Why prostitutes.

And while members of the world's oldest profession have been targets for violence throughout history, in the examination of the Armstrong case, the city of Detroit with its prostitution culture is just as much a player in this story as the perp and the five female lives he claimed.

A PHOENIX JUST BEGINNING TO RISE

Founded in 1701 by the French explorer Antoine de la Mothe Cadillac, and once the nation's fourth largest city, Detroit is known for a lot of things. The auto industry that drew folks from the South with the promise of a better life, an industry that flourished through the '50s and '60s. The Motown recording studio that catapulted the career of quite a few music legends. The 1967 riots and ensuing white flight to the suburbs. The fires of the annual Devil's Night so deftly punctuating the anger and disillusionment the riots left in their wake. The largest Middle Eastern population in the US. The city bankruptcy filing of more recent years. The former mayor in the clink. (And back out again.) Economic turns felt more deeply than in other cities. Racial tensions more marked. Even the coronavirus pandemic hitting this place a little harder.

In his book *Devil's Night and Other True Tales of Detroit*, a rather fascinating sociological study of the city in the wake of the riots, Ze'ev Chafets quoted former

Detroit City Council member and US Representative Barbara-Rose Collins as saying in the '80s, "Most of this city is like a national disaster. Drugs, crack, assembly lines shutting down—it all comes here first, the good and the bad. Whatever happens in America happens here first—Detroit is like a laboratory for the rest of the country." Chafets wrote of a white town that changed color almost overnight, of the Middle Easterners who moved in and purchased up convenience stores and gas stations at what he called "fire-sale" prices, and the Blacks who resented it, of the drugs (like crack) that took such a hold the police could do nothing about it, of the youth turned to violence. A city in strife, though still determined.

Detroit's seedier underside provided more than ample hunting ground for John Eric Armstrong's proclivities. The city had (and has) multiple pockets with a high degree of prostitution. For one, the Cass Corridor, the stretch of Cass Avenue near Wayne State University, that at the time of this case, had potholes big enough to swallow your car (maybe still does) and that was definitely a walk on the wild side. Woodward Avenue. Warren Avenue. Fort Street. And of course, Michigan Avenue.

At the time of these five murders, I was living downtown, just a block from where Michigan Avenue begins. I was working in the features department of *The Detroit News*, located at the time just a few blocks from my apartment. Detroit was something this former farmgirl had sought after, the biggest city in Michigan, a sign of having "made it." *The News*, the biggest newspaper in the state at the time, was a goal I had set in college. I was going to love this town no matter what. It didn't really want to love me back but that didn't matter. I felt I understood it. I identified with it. And I loved it nonetheless.

The Detroit I saw—and felt—around me in the latter 1990s and early 2000s was a hardened, determined city with an edge of anger. I could feel it when I went to the corner store or when I gassed up my car. Above all else, though, Detroit was and always has been *real*. No pretenses. Take it or leave it. The underdog, some have called it. And there was plenty of the idea there, around the turn of the millennium, that the city was on a comeback. They had been talking about that—more overly optimistically than anything—since the mid-1970s construction of the Renaissance Center office complex right on the river, which became the home of Ford Motor Company, then later General Motors. They were onto the right idea back then, but the timing was a bit too soon. A couple decades later came casinos and ballparks like the Detroit Tigers' new home, Comerica Park, which I watched going up via binoculars from the balcony of my high-rise apartment a couple blocks away. When the three casinos arrived, around 1999, I could drive home from visiting my family in mid-Michigan late on a Sunday night, hop off the Lodge Freeway downtown, and actually see *people* around. There were *people* there, where before it had been desolate. My Detroit had suddenly become a twenty-four-hour town.

By that point, Little Caesars czar Mike Ilitch had already restored the fabulous Fox Theatre on Woodward Avenue and had given suburbanites a reason to come to the 'hood. His Red Wings team was rockin' it—two consecutive Stanley Cups and another one soon after that. Devil's Night had its angels basically stomping the crap out of it. Things were looking up, amid the decay. Heck, even Starbucks opened up a downtown location, very daring for the time.

Nowadays, I know that the comeback tale was just beginning when I lived in downtown Detroit back in the latter 1990s. I could drive downtown after my years away in Atlanta and Washington, DC (at least before the COVID pandemic), and see a whole new city emerging. I actually have half-jokingly referred to it as New Detroit, but it's no joke. Lately, Quicken Loans king Dan Gilbert has been the one pouring money into the city, buying up abandoned properties, refurbishing historic buildings, and he has poured far more in than one would have expected from the awesome legacy Ilitch indirectly passed on to him from the '90s. There has lately been a vibrance downtown, people milling about, people actually *moving into* downtown again. People working, not only having coffee at the coffee shop, but heading to Hart Plaza for an event, walking along the riverfront. Grabbing an ice cream at the ice cream shop or a pop at the drugstore. I remember how excited I was, back when I lived downtown, at that first Starbucks opening up, right near the then NBD headquarters (that was National Bank of Detroit, as mentioned earlier). It was my Friday-morning treat on my walk to work, a Starbucks to greet the last day of the workweek. An actual big franchise setting up shop here. Now, there is a Subway and a CVS and what-have-you all over downtown.

So yeah, Detroit has been coming back. And it was somewhat on its way, back then, as Armstrong hunted on Michigan Ave.

INSIDE THE CALL-GIRL CULTURE: ONE OF DETROIT'S SEEDIER SIDES

Amid the ups and downs of Detroit, prostitution has been a constant. It's big business. And the accompanying drugs like heroin and cocaine feed into it, and vice versa. These two elements, drugs and prostitution, intertwined in any big city, have been ever present in Detroit, supporting each other like two parasites that barely even realize they're both on a mission to destroy lives.

"Detroit is an interesting animal, you know?" said former Detroit cop Ira Todd. "It's a real interesting animal. Detroit is different than a lot of cities. Especially when you look at it from the underground economy. Because our underground economy is all about blind pigs and prostitution and drugs and things like that. And people don't realize there's a complete underground economy here in Detroit."

This world of Michigan Ave, particularly the couple-mile stretch between Wyoming and Livernois, has stood far away from downtown's velvet-and-fur-clad Fox Theatre-goers and the like. Because no matter how *real* Detroit is, things have still fallen into a certain class order. Haves and have-nots. And where John Eric Armstrong plucked up his victims was the land of the have-nots.

At the time, and perhaps still true, the strip clubs along this stretch often belonged to a larger network and brought in girls from Las Vegas or Los Angeles to get fresh faces on the stage. White, Black, brown, whatever. Race didn't matter here, just as it didn't matter to Armstrong as he hunted. This is an equal-opportunity biz. These women would rotate around to the different local clubs so that fresh bodies were kept working in each place. A woman might have to rent that space on the stage to make her living. And after getting hooked on drugs, they tended to gravitate from stripping to streetwalking. That's how things evolved in this life.

Prosecutor Elizabeth Walker got an education about the Michigan Ave mystique when she prepared the case against Armstrong. One of her assault-survivor witnesses in particular, Avon aka Cynthia Smith, gave her the rundown. "That strip of Michigan Avenue, she said that is like the crème de la crème of prostitution. She came there to work that—she and her boyfriend came there for her to work that strip and make a lot of money before they went back wherever they were from … She said, 'Oh yeah, there's a lot of money that can be made there.' They were going to work that strip for a couple of months, and then go back, and then live well for a while."

This educated, accomplished woman found it quite astonishing. "People come from all over to go prostitute in that area. And I'm like, really? It's a dark, derelict, ugly-looking area. I don't get it."

Kimberly Sanders was a Detroit police officer from 1986 until her retirement in 2009, retreating into the much quieter world of gardening, having been a certified master gardener after studying horticulture at Michigan State in the '80s. While with DPD, she worked homicide and saw lots of things that can't be unseen. There were always runs to that stretch of Michigan Ave and the various motels and strip clubs along it. Sanders remembered a body being found at the notorious Victory Inn, since demolished but quite the den of iniquity on Michigan at one time. The Victory Inn sat on Michigan Avenue at Wyoming, right next to the Venus topless club and right at the city's border with Dearborn. Shootings, robberies, and assaults often happened there, and federal agents got wind of human trafficking going on as well. Women were being drugged and forced to have sex in the rooms, it was reported. One of the largest federal raids in Detroit history finally shut the place down in January 2017, rescuing several women, and the motel was razed not long after. It was reported in 2017 that the raided drug and sex operation had occupied forty of the hotel's forty-two rooms.

Sanders recalled a prostitute giving birth in a toilet and trying to flush the baby. She saw "things that can be done with the human body that most people couldn't imagine." And at one time, she did decoy work posing as a prostitute. She worked what she called OTEs—offers to engage.

"I was on a morality crew that drove around," Sanders explained, "and sometimes we used male decoys. And that would be our sergeant or someone else. And they would play the role as the john. And they would drive up and down the street and if they were signaled by a prostitute, they would lock them up." This was what she referred to as an "offer to engage" and sometimes the charges would involve disorderly conduct as well. "If they waved or made eye contact—whatever was necessary within the law to arrest them, to get them off the street, we did. And then myself and three or four other officers, partners, we worked the decoy unit."

Sanders explained, "We would stand out in the street, and guys would pull up and ask us if we were police officers. 'Of course not,' we would say, or regardless of the language we used, we would convince them that we weren't. And we'd ask them what were they looking for. And the minute they said sex, it was like, well, 'Okay, what do I get for it?' You know, 'You offered sex: what do I get for it?' And they would make an offer. And so once they offered money, boom. It was a set deal. So we did decoy operations along Michigan Avenue. We did them in Brightmoor. We did them on Livernois. We did them on Fort Street. We did them in a lot of places."

She remembered standing out there in the cold and sometimes seeing a guy drive by her a couple times, real slow, only to come back and offer her a cup of coffee. He'd say something like, "I got this for you just to warm you up." Sanders would politely take it, say thank you. "And he'd stand there for a minute," she said, "and I wouldn't respond. Like he wanted me to drink it, but I damn sure wasn't going to drink it, so I sipped it, and I said, 'I gotta get moving because my kids need some food tonight.' And I'd walk away, and if he didn't pursue me, then he would just drive away, and I'd pour the coffee out."

She went on, "But yeah, it was a myriad of weird situations that all blended together into one job that provided me with lots of memories and lots of different views on what different people do in any given situation. Any class. You could find any class of person on Michigan Avenue. The addresses varied from Farmington Hills to around the block. I got a guy on a bicycle. And there was a guy in a very expensive—I can't remember what, I can't remember the type of Jaguar but it was a Jaguar. He was a very attractive man. And I'm like, come on, dude. You don't need to be buying prostitutes. I think I was mad at my sergeant because I told him I was a cop, to go home. I said, you'll never know because some officers actually really did it up.

I mean, really did it up. I mean, I had a fake nose ring. But some officers would take an eyebrow pencil and blacken out a couple teeth or stuff like that."

Sanders remembered the drug of choice at the time being crack. "Heroin had just started getting cheap enough for prostitutes to buy. But then again, there was a lot of trading going on. We had a house on Cottrell, in my area, and a lot of them would come down there, and the house was raided over and over and over again. But yeah, they were mainly into crack, and when I went to pat them down, I was like, 'If I get cut on a crack pipe ...' Because all they use is a broken tube. Stores in the area would sell those little rose flowers in the glass tubes. And of course, that was a crack pipe. But they sold it with a rose in it so they could pass that it wasn't paraphernalia. But so many times I would pat 'em down: 'Do you have anything on you that's going to cut me, stick me, or anything?' 'Nope.' Pat 'em down and sure enough, there's a broken piece of glass in their pocket. And it just frustrated me. But yeah, it was very prevalent. Crack use was very prevalent back then. Very, very prevalent. And you could tell it because heroin had a different effect, whereas crack just made them very jittery and they would always have this nasty smell about them. They would have this nasty spittle, a type of sickening spittle around their mouth and their lips."

There were a lot of prostitution busts back then, as John Eric Armstrong was doing his hunting. Sanders remembered it and so did Carl Day, who came aboard the Detroit force in 1967 and worked in various precincts over the years, including the area of Michigan Ave around the time of Armstrong's crimes. Day worked Woodward Avenue at one time too and was responsible for a lot of arrests over the course of his career, a whopping twelve hundred in teaming with his partner, he estimated.

"I used to interact a lot with the prostitutes on Michigan Avenue when I was not working Liquor, Gambling and

Vice, but when I was an FTO, a field training officer," Day said. "And I had all the new people working with me, and I was working midnights, mostly, at that time. And we used to get 'em off Michigan Avenue all the time. Virtually at Wyoming and Michigan Avenue, we used to herd 'em across the street to Dearborn. It would be nothing to have twenty-five or thirty working between Livernois and Wyoming, just on Michigan Avenue, at one time."

As nasty as Armstrong's hunting ground was, Day believed Woodward Avenue, slicing right up through the heart of Detroit, was worse. "We had a lot more of it on Woodward than they did on Michigan Avenue. Woodward Avenue and Michigan Avenue were the two places that catered to suburbanites. The johns all came from the suburbs."

Day, who retired from the force in 2002, recalled that time well. "Oh yeah, there were a lot of johns that were arrested, because when you arrested them, you took them in, they had to go to court, they had to post a bond, they hired an attorney." And then they were right back out there. "I mean, Detroit had a lot of police officers working prostitution in the city. Liquor, Gambling and Vice flourished very well."

He agreed that crack was the big thing. Crack houses were everywhere. "Prostitution was a means to support their drug habit," Day said. "And the people providing their drugs for them were their pimps. And everything was all about money. The drugs were money. The prostitution was money. The girls were worth money. And they used to beat the shit out of them if they didn't make enough money."

But Day didn't necessarily believe the pole dancing was at the heart of it. He saw some other angles of Detroit's prostitution biz.

"Well, you know, everybody wants to blame the strips clubs," he said. "The strip clubs weren't as bad as—hey, what about the drug houses? What about the people that were coming from Brownstown Township and coming in from the suburbs into Detroit with their girls, putting them out on the street, picking them up, and taking them home in the morning? And coming around every hour or two to relieve them of what money they had?"

And if it blows your mind that any woman in a suburb or anywhere else would subject herself to that, at least any one of age, Day said, "They didn't have a choice! They were on drugs. You know, crack cocaine, they could go on in and smoke a little bit of crack and go right back out to a hundred feet away. A lot of your crack houses were within one hundred or two hundred feet of Michigan Avenue."

One establishment that Day often frequented on Michigan Ave as he was working the prostitution beat was a popular twenty-four-hour hamburger joint that will respectfully remain nameless, a local landmark that has always done big business in the city. And working at that burger joint at the time was Sheryl Yike, who remembered Officer Day well, used to joke with him a lot, saw him come in all the time.

Sheryl remembered seeing lots of johns busted back then, their cars taken away. And prostitutes would be apprehended, then recruited to bust more johns. A lot of arrests going on. And she saw each one of Armstrong's three railroad-track victims wander into the tiny restaurant at one time or another in the months leading up to their deaths. Sheryl remembered Kelly as the skinny one that the morning shift workers said had kids. She remembered Rose as a bit heavier and a loner. Didn't talk much. She knew Nicole as the out-of-state girl new to the Detroit streets, not out there for very long at all before she disappeared. She remembered a pimp coming in with one of them. He would also hang out at the door of the restaurant while he was waiting for his girl to return from a job. Sheryl had to wonder what good he was, that he just seemed to be collecting cash but wasn't at all trying to make sure the girl was safe.

When these girls weren't high, they were fine, Sheryl said. They were pleasant. But they often did come in high. One time, one of them teased Sheryl that she must be jealous of her job since she made so much more money. And Sheryl actually got into a verbal fight at the counter with one of the three victims just shortly before her disappearance and the discovery at the tracks. The boss told the staff that when prostitutes came in, they were to be served quickly so they didn't linger inside the restaurant and they were not to be sitting at the counter. This woman came in one night, flailing and clearly high, hands purple from the drugs, and going every which way.

"She was putting her hands all over the counter, where we've got to put food," Sheryl remembered. "I'm supposed to say something. I didn't want to. I knew it was going to start something. But the boss was standing in that corner looking at me, like, what are you doing here? So I said, 'Listen, hon, I'm not trying to be mean. I don't know if you got something, what your hands have been up on. But they can't be on the counter where the food goes. It's unsanitized.' I said it real nice. She said, 'I'm not nasty! I don't got anything!'"

Sheryl wasn't sure what to do. "Yeah, she went 90 at me. She would not stop. And then I hurried up and got her out and whatever." Later, at the end of the shift, the girl was standing at the front door of the restaurant when Sheryl was leaving. "I'm like, *aww*. I worked a double. Two o'clock to six in the morning, so I was tired… I said, 'I'm so dang tired. I only did what my boss told me to do.'"

Thankfully there was no physical altercation that night and Sheryl was sickened and remorseful when she later learned of the girl's body being discovered at the tracks. And she recalled, amid all the talk about the case at the time, that things got a lot quieter around the burger joint. Her boss didn't have to worry so much about the hookers coming in and lingering—they were laying low, at least for a little while. One prostitute who did still come in, however, was one of Armstrong's survivors, Devin Marus. Having lived to tell the tale, she definitely told it at the burger place, Sheryl said. It was fascinating fodder for the prostitution culture of Michigan Avenue, a culture that continues to this day. Neither Day nor Sanders believe there's been any change in that in the decades since Armstrong's arrest. It's not any more prevalent, or any less. Just constant.

"It's the oldest profession and I don't think it will ever disappear," Sanders said. "And you have your classes, where a woman that has a separate idealism about what prostitution is may meet people from different places. And then you have those with no home, no place to meet people and, I mean, five dollars or a rock of crack or something just to get through to the next person. I was even threatened by one particular prostitute twice when I was doing decoy work. She was driving one of her john's cars and saw me walking and said, 'Bitch, get off my corner.' And I, of course, replied in kind. And then she tried to run me down the street, so she got arrested for that." It was pretty common for a prostitute to steal a john's car after telling him she'd go out and grab something, maybe booze, for the two of them, Sanders said. The john would then sheepishly try to pass it off as a car stolen by some random stranger.

"So yeah, they get aggressive," Sanders said of the prostitutes. "I don't know if it's because their mind is gone because of the drugs or because they're so depressed of their way of life and their status in society. But as far as the income in that area is concerned, I don't think too much would have changed. Unfortunately. And I've had guys in very expensive cars, with baby seats in the back seat, stop and try to solicit me. So I guess they find where to go and they go, regardless. I mean, I've had a guy on a bike ask me to do it in an alley."

Mark Bando was an officer on the DPD force in the 1970s, '80s, and '90s, and he worked the prostitution beat. He and his partner made a high volume of arrests of prostitutes, johns, and pimps from what was nicknamed the "whore car." And in that squad car, he brought along a homemade cataloguing system he devised for all the prostitutes and suspected prostitutes he encountered in the seedy Cass Corridor. He handwrote them all out by name in multiple binders, sometimes with snapshots, a birthdate if known, height and weight, little notes of observance, any family members and associates. He did this for his own reference, as well as for his fellow officers, to keep track of these women since they so often used fake names. There are a few pages in one volume of the binder set (which was nicknamed—you guessed it—the "whore book") dedicated to fake IDs. It was not uncommon for a prostitute to carry no identification at all but for many in this pre-Internet age where it was so much easier to exist off the grid (to the earlier point about finding Rose Felt), it was super easy to get a fake ID. A piece of cake. Many of the women carried them.

Bando also collected an array of other cards the women carried in their purses. "Want a date? Call me" one card said, along with the name Lynda and a phone number. Another said simply, "Call me" in the center, with a phone number off in a corner, no name. A business card. So in-your-face.

It was chilling to look through Bando's books, which this author prefers to term a "call-girl catalog" rather than that other name, and see these young women, most of them photographed in the 1980s. Like Kelly Hood, they wear clothing I can remember from high school. Their hairstyles are decidedly '70s and '80s. In the snapshots, some of these girls are hanging in the window of the squad car, smiling for the camera, and they look like '80s prom queens. Fresh makeup. Fluffy hair. So young. If you drive down Michigan Ave—or the Cass—now, you see women looking twice their age after just a few years out there. That's due in part to the difference between heroin and crack.

Bando had both an edge and a heart as he talked with me about them. A mix of disgust, frustration, disappointment. Even hurt, as he talked about one woman in particular that he came to know a lot about, a young girl whose alcoholic mother moved them into the Cass Corridor when she was younger. A girl who went to bed hungry a lot of nights and fell into prostitution as the easiest way to get some cash. One day she was snatched up and taken into a motel room and gang raped for three days by members of Young Boys Inc., or YBI. After that, she didn't want to live. She OD'd, leaving behind a two-year-old girl she'd had at seventeen.

There were those girls whose stories touch your heart, and there were other girls. Bando echoed Sanders' perceptions of aggression on the part of prostitutes who could be stealing your car or acting out in other ways.

"I saw another aspect to that which I interpreted as their contempt for males in general," he said. "They were accustomed to being in charge with their tricks, dictating the terms of each encounter, and came to despise the passivity of their customers. This inflated their ego and sense of power so it was real difficult to deal with types like that in a police encounter, because they were so arrogant and felt that nobody could rein them in because they were accustomed to being tyrannical objects of adoration. Those types were not the majority, but they were usually the more decent-looking ones, who were not yet eaten up by drugs."

What caused me to even be looking through Bando's call-girl catalog in the first place, to be talking with him, is I was looking for my victims. Rose, Kelly, Monica— Wendy was the likeliest possibility since she was older and most of these women were catalogued in the '80s. Even though Bando worked the Cass and not Michigan, a lot of women would wander. One high-profile woman from his binders, Dawn Marie Spens, one of the subjects of the book *Masquerade* by Lowell Cauffiel for her involvement in the murder of a Detroit psychologist, worked both Cass and

Michigan at different times. Kelly, Rose, and Monica were in their thirties when they were killed and could have been out there off and on for several years. But alas and alack, none of the girls were in the binders. Not even Armstrong's assault survivors were in there. Out of curiosity, I tried finding the victims of Benjamin Atkins, who killed earlier than Armstrong, in 1991 and 1992, and had more victims. Not a single one of those women were in there either. Bando's catalog covered about twelve hundred women. But there are just that many sex workers in Detroit, at least there were at the time. Bando sees that as changing in more recent years, in terms of the visibility on the streets.

"Today, with them being mostly off the streets and invisible due to escort services and online and smartphone contacts," he said, "it is impossible to know if that business is still thriving as much as it was thirty years ago, or what the actual current situation might be. When all those hookers were out on the streets, well, it was an era when they were quite visible, but unless technology collapses, it's an era we will never see again."

And always with some trying to go legit. Trying to get themselves off the streets, like our five Detroit victims often were. Getting themselves more civilized employment. Getting off the drugs, for a time. Trying, then failing. Maybe trying again.

One of Armstrong's arresting officers, Rodney Durham, had his own special case he was sorta keeping tabs on, much like Bando's Cass Corridor teen. Her name was Stella and she was from the Grosse Pointes. Durham's partner at the time had actually gone to school with the girl there in the Pointes. She was one of the girls everybody wanted to date, he said. She had been a cheerleader. She came from a prominent family. They were well-off; her dad was in the oil biz. Stella had everything going for her. A bright future. She was pretty. But she got hooked. Durham and his partner were continually running her in, locking her up. Then her family would have someone come get her, take her to rehab. Sometimes they had to hire a private investigator to find her.

"She would be gone for three or four months," Durham said. "She would come out, and you would catch her the first, second day she got out. She looked really good, put on a lot of weight. But then she was right back at it, you know? She'd just look like shit again for the next couple weeks. And somebody again would haul her off. This was a repetitive process that just kept going on and on and on."

Until the day Durham and his partner got a particular run to a motel on Michigan Ave. Report of a dead body.

"Sure enough, it was her. They had put cigarettes out on her. They sodomized her with a screwdriver. All kinds of terrible stuff. They cut her nipples off."

This was not long after the Armstrong case, he recalled, maybe 2001 or 2002.

"It was one of the more brutal crime scenes that I have ever had to see. It was one of the tougher ones to look at. It was really, really sad, and that's because we had reached out to her so much. Just a sad story all the way around, because so many people don't even get any recognition. That happens every day in that city."

But the culture of the street is just not easily explained.

"What desperation drives people to do sometimes takes a lot of understanding and a lot of empathy and a lot of compassion," Sanders said. "You can judge, and you can decide what choices should have been made when, but sometimes people get in positions where they are so desperate they don't have time to think about it."

At the heart of it all, we have to come back to the reality of addiction.

"Once it's there, without any backup, without any support, without any ..." Sanders said. "But a lot of times, we would come across people and say, 'We can get you here,' 'we can get you there, 'would you like to go to this shelter.' A lot of people don't want to get off the streets because their freedom is restricted. It's a choice. And if you say, 'Listen, you can clean up, we can take you to this shelter,' a lot of women are abused, and so they need the narcotics to numb the pain, the physical and emotional pain from the abuse. However, like I said, it comes down to a choice. Do I want to risk going into a shelter and rehab and feeling the effects of withdrawal, or do I want to risk staying on the street and just dealing with it because I know I can get something to numb it? It's like being in hell, you know?"

CRIMES OF OPPORTUNITY

"Prostitutes are pretty easy targets. They go with whoever's got the money. They anticipate a certain amount of violence. And sometimes it winds up being fatal for them."

Those are the words of Elizabeth Walker, who successfully prosecuted John Eric Armstrong, as quoted in ID's *Very Bad Men* episode about the case. It sums up one aspect of the "why prostitutes" question pretty well.

Detroit Police Chief Benny Napoleon speculated simply, at the time of Armstrong's arrest, as quoted in *The Detroit News*, "He may have targeted prostitutes because he didn't believe police would investigate those murders as aggressively."

James Alan Fox, a criminology professor at Northeastern University in Boston, theorized about Armstrong at the same time: "For him, preying on prostitutes was a hobby. He did it when he had some free time to kill." (Pun intended?)

You have to consider, though, that there's a paradox to that idea of prostitutes being willing to go with anyone who's got money. "Street walkers are probably the most paranoid people (short of cops) that you will ever meet," said Gerald Cliff, who as a beat cop in Detroit in the 1970s would sometimes glean valuable intel from prostitutes. "For them, it's a survival skill they need to master in order to continue to function. They need to fear the sexual predator *and* the cops when they work. Getting them to trust you requires a master of deception." That meant some skill on Armstrong's part, he believes. "Everything I've read about serial killers, they were all very personable and very adept at deception. This is one of the required skills for this type of crime. Armstrong had to be a practiced liar to have been able get all these victims to trust him enough to go with him to wherever he chose to kill them."

Jim Izeluk retired from the Dearborn Heights Police Department in 1999 but was called in as a consultant to work the Armstrong case in 2000 when Wendy Jordan was discovered in the Rouge River. Having witnessed or worked the cases of between one and two hundred prostitutes found murdered over the course of his career, the Jordan case wasn't unusual to him. He recalled one particular unsolved case of a prostitute being found at a truck stop at Van Born between Beech Daly and Inkster, near the city border. This was earlier in the 1990s. And the idea, when a body was found, that it might be a serial killer would come up sometimes, so Izeluk was consulted on the possibility of there being a connection between Wendy and any of the other cases he had investigated. Yes, prostitutes are easy prey, he agreed. But, Izeluk said, "I think it goes deeper than that, myself. Maybe I'm reading too much into that stuff. But I think it goes back to childhood or something. If you look at these serial killers—I did a research paper on psychopaths and sociopaths—and it all goes down to their first eighteen months of life, and how they were treated by their parents, lack of love. And then you see these kids burning and torturing animals and all that; it's a surefire thing."

Izeluk said, "They say most serial killers are very, very pleasant, good-looking guys. They're very convincing to people. You want a prostitute, you got a twenty-dollar bill, they're going to jump in."

One interesting phenomenon Izeluk saw often in his work in this Detroit suburb was a spillover from the city, actually. Prostitutes dumped within the Dearborn Heights city limits that police figured were killed in Detroit. So the Wendy Jordan discovery wasn't surprising in that aspect either. That accounted for a good chunk of the cases he investigated.

"We think they were probably just dumped," he said. "We don't know where they were murdered. But we had some prostitutes that used to work Telegraph, or Michigan Avenue, something like that. Even Van Born on the south end. Mostly they worked Michigan Avenue and Inkster, Michigan Avenue way down in Detroit, sometimes Telegraph in Redford, down that way. We don't know where they come from, but we know they are prostitutes."

He added, as a joke: "I think the cops dumped 'em instead of the people." A joke with perhaps an edge of truth? "Well, it's like, you get a whodunit in Dearborn Heights, you know it's going to get worked. In Detroit, they're not going to work it. They just don't have the manpower or the time, you know? Unless it's a smoking gun in Detroit, you're not going to get much of an investigation, unfortunately."

Another police officer who worked the Armstrong case, Everett Monroe, was asked, from his own perspective in law enforcement, why did he think this killer chose prostitutes as victims?

"Maybe something in his earlier years caused him to lash out. I know Benjamin Atkins used to go with his mother—his mother was a prostitute and she used to take him with her when she did her tricks. And he developed this hatred for prostitution. John had a hatred for his dad and the way that his mother was treated. I don't know. Maybe he just picked an element of society that he felt was bad."

In 2018, in trying to explain his own targeting of prostitutes, incarcerated serial killer Joel Rifkin told journalist Chris Cuomo: "A total stranger is willing to get in a car and then park in some dark, way-out-of-the-way place." It was just easier, as he explained it. "There is no family; there are no friends. There's no relatives."

Rifkin, who was very forthcoming in the prison interview about his crimes for this episode of the TV series *Inside Evil*, said he did not kill every prostitute he was with. There was no rhyme or reason why he killed one and not another.

So we've got the idea that prostitutes will get into a car with anybody who has got money. These girls are easy to get alone. And their desperation may be sharpened by drug addiction. They have no issue with going to secluded places where crimes can more easily be committed. We have the idea that prostitutes are on the lower rungs of society and wouldn't be missed, that their cases would not be investigated so aggressively. That they're in a high-risk profession and are accustomed to violence anyway; sometimes their tricks are "jumping bad," or turning violent. That public sympathy for their deaths is not as great. Maybe even the idea that they're evil or bad, the subject of hatred and should be eliminated, as once indicated by the so-called "Butcher Baker" Robert Hansen and the "Green River Killer" Gary Ridgway. These are referred to as mission-oriented serial killers who target prostitutes to clean the streets. Added to all of that supposed rationale, we've got Armstrong's own practical reasoning that prostitutes can be easily controlled. And that he just plain didn't like them.

Dr. Lawrence Simon, the psychologist mentioned earlier who studied serial killers, begs to differ on the idea that prostitute murders are not investigated so heartily by police.

"I do want to tell you, this is a big misconception," he said. "And I always hate hearing it. But this is a misconception that you hear, but it's from the general public, whereas their cases, when they disappear, they're not concentrated on as much or they're kind of low-risk victims in the sense where they're not going to be missed as much as someone like a teacher or an accountant or a lawyer. Somebody that's out there, you see, and maybe viewed as a respected member as far as that's concerned. Law enforcement has got that bad rap. Generally, the homicide detectives that I've met throughout my ten years, twelve, thirteen years of doing these seminars, not one of these detectives has not taken each homicide seriously. It's just the general public kind of views it that way. The fact of the matter is that these cases are extraordinarily difficult. The average lifespan of a serial killer in the '80s was ten years. Now it's about two years. But that's because of the advancements of law enforcement. It does make it a little more difficult with known prostitutes because they do disappear sometimes, and they're not kept track of as much as let's say someone else. And that is the reality, unfortunately, of the situation. But their cases are taken seriously. Each case is taken seriously. It's just that unfortunately they do make a victim that's not going to be recognized that they're gone the next day. It may take like a week or two, and by then—you know what I mean?"

On the opportunity issue, Simon points to changing cultural trends over time. In the 1970s, hitchhiking was popular, for instance, and he has talked to serial killers who once used that opportunity to pick up victims. But hitchhiking was recognized as dangerous and has since become unpopular and largely disappeared from our culture. Jogging, on the other hand, is something that was popular back then and is still popular these days, and he has seen that as an opportunity for this brand of criminal.

"When I do my classes, I tell folks, especially women, when they're jogging, don't jog at night. Things that may not seem so simple. Not jogging in the evening with headphones on. Getting in a car where there's a guy that's in the passenger seat. These are all stories that I've actually heard from serial killers on how they get their victims. That's how they get them nowadays. I mean, back in the day—especially I wouldn't be surprised with, obviously, some of the prostitutes—they're hitchhiking. It's like shooting fish in a barrel. But nowadays, things are a little bit different. Even with prostitution nowadays, unless, of course, they're addicted to drugs, you have folks that are operating with madams and pimps and things like that that make it a little bit more challenging for a serial killer. But it's not that difficult. That area of profession, if you will, is always going to be targeted much more than let's say a random jogger. However, that's why I say that that's what you have now. Those are the high-risk folks, folks that are jogging, folks that are camping, things like that, and parks. And I tell my own daughter that too, to avoid these things. Especially, obviously, the camping. I mean, if you're going to jog, then you should make sure that you take the safety precautions. I'm not advocating any particular product, but there's at least four or five out there on the market that are specifically designed because of the predators that are actually out there. Not just obviously serial killers, but rapists and things like that that are out there actually looking for vulnerable victims."

Unlike Joel Rifkin, it was said of John Eric Armstrong at the time of his arrest that he killed or attempted to kill every prostitute he was with. We have no way of knowing that, but it's another point Simon is doubtful of, with both Armstrong and other killers he's profiled.

"I have one serial killer, he didn't kill every prostitute he came into contact with; however, the ones that he did kill, either he perceived being, or was literally, ripped off. So for example, if getting fellatio cost sixty dollars but he didn't have an orgasm, he didn't like the way she did it, yet she wanted the money, he'd kill, you know? If he said that somebody charged forty dollars but then said that it would be eighty dollars, you know, then they're going to die."

Armstrong spoke of being cheated out of his money in some of his confessions to police. And often he would flat out take the prostitute's money.

THE 'BABY DOLL' SERIAL KILLER   335

How much does social class or structure come into play with serial killers like Armstrong? Does targeting women who work the streets venture into the idea of eliminating those on a lower rung of society whom the killer believes should be eliminated or who are deemed powerless to defend themselves? Some have wondered. The paper "Researching Serial Murder: Methodological and Definitional Problems" by Ronald Hinch and Crystal Hepburn argues that there is good reason to question the assumption that the victims of serial murder are powerless people who are on a lower rung of society, but this has changed over time. They point to the work of another researcher, Elliott Leyton, in arguing whether or not the modern multiple murderer is attempting to level the social structure. "Multiple murderers of previous eras had been members of the higher strata who primarily killed members of the lower strata," the paper says. "By contrast, the modern multiple murderer comes from the lower strata and kills representatives of the higher strata."

Leyton explained, "The major homicidal form of the modern era is the man who straddles the border between then upper-working class and the lower-middle class. Occasionally ... they continue a metaphor from the earlier era and discipline unruly prostitutes and runaways. Much more commonly, however, they punish those above them in the system—preying on unambiguously middle-class figures such as university women." Ted Bundy, for instance. But not really Armstrong, though he fits the first part of Leyton's explanation.

Whatever the reason, whatever the social standing, whatever the likes or dislikes of the perp, it all comes down to the value of a human life. It's an idea that was well represented by the sisters of Wendy Jordan, who stood strongly like bulldogs throughout the case, sternly staring down all involved until justice was served. Until law enforcement completed its job, until a jury agreed. Until a guilty verdict was given.

On the *Very Bad Men* episode, Judy Jordan said, "I knew that they knew Wendy was worthy. This was not a throwaway that nobody wanted."

WHY, AT ALL?

It was a long series of confessions at Detroit police headquarters through the early morning hours of April 12, all day, and into the morning of April 13, 2000. The more questions the police officers asked, the more information they got back. Details—places, timeframes, victims' clothing—came flowing forth from John Eric Armstrong, flavored with remorse and a mix of other emotions. Rising to the surface at times, in certain confessions, were glimmers of insight into just what might be in back of this career of killing that was thankfully brought to a close.

There was the very interesting detail that came out during Armstrong's confessions of the Virginia killing and the Cynthia Smith assault. He said he saw his father's face on the woman in Virginia. But that's not all.

"Why do you kill?" asked Ira Todd and Everett Monroe of the Violent Crime Task Force during the confession for the male victim in Seattle, Washington, in November 1996.

"I like to be in control."

"Why do you like being in control?"

"Because my father was in control of everything."

"Was he in control of you?" they wondered.

"He was in control of everybody," Armstrong confirmed.

"How does killing people put you in control?"

"Because I'm the stronger type and they're the weaker type."

"Who do you prefer killing, men or women?"

"Women."

"Why?"

"Because I can control them more."

"How do you control them?"

"Making them being submissive."

"Have you ever killed with a weapon other than a metal pipe?"

"No."

"What do you normally kill people with?"

"My bare hands."

"How?"

"By strangulation."

"Have you had any special training with your hands?" they asked.

"No."

An hour or two later, after Armstrong told police he killed a prostitute in Hawaii to get back at his wife after they'd had an argument, the officers asked if he enjoyed killing this woman. He replied no.

"Did you see fear in her eyes?"

"Yes."

"How did it make you feel?"

"Scared."

"Did she know she was going to die?"

"I don't know."

Several hours earlier, during that afternoon, when confessing the 1996/97 murder of the Asian transgender prostitute in Thailand, Armstrong wrote in his own hand on the statement paper, followed by his signature:

The reason why I threw her out the window was because I felt humiliated, frustrated, angry, out-of-control. I have no control in killing hookers, except I have control and I will never kill my wife, or my child. I have killed only nine people that I can remember. Most of my victims I've strangled because I hate hookers. I don't want to have my son become fatherless like I was. I love my 14-month-old son very dearly and I have one on the way. I would like to watch my children grow up.

Control has been a key element in the psychology of John Eric Armstrong, for sure.

HIS HUMBLE BEGINNINGS

Settled in 1710 and named after a town in Switzerland, New Bern is located along the eastern coastline of North Carolina. It's characterized by a few different things. Because of its location, it often falls prey to hurricanes charging in from the Atlantic. It is also known as the birthplace of Pepsi-Cola, first developed in 1893 by Caleb Bradham at his drugstore. Plus, the city, with a population of about 31,000 nowadays, is the setting for resident Nicholas Sparks' popular novel *The Notebook*. Fox's TV series *Sleepy Hollow* shot there. But beyond all of that, it was in this small Southern town draped in about two thousand crepe myrtles—its official flower—where John Eric Armstrong grew up.

"New Bern is a historical town," said Dana Dixon, who attended school with Armstrong. "The first capital of North Carolina and birthplace of Pepsi Co." She also noted the town is home of Tryon Palace, where North Carolina's British governors resided in the 1700s and which now houses a historical center and some palace grounds that set the scene for *Sleepy Hollow*.

"Growing up we could roam most of the town without worry," Dana reminisced. "The go-to restaurant was the old Billy's Ham and Eggs. The teenage hangout was the mall, the theaters, or 37th St. Pizza. I was born and raised there until I moved to Alabama in 1989. I went back to visit in 2017. A lot has changed but it's still my hometown. I really miss it."

Born in November 1973 to John and Linda Armstrong and growing up there in New Bern through the 1970s, John Eric Armstrong attended the local schools with Dana: Trent Park Elementary, J.T. Barber Elementary, H.J. MacDonald Middle, West Craven High, New Bern High. His mom Linda was a licensed practical nurse but later worked as a teacher's assistant for Craven County schools. As a child, he fished and played Nintendo, said news reports at the time of his arrest. His family went to the beach a lot, which he enjoyed, he would later write in a letter from prison. He was a student of B and C grades who talked of someday becoming a police officer.

"John was just a goofy kid who happened to be taller than everyone else," Dana recalled. "He was always polite, a little standoffish. We'd goof off in class and the lunch lines. He used to say jokingly, 'God named me Armstrong 'cause I have strong arms.' He'd slap his forearms as he made a fist to prove his point. I vaguely remember, but I do remember him changing his name to Eric around sixth or seventh grade. It was hard for us to remember because he'd always been John to us. He'd get real upset if you called him John. I think that's why most people continued calling him John. I lost touch with him after eighth grade because my family moved to Alabama. Next time I heard anything about him was when my cousin called telling me about the murders. I was truly shocked. He did have a bit of a temper but he would have never hurt anyone, or so I thought."

Bill Taylor attended Trent Park Elementary with Eric Armstrong and was friends with him. "We were always cool with each other (probably since we weren't part of the 'cool kids')," Taylor recalled. He did not recall Eric being involved in any school activities. "He was always fairly quiet. Never one to stand out in the crowd except being a big guy and the red hair."

Trinity Kathleen Lee, who was in a youth group with Eric at what was then National Avenue Baptist Church (later Crossroads Baptist Church), echoed that. "I remember he was fairly quiet and a little reserved," she said. "He seemed nice, just not too talkative, and I was surprised when he and my friend also from youth group started being boyfriend and girlfriend."

Her impression of Eric, years later, follows right along the lines of anyone else who knew him. Knew him in passing, at least. "I can't remember him talking about his family or other friends, or anything that he genuinely liked as most people would (sports, music, movies) or even other events and such that took place outside of youth group. He did come most every Sunday and any outings we went on, but there isn't anything that sticks out, like, oh, he really talked about this or that. He really was that quiet. He seemed sweet, just reserved."

Trinity's grandmother, Judy Avery, was closer to Eric as one of the leaders of the church's youth group. She and her husband Les would shuttle kids to and from the Sunday night church activities and the various outings. In her eighties when interviewed via phone for this book, she easily remembered the tall, sweet boy who faithfully came to the youth group back then.

"He attached himself to me," Judy recalled, her well-spoken, polite voice resonating with a certain Southern belle flavor. "He was a very endearing person at that time, but also very troubled."

The Eric she knew for several years in his teens would be waiting patiently outside for her to pick him up for church, and when she got out of the van, he would come up and kiss her on the cheek. Les would joke that Eric now owed him a dollar for kissing his wife.

"He was very good, sweet, attentive," Judy said, "and would do endearing little things, like bring me a little rosebush for Mother's Day or something like that. Write me little notecards." She remembered one of the notecards, which she had tucked away in her Bible for years, that said, "Don't worry, be happy."

At the time, Eric's family lived in a trailer park just on the other side of Bridgeton, an area of New Bern across the river. Judy met Linda a time or two at special church services, but never met Ron, as he was on the road a lot for his driving job. And as Judy got to know Eric, this neatly dressed kid who never used bad language, she remembered that he had dreamed as a teen about someday joining the Navy Seals. "He would talk to me on end about it."

Miss Judy, as she was known, led young Eric to the Lord, as she no doubt did with others in this group of twenty-five or so kids in her care for church activities. And she recalled that day in church, after Eric had made his profession of faith when he was about to be baptized.

"He came to where I was sitting in the congregation," she remembered. "And he was just wringing his hands, and he said, 'Miss Judy, you've got to go back there with me. You've got to go back there with me.' And I said, 'Eric, they don't do that. They have one side for the men and boys, one side for the women and girls.' And I said, 'There will be some men back there that will help you. They'll help you down into the water.' And I said, 'But I will be right here, and you're going to be just fine.'" And though Eric did find the courage to go to the baptismal water without her, she remembered that incident showing this teen's more tender side.

One event that we know had a deep effect on Armstrong was the death of his baby brother Michael, born in 1978. The baby was only a couple months old when he died in his crib, a death determined to be from sudden infant death syndrome (SIDS). The trauma of losing his baby brother, whom mother Linda has said Eric saw as his own baby, was devastating. Judy remembered that Eric did not share many details with her about his little brother's death, but he did tell her that it was very difficult for him.

Linda did not let him go to little Mikey's grave on the day of burial. "The therapist felt like he never had closure," she would tell the media years later when he was arrested. "You do what you think is best … I made a mistake."

Plus, Eric, only five years old, was said to have blamed his father John for his brother's death.

"Even as a teenager, he felt (his father) killed the baby," Linda told the media. "I don't know where that came from. We had an autopsy. But he never did believe it."

The story that Kevin Gray wrote about Armstrong for *Details* magazine in March 2001, however, just as the trial for Wendy Jordan's murder was beginning, dropped a bomb regarding the death of the baby.

"One night, in January 1979," Gray wrote, "when Mikey was 2 months old, Armstrong says he found his little brother dead in his crib. Then he crept back to bed and feigned sleep. The coroner's report states that the cause of death was SIDS, sudden infant death syndrome. In a recent letter to his wife, Armstrong suggests this may have been his first victim. 'There is no way I can live with that guilt,' he wrote. 'Knowing that I killed my little brother, without knowing it.'"

Gray's story, also posted on his website, is the only place this tidbit can be found. Though the idea—perhaps just speculation on Armstrong's part—seems quite weighty, it never came up anywhere else. Perhaps it was halfway mentioned when at the first trial, Dr. Calmeze Dudley testified that Armstrong blamed himself for the death of his baby brother. But it was not really explored then, the inference being more that he blamed himself in another way—like maybe he didn't do enough to protect his brother, as he had discussed with Officer Donald Johnson. But which was it—he blamed his father or he blamed himself? Could his own baby brother be the very first victim in North Carolina that Armstrong mentioned to Detroit police right after his arrest but did not give any details about?

Years after Eric was tried and incarcerated, Judy Avery was told by a friend that there had been a rumor in New Bern that Eric had something to do with his baby brother's death. Judy had not herself seen Gray's story, so it's unclear if the story was the source of the rumor or if there was something else that started it. Perhaps it was just the idea that someone who has been convicted of murder happened to have a baby brother who died in the crib? A sort of guilt-by-association conclusion and the standard workings of a rumor mill in any town?

Eric's family found in his childhood Bible that he had recorded his brother's death there four times.

It was also during this time in his childhood that, Armstrong alleged, his father abused him. John Armstrong left the family shortly after the death of baby Mikey. But was the claim of sexual abuse at the hand of his father just a tactic to get him acquitted, or did it really happen? Eric was quoted in Gray's story as saying he once walked in on his father beating and strangling his mother. There are also some uglier details about his own alleged abuse in that story. Gray said he based his article on not only interviewing and corresponding with Eric, but also talking with his wife and others in his life. And in later years, Eric would write a female acquaintance from prison that his biological dad "was married to five women at once" at the time his parents divorced.

Added to that gruesome-sounding childhood, Linda claimed that Eric broke his leg when he fell out of a window at age two when his father was supposed to be watching him. "He was abusive to Eric. He was abusive to me as well—and Eric saw that," said Linda, forty-nine at the time she was quoted and living in a mobile home in New Bern. "I always thought Eric and I had a good relationship," she said. "Why didn't he tell me? I would have done something to help him."

Jennifer Westberg, Armstrong's friend and co-worker at Target, remembered him talking about his childhood in North Carolina, and she remembered that he hated both parents, not just his biological father.

"Whenever I would tell a story about my upbringing," she said, "he would match it with a story about his childhood. Unfortunately, I don't remember any specific stories. What

I remember most was how much he hated his parents. His stories would always make me feel better about my own life. Like, 'Well, at least I don't have it as bad as he did.' He did mention his brother dying, once. He also blamed his parents for his death."

A few years after Eric's biological father left, he gained a new dad, Ron, whom his mother married in 1984. Ron already had a daughter, and together he and Linda had a son in 1985.

It came out in *The Detroit News*' coverage of the case that Eric had been admitted to a psychiatric hospital as a teen. He was said to be suicidal after trouble with his girlfriend at the time. Linda told the media that he spent thirty days in a North Carolina psychiatric hospital as a high school sophomore after locking himself in a bathroom with a knife. "A girl in high school was pressuring him real heavy for sex," she said. "He didn't want nothing to do with her. I couldn't trust that he wouldn't hurt himself." Earlier that same year, Eric had visited a psychiatrist because he was still fixated on Mikey's infant death from eleven years earlier. The timeframe for this apparent suicide attempt and hospitalization matches the more recent blog post comment by "Elizabeth," who claimed to have been the girlfriend.

Also as a teen, Eric was said to have a girlfriend named Kelly that he was very much in love with and whom he grew apart when she went to college, his family remembered at the time of his arrest. Some of the details Eric told police about his childhood were not really corroborated by his family members when interviewed by the media but it's possible they just weren't privy to those details.

"He was very quiet and didn't have a lot of friends," high school classmate Sami Marsh told *The Detroit News*. "He was an introvert."

Judy Avery had the inside track during that time of the suicide attempt, one of two suicidal incidents she remembered for Eric. The girlfriend that Eric had at the time, whose name was neither Elizabeth nor Kelly, was also a member of the church youth group. In an interesting detail, the girl had raised allegations that her father was abusing her. She later recanted those allegations, despite being very adamant about them at the time, but in the midst of them, the situation had Eric tied up in knots, Judy recalled. He didn't know how to deal with the emotions he was having. There was an incident one particular night where Eric ran the six or so miles to Judy's house all the way from his own house on the other side of Bridgeton. She was not home at the time, but he waited for her a while, then took off. The sheriff, alerted by Eric's mom Linda, finally found him— standing over the edge of one of the bridges in town. Eric never talked to Judy about this incident.

Judy also recalled an incident on a church youth trip to the beach. She and another youth leader took a couple vans full of kids there and back for an enjoyable day swimming. She was driving the van in which Eric rode.

"When we got back to Havelock, which is about fifteen miles from New Bern," Judy said, "somebody told me we had to stop, that Eric was about to pass out in the back. So we did, pulled over at a shopping center. And of course, the other van pulled over too. And Eric was hyperventilating and couldn't get his breath. And so we finally had to take him out of the van, and I went and talked to him and got him to do the breathing exercises that you do when you're going to like have a baby. You know, to calm him down. And eventually he did."

Whatever was going on in Eric's head, he otherwise seemed to live a normal teenage life. He went to two of his high school proms, his family said. He worked at a Food Lion grocery store in New Bern while still attending New Bern High School, where he graduated with a class of about three hundred and fifty in June 1992. He never got into trouble with police; they had never heard of him during those years.

Stephanie W. of New Bern worked with Eric at the Food Lion, getting to know him there for more than a year. She became a sort of second mom to him, taking him under her wing, as she recalled years later for this book. And now she feels like she almost knew a different person back then.

"At that time, the Eric that I know was just one of the sweetest guys you could ever know," Stephanie said. "He was tall, lanky, kind of not really self-confident. But had a great sense of humor. A hard worker. I mean, he would do anything. He never complained when he was asked to do duties that weren't actually his. And just had an extreme love for his family."

Eric and the younger half-brother he gained after his mom remarried were very close. "He was very protective over him. His brother just adored him. Just a really good kid."

Linda was actually the Avon lady of Stephanie's mother-in-law, not surprising for this small-town setting. Stephanie's impression of Eric and his family was very positive. They were a tight family, a good one, she recalled, with Eric being not only a great older brother but a great son too.

Something Eric struggled with as a teen were migraines, as she remembered. She heard that they were doing tests on him to try to ascertain why, and that the migraines were pretty debilitating for him, requiring him to leave work.

Eric enlisted in the US Navy in April 1992 under a delayed entry program, then completed boot camp in Florida in November 1992. He reported to the *USS Nimitz* warship and aircraft carrier, designation CVN-68, for duty in March 1993, where he served until he was honorably discharged in April 1999. He enlisted for an initial four years, then reenlisted in October 1996 for two more years. While aboard he worked in the ship's barbershop, among other duties. He was an aviation fueler when he first got to the *Nimitz*, one of his shipmates said, though another disputed that, saying he was a ship's serviceman, meaning one of the ones in charge of the ship's stores and barbershops. Indeed, records show Eric was designated Ship's Serviceman Third Class Petty Officer (SH3) in June 1995.

And he got to travel all over the place, during his time aboard the *Nimitz*. He would later say that he loved Dubai in particular—and visited there thirteen times. He talked about the vendors with gold and silver chains you could buy, wound around big spindles. He bought his wife a couple rings there for about fifty dollars each but they might be worth more like five hundred, he said. You could get a good deal there. He bought his stepdad a leather horse statue that was probably a foot high. You could see the muscles in the horse, it was so detailed.

Hawaii is a nice place to visit but you wouldn't want to live there, he would later say, because it has such a high cost of living. He enjoyed seeing the memorial for the *USS Arizona* battleship, however, which is still there at Pearl Harbor. It leaks oil and they say that's the "Arizona's tears."

He loved Seattle, near the *Nimitz*'s home port. He would take a ferry from where he was stationed, about an hour-long trip up to Seattle. He liked it there even though it rained nine months of the year. He said the people there were really nice.

He kept up with his friend and second mom Stephanie during those years. He occasionally called her from different ports, she said. She remembered one particular call, when Eric turned twenty-one. He called to tell her that for his birthday, his shipmates had gotten him a hooker. Before that, he had been a virgin, from her understanding.

Judy Avery also recalled Eric calling her from different spots while he was in the Navy. Though she never saw him again after he enlisted, she would get a phone call from him once or twice a year.

NCIS records indicate that in July 1994, just about a year and a half after Armstrong came aboard the *Nimitz*, he was having some issues and was referred to the senior medical officer. Armstrong explained that overspending was causing him some financial problems and he was having trouble with a best friend. On top of that, two of his close friends back in New Bern were murdered due to "drug problems," he said. Under evaluation, Armstrong admitted to "fleeting suicidal ideations," but said he would never actually commit suicide. The medical officer found no evidence of pathological behavior. Armstrong also complained of migraines at this time; a CT scan revealed no abnormality. Among other reported issues: carpal tunnel syndrome, ankle injuries, chest pains with shortness of breath, vomit containing blood, and difficulty tolerating physical training.

Since his arrest, all kinds of fellow servicemen have spoken up about Eric Armstrong, who was referred to as "Opie" aboard the ship. Some of them have spoken to the media. Some have posted to online message boards and news articles.

"'Opie' as we called him worked for me," one commented on a blog post about the case. "I was stationed on the USS Nimitz for just 18 months. I would have never guessed he was able to [do] something like this. He always seemed so timid and would cry at the drop of a hat."

"I was on board the USS Nimitz when Armstrong first reported and I left in 1994," another said. "Everyone I have spoken to who were shipmates have all said the same thing, we all thought he didn't like girls, ANY GIRLS. During his first WESPAC (deployment) we tried to get him to go out drinking but he refused. He did make it clear his dislike for prostitutes, but we never saw him angry. Really weird knowing that I shared a berthing with this guy."

One woman commented, "I was stationed with Opie on the Nimitz as well and worked closely with him. For a while I was the only woman in the S-3 division and Opie was one of the men that trained me to do my job. There were several times that Opie and I would go out drinking and end up getting a piercing or tattoo. I always felt that he was a close friend and since I've found out about this there have been several moments I look back and wonder how the hell I got away with treating him like that and lived."

"I too was stationed on the *Nimitz* with Opie," said another commenter, Tony Palmer, also quoted in the media at the time as noted earlier. "We got there around the same time but I ended up leaving before him. I liked hanging out with him because he always had a way of talking to you, it just made you feel a bit better. He had that boyish laugh and personality that made you think that he couldn't hurt a fly. I even had him at my family house sometimes for dinner. But when I was told about what had happened, I just thought that someone was playing a really bad joke. Then I saw it in the papers and reporters were leaving messages asking for interviews. People still ask me questions today about him. I just really hope that his family will get through this. And I do hope that someone can crack the code of WHY he did all this to begin with."

Still another said, "I was onboard the *Nimitz* from '94 to '97 with Eric. He was always a great guy. He used to hang with a lot of us on port visits and in fact I still have many photos of all us hanging out. I would have never thought of Eric as a serial killer. He never acted in a way that I thought strange. He met his wife Katie on the *Nimitz* and they always seemed so happy together. After they met, that was pretty much how his time was spent, with her. I hate to hear that all this happened and never knew anything about it until the story broke. I wish the best for Katie and the kids. I can only imagine how awful it is for them to have to go through something like this."

"He was a nice guy, worked just as hard as the rest of us," another commented. "Always had an answer to explain the scratches (on) the neck!" (But who knows if that last bit is just an add-on, joining in with the conversation and getting a little carried away?)

Blogger Lance Lambert posted on his own blog about how Armstrong was his barber on the ship: "Our exchanges in the barber chair were brief and lively. I liked Armstrong, particularly his penchant for making light of serious subjects—often himself—which suited me just fine. His shipmates called him 'Opie' after the *Andy Griffith Show* character, for his red hair, freckled complexion and country demeanor."

Blake Hempstead, who served with Armstrong aboard the *Nimitz*, had to wonder if the teasing atmosphere on the ship had in some way been a trigger for Armstrong's crimes. They were all in tight quarters. They spent sixteen hours a day with each other. They didn't have any friendships but each other. And Opie was known to be pretty "soft," Hempstead said.

"When you're a bunch of guys together wrapped up on a ship and nowhere to go," Hempstead said via phone in 2020, "I mean, quite honestly, you have a lot of competitions. And the competitions thus usually resulted in wrestling or anything like that. The funny part was, we kind of beat up on him a little bit. He was bigger than us, but he wasn't really strong or he wasn't intimidating or anything like that. We kind of pushed him around a little bit. Not in a mean way, but we weren't exactly the nicest people to him."

Sometimes they would blow off steam by having a sort of wrestling match around the ship's laundry chute, he said. "The main laundry, we would always throw down the chute when it was done, and that's where people would go to pick it up. The wrestling contest was, the last one to go down the chute won. And the chute was a big metal square and it wasn't nice to get thrown down because when you hit the bottom of it, it was a metal deck underneath. He was always the easiest one to get through the chute."

When Hempstead reconnected with his Navy buddies on social media years after his service and learned about Opie's arrest, he was surprised and intrigued. He had to speculate if it was all the result of an inner rage well-hidden beneath the surface of his shipmate but nonetheless surfacing at times. And could his experiences on the *Nimitz* have had anything to do with it? No, probably not, he decided.

"I always kick around the idea. Of course, bullying is now becoming more of a talking point with youth. And I thought because of some of the things that we did to him in terms of—not necessarily being his friends, but being his work colleagues—kind of beating up on him a little bit. I kind of thought that might have brought out some of the rage … When I read about some of the things that he was doing and how it was attributed to his growing up and some of the things that … he was dumped by girlfriends or some of the experiences that he had growing up, I knew that that wasn't the case. I knew it was just guys being guys and doing just stupid stuff, you know, nothing else to do, so you wrestle or fight or do whatever. You know, we never did any harm to him. It was more or less degrading. You lose a wrestling match and somebody is going to flick you a little shit about it. It wasn't anything to where we put any physical harm on him."

Indeed, and even while Armstrong was being interviewed by Dearborn Heights police in January 2000, he spoke well of his time in the Navy, as it not being a negative experience at all. He spoke of it with a hint of pride.

All in all, to his shipmates, Armstrong seemed like a nice guy, an innocent guy, kind of like a babe in the woods. As befitting his moniker.

"Yeah, he was Opie," Hempstead said. "I have red hair. I have freckles. *My* nickname was not Opie. You know?"

It was aboard the *Nimitz* that Eric, of course, met his future wife Katie, a 1994 graduate of Dearborn High School in Michigan who swam on the swim team and tended to keep to herself, schoolmates have said. She didn't pal around with the rest of the swim team, she aspired to join the military, and she was "drawn to the peculiar." She "played to the tune of a different drummer," one person who knew her told *The Detroit News*.

Hempstead remembered Katie as being similar to Eric in mannerisms and appearance. They got along well together, spent a lot of time together on the boat. Katie was part of the air wing unit, a group of additional personnel that would join the ship's crew to maintain the aircraft when the ship went out on a tour such as the WestPac tour where they met. For that time period, it would have been Carrier Air Wing Nine (CVW-9) that was attached to the *Nimitz*.

Again, Eric placed a call to his friend Stephanie, telling her he had fallen in love and that he and Katie planned to leave the Navy, get married, and have a family.

The couple married in September 1998 at South Redford Christian Church, Katie's childhood church in Michigan. The minister who performed the ceremony, Reverend Fred Zimmerman, would later tell *The Detroit News*, "We knew him as Eric and he was a nice guy, nothing out of the ordinary."

When the *Nimitz* docked in Virginia for a while, Eric and Katie got an apartment on Field Stone Lane in Newport News, right by Interstate 64. They lived there from October 1998 until the spring of 1999, when they were discharged. When their son was born in 1999, Eric asked Stephanie if she would serve as the baby's godmother. He and Katie made a trip to North Carolina to have the baby baptized there, Stephanie recalled.

It was during this time the *Nimitz* was in Virginia that another shipmate, Kym Jones, knew Eric. She spent a total of twelve years in the Navy but only arrived on the *Nimitz* in December 1998, meeting Eric then. Her memories of the *Nimitz* are not pleasant; she was the victim of bullying and hazing incidents herself. She described one incident involving feces that was particularly traumatic. And truth be told, the *Nimitz* had some negative press over the years for antics that went on there. The ship's captain while she was there, Jones said, was a racist and sexist who believed women did not belong on the ship. Eric Armstrong, however, was a friendly face in what she remembers as a hostile atmosphere.

"He was literally one of the best people I had met on that ship," she said. "My time on that ship, I referred to it as a berth you forget. My time on that ship was a complete nightmare."

Beyond his helping train her on the ship, Eric and Kym palled around Newport News a bit. He showed her where the movie theater was, and where the bookstore was, because she had an interest in that. He showed her the bus routes. Kym met Katie a couple times. Eric and Katie sometimes had other family members staying with them, she said, and she babysat for them a time or two. She remembers Eric working in the barbershop and the store of the *Nimitz*.

Kym Jones was still serving on the *Nimitz* when the news broke about Eric's arrest in Michigan.

"Everybody was in shock," she said. "Nobody could really believe that this was the same guy that we knew. There were a few people I remember saying that, oh yeah, they knew that he had this in him, that he just seemed like that kind of person. But overall, nobody could believe that this was the same person that we knew. The people that said that, oh yeah, they knew it—they didn't know him. These were people that just had gotten to the ship or people that were just trying to I guess make themselves feel good about stuff. Oh yeah, they 'knew,' whatever. Those that actually knew him and spent time with him, we were all in a complete state of shock."

NCIS interviewed Jones as part of their investigation, pretty intensely, for about an hour and a half to two hours.

"It seemed like they wanted me to admit that I'd had a sexual relationship with him," she said. "They didn't want to believe that he was just somebody that I spent time with learning my job. Like a female can't just learn from somebody and spend a little bit of time with somebody who's married."

Like Blake Hempstead, Kym Jones has wondered if Armstrong's time aboard the *Nimitz* had some kind of influence over his actions. But she also only wondered that to a certain extent. "Now, I know that the experience is not the only thing. He had to have some sort of mental issue to begin with. It has to do with nature versus nurture and stuff like that as well. But yeah, to a degree I wonder if something might have triggered it."

After leaving the Navy, Eric applied for a job unsuccessfully with the Virginia State Police. He and Katie then decided to make the move to Michigan, where she was from and where her parents still lived. During the summer of 1999, they moved into the fifteen-hundred-square-foot brick bungalow on Fairview Drive in Dearborn Heights with Katie's parents.

And that's where we pick up our story with Armstrong, as he settled in to this new place, getting a job at the Detroit Medical Center in Novi, then Target, then Signature Flight Support at Detroit Metro Airport. He took classes at Schoolcraft College in Livonia, another suburb west of Detroit. He studied zoology and veterinary science, he would later write to a female acquaintance from prison, because he loved all animals, especially the tiger. (One police officer interviewed for this book, however, remembered his area of college study being law enforcement, and Armstrong told the Dearborn Heights police he was studying biology.)

Enjoying his toddler son during those months in Michigan before his arrest, Eric was about to become a father again: a baby girl would be born that October in 2000. Katie was reportedly working as a lifeguard at a local YMCA. The two were in their mid-twenties, seemingly living a good life as a normal family in the Midwest. For the most part.

During those months, Jennifer Westberg remembered Eric talking about not only how hated his own mother and father growing up, but he didn't like his wife's mother either. And she definitely recalled the deal Eric had about his name.

"Yes, he told me pretty soon in our friendship but it came up naturally. I was talking about my boyfriend, John, and he said his name was John also. But he didn't like to be called John because his father was John and he was a terrible man. So he went by his middle name, Eric, instead. But he let me know that he really hated when people called him the wrong name."

And among the other things they discussed: "I remember Eric complaining about a lack of sex from his wife. She was always too tired or didn't want to do it because her mom and son were in the house. It was part of the reason he was so gung-ho to move out."

When Eric was arrested, shock waves ran through those who knew him.

"It's a real shame," schoolmate Dana Dixon said. "I think about those poor girls and his family from time to time. I just shake my head in disbelief. He isn't the John I grew up with. I started to write him a few times but really, what would I say to a serial killer? Also, my cousin and her best friend were kidnapped, raped, and killed by three Marines in North Carolina; what would her mom and my mom have thought if I wrote a man who has killed so many other daughters? It was best to leave it alone."

Eric and Katie visited his friend Stephanie and her family when they made a trip to North Carolina in 2000, not long before his arrest. They had dinner at Stephanie's house and Eric told her the story of his "discovery" of Wendy Jordan's body in Dearborn Heights. But Eric had been cleared in the investigation, both he and Katie explained, and they were glad that ordeal was over.

Then Stephanie saw the news while she was making coffee one morning a few weeks later.

"I thought they had the wrong person. Because the things that they were saying—they were saying that he had confessed to killing women all over the world and all of this. And I'm like, that can't be. That's just not who he is. It was almost surreal. Because he never ... you know how sometimes people just give you the willies? He never did that."

Stephanie, who after her time at the Food Lion store had become a youth pastor, then went on to become a therapist, had several thoughts running through her head. One was that a couple years before, she had invited Eric to chaperone her church's weekend youth trip to the Outer Banks of North Carolina. Eric had even brought along his little brother. She felt compelled to explain herself to the church's pastor because she never would have asked if she had known ... But how could she know? How could anyone know?

"What happened when he was arrested," she said, "those of us that did know, everyone was like, there's no way this could be Eric. And I still think about it as, was that just a bad dream? The Eric that I know was just a kind, giving, loving young man who would never hurt anybody. Who would go out of his way to help people. And then all of a sudden ... *that*. And then when I found out that they actually had DNA and I heard more of the story, and more about his abuse, when he was younger, and things like that, and then being in the mental health field, I understand a little more now."

Stephanie also thought about the visit just weeks earlier, when Eric talked about finding the body in Dearborn Heights. About how sincerely grateful Katie was when talking about it, grateful that Eric had been cleared of this. Stephanie's impression of Katie was that she honestly had no idea.

"It still breaks my heart when I think about it," Stephanie said. "That had to have been a horrific thing for her to go through too."

Like others who have known Eric, Stephanie has considered contacting him in prison. "I love Eric and I love the Eric that I know. And I know that something snapped, to make him do what he did. I believe that he did what he did. But that's not the Eric that I know. And I guess it was all just kind of hard for me to—I don't know why, I don't know why I didn't keep in touch with him. All these years I have wanted to but I just haven't."

She added, "It's like a bad dream. It's like, did that really happen? I know he did it. It's been proven that he did it. But it's still unbelievable."

Judy Avery, Eric's one-time church youth group leader, also found the news unbelievable. In fact, when the news report came on and she heard Eric's name, she had almost convinced herself it couldn't be the Eric she knew, since the man they showed on TV had a beard. "I just couldn't imagine him being that violent," she said. "He never showed that."

For Jennifer Westberg, the question that has been lingering all these years is not whether or not it happened or why. It's actually, why not? Why didn't Armstrong kill her too?

With apologies for the creepy factor, I asked Jennifer her feelings about that seat in which she once sat on her way to work, the passenger seat of the dark bluish-gray 1998 Jeep Wrangler. The seat where other women lost their lives.

"LOL, it's OK, it's actually the most often asked question when I tell people. And it was one of the first things that crossed my mind. I sat where women died. I sat where he not only killed people, but screwed around with them first. Then I thought about the news article I read where it said he used to make his wife dress as a prostitute and 'pick her up,' as well. Then I pictured her there. It was part of what messed me up so much. Why kill all those women but not kill me? And did he want to kill me too? Did he not do it because I wasn't a mom? Because I wasn't a prostitute? What did I do right to get in and out of that Jeep where other women weren't allowed to get out? I had nightmares for months after. Nightmares where he would call me on the phone and tell me he's coming for me as soon as he gets out."

Years later, Jennifer's thoughts of Eric Armstrong are not what you might think.

"I use my story as an ice-breaker when I meet new people. I try to think of the kind man who was there for me. I try to think of the father who loved his son and was so excited to have another child on the way. I try to think of Eric the friend and not John Eric Armstrong, the serial killer. Also, when I vouch for someone now, I preface with, 'But I was friends with a serial killer so I'm not the best judge of character.' It's funny but it's true. And when anyone asks about him, I share all the good things. He really was a kind and generous man ... to me."

Has she ever thought about contacting him in prison?

"I've thought about it but don't know what I would say other than, 'Why didn't you kill me too?'"

THE OTHER SIDE OF THE STORY: A HALF-BROTHER SPEAKS

Kelly Hood's sister Shannon sat through the whole trial for her sister's murder, and years later, one of the impressions she would still be left with is that John Eric Armstrong "threw his family under the bus" to try to gain his freedom.

"But he didn't have a bad family life," she said. She didn't know Armstrong personally. But that was her impression as she listened and observed throughout the trial. This defendant sitting in court had soiled the name of a father not there to defend himself, a man he couldn't possibly remember a whole lot about from the tender age of five. And truth be told, had this defendant been much kinder to the mother and stepdad faithfully sitting behind him, in his bid to be free?

In spring 2001, Eric's biological father John had no idea this trial was taking place, had no idea what had happened with his son all these years since he left. By all accounts, he and Linda had not been in any communication, and the family he had built after leaving North Carolina evidently did not know about his previous life. Thousands of miles away to the west, whatever national headlines might have filtered their way about the case evidently went by unnoticed. It wasn't until more than a decade after Eric was incarcerated that his father learned of all of this. And more recently, a half-brother whom Eric has never met, having also realized the details of the case, decided to have his own say. To speak up and give another side of the story for the father he has loved dearly all of his life.

John Ezra Armstrong was born in April 1946 to John Clayton Armstrong and Florence Glendola Myers Armstrong and grew up in a small town called Pryor in Oklahoma.

After graduating from Strang High School in Oklahoma, he went on to the Marine Corps, where he served in Vietnam.

"I'm not real sure where or how long he was over there," said Mike Armstrong, who bears the name of another half-brother he never met. "But I do know he was honorably discharged. He had several scares he got from over there. Mortars and explosives left him with pieces of shrapnel all through his body. He would show (them) sometimes. The little pieces that would move around under his skin. He wouldn't tell me much about what happened over there. You see, Dad didn't like what he had to do in Vietnam. But he did it anyway in the name of doing what he had to do."

His son went on: "He had a pet monkey that he rescued out of a perimeter fence once. It wouldn't leave his side after rescuing it. Until fighting happened. Then it would disappear for a bit and show up later and find Dad. Until one day it didn't come back. Dad was heartbroken. He worried every day about the things he had to do in war. Worried it would keep him out of heaven."

John Ezra came home after his military discharge and started the next chapter of his life, beginning a family and living for several years in Oklahoma. He had his first son, Shawn Armstrong, with a woman named Pat. They eventually split up, and then he met Linda, whom he called Lynn. Settling in North Carolina, they married and in 1973 had a son, John Eric. A few years later, in 1978, came another son, Paul Michael, who then died in his crib at two months old.

Mike explained what he knew of this other half-brother: "Dad came home from working the night shift and Michael was crying. Dad fed and burped him, then changed his diaper and put him to bed. Later they found Michael had passed away. Linda blamed Dad, so there was an autopsy and they confirmed it was in fact SIDS. *Nothing more.*"

Eric's allegations about his father being responsible for the baby's death are completely false, Mike said. "Dad couldn't kill an animal to feed us, let alone his own child."

And what broke up John Eric Armstrong's family? Here is Mike's understanding from his father's perspective: "He told me Linda had a very bad problem of being an 'easy woman.' He found out later that she was cheating on him, again. So he left her and came back home to Oklahoma, where he met my mother, Loretta Smith. He married her and took my two other siblings to raise as his own. Steve, Amy, and myself all grew up together." Even Mike's older half-brother Shawn lived with the family for a while until he got married and moved out.

But Mike's parents did not stay together. "My mom eventually cheated on Dad while he was driving a truck for CFI (Con-way Truckload). They got a divorce when I was about 8, I think. He stuck around for a bit and I went over there on weekends. I loved my dad. He was, is, and will always be my hero."

John Ezra eventually decided to leave Oklahoma. He went to Phoenix, Arizona, to live with his brother for a while. He worked there as an electrician wiring—ironically—all of the new Target stores in the state.

Mike and his father, John Ezra Armstrong.
Photo courtesy of Mike Armstrong.

"It was several years that went by that I didn't see or hear from him," Mike said. "That was extremely hard for me. My hero was gone and I wasn't sure why. He eventually met a woman named Charlene. They moved to Pryor and Claremore, Oklahoma, for a few years. Then moved to New Orleans, where she was from. Later on, my grandma, Dad's mom, passed away and Dad came home for the funeral. I met up with him there and it was like he had never left. I decided to move to New Orleans with him. I needed my dad back in my life badly. He worked on offshore oil rigs then, so he wasn't home very much."

Mike said, "I got into an argument with Charlene one day and moved back to Oklahoma. Later, Charlene passed away and Dad moved back to Oklahoma, where he met up and eventually married his high school sweetheart, Shirley. They lived together for a little bit and then moved to Kansas. Her family all lived there. Her oldest daughter eventually passed away from breast cancer, leaving her four children behind. So Dad and Shirley stepped up and adopted them. They raised those children until my dad passed away in 2015. He died from chronic heart failure and Agent Orange."

John Ezra remains the man this little boy looks up to.

"My dad was a great man. He was one of the most gentle giants you'd ever meet. Until someone messed with his babies. Then papa bear came out. Nobody messed with his kids."

Mike strongly rejects the allegations against his father that came out during Eric's arrest and trial. "My dad has three boys that are his: Shawn, John Eric, and me. We're all half-brothers. He also raised my other half-brother and sister and his four grandkids. Not one of us has ever been touched by him. My dad was not the kind of man that beat his family. He spanked me only a handful of times *ever*. And I had it coming. I've seen him poke my grandpa (my mom's dad) in the chest for spanking me once. He was very protective of us all. Even my brother and sister that weren't his kids. He raised all three of us. And all three of us and my mom all agree. There is absolutely, undoubtedly, no way on God's green earth that my dad, in any way, shape, or form is a sexual predator or child molester."

Mike has other theories about his half-brother's upbringing and the motivations behind the abuse allegations. And they're formed from what his dad told him about Eric's mother.

There are shades of what John Ezra told Mike in some things Eric said to people he knew. He said some unsavory things about his mother to a coworker and to one of the officers who interviewed him after his arrest. He even reportedly made an allegation about a grandmother. It's impossible to know, though, if these were just fabrications, as we certainly know of this perp's ability to lie. Were these merely the ramblings of an extremely contrite man who had just been arrested? Who was confessing things right and left, with plenty of tears and apologies? Just some lies, some subterfuge, and perhaps a bid to rationalize the murders in the wake of his arrest?

"He always talked about his mom," Ira Todd said in mentioning one particular story of Armstrong's. "I never really confirmed that at all. But that's what he said. It kind of messed him up, you know… So I didn't know if it was a sob story or it was real. But he kind of gave us a picture of a real bad childhood." A lot of the time, stories like that will come up in interrogations as part of what cops call *minimization*—efforts to minimize or lessen the crimes, or the responsibility for them, by placing blame on a bad childhood or whatever. Placing blame on others. Todd recalled that Armstrong would bite on this idea, would run with it, if Todd asked about his childhood.

We know the abuse allegations against Armstrong's father came out in court as part of his defense. The psychologists who spoke with him accepted it as true, presented it as true in court, though it can never be proven, and is vehemently denied by others. But amid the personal things Armstrong shared with his coworker, Nancy Miller, which included comments about his mom, she did not recall any abuse allegations about his dad. Neither did his coworker, Jennifer, with whom he confided about his "bad" childhood in this calmer period before his arrest. Jennifer only recalled that he hated both his parents.

Another thing to consider, post-arrest interrogations aside: Nancy recalled that the way Armstrong told her his little brother died was by drowning, not in the crib. "He drowned in a lake," she remembered him saying. "And he said he saw, unfortunately, he told me that he saw his brother drown." So assuming that Nancy is remembering this correctly after all these years (which is another variable because we're all human), what were the lies and what were the truths in all of this? Did this killer just lie about anything he said about his family, like he lied about "finding" Wendy

Jordan's body and about the alleged break-in at the medical facility in Novi?

Mike Armstrong believes his dad served as an easy scapegoat when he left the family and was no longer there to defend himself, and that what went on in the household after he left is really the motivation behind Eric's crimes.

"Now, research has showed me that people with issues like John Eric tend to project their anger and/or problems on victims that remind them of their abusers," Mike said. "So if he was allegedly choking female prostitutes, that would immediately make me look at his mother." Mike believes something went on that Eric won't admit to. "He blamed Dad, who wasn't in the picture and made an easy scapegoat."

Mike Armstrong grew up barely aware that he had a half-brother named John Eric, that he had once had another half-brother who bore his own name. He knew scant details about this other life his dad had lived in North Carolina. And then, far into his own adulthood, he was shocked to learn what his half-brother had become known for.

"My dad found out about John Eric and what he did only a few months before he passed away. All of us did. We found out about what John did in, I'd say, sometime in 2014-2015. My Aunt Fern found out and told Dad what happened. He was disappointed and angry, to say the least."

Indeed, on a blog post about the case, a comment can be found attributed to Fern Armstrong Smith and dated March 31, 2015: "I am the sister of John Eric Armstrong's biological father. He left because his wife was having an affair with his best friend whom she married (Ron). His father did not abuse John Eric when he was younger. His father is alive and sick living in Grove, Oklahoma. He has never seen John Eric since leaving all those years ago!!!! If you want a different story come to Oklahoma and talk to his father!!!"

John Ezra passed away that following July. Having visited and lived in several parts of the country and world during his lifetime much like his namesake son, John Ezra, living in Grove, Oklahoma, at the time of his death, was then buried in a small cemetery in Boatman, Oklahoma, next to his parents, two brothers, and a sister.

And now, a few years after learning what he has learned about his father's son John Eric Armstrong, having suffered the shock of this knowledge, having even gone to online blog comment sections and essentially apologized for his half-brother's behavior...

"I wish I could express my deepest condolences to the families of his victims. Tell them I'm sorry that this nasty human being took away their stars, their hearts, and their peace. When I found out what he did, I went straight home and looked him up. My jaw hit the floor. For the first time in my life, I was seeing what my long-lost half-brother looked like and what he really was ... a monster. He killed poor, innocent women in a very personal, savage, and brutal way. He looked nothing like us. He didn't look like what I had pictured all my life. He looked evil, and dirty. He made me sick."

Has Mike Armstrong ever considered contacting his half-brother in prison? What would he say?

"I've thought several times about talking to John Eric. Not sure what I'd say to him. I know it wouldn't be pleasant. Because I'd like to really hurt him for what he's done. I am a defender and protector of people like Dad was. If I see someone in need. I feel obligated to assist them. I can't stand bullies or bad guys. This made me want to join the Marine Corps. I wanted to be a hero, a soldier, a Marine just like my dad. But he talked me out of it. He didn't want me to see or go through what he did. He wanted me to make a better life for myself and raise a family. So I did. I've been married to one woman for almost 19 years now. We have two boys. Erik and Cash, and they're my everything. And they sure did love their Papa John."

He might still contact his half-brother in prison.

"I would ask him why he did the things he did and why he lied about Dad. I'd tell him exactly what I think of him and his actions. I think he is an evil man. He makes me sick to think of what he's done and how he did it. And he needs to tell the truth about everything, including Dad. Because he damn well knows it's a lie. I grew up with Dad, on and off most of my life. But one thing I know for sure is that he was NOT a child molester."

NO EASY ANSWERS

The death of a beloved baby brother. Alleged abuse in the childhood home. Possibly some other questionable behavior in the home. A certain hatred for prostitutes. Jilting girlfriends and Dear John letters. A claim of lack of intimacy with his wife. Maybe a little bullying along the way. We've got some interesting background details but no real explanation for why John Eric Armstrong killed, other than his claim about needing control. And the perp himself, at least as of this writing, is not willing to shed any light.

"The Eric we raised could not have done these things," Armstrong's mother Linda told the media at the time of his arrest. "This is just not the person we know."

Stepping back for a moment, there is a lot we know about serial killers from research done over the decades.

At a 2005 symposium in San Antonio, Texas, the FBI set this definition of a serial killer: "The unlawful killing of two more victims by the same offender(s), in separate events." Other definitions put that at three victims in separate events, with a pointed break ("cooling off") in between. FBI agent and profiler Robert Ressler, who studied many serials in his career and is often credited with coining the term "serial killer," subscribed to the definition of at least three victims in three events. His fellow FBI agent John E. Douglas, with whom he authored books and papers, agreed on the three-victim idea.

According to the Radford University/Florida Gulf Coast University Serial Killer Database containing data on 2,715 serial killers from the US (including Armstrong) and 1,292 from other countries, about 52 percent of serial killers are white and 92 percent are men. About 21 percent have a military background. A large chunk, about 12.5 percent, are white males in their mid- to late twenties like Armstrong was.

The US has about 4.4 percent of the world's population but 67 percent of its serial killers, the database says. Other sources put that number at more like 76 percent.

Serial killings in the US were just riding off a high of several decades, from about 1960 to 2000, when Armstrong was active. This peaked at 689 serial killers in the US. in 1980, the Radford/FGCU database says. It has dropped rather dramatically in the past decade, with only 87 in 2010, but has been declining since the 1980s.

James Alan Fox, criminology professor at Northeastern University and co-author of *Extreme Killing: Understanding Serial and Mass Murder*, keeps his own database of confirmed serial murderers starting in 1900 and corroborates those figures. Numbers increased in the '70s and '80s and started declining in the '90s.

Can we attribute this decrease to better crime detection tools such as DNA testing? Greater technology? (How on earth can a potential serial actually kill a second person nowadays since almost everything we do is on camera?) Maybe there's been a sociological shift away from this sort of crime? Or some fault in reporting? Who knows. The Radford/FGCU study speculates that there are fewer targets for serials because we have changed our behavior: less hitchhiking, kids better monitored/not left alone to go to the playground, etc. (And yes, any of us kids of the '70s know that we could disappear for a whole day on our bikes and no one would blink an eye. Not so now!)

You could certainly make the argument for better technology nowadays, though. In this case, first victim Monica Johnson aside, if the technology of DNA testing would have been back then what it is now, Armstrong would have three fewer fatalities in Detroit. Dearborn Heights PD had him pegged; they just didn't have the DNA evidence in hand to arrest him after Wendy Jordan's murder.

Radford/FGCU formulated a general serial killer profile that includes the characteristics of an unstable home, the absence of a loving and nurturing relationship, physical ailments and disabilities, and head injuries. Then there is the commonly known triad of early indicators that some subscribe to: bedwetting, fire starting, animal torture.

In comparing serial killers to the general population, a 2005 study by Heather Mitchell and Michael G. Aamodt of Radford University estimated that six percent of the general pop have suffered physical abuse while 36 percent of serials have. About three percent of the general pop have suffered sexual abuse while 26 percent of serials have. And the numbers for psychological abuse, which you would think would be a bit difficult to quantify, are two percent for the general population and 50 percent for serial killers. Ressler believed that all serials have some kind of abuse—violence, neglect, or humiliation—in their childhoods.

Unlike Armstrong, most serials have a criminal history: 84.7 percent were previously arrested and 76.8 percent had spent time in jail or prison. Many had received prior psychiatric treatment and 1.8 percent killed prior to their actual killing series.

Strangulation is the second most common method for serials at 23.2 percent, behind shooting at 41.8 percent.

But what about motive? That's what all of this is leading to, right? The Radford/FGCU list of broad motives based on 3,646 killers in its database lists at the top: enjoyment (thrill, lust, power) at 40.3 percent. It's followed by financial gain at 28.5 percent. Anger is third at 14.9 percent.

And relating to motive, several varieties of serials have been identified. Would Armstrong fit into the category of "Missionaries," determined to rid the world of unwanted types like prostitutes? There are also "Hedonists," who kill for fun or profit, like lust killers or thrill killers. Based on his own words, Armstrong would certainly fit the category of "Power Seekers," killing to exert power over strangers, with the examples of Ted Bundy, David Berkowitz, and Ed Kemper. There are also "Revenge Killers" and "Antisocial Personalities."

Many who have studied serials classify them as organized or disorganized. The Radford/FGCU study cites an organized killer as one who has sex before killing, brings the weapon(s) with him, is quick in his viciousness, hides the body, and learns from each kill. By contrast, the disorganized serial finds his weapons at the scene, tortures the victim, disfigures the body, has sex with the victim after death, and shows a lower degree of sophistication and learning from the kills. Organized killers take a memento and then follow the case in the news; disorganized killers do not. An organized serial drives to commit the crime while the disorganized tends to walk or take the bus, strangely enough. And an organized killer targets low-risk victims, while a disorganized one targets high-risk. You could assume that means a college coed, as in the case of Ted Bundy, as opposed to a sex worker. In general, while organized killers tend to be more intelligent, attractive, outgoing, and better employed, disorganized killers work menial jobs or no jobs, are less attractive and intelligent, tend to be loners, and feel they are inferior to others. In the course of the research for this book, I had assumed—and even read—that John Eric Armstrong would be classified as an organized killer, but given this information, he might better fit the profile of a disorganized one. A disorganized killer also tends to keep anger inside while an organized killer is more likely to act out through bullying or by being the class clown.

In their paper, "The Incidence of Child Abuse in Serial Killers," Mitchell and Aamodt of Radford note that there is a "mixed" category in addition to organized and disorganized. They also note that an organized killer not only follows the killing on the news, but may offer tips or help to the police. They zeroed in on lust killers for their paper, even contacting some perps in prison to fill in the blanks on their data. They concluded that childhood abuse or other abuse in the life of a serial killer was definitely a factor, though not the only one in the motivation for killing.

"Serial killers have a type of cycle during which they kill, presumably during some period of stress," they wrote. "After the cathartic experience is accomplished, they feel temporarily relieved of this pressure."

Some researchers are leery of certain serial killer typologies, like a killer who always targets prostitutes because of some element in his background or makeup. Situational and random factors have to be considered, they argue. "Typologies based on motivation assume that serial killers always act according to a plan," wrote Ronald Hinch and Crystal Hepburn in their paper, "Researching Serial Murder: Methodological and Definitional Problems." In real life, they said, random, unpredictable environmental factors come into play. They cited David Berkowitz, who ran away after his first victim screamed and bled, and Dennis Nilsen, who dropped his usual M.O. and killed a man simply because the man was annoying and in his way. This is much like Armstrong's confession of the man in Seattle that he said he beat with a pipe when the guy kept following him asking for money.

Cindy A. Pokel authored "A Critical Analysis of Research Related to the Criminal Mind of Serial Killers" for her master's degree at the University of Wisconsin–Stout. In it, she looked at a number of studies and theories by various researchers as to why serial killers kill. She cited a 1985 study by the FBI in which they found that most serial killers spent their childhood in unhealthy, uncaring, and abusive homes. "The study also found that family histories of serial murderers highlighted multiple problems to include alcohol and drug abuse. The study found that most of the murderers evaluated had a weak attachment to their family members, and that there was present a parent whom suffered from problems of substance abuse, criminality, and aberrant sexual behaviors. A common theme among all the murderers was a childhood with the absence of the development of self worth."

She goes on, "The absence of meaningful relationships also impacts the aspect of sexual relationships." She says some theorists have proposed that a serial killer can harbor a deep hatred toward women due to an underlying hate for some significant woman in his life. "In psychological terms this is often referred to as 'displaced aggression.'"

Using the example of well-known serial Ed Gein, the inspiration for *The Texas Chainsaw Massacre* and *The Silence of the Lambs*, she writes, "Relationships with mothers have been found to be an important indicator. Research has found that serial murderers frequently are found to have unusual or unnatural relationships with their mothers."

Dr. Lawrence J. Simon, from his great deal of research on serial killers, said that sometimes there is a flawed object relations concept referred to as "mirroring" from an idealized figure, such as a mother's verbal or nonverbal behaviors and overall relationship with the child, which encourages positive self-worth and value. It is opined that many serial murderers didn't get that positive recognition, intimacy, or emotional nurturing, and the residue of that literal or perceived adverse relationship with the primary caregiver impacted the child's sense of self-worth; that later affects issues of trust, anger, and resentment.

He explained: "Inconsistent parenting is really big, whereas they don't know one day to the next what's going to happen. As a brief conceptual description of this object relations concept that in my experience is applicable to many serial predators interviewed over the years, is the overwhelming childhood dysfunction between mother, father, and son, particularly the lack of positive recognition from primary caregivers, which consequently within the first several years of life, personalize feelings of distrust, humiliation, anxiety, lack of moral grounding, and inadequacy. These feelings resurface during early adolescence and without some type of intervention continue into adulthood, where at some point anger becomes sexualized. He has a propensity to view others as threatening and develops a sense of mistrust for the outside world. Through the acts of tormenting and killing others, his feelings of low self-worth as a small child are altered into grandiosity that is reinforced through acts of sexualized violence and continued to be observed by others. During my interviews with many serial-type predators, I observed the subtle and not-so-subtle grandiose and narcissistic idiosyncrasies, but again keep in mind they are usually compensating for feelings of psychological frailty.

"For example, I told a serial killer one time, you know, I have a daughter. So I go home, and I'm divorced, and I see my daughter as much as I can. I know my daughter, obviously, she loves and adores me, and I love and adore my daughter. She sees it in my face and I see it in hers, as well. So when you're trying to explain that to them, and I remember, this guy was like looking at me like I was crazy. And I was like, what, you never felt that? These guys never felt that connection, that realm, whereas they don't feel recognized. Essentially, in a nutshell, it appears, at least in my experience, that serial murderers do not light up their mother's face, including a general absence of affection and attachment, particularly during early childhood years. So, as small children they're just not getting that recognition right off the bat, for the most part, from what I've seen. I can't say that Armstrong falls into this category because I don't know the relationship, but at the end of the day, perceived recognition is really important."

It is conceivable that both the trauma of Armstrong observing the death of his brother and the perceived relationship with one or both parents are big things, but of course not the only factors that led him toward a path of destruction. These are just possibly two ingredients that may have unfavorably impacted his thought processes as he navigated through life and ultimately made the choice to act on his impulses.

"Certainly trauma and that's one of the things I talk about," Simon said. "Trauma is manifested in different ways perceptually by anybody. And that's really the focus point; when you are looking at serial killers, you're looking at trauma. They suffer from some trauma. But again, it may not be the same traumatic experiences for us. For example, with the boy dying, there's people who have witnessed other family members die in horrific ways, and then, of course, don't go down any kind of beaten path and things like that."

And the relationship between sex and violence is a very interesting one for many serial killers. "See, all these harsh chaotic life encounters during a lifespan, whether real or imagined," Dr. Simon said, "sooner or later, the anger is absorbed, internalized and fused with sexual fantasies, which are then externalized into obsessive thoughts about harming others. Their masturbatory fantasies are primarily sadistic, frequently reinforced through masturbation whereby they contemplate and do take some steps moving forward before harming others, that we sometimes are able to observe in their previous offenses that they get caught for.

"For example, attempted kidnapping, peeping, trespassing, breaking and entering, just to name a few. Very rarely will we see a serial murderer abruptly jump into sexual homicidal rages without leaving a few footprints behind, by either committing some type of bizarre offense, or other deviant behavior someone close to them observed after he was arrested. Thankfully, serial murder is a rare phenomenon, whereas most homicide investigators will never cross paths with one. But when they do commit a series of murders, it is their psychological failure in navigating around deviant fantasies and obsession, a lack of moral culpability, and strong desires to up the ante due to sexual dissatisfactions. The ongoing environmental stressors and tensions lead to a breaking point, coupled with some predisposing biological factors, where to maintain relief is through violent acts and harming others."

It's kind of like the way many of us will look up to one or both parents. "But looking at it characterologically, is probably more accurate, where you have that familiarity. That's what you feel comfortable with. It's kind of like turning on a song, and you don't know why you like that song. Maybe your mom or dad had played that. The reason I'm focusing on this is this is where it all begins. You see, as young children we rely on our caretakers, or the absence thereof, of any kind of connection, or our self, becoming our self."

Like Pokel, Simon cited the example of Ed Gein. "His mother was devoutly religious. He was highly infatuated with Mom. Mom's bedtime stories to Ed and his brother were from the Bible. And in the Bible, there's quotes of harlots and stuff. His mom made very clear to Ed and his brother at the time that women are the devil. That they're dangerous and never to be with women, and you know, basically demonizing all women. Okay? So early on, unbeknownst to Ed's mother, Ed Gein feasibly felt trapped inside the opposite sex's body, as one of the rationales in constructing a body suit made of female private parts. He also perceived women as the devil, thoughts that were nurtured and strengthened by Ed's mother by her early teachings. He was also a paranoid schizophrenic, the symptoms of which begin to manifest earlier in men at about 16-25 years of age. So, here we have Mom unexpectedly dying, and later, Ed attempts to excavate his mother's corpse, to likely pacify his undying love for his mother because of his unusual attachment to her. Ed was not able to unearth his mother's body, but instead engaged in extremely odd behaviors that have been well-documented. Importantly, it was noted he found erotic pleasure in using female body parts of the women that he murdered and others he would find in the obituaries to decorate his home. The long story short is that he perceptually and literally demonized women throughout his childhood and adult years, including a love-hate relationship with his mom that was cultivated by his mother, but also reinforced by his progressive psychotic state of mind."

Regarding the caretaker role for serial murderers, both Mom and Dad play a critical role in their emotional development. Dr. Simon said, "There is an abundance of documentation and self-reporting that many serial murderers were either emotionally, physically, and/or sexually abused independently or in combination by a male or female caretaker, father, mother, or both. The specific types of neglect or abuse that has been self-reported or read about in newspaper articles or books can be appalling and sometimes clearly understood as being just that. But what about the not-so-obvious behavioral incidents that do not meet any normal standard of abuse or neglect, either in a legal or moral sense. Basically, I am referring to the compilation of nonverbal and verbal subtleties during childhood that exist between mother, father, and child having a lasting impact on the psyche.

"Unlike many serial murders who have been abused, Jeffrey Dahmer was not; however, his formative childhood and adolescent years were problematic and mostly spent alone, with his father being largely absent and preoccupied with his educational endeavors and reportedly his mother having emotional issues, coupled with cruel and frequent arguments in the home that eventually led to a nasty divorce. Of course, this is not a direct correlative factor in Dahmer's killings, nor would it be to anybody, as many households have this dynamic. Instead, it was the frequency and intensity of Dahmer's deviant obsessions, facilitated through alcohol consumption, that invariably cemented his path toward depravity."

In any case, Dahmer, Armstrong, or any other male during their formative childhood years passes through what Sigmund Freud described as Oedipal conflicts and urges toward Mom and jealousy of Dad, along with the perception of the mother-son, father-son relationship, or lack thereof. Dr. Simon said, "These relationships are not only crucial in character and identity development, but are influential later in life, whether the relationship with caretakers is perceived as negative, or positive, or whether the caretakers are symbolically or literally absent in their life. Regardless, most of us 'idealized' and overemphasized our fathers as to physical ability (e.g., my dad can lift a car off the ground), or emotional strength and stature (my dad is greater than anyone else's dad). Although in some cases unrealistic, there seems to be a negative and positive continuum of these illusions that establish Dad as hero, envy, power, failure, perfectionism. These perceptions are facilitated and reinforced throughout their childhood years that simultaneously establish his own sense of value and self-worth. Essentially, the father being perfect and 'a part of me' experience is important in cultivating initial positive feelings, moral development, and self-confidence, as similarly as it is with the concept of mirroring or recognition with the mother and son relationship."

And the idea of Armstrong picking up both men and women—although the men identified as women—is another interesting aspect. "Serial murderers are known to have multiple sexual inclinations and deviancies," Dr. Simon said, "which includes and is not limited to sexual sadism or sadomasochistic tendencies in combination with the same or opposite sex, and not uncommonly, experiment on themselves, or even have a history of sexually experimenting with both men and women. These sadomasochistic urges are initiated to either satisfy a sexual fantasy in receiving pain or can merely be practice prior to choosing to victimize a stranger. Dennis Rader, aka the BTK killer, likely fell into this category, as a sadomasochist, as he had many reported sexual proclivities, including engaging in autoerotic fantasies, bizarre bondage selfies, and hanging himself. He killed men, women, and children with the same disregard and it pleased him the same."

Katherine Ramsland, Ph.D, explored the dynamics of power and control in her article "Shame and the Serial Killer" in *Psychology Today*, theorizing how deep feelings of past humiliations could motivate a serial killer. "Victims are symbolic," she wrote, citing a 1994 paper by researcher R. Hale. "They trigger embarrassing internalized memories about being taunted, threatened or abused that continue to enrage the killer. He strikes out in an attempt to decrease the impact—but since the victim is not the offending person, there is no resolution, so the murders continue. The killer does not make the association between his past and what he's currently doing. He's just trying to feel empowered within a familiar context."

Wendy Jordan's sister Bonnie, as she sat in the courthouse day after day watching the proceedings on Armstrong, was struck by how his wife Katie behaved in court. To her, the behavior seemed demeaning toward Armstrong, she later said. It struck her as a huge contrast to the behavior of Armstrong himself, often shown in TV news clips and photos as crying as he was led in and out of his court dates by police.

"He was whimpering," Bonnie said. "I was like, what the??? I told Nancy Grace, I said, he was whimpering at the arraignment. By now we know he at least killed Wendy and one other person. We didn't know all the rest of that stuff. And I'm like, what the hell? You're killing people and you're whimpering? Can you imagine? And I told Nancy Grace, I said, he killed my sister, but I said, I know this might sound crazy but I felt sorry for him because he reminded me of a person that has been bullied, as big as he was."

Prosecutor Elizabeth Walker and Detroit Police Officer Donald Johnson had the same impression of Katie as she testified on the stand. Johnson in particular had listened to Armstrong's own perspective of his marriage and his life as he talked with Armstrong in those first several hours after his arrest. Listening in awe to everything this perp was willing to reveal about his life, Johnson formed his own impression of the "why" of it all. To him, this was not a brain chemistry thing, a serial killer gene, or anything like that; this was a matter of environmental factors that built up to a point where the pressure had to be released.

"He would start picking up prostitutes and paying for sex and stuff like that," Johnson said. "And so he would have these encounters with these women, but at the same time, because of the rejection and other things that were going on in his life, he said he would start having visions. And so one in particular, he said, the young lady, they were in his car, and the young lady was on top of him, and he was like literally, at that point of ejaculation, he just reached up and put his hands on her throat and started strangling her. He said he couldn't stop. He strangled her until she was out. And so he just said that became the norm for him. And then he would go back, like the three bodies that were found at the railroad tracks, and he would go back to the railroad tracks and have sex with them, because he knew that they couldn't reject him. And I was like, holy crap, just to know the guy's going back and having sex with dead bodies, I was like, this guy has got some various, you know, psychological issues. Is sick … And I tell you, it took me about three weeks to kinda get to some normalcy in my own personal life, after just ingesting so much information and looking at each, and going through each and every one of those cases with him, in reference to, you know, the unfortunate taking of someone's life. And the reason, what were the reasons behind it. It was more than just, 'I'm just going to kill someone.' It was some underlying issues that he had dealt with since childhood. And all these things were coming into play in his life, with the rejection and with the sexual abuse by his dad. All these things were just adding up, adding up. And the pressure just got to him. And it became, unfortunately, it became for him to target, you know, what they referred to as street walkers."

And it was very deceiving, what was lying beneath the surface of this boy next door. "You would never know that he had this monster type of attitude that came out. That rage, that silent rage, is what I like to refer to it as. He had it, you know? And it's just like they say, never judge a book by its cover. You know? And so that rage was just there. And that was his outlet, unfortunately … Just a lot going on. And the rejection, those type of things. And so this was his way of letting it all out, unfortunately."

Right after Armstrong's arrest, it was reported in the media that Detective James Hines, Johnson's partner in the initial interrogations, had to hang up on Katie Armstrong after a minute-long phone conversation because she wouldn't stop yelling.

"She's in extreme denial," he was quoted. "Apparently she didn't want to hear what I had to say." He added, "She was a very loud and rambunctious woman."

Hines confirmed it for this book, decades later. "She called me and cussed me out, said I was framing her husband."

Kevin Gray wrote in his *Details* magazine story that friends said Katie had a way of bludgeoning Armstrong's feelings. She criticized his "redneck" haircuts and dismissed his "hillbilly" wardrobe. She chided him for being too passive.

Katie, who did not respond to the request to be interviewed for this book, spoke only with Gray during the time of her husband's arrest and trial. Gray described her as a compulsive talker who wavered between disbelief and "sneaking suspicion" of Armstrong's guilt.

"My husband is the kind of person who cries when he sees a dead animal in the street," she told Gray. "If you yell at him, he cries." She also told the writer that her husband insisted she dress up like a prostitute during sex.

And for the big question of whether or not Katie had any idea what her husband was doing, she told Gray that she didn't know and she didn't want to know. "I guess I'm just afraid," Gray quoted her. "I'm afraid of Eric's answer."

One interesting comment Armstrong offered during the questioning right after his arrest was in the discussion on Kelly Hood. He was asked if he got pleasure out of strangling women. He said no. Why do you do it, police then asked. "I don't know. It just happens."

Another interesting aspect of this case is the necrophilia element, as mentioned by Johnson. Former Detroit cop Everett Monroe remembered this aspect pretty well, as did others interviewed for this book like Conrail conductor Denis Kupser, who recalled the rumors going around the railroad staff at the time. A detail that's bound to stand out about the case, for sure. And Monroe remembered not only that about Armstrong, but also that police had seen indications at the railroad track scene that their perp had actually changed the clothing of the victims. Almost like he was playing with dolls? One might wonder.

Ira Todd remembered this idea as well, from his interrogations with Armstrong. "And when I asked him about that, he said he was just changing their clothes around because, you know, he was trying to make them presentable and stuff like that. And I think it was the Black girl—he had propped her open and left twigs between her legs. I even asked him, I said, why did you do that? He said I wanted to see if anyone else was coming, tampering with her. Isn't that sick? Like he thinks somebody else is going to come by and have sex with these dead bodies while he's away. He was a jealous monster too. So it's crazy. But you know, those kinds of things are just weird."

Another impression that remains in Everett Monroe's mind, years later, is of what he considered a dual personality in the perp: "He seemed to not fit the profile of anyone that would take someone's life," Monroe said, "but I say, I've been doing this long enough to know that there are many motivating factors that cause people to commit homicide. To look at him, you would say that he is not a person that would kill. He's just the opposite. So it was amazing for him to have such a mild personality in interviewing him, and he would show remorse while he was explaining the incident, but he was a serial killer. There was no doubt that he was responsible for those crimes."

What was going through police minds about this at the station? I asked. Had this sort of thing been encountered before, at least in recent times? What was the thinking around the investigation about this?

"It was just bizarre. The behavior just ran the gamut. You had a guy that was a serial killer. You had a guy that had a fetish for sexual encounters with a corpse. You had a person that liked to change the clothing on a corpse. I mean, it was a very learning experience and it pretty much taught me how to profile my suspects in additional cases. But it was bizarre. It really was."

Benny Napoleon, the Detroit police chief at the time of Armstrong's arrest, told the media, ''We initially thought that he was posing the young ladies for a photograph, but he was actually leaving them in the position where he could come back and have sex with them again. And he did.''

Necrophilia is defined as a sexual attraction or sexual act involving corpses. Believe it or not, it's been documented since ancient times.

"He had some necrophiliac impulses; that's not too much of a surprise," Dr. Simon said of Armstrong, "because many of these guys do. You know, they've got the sexual sadistic component and the necrophilia. And you have multiple deviancies. As far as the strangulation is concerned, I would venture to say that that really turns him on. I would almost in many ways doubt that he had an orgasm before … You could explore this anyway through his sexual relationships and things like that, if he is a sexual sadist. For example, talking to folks that previously dated him. Did he like to be tied up? Did he like to be in pain?"

"A New Classification of Necrophilia" by Anil Aggrawal, from the *Journal of Forensic and Legal Medicine*, includes various classifications of necrophiliacs. Categories include role players (those who get aroused from pretending their live partner is dead during sexual activity), as well as romantic necrophiles (who remain attached to a dead lover), or even exclusive necrophiles (who cannot perform with a live lover). Of the categories, Armstrong might fit into the opportunistic necrophiliacs: those who normally have no interest in necrophilia but take the opportunity when it arises. There are also those who get aroused by touching or stroking a corpse without engaging in intercourse, those who just fantasize about it without any physical contact with a corpse, those who mutilate the corpse as well, and those who kill specifically to have sex with the corpse.

According to "Sexual Attraction to Corpses: A Psychiatric Review of Necrophilia" by J.P. Rosman and P.J. Resnick, informed by a study of one hundred and twenty-two cases of necrophilia, the necrophile often develops poor self-esteem, perhaps due in part to a significant loss. In Armstrong's case, he suffered the death of his baby brother as well as the departure of his biological father. Necrophiles tend to fear rejection and want a partner who cannot reject them, the authors found. They also may fear the dead and thereby turn that fear around by making it a desire. Most necrophiles are heterosexual males and between the ages of twenty and fifty, sociology students at University of California—Santa Barbara have found.

Rosman and Resnick found a large percentage of their necrophiles (68 percent of what they consider genuine necrophiles) were motivated by a desire for a non-rejecting partner. A reasonable chunk, 15 percent, reflected a desire for comfort or to overcome feelings of isolation, and among the other factors, 12 percent showed a desire to remedy low self-esteem by expressing power over a corpse.

"It is sometimes mentioned in the literature that necrophilia stems from the need for an unresisting partner," wrote Jack Pemment, MA, MS, in an article for *Psychology Today*. "This can be unpacked in various ways, but it is possible that this stems from the need for a non-judgmental partner, which is something many people desire from their own healthy relationships."

But he said, "Those who commit rape and homicide, and then further mutilate and assault their victim, I think have different motivations. Stein et al. [M.L. Stein, L. B. Schlesinger, and A.J. Pinizzotto; *Journal of Forensic Sciences*] include these as discussion points in their paper 'Necrophilia and Sexual Homicide,' and they include the need to further destroy and degrade their lifeless victim. However, I would argue for most of these cases, as the violation happens very soon after death, that the offender, due to their extreme objectification of the victim, doesn't register the death on a deep level, and just continues to destroy the person through lustful violence. But of course, due to the infinite nature of human experience and thought, there would be exceptions. Bundy, for example, continued to visit his grave sites long after the act of homicide, and others have killed specifically to mutilate and to enjoy the experience."

Dr. Simon has seen cases of serials changing the clothing on their victims. "Look, you've got to remember," he said, "when these guys go back to the crime scene, these guys don't want to leave at the end. You know? To them, it's like their glory, it's the one thing that has given them power and control over their life. And of course, it provided recognition. Think about it. Think of going to a theme park, you know? You go to a theme park, you don't want to leave at the end. I took my daughter to Disney World, and you go to Disney World, you want to leave at least with a balloon. So that's the thing. These guys, kind of like a similar type of thing."

And then there's the aspect of Armstrong reporting his own kill, in the case of Wendy Jordan. Did he want to be caught? Retired Dearborn Heights cop Jim Izeluk, who once wrote a research paper on psychopaths and sociopaths, said it's common for them to call in tips and want to be a part of the investigation.

"Him making the call to the police department is very common with psychopaths too because they want to be aware of the investigation, what's going on, and be part of it," Izeluk said. "And him, talking about, confessing up to the other ones—he was proud of them. You know what I mean? He was proud of it. And he was prouder yet if he would beat it, you know, what I told you, if we didn't link it with the evidence. Or lack of the evidence, I should say. That's how they work. They're pretty sharp, to think of all this stuff. But they want to be involved in the investigation. That's one thing these guys like to do. So a lot of times somebody would stop around the police station or meet cops in the doughnut shop and ask about the case. Just call the station as a tipster, a lot of the times, to see if they had any other tips. They just want to know what's going on."

Armstrong's Target coworker, Nancy Miller, for one, believed he was trying to turn himself in by "discovering" Wendy Jordan's body.

An FBI report on serial murder found that as serial killers continue to offend without being captured, they can become empowered, feeling they will never be identified. As their series continues, a killer may begin to take shortcuts when committing his or her crimes. This often causes the killer to take more chances, leading to identification by law enforcement. It is not that serial killers want to get caught; they feel that they can't get caught.

Of course, in his confession on Nicole Young, Armstrong said he had left the body there to be found, so he could get help. So you could argue that his reporting Wendy's body was a cry for help as well.

Dr. Simon said that there is often another motivation for a serial to keep killing. "I think that definitely the first time that they killed or attempted to kill, a lot of times that hurt. It's a mess, or they didn't do it right. You know, they don't even imagine how much blood volume (there is). This isn't where the Wolfman in *Pulp Fiction* comes and cleans up. So these guys, what they have in their illusions and how it's going to turn out, it never does the first time. That's one of the reasons why I think they keep trying, they keep killing. Because the fantasy doesn't match up to reality. So they've got to keep that illusion going. They're trying to get that perfect fantasy. And that's why the more brazen they get. They'll keep the victim alive a little longer; they'll maybe use some dialogue and things like that."

And what about the blackouts Armstrong seemed to have, claimed to have, in at least some of these killings?

"And the blackout tendency, some of that is believable only in the sense because when they're in that frenzy, it's hard to kind of remember every detail," Dr. Simon said. "I have actually gone into those depths before with serial killers to where I talk to them about what their physical experience is like. I had one guy tell me, and he remembered everything; he remembered the body shaking, he remembered them urinating, defecating, he remembered that as well. So there were things that he was able to recall … I like the word 'blackout,' because in a way, it is. They just can't remember every detail of it. And that may also explain why a lot of these guys go back to the crime scenes. Or have sex with the bodies. Other than the fact that they'll tell you, well, I wanted to see if the body was discovered yet. Or what have you. But other than to go back and relive the experience, because they really didn't have that experience because there was a blackout. And this way they can go back and kind of relive that experience to see what they really did, and then of course—it's their body at that point. They take ownership of that victim at that point. That's one of the reasons of going back. I mean, you know. And those are the details that they do remember."

During Armstrong's trials, a diagnosis of intermittent explosive disorder was brought up. Did he really have this disorder, and how does that fit into all of this? As a cause, or a symptom?

IED, as it's often called, is a thing, and you may see it pop up on the occasional *Criminal Minds* episode or whatever. According to *Psychology Today*, IED is characterized by a failure to resist aggressive impulses. Individuals with IED, the magazine says, "often seriously damage property or assault others, and react in ways that are entirely out of proportion to the provocation." It can mean a spell or an attack of anger, after which there's a moment of relief, that is then followed by remorse. The Mayo Clinic describes it more as a temper tantrum sort of thing, like road rage, not necessarily a murderous rage. It's often preceded by tremors, tingling, or tension in the chest or head.

IED typically begins in childhood, and it may affect as much as 2.7 percent of the population. Other experts have a slightly higher estimate, three to four percent. To be diagnosed with IED, *Psychology Today* says, "an individual must have displayed verbal or physical aggression toward property, animals, or other people, approximately twice weekly for a period of three months … A person can also be diagnosed with IED if they have three aggressive outbursts that result in damage to property or physical assault that involves injury within a 12-month period. In general, outbursts last for less than 30 minutes and are impulsive, not premeditated."

Someone with IED might be involved with drugs and alcohol (by all accounts not really the case for Armstrong), and might try to commit suicide (bingo there—we do know that Armstrong contemplated, and even attempted, suicide multiple times).

Both heredity and environment can play a role in causing IED. A person may have grown up in a violent environment, or they may inherit the genes from a violent parent. People who were abused as children or experienced multiple traumatic events have an increased risk of the disorder, the Mayo Clinic says. There may be a brain chemistry element: there appears to be abnormalities in the limbic system (which controls emotions) and the frontal lobes of the brain that are responsible for impulse control of those with IED. It seems to be more common in men and the majority of those who suffer from IED are younger than thirty-five. Treatment involves medication and psychotherapy. The psychotherapy, the Child Mind Institute says, involves determining what situations trigger the attacks. That would seem to indicate that a person has specific triggers, like perhaps having sex with a prostitute. During the second trial, Dr. Dudley testified that Armstrong's interaction with sex workers served as the "pivotal feature, pivotal precipitant to causing his underlying anger to come out." So what was at the root of that anger? Just what was it really about? Why would being with a prostitute ignite it for him? Dudley had also mentioned general problems with intimacy and a specific lack of intimacy with his wife. So was the implication that he was going out and getting prostitutes because he couldn't be intimate with his wife, and this in turn caused an intense anger to arise?

Zelda Jakubowski experienced that anger firsthand and she felt that there was something quite calculated about Armstrong's behavior. He had scoped her out; he had sighted her before she saw him. He had watched her approach his Jeep. She believes the attacks were a daily thing for him. He struck her as very seasoned at this. "I believe that. That's what I feel. I don't have any proof to validate that, but I just felt that all along."

She added, "I believe that he was a narcissist, a little bit. I believe that he knew what he was doing. I felt very violated. I mean, here you're a Navy guy, and a big guy ... It's predatorial. Very predatorial."

Then when he suddenly snapped as they drove along, she believes what she saw was a "murderous spirit." It's similar to a split personality "but all of that is spiritual," she said. "That's a fragmented soul with a bunch of demons up in there."

And in a more secular sense, men are able to more easily compartmentalize the aspects of their lives than women are, Zelda reasoned. Men think in boxes; women think in streams. For this guy, he kept his murdering self separate from his family self, his job self, whatever.

Ira Todd saw Armstrong's rage while taking his confessions, and there was certainly no prostitute or wife present in the small room where they were questioning him. It was during this time as he was learning more about this freshly arrested suspect that he felt something was going on here that went way beyond anger. He could push Armstrong's buttons, particularly when it came to his childhood. It actually scared Todd at one point.

"I really believe something happened to him," Todd said, "because when he hit that file cabinet, I was actually trying to take on the father's role. And I remember, that was one of the first times in my whole career of interrogating somebody, I knew I wasn't quite qualified for him, because more than like deviant behavior, just a bad, mean person, I could tell he had some mental things that were really going on with him. And I remember, I would scold him because a couple times he would get a little reluctant and checked out. I said like, now, Eric, I want you to tell me about some of these other ones you've done. Tell me about the ones in Japan, and this and that and this and that. And he would shut down and kind of like pout like a kid. I said like, I was scolding him, 'Look, you know, you're just like your dad told me. You start something, you don't finish it.' And I could tell his dad always complained about him. And that's when I remember scolding him like his dad. I was trying to push buttons and I guess I pushed the wrong ones because he stood up, and I just remember him shaking. He punched the file cabinet but he's shaking afterward. And all I remember was, *let me get out of this room.* That was the scariest thing there was. I'm tellin' you, I was about two hundred maybe ten pounds, about six feet. Two hundred ten pounds. I was in one of my better shapes then. I could have maybe taken somebody that's the average guy. This guy, you could tell, he was enraged. And I could tell if he got his hands on me, it would have been nothing I could do. Because you could just tell how big and strong he was. He was one of those big guys—big arms, you know, back then. But I was like shaking. And I said, you know what? I'm not qualified for this one. This is somebody that's really—you know, something's really wrong."

There were minute-to-minute changes in Armstrong, Todd remembered, and it wasn't just about what was said out loud.

"He would go out into a rage, and you could see that other side of him. He went into a rage, even his non-verbals, his facial expressions. And that's what I read most during interrogation. You read the non-verbals, the facial expressions, the hand gestures, those types of things. And even when he changed, it was like he morphed into something different. I'm not saying he wasn't there, but you could tell it was a—his mean side was there. And when he hit that file cabinet, I'm telling you, it wasn't like he—he didn't try to—you know how people hold back because, like, 'I'm about to hurt my hand'? He *punched* that file cabinet. I was expecting his hand to be broken. But that file cabinet moved. I just remember, this heavy file cabinet—I remember, we used to move that—it was a little storage room we had. We used to move stuff around; I just remember how heavy it was. He moved this file cabinet; that's how much force he hit it with. And I was like—I was thanking God that wasn't my head or something. Because I didn't have a gun in there with me or anything. We went in there without guns. And I would take the cuffs off of him because I wanted him to relax. And I was feeding him and stuff, giving him food. You would see, when he was in a calm state, he had no problems. Chowing down."

And to this experienced interrogator who had observed suspect behavior for years, Armstrong didn't seem to follow the pattern. Todd believes that people grow up basically knowing the difference between right and wrong and that when they do wrong, they more often than not want to tell someone about it. It hurts, he believes, and they want to get it off their chest. But Armstrong didn't seem to react the way most perps do.

"You know, none of this stuff was so emotional to him where, you know, most guys, once you've caught them and once they confess, you can tell that there's a drain on them, like immediately after they've given it up. I mean, they're so emotionally drained by it—'I can't eat, I don't want anything to drink.' But this guy, he was pigging out. It was almost like it wasn't really bothering him, you know, unless he was trying to portray that a little bit. You know, make you feel a little sympathy for him. It was interesting. It was one of the cases that made me want to get more into psychology. Because I was thinking like, I'm used to interrogating hit men and street killers and armed robbers, sex offenders and stuff like that. But a real serial killer, a guy that really had some sort of problems, had these patterns and behavior, you know, we were just getting into those types of investigations. And I'm telling you, it opened my eyes. It did show you that a lot of mental health issues are crime issues."

And the range of emotions—from intense anger to no emotion at all to then perhaps a play for sympathy—was so varied in this subject he interviewed. Armstrong followed the prompts of Todd and the others on the task force, played on them, even. It was Todd's impression that the statements of remorse in the confessions—"I'm sorry for killing this female" and the like—were for the benefit of the written record, as police would sometimes remind him that what he was saying would be part of a permanent record and could wind up being read in court. And the confessions were, at least for Wendy Jordan and Kelly Hood.

"He was one of those guys that, you could tell, he was smart," Todd said, "and he was playing to everything that we were saying to him. But he was planning his defense the whole time. I could tell."

The guy who wanted to take a teddy bear on his perp walk.

"I think he was just an angry person. And he was hurt when he was younger and he wanted to hurt other people."

Another of Armstrong's interrogators, James Hines of the Wayne County Sheriff's Department, saw Armstrong's range of emotions and had his own theory about what might have helped motivate these crimes.

"All that meekness and passiveness went away when I asked him how did he feel when he was killing the women," Hines recalled. "And he hesitated, didn't have an answer for me. And he said, 'I'm sorry.' And I said, 'What is it about it? Was it when you were choking them, when you were inside them? Or was it because they were making fun of you?' And he got extremely upset about that. One of the problems that he had with women was he said he killed one of them because she laughed at his penis size."

Indeed, that was Nicole Young, Armstrong's last fatality.

"I think that was the catalyst for all of them," Hines said. "He didn't say it about all of them, but just my gut feeling says that if they had a problem with his penis size, either by making comments or laughing at him, or he couldn't function, couldn't get his activity off because of the size of it, that infuriated him and caused him to kill them. Because he didn't kill everybody."

But whatever the motivations, whatever considerations we have in this land of no easy answers, taking the life of another means crossing a big line. A line that many of us would never cross, or at least we don't believe we ever would. What was so different about Armstrong?

Really, it all comes down to … why could he cross that line? Dr. Simon said that sometimes that's an easy question—it's a stressor. It's something, or a combination of things, that happened in this perp's life. A trigger. Or many triggers.

"It's everyday things that happen to us," he said. "Think of myriad things that occur in life, but they're not really prepared psychologically to take on these challenges and things like that. You could almost equate it to, okay, I'm ready to commit suicide, I'm ready to die, and I'm ready to go along on my fantasy because look, at the end of the day, I want to get this thing going. And they've accepted the fact that prison is going to be their reality. Or death. They don't do it when things are going very well. They do it when they're at a point where it's like, you know, do I blow my brains out or do I kill? Almost like the mass shooters kind of thing. Except with these guys, they more want to get their groove on. They want to live, but they want to experience the ultimate power. They want to experience what it's like, in their view, to be alive. Because they've been dead all these years, and the illusion they've had, which is they're omnipotent, once they kind of snap into reality and realize they're not, they don't want any part of that. So they want to get back to that illusion of omnipotence. And the way that they're going to do that is they're going to take control of these victims. They're going to say when and how they're going to die. And with that power becomes that illusion of omnipotence."

The idea of a single trigger, or maybe even a couple traumatic events, seems so simple. It couldn't be that simple, could it?

When we spoke on the phone, Dr. Simon began answering the question of *why* with an analogy that perhaps says it all: "I'll tell you, that's the magical question: why. If there was an easy, two-plus-two answer. I always tell a story. I sat next to a guy who flew one of those triple-7s, you know, those big, huge jetliners, on one of my routes to do a seminar. And I asked him, I said—probably not the best question in the world—but I said (I was always nervous on the takeoff), I said, what does it take really for a plane to go down? And he looks at me, he says, well, you know, the flaps gotta go, hydraulics, the pitch, the nose, and you know, all that, that kind of … he named about nine or ten different things. And then as we're at about ten thousand feet and they tell you to turn on those electronics, he asked me what I do for a living and I told him. And the first thing he said is, I watch *CSI* and all that good stuff, but what does it take for somebody to go down that path? I looked at him and I said, well, the flaps have gotta go, the hydraulics, and all that ..."

KILLER COMPARISONS

So in the life of John Eric Armstrong, convicted serial killer, the mysteries as to the *why* of it all can still remain. You could certainly draw your own conclusions, from the information above, or from other information you've seen. Or you could decide that we just can't be sure of the why.

Amid the theories and allegations and counter-allegations, sometimes a case like this cannot be easily explained.

One of the more famous serial killers, Jeffrey Dahmer, convicted in Wisconsin after murdering and dismembering at least fifteen men and boys in his apartment between 1978 and 1991, laid it all out in a prison interview with TV journalist Nancy Glass in the 1990s. His manner was straight, no-need-to-be-charming, analytical, unsmiling. But very honest.

"To this day I don't know what started it," he told Glass, "and the person to blame is sitting right across from you. That's the only person. Not parents, not society, not pornography. I mean, those are just excuses."

There was no abuse evident in Dahmer's childhood, though it's been said his mother took a lot of pills while pregnant with him, and that he didn't have a lot of human contact as a baby. Still, Dahmer said he had a normal childhood in a good home. "Something went awry in my thought life," he said. "I don't know why."

As others have said about Armstrong, Glass said of Dahmer: "He appeared to be completely normal."

A lady who lived in Dahmer's apartment building, Pamela Bass, was also interviewed for the TV special airing Glass' story. "I knew Jeffrey who used to stay across the hall from me," Bass said. "That Dahmer guy is somebody else." These thoughts were very echoed by Armstrong's friend Stephanie.

Convicted serial killer Joel Rifkin, who, like Armstrong, targeted prostitutes, had been a loner in school and in his early adult years, often disheveled in appearance, often picked-on. He had suspected his birth mother was a prostitute. He was believed to have murdered up to seventeen women in New York, beginning in 1989, and he was serving a 203-year sentence when interviewed by Chris Cuomo in 2018.

"It was a lot of self-lying," he said. In a resigned, straight-up manner similar to Dahmer's, Rifkin explained that once he had killed one woman, he figured that would be enough, he wouldn't go back. He was wrong. "It was almost an addiction, seeing these women," he said. (In his own interview, Dahmer had also mentioned the addiction aspect of killing.)

As noted earlier, Rifkin didn't kill every prostitute he was with, and like Armstrong, he chose rather hands-on methods: strangling, suffocating, hitting. "With a handgun, you don't feel it," he explained. Rifkin and Dahmer also were said to have engaged in necrophilia with their victims.

An expert in that same *Inside Evil* episode where Rifkin was interviewed pointed to the 1972 Alfred Hitchcock movie *Frenzy* and its explosive strangulation scene. The argument was that pop cultural elements like this have an influence on real human behavior, this one in particular pairing female sex appeal with murder. This expert suggested that there should be a few minutes of screen time between the male viewer's arousal/erection and the murder scene so that the two are not intertwined.

Contrast the killers Dahmer and Rifkin with someone like Lorenzo Gilyard, another serial who targeted prostitutes. In his own prison interview with Piers Morgan airing in 2018, Gilyard, known as the Kansas City Strangler, vehemently denied any wrongdoing. He insisted he had nothing to do with the thirteen women he was accused of killing between 1977 and 1993, despite his convictions, despite the evidence against him (including DNA), even threatening to walk out of the interview if referred to by Morgan as a serial killer.

Prolific killer Ted Bundy played the same denial card for years, insisting he was innocent until he apparently thought he had something to gain with confessional details that could lead to the recovery of other, unknown victims from his 1970s and '80s killings. Just buying a little more time on death row? Whatever the motive, it didn't work, ultimately. He was executed in Florida in 1989. But the handsome, smooth-talking, former law student Bundy is interesting because, like Armstrong, he strangled (sometimes, but he also bludgeoned with objects), but unlike Armstrong, he targeted pretty young college coeds and other lower-risk women who would immediately be missed by their families. He made great effort to not leave any DNA evidence and to hide the bodies of (most of) his victims, not simply heaving them out of the car wherever it happened to be parked.

As far as Bundy's own background, he was born in a home for unwed mothers and raised at first by his grandparents, and it's rumored that his violent grandfather might actually have fathered him. Bundy reportedly had a lifelong resentment toward his mother. It's been said that feelings of rejection and lowliness caused this rather intelligent perp, despite heading toward a promising law career at one time, to begin killing pretty girls.

Sexual assault fulfilled his need to "totally possess" his victims, Bundy's page on Wikipedia says of his prison confessions. At first, he killed his victims as what he termed "a matter of expediency ... to eliminate the possibility of [being] caught." Later, murder became part of the "adventure." "The ultimate possession was, in fact, the taking of the life," he was quoted as saying. "And then ... the physical possession of the remains." Like Armstrong, Bundy was a necrophiliac, as mentioned by Dr. Simon earlier.

Another convicted serial, Charles Albright was believed to have killed three prostitutes in Dallas between 1990 and 1991, though he was convicted of only one. He's known for his fascination with eyes, having carefully cut out the eyeballs of his victims. At a young age, he was interested in medicine and enrolled in college for premed, but some run-ins with the law derailed that. At one point, he lived a pretty normal life with a wife and child. He was fluent in other languages, was a painter, and he tended to leave people with a good impression. Though like Armstrong, he targeted sex workers and witnesses say he had a hatred for them, his method of killing was less hands-on—shooting them. He did display their bodies for police as he arranged them in public areas and he was pretty good about not leaving evidence behind. He was older than the stereotype, however, in his mid-fifties when convicted. When interviewed for TV specials on the case, such as a 2001 episode of *Forensic Files*, Albright has denied the crimes. A May 1993 story in *Texas Monthly* asked, "How does a perfect gentleman become a vicious murderer?" Indeed.

Edmund Kemper, featured on the TV special *Kemper on Kemper: Inside the Mind of a Serial Killer*, was the subject of an extensive FBI study on serials. Kemper had an abusive mother when he was a child, along with a father who left the family evidently due to the mother's behavior. Kemper showed an early red flag of a serial—he abused animals as a kid. He also was interested at a young age in going into law enforcement. He even had drinks with the local cops at the bar. Though he spent several of his teen years in a psychiatric hospital, he was later deemed sane and intelligent, with an IQ of 145. Like Armstrong, his pleasant demeanor belied his murderous acts. Preying on women, he said, was like a drug to him. He also was a necrophiliac.

Detroit serial Benjamin Atkins, whose name was brought to mind at the discovery of Armstrong's three railroad track victims as another predator of prostitutes, was reportedly raped at age ten and had witnessed his mother engaging in prostitution.

John Wayne Gacy, who spent fourteen years on death row before being executed in 1994 for murders in the Chicago area, also showed abuse in his childhood. His alcoholic father would beat him and was reportedly very disappointed in his son. Gacy was molested as a child by a building contractor known to the family. He sought to please his father, hiding feelings of homosexuality from an early age and continuing to hide them into adulthood, getting married and working a respectable job. But beneath the façade, he lived a secret life, and he began not only to pick up young boys for sex in the 1970s but also kill many of them. He's believed to have killed at least thirty-three people. He confessed to the murders at first, then claimed innocence, like Armstrong. He staunchly insisted he was innocent right up to his execution.

Todd Kohlhepp, convicted in South Carolina in 2017 of killing several people and probably best known for the female captive found alive in the storage container on his property, also claimed abuse in childhood. He said his grandfather would shock him with a cattle prod. He said his father was negligent. His father denied that, saying Todd's behavior in his youth was very bullying toward others. Kohlhepp's former defense attorney even said that Kohlhepp lacked empathy for others. While Armstrong fought the charges against him in court, Kohlhepp pled guilty and seemed to want to claim more victims than he had on record and claimed them without emotion.

Andrew Urdiales, a more obscure killer who ended up on death row in California's San Quentin after a years-long murdering career under the radar that left at least eight women dead, targeted some sex workers but also other women. He said at one time that he'd been with hundreds of prostitutes, so he certainly didn't kill every hooker he was with—only the ones who in some way had angered him, he reportedly said. Urdiales had anger issues, for whatever reason, and he described killing as a release of pent-up tension. In a 2018 prison interview with Cuomo for *Inside Evil* airing in summer 2019, Urdiales shed no light on his background or upbringing and was not outwardly remorseful about the crimes he was convicted of because he was still denying them, still holding out for appeal. But in court, he expressed condolences for the family members of the victims and he apologized to the one female assault victim who got away. He even said he agreed with the jury's guilty verdict and would have come to the same conclusion himself. A bit of a mixed message that Cuomo tried to pin him down on without success. Urdiales died by suicide in prison in fall 2018. Interestingly, Urdiales was a former military man like Armstrong and killed a few women while a Marine stationed in California. His killing methods varied—stabbing, shooting, even strangling. During an interview with police, he brought up how he was trained to kill in the military.

Samuel Little, more recently credited as the most prolific serial killer in the US with a victim count believed to be more than ninety, also targeted prostitutes, and like Armstrong, he left survivors. This serial killer, born in 1940, said he originally felt the urge to kill at only age seven or eight, but only fantasized about it for years until age thirty when he first committed murder. He called it a curse. Little's case highlights an aspect of manual strangulation so evident in the Armstrong case: sometimes the victim might wake up. And for Little, it was an element of torture he evidently enjoyed. If she woke up, he would strangle her again, and she even might wake up again, then get strangled again.

Little traveled all across the country, leaving victims in many different towns and states. And Little provides another interesting comparison with Armstrong in that when law enforcement—specifically a Texas Ranger teamed up with a couple FBI agents—convinced him at age seventy-eight and serving multiple life sentences to finally come clean about his crimes, he burst forth with a startling level of detail. The FBI agents had been pulling case files they suspected Little for and when the towns came up in the interviews, Little brought out details matching the case files that only the killer would know.

For Armstrong, however, we're going in the opposite direction—we're starting with confessions and their myriad details and trying to pair them with actual cases or bodies. Perhaps that's more difficult. But for Little, there was one particular case in Las Vegas where law enforcement was in that same predicament: they had Little's account of a woman he said he murdered, even the detail of meeting her son that night, but they didn't have a case or a body. He had been so accurate in the rest of the accounts given to police that they had no reason to doubt this Las Vegas incident. And it should be noted here, as it was in the ID special about Little airing in summer 2020, that though this aging serial had amazing details still front and center in his brain about the murders—he even remembered and drew their faces—the only details he jumbled were timeframes. As Armstrong did.

Dennis Rader, who dubbed himself the BTK (bind, torture, kill) killer during his 1974-1991 span of murders in Wichita, Kansas, was a husband and dad like Armstrong. A family man whose wife and kids had no idea the secret life he led. Rader didn't target prostitutes, though—he targeted whoever was convenient, and he stalked each person for a while before striking. He invaded the victim's home. And besides playing the family man by day, he held a good job and even served as congregational president at his church (a fact that helped identify him in 2005 when he submitted a floppy disk of information to the police that was traced back to the computer at the church office). Like Armstrong, Rader was willing to confess his crimes when cornered but unlike Armstrong, he did not show remorse. He stood in court and recited horrific details like he was talking about going to the grocery store, as one anchor at the local TV station put it. In the *20/20* special, "My Father BTK," it was said Rader played cat and mouse with police and the media before his arrest and seemed to crave the attention and infamy associated with serial killing. It was a thirty-year retrospective of his BTK crimes in the local newspaper that spurred him to resurface and communicate with police after being dormant for years. He didn't want to be forgotten, essentially.

One of the most interesting things to note about the *20/20* special on Rader is that nowadays, his daughter has forgiven him and continues to communicate with him. She is able to successfully compartmentalize (much as her father did during those years he killed) between the dad who raised her and the public persona of a killer who she doesn't really know, never really met. This was a man who always seemed like a pretty normal dad to her, despite a violent outburst or two over the years. And the forgiveness daughter Kerri offers to her father doesn't rely on his behavior—it's an effect of her relationship to the Lord. It's a symptom of the condition of her own heart. John Eric Armstrong has yet to experience that, however—as of this writing, he has not seen his wife or son in many years and he has never met the daughter who was born after his arrest.

At any rate, with all of these serial killer case studies, where does this leave Armstrong? Somewhere in between? Indeed, years later, he is. Though he was thoroughly penitent when arrested in 2000, rattling off confessions as soon as his brain could lock onto the details, nowadays he would rather not discuss the case. He's still the kind of nice guy who, amid casual conversation, you just cannot reconcile with his crimes. Much like Dennis Rader and so many others.

Perhaps Katherine Ramsland, who wrote *Confession of a Serial Killer: The Untold Story of Dennis Rader, the BTK Killer* and was interviewed for the *20/20* special, summed it up nicely: "I think to dismiss Dennis Rader or any other serial killer or mass murderer as a one-dimensional being is to make yourself unsafe, because you will not spot the real monsters if you think they're so easy to see."

JOHN ERIC ARMSTRONG TODAY

This will, unfortunately, be the shortest chapter in the book because our subject, as of this writing, does not want to discuss the case.

I have visited John Eric Armstrong in prison a couple of times. We have sat next to each other and chatted, no barrier, nearly touching shoulders in plastic chairs in a common meeting room at the G. Robert Cotton Correctional Facility in Jackson, Michigan. We've chatted a couple hours each time, actually. He's talked about life in the prison, his job in the bakery, his time training support dogs in the prison's special program, his former life in the military, and traveling the world. He even offered a few tidbits about his childhood. But nothing about the crimes.

He doesn't say he's not guilty. In fact, he carries himself as if he is and you know it and he knows it. He just doesn't want to talk about it.

You could think John Eric Armstrong is one of the nicest guys you ever could meet. As many have said for this book, you would just never believe this could be a serial killer. I found myself wondering that, as I sat and talked with him, and watched his mannerisms, his easy smile, the friendly way he has about him. *Did they give me the right prisoner?* I actually wondered that when I first visited him. *What if there's been a mix up?* He doesn't even look like he used to, now bald and much thinner. And I could not see any of his trademark tattoos for his long-sleeved prison garb. I really had to wonder if this was the right guy.

It took a little coaxing to get him to respond to my initial emails. He was hesitant. Cautious. And as it turned out, he would be okay with a new friendly acquaintance, just not a journalist interviewing him. He'll chat, no issue with that. And he's conversed with a few other women over the years, whether they were driven by curiosity from reading about him online or whatever. But he really doesn't get visitors. His mom Linda and stepdad Ron faithfully arrive from North Carolina about every year or two. But from what he told me, it sounds like that's it. He doesn't hear from his now ex-wife. Or his son. And he's never met his daughter. It's the saddest part of his life. It's all too evident as he mentions it.

Does he have those "nightmares that wake you up shaking and crying," as Judy Jordan wished upon him at his sentencing? It's hard to say. With everything I've learned in researching this case, though, I am inclined to say yes.

It's difficult to tread the line here. To try to shoot this thing down the middle, as I told him I would do when I first explained the book project to him. To offer him his own say too. To look at gruesome crime scene photos in one moment, or maybe reread an assault survivor's horrific account and feel so much of what she was feeling in that moment, or to listen to the tears of a victim's family member, then sign onto my email a couple hours later to a friendly Jpay message like, "Hi, how are you, sorry I haven't written in the past few weeks …" It's hard to reconcile those two perspectives. But this perp, I have certainly learned, is a complicated man. A man of many contradictions.

And I guess that's where we have to leave it.

ACKNOWLEDGMENTS

This author admires those true-crime writers who use footnotes and endnotes to indicate their sources. I've read a couple good ones lately. That kind of transparency really serves the reader well because I've also read a couple true-crime authors who indicated nary a source other than directly quoting people they interviewed. Then when you read any intimate details in the story—secret conversations or individual thoughts and feelings—you have to wonder where on earth that stuff came from or if it was a slight bit of poetic license.

Though I like it when footnotes are there, I also find them a bit jarring. I have tended to carry over my journalistic (newspaper!) training into my books, citing sources in the same sentence as the material, generally, throughout the text. So you'll find that approach here, in my first true-crime outing.

Plus, I'll note that a lot of the material in this book, whether noted in the text or not, comes from sources such as court transcripts, police records, autopsy and toxicology reports, and other official documents obtained through the Freedom of Information Act. These were used as the primary sources of the information herein, wherever possible, along with the personal interviews of the folks below.

For some other sources, often specifically named in the text, I am including a bibliography below to indicate where you can read more, if desired. These sources were considered secondary, to fill in gaps from the more official sources above.

And with all that being said, I'd like to issue a special, heartfelt thanks to the following folks who assisted with this material, in ways small and large.

First and foremost:
Gerald Cliff, Ph.D, whose expertise was indispensable

Along with:
Detroit Police Department
Dearborn Heights Police Department
Dearborn Police Department

As well as these individuals for their kind contributions and assistance:
Alex Henderson, Amanda Rakos, Monique Smith, and the City of Detroit Law Department
Alex
Ann G.
Art
Avon/Cynthia Smith
Benny Napoleon
Bill Taylor
Blake Hempstead
Bonnie Jordan
Carl Day
Craig Schwartz
Dana Dixon
Daniel Hollis
Dave Babcock
Del Christian
Denis Kupser
Dennis "Doc" Richardson

Donald Johnson
Donald Pace
Donald E. Riley
Ed Yike
Elizabeth of the National Association of Police Organizations staff
Elizabeth Walker
Everett Monroe
Gary Tomkiewicz
George Hunter
Gregory Geider
Grigg Espinoza
Ira Todd
James Hill
James Hines
Jeniffer
Jennifer Westberg
Jim Izeluk
Judy Avery
Kathleen Fitzmaurice-Ward
Kenny J.
Kimberly Sanders
Kyle C.
Kym Jones
Lawrence J. Simon
Library of Congress staff
Loretta
Marilyn Hall-Beard
Mark Bando
Mike Armstrong
Mike M.
Mike Petri
Monica Johnson's siblings
Nancy Miller
Natasha Olejniczak
Nathaniel Womack Jr.

Norfolk, Virginia, Police Department
Richard Tchorzynski
Rodney Durham
Rose Mary Tchorzynski
Russell Walls
Sarah Hillig Hugus
Scott Felt
Shannon Wilson
Sheryl Yike
Stephanie W.
Thomas Berry
Tina Carroll
Todd Learst
Tom DeSimpelaere
Trinity Kathleen Lee
Virginia Office of the Chief Medical Examiner, Tidewater District
Wayne County, Michigan, Office of the Medical Examiner
Zelda Jakubowski

A note that all names in this book are actual (even if it's a street name like Robin Brown or Cynthia Smith), but for people who could not be reached and spoken with firsthand, sometimes only first names are used if their name was not part of the public record.

SELECTED BIBLIOGRAPHY

20/20, "My Father, BTK," ABC. February 1, 2019

The 93 Victims of Samuel Little. Investigation Discovery. August 2020

Aamodt, M. G. (2014, September 6). Serial killer statistics.

Aggrawal, Anil (2009). "A new classification of necrophilia." *Journal of Forensic and Legal Medicine*. 16 (6): 316–20. doi:10.1016/j.jflm.2008.12.023. PMID 19573840

Chafets, Ze'ev. (1990) *Devil's Night and Other True Tales of Detroit*. New York: Random House.

Child Mind Institute, "Quick Guide to Intermittent Explosive Disorder (IED)," https://childmind.org/guide/intermittent-explosive-disorder

Crime Stoppers of Tacoma/Pierce County, Washington, http://www.tpcrimestoppers.com/

Dead Silence: The Serial Killer Blog, "John Eric Armstrong: Psycho Sailor," https://deadsilence.wordpress.com/2006/07/31/john-eric-armstrong-psycho-sailor

Detroit Free Press. (2000-2001) Coverage of the arrest and trial of John Eric Armstrong by Suzette Hackney, Dennis Niemiec, Joe Swickward, Jack Kresnak

The Detroit News. (2000-2001) Coverage of the arrest and trial of John Eric Armstrong by George Hunter,

Wayne Woolley, Norman Sinclair, Jodi S. Cohen, David Shepardson, Kim Kozlowski, Santiago Esparza, Mike Martindale, Charles Hurt, Oralander Brand Williams, Ron Hansen, Steve Pardo, David Josar

The Disaster Center, "Hawaii Population and Number of Crimes 1960–2018," http://www.disastercenter.com/crime/hicrime.htm

The Disaster Center, "Washington Population and Number of Crimes 1960–2018," http://www.disastercenter.com/crime/wacrime.htm

DoeNetwork.org and its accounts of Jane Does:
  http://www.doenetwork.org/cases/1590ufhi.html
  http://www.doenetwork.org/cases/168ufhi.html
  http://www.doenetwork.org/cases/558ufnc.html
  http://www.doenetwork.org/cases/1553ufnc.html
  http://www.doenetwork.org/cases/560ufnc.html
  http://www.doenetwork.org/cases/922ufwa.html
  http://www.doenetwork.org/cases/923ufwa.html

Hinch, Ronald; Hepburn, Crystal. "Researching Serial Murder: Methodological and Definitional Problems," Electronic Journal of Sociology (1998), ISSN: 1198 3655.

Honolulu Police Department Criminal Investigation Division, Cold Case–Homicide, https://www.honolulupd.org/

Inside Evil with Chris Cuomo, "Edmund Kemper," CNN, 2018

Inside Evil with Chris Cuomo, "Andrew Urdiales," CNN, 2019

"Intermittent Explosive Causes and Effects," Piney Ridge Treatment Center, https://www.pineyridge.net/behavioral-disorders/intermittent-explosive/causes-effects-symptoms/

"Intermittent explosive disorder," Mayo Clinic, https://www.mayoclinic.org/diseases-conditions/intermittent-explosive-disorder/symptoms-causes/syc-20373921

Janos, Adam. "Why Are Sex Workers Often a Serial Killer's Victim of Choice?" https://www.aetv.com/real-crime/why-do-serial-killers-target-sex-workers

Kemper on Kemper: Inside the Mind of a Serial Killer, Oxygen network, January 1, 2019

King County Sheriff's Office Cold Case Files (1960-2010), https://www.slideshare.net/elisanitz/cold-cases-1960-2010

"Lambasted" blog post, "My Serial-Killer Barber," Lance Lambert, October 1, 2011, http://lancelambert.blogspot.com/2011/09/my-serial-killer-barber.html

Leyton, Elliott. (1986) *Hunting Humans: The Rise of the Modern Multiple Murderer*. Toronto: McClelland- Bantam Inc

Leyton, Elliott. (1996) "Second Thoughts on Theoretical Approaches to Multiple Murder," in Thomas O'Reilly-Fleming (Ed.) *Serial and Mass Murder: Theory, Research and Policy*. Toronto: Canadian Scholars' Press: 37-51

Mayo Clinic, "Intermittent explosive disorder," https://www.mayoclinic.org/diseases-conditions/intermittent-explosive-disorder/symptoms-causes/syc-20373921

Mitchell, Heather; Aamodt, Michael G.; Radford University; "The Incidence of Child Abuse in Serial Killers."

MJA Inc. Investigations, "Missing Persons & Unsolved Crimes & Doe's, formerly at https://mja--inc--investigations.webs.com

Murder in Hawaii: 1992-1997, Volume 6, Issue 2 (June 1998), State of Hawaii Crime Prevention and Justice Assistance Division special report. http://ag.hawaii.gov/cpja/files/2013/01/Murder-Data.pdf

New York Times. 2000. "Coverage of the arrest and trial" of John Eric Armstrong by Nichole M. Christian.

North Carolina State Bureau of Investigation Cold Case list, https://www.ncsbi.gov/Divisions/Cold-Case-Investigation-Team/Unsolved-Homicides

Pokel, Cindy A. (2000) "A Critical Analysis of Research Related to the Criminal Mind of Serial Killers." Research paper, University of Wisconsin—Stout. http://www2.uwstout.edu/content/lib/thesis/2000/2000pokelc.pdf

Psychology Today:
   "Intermittent Explosive Disorder," https://www.psychologytoday.com/us/conditions/intermittent-explosive-disorder.
   "The Appeal of Necrophilia," by Jack Pemment, September 2018, https://www.psychologytoday.com/us/blog/blame-the-amygdala/201809/the-appeal-necrophilia
   "Shame and the Serial Killer," by Katherine Ramsland, Ph.D, September 2019, https://www.psychologytoday.com/us/blog/shadow-boxing/201909/shame-and-the-serial-killer
   "3 Reasons Serial Killers Claim They Have More Victims," by Katherine Ramsland, Ph.D, August 2018, https://www.psychologytoday.com/us/blog/shadow-boxing/201808/3-reasons-serial-killers-claim-they-have-more-victims

Quinet, Kenna. (2011). "Prostitutes as Victims of Serial Homicide: Trends and Case Characteristics," 1970-2009. Homicide Studies - HOMICIDE STUD. 15. 74-100. 10.1177/1088767910397276

Rosman, J. P.; Resnick, P. J. (1 June 1989). "Sexual Attraction to Corpses: A Psychiatric Review of Necrophilia." Bulletin of the American Academy of Psychiatry and the Law. 17 (2): 153–163. PMID 2667656

Serial Killer: Devil Unchained. Investigation Discovery. August 2019

Serial Killers: "Victims of John Eric Armstrong," formerly at http://serialkillers.briancombs.net/1208/victims-of-john-eric-armstrong/

"Serial Murder: Multidisciplinary Perspectives for Investigators," Behavioral Analysis Unit-2, National Center for the Analysis of Violent Crime, Critical Incident Response Group, Federal Bureau of Investigation, https://www.fbi.gov/stats-services/publications/serial-murder

Snohomish County, Washington, "Cold Cases," https://snohomishcountywa.gov/319/Cold-Cases

StatisticBrain.com, formerly at http://www.statisticbrain.com/serial-killer-statistics-and-demographics/

Texas Monthly, "See No Evil," 1993, https://www.texasmonthly.com/articles/see-no-evil-3/

Uniform Crime Reporting of the FBI, 1999, https://www.fbi.gov/services/cjis/ucr

University of California, Santa Barbara article on necrophilia, 2019, https://www.soc.ucsb.edu/

US Navy, *USS Nimitz*, https://www.airpac.navy.mil/Organization/USS-Nimitz-CVN-68/, formerly at https://www.nimitz.navy.mil/

Very Scary People, "John Wayne Gacy," HLN, March 17, 2019

Washington State Statistical Analysis Center, Criminal Justice Data Book, data sets for crimes by county, https://sac.ofm.wa.gov/data

Weather.com

Wikipedia.org
   Benjamin Atkins, https://en.wikipedia.org/wiki/Benjamin_Atkins

Ted Bundy, https://en.wikipedia.org/wiki/Ted_Bundy

John Wayne Gacy, https://en.wikipedia.org/wiki/John_Wayne_Gacy

Necrophilia, https://en.wikipedia.org/wiki/Necrophilia

New Bern, North Carolina, https://en.wikipedia.org/wiki/New_Bern,_North_Carolina

Pepsi, https://en.wikipedia.org/wiki/Pepsi

Wunderground.com

For More News About B.R. Bates,
Signup For Our Newsletter:

http://wbp.bz/newsletter

Word-of-mouth is critical to an author's long-term success. If you appreciated this book please leave a review on the Amazon sales page:

http://wbp.bz/babydoll

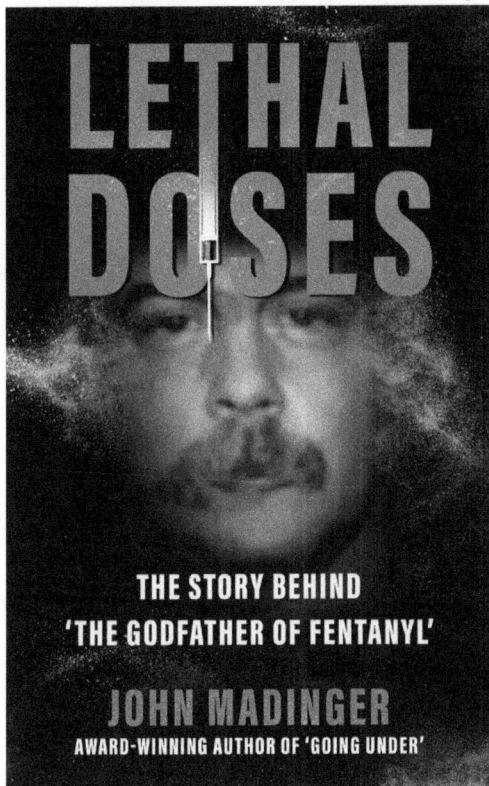

www.ingramcontent.com/pod-product-compliance
Lightning Source LLC
Chambersburg PA
CBHW070050030426
42335CB00016B/1844